# The Beauty Of the Righteous & Ranks of the Elite

A Collection of 1000 Rare Accounts of
The Blessed Companions of
God's Messenger Muhammad ﷺ
Based On the Classic 10th Century Work of
Imam al-Hãfiz Abu Na'ïm al-Asfahãni (948-1038 C.E.)
*Hilyat-ul Awliya Wa Tabaqãt al-Asfiya*

Translated from The Original Arabic
& Edited by
SHAYKH MUHAMMAD AL-AKILI

PEARL PUBLISHING HOUSE

Title: The Beauty of the Righteous
& Ranks of the Elite

Subtitle: *Hilyat-ul Awliyã wa Tabaqãt al-Asfiyã'*
by
Imam al-Hãfiz Abu Na'ïm al-Asfahãni (d. 430 A.H.)

Translated from The Original Arabic
& Edited by
Shaykh Muhammad Al-Akili



All inquiries must be addressed to:
Pearl Publishing House
P.O. Box 28870 Philadelphia, PA 19151 U.S.A.
Tel. (215) 877-4458 / Fax (215) 877-7439



Library of Congress Cataloging in Publication Data:
1- Abu Na'ïm al-Asfahani; 2- Asfahani; 3- Islam;
4- Companions of the Prophet;
5- Prophetic Traditions; 6- Al-Akili
(Indexed)

Library of Congress Card Number 95-074798

**ISBN** 1-879405-11-3

Cover Photo: Dunes, © 1995 PhotoDisc, Inc.

First Printing, April 1996

Published in the United States of America
Printed in Canada

# Table of Contents

*Contents*

All praises belong to Allah, the Creator and Sustainer of the universes, and the unfathomable Lord of grace. May we all delve to join the everlasting praises His angels and the blessed ones are constantly celebrating, and may His eternal and most effulgent blessings shower upon His last messenger and the seal of His prophets, Muhammad ﷺ, upon whom and upon all of God's prophets and messengers be peace.

This is the first attempt to bring the work of the renowned 10th century Imam al-H̲āfiz Abu Na'ïm al-As̲fahāni, God bless his soul, into English, and I am extremely thankful to my Lord for allowing me to share these jewels of testimonies of the chosen ones and the elite, the blessed companions of God's messenger ﷺ, upon whom be peace, whose knowledge, testimonies, and deeds are the true map for those aspiring for the eternal gardens of bliss.

The sincere godly reader will surely recognize this work as a guidebook for the seekers on God's path, a shield to win the battle against the trials and adversities of this world, and a strong warning for the heedless and the innovators, to spare themselves the just and afflictive eternal punishment in hell-fire.

The knowledge of the enclosed over 1000 accounts, prophetic traditions, and sayings of the blessed companions was given to their hearts by none other than God's messenger ﷺ, upon whom be peace, himself, a task he was sent by Almighty Allah, blessed be His Name, to deliver to humanity. Having delivered the divine message to his companions, in turn, God's messenger ﷺ also asked them to disseminate the revelation to all nations. Hence, these testimonies, which represent an important episode of human history, were first transmitted through oral traditions by the illustrious companions, and then by the scholars, the shaikhs, and the pious ones who remain to this day our strong link to the blessed era of the last and final divine revelation, and therefore, our path becomes illumined and most inspiring by their commitment and love for their Lord, and by their continuous efforts to deliver the authentic divine message to humanity until the last day.

This work represents a drop in the ocean of knowledge the blessed companions cherished, and their testimonies will surely help polish a tarnished heart, as well as they will beautify a pious one. In fact, although the legacy of our righteous predecessors (*salaf sãlih*) is unique and their devotion surpasses the common, yet, their wisdom, example, and teachings will surely fill a yearning heart with the love and grace of Allah.

The exalted model (*sunna*) of our righteous predecessors provides us with a most awe-inspiring high moral standard, and therefore, it is our duty and responsibility to learn from their testimonies, and to pay homage to such blessed and rare human beings, and pray for their souls to ever remain exalted in Allah's pleasure. Furthermore, once we have learned and acted upon what we have learned, it is our duty to pass on this exalted and unadulterated knowledge to our children, and as much as possible, we must share it in our immediate circles through good example.

Hamïd bin Anas narrated that God's messenger ﷺ, upon whom be peace, said: "With this knowledge, Allah will raise some people in stations, and He will make them eminent leaders and illustrious models. Their work will become widely known, and it will be admired and studied by others for ages. The angels will seek their company and huddle around them, and the angels' wings will constantly rub against their shoulders." (*Cf. Account #966*)

The events reported in this book took place over fourteen hundred years ago, and they helped change the course of history, as well as they were the answer to the prayers of God's messenger ﷺ, upon whom be peace.

On this subject, it is reported that God's Messenger ﷺ once saw a young boy called Ibn 'Abbãs, and he prayed for him: "O Allah, endow him with the knowledge of understanding and correct interpretation" (*Allãhumma 'Allimhu 'Ilma-Ta'weel*). At another occasion, God's Messenger ﷺ prayed for him, saying: "My Lord, strengthen him with the holy spirit," (*Allāhumma Ayyidhu bi-Rūhil Quds*, e.g. the comfort and strengthening support of the archangel Gabriel, upon whom be peace). Hence, Ibn 'Abbās grew up to become the most renowned interpreter of the Qur'anic revelation and of the prophetic sayings (*hadith*).

God willing, and as long as we are inclined to allow our hearts to hearken to this divinely inspired and most exhilarating guidance, we will become the embodiment of its blessings, and we pray that such advantage saves our souls, those of our children, and future generations from an awesome day of exact and just reckoning that will infallibly come.

Upon reading this most valuable reference book, — this manual of faith, blessed traditions, and high moral code, — God willing, one can draw a concise map of the environment of the sacred city of light, Medina, as it emerged over fourteen hundred years ago during the blessed time of the divine revelation, and then, one's heart can travel back in time to meet the blessed teacher, God's messenger ﷺ, upon whom be peace, and his beloved students, the companions, God be pleased with all of them. Thereat, one's questions will receive over one thousand answers relating to his or her spiritual quest, he will learn about the advantages of the life of a believer, the ultimate salvation of one's soul and that of his family and children, and moreover, one will learn how to conquer the constantly rebelling mind, he will discover the correct medicine to cure his weaknesses and attachment to this world, and he will learn how to dispel its darkness to reveal the light of divine guidance.

Once this knowledge becomes the embodiment and guiding light of one's life, one will also recognize his birthright, his true worth in the sight of his Maker, and it will reveal the reality and purpose behind his ephemeral existence in this world, and how to effect one's destination in the permanent life to come.

In closing, I pray to Allah, the Almighty Lord of the universe, the Lord of the divine Throne, Who has no partner or helper, and Who controls and manages every atom in existence, to help us reap the benefits of this reading, and I implore Him to forgive us our sins, those we commit knowingly, and those we commit in ignorance, to grant us His good pleasure in this world and in the life to come, to guide us, and to make our last actions in this life pleasing to Him, to make the conclusion of our lives in this world blessed by Him, and to make the best of our days the day we meet Him.

Lord, I seek refuge in You from the withdrawing of Your gracious bounty, I seek refuge in You from Your sudden retribution against the heedless, and the loss of our good fortune which You bestow upon us. Lord, I seek refuge in You from the pit of wretchedness, from the alteration of Your favors towards us, and from any evil destination. Lord, I seek refuge in Your protection from all calamities and afflictions, and I beseech You to grant us Your bounteous eternal gifts.

Lord, cure our sick, remove our infirmity, have mercy upon our dead, grant us healthy bodies and engage them in Your service. Lord, expand our understanding, guide our affairs in this world and protect our children. Lord, and cover up our sins, help us correct our actions and thoughts, guide our forgetful ones, bring back safely to You our loved ones, keep our faith in You strong, and grant us to be rightly guided.

Lord, grant us the benefits of good deeds in this world, the reward of good deeds in the life after, and save us from punishment in Hell-fire. Amen.

*Muhammad Al-Akili*

# About
# al-Hãfiz Abu Na'ïm al-Asfahãni
## 336-430 A.H. / 948 - 1038 C.E.

The compiler of the original work is Ahmad bin 'Abdullãh, son of Ahmad bin Ishãq, son of Müsa bin Mihrãn al-Asfahãni, patronymed Abu Na'ïm, who was born in the city of Isfahãn the year 336 A.H. (948 C.E.).

Isfahãn, also pronounced Esfahan or Asfahan, is located in the central mountains of Persia. Al-Sam'ãni wrote that Isfahan was originally built around 335 B.C.E., by Iskandar zul-Qarnain (Alexander the Great, 356-323 B.C.E.), and later on, it was captured by the Sassanid (224-640 C.E.). Isfahãn reached its apogee under the Persian king, Shah 'Abbãs I who made it his capital in 1598, and he embellished it with magnificent buildings such as the Imperial Mosque, the Lutfullah Mosque, and the Royal Palace. The city later on declined after its capture in 1723 C.E. by the Afghans.

Several renowned scholars and historians spoke of Abu Na'ïm al-Asfahãni in their writings, including Muhammad bin Ahmad bin 'Uthmãn al-Zahabi (d. 1360 C.E.) who mentioned Abu Na'ïm al-Asfahãni in his book *Mizãn al-I'tidãl fi Naqd al-Rijãl* (The Balanced Criterion in Literary Criticism; first published by *Dãr Ihyã al-Kutub al-Arabiyya*, Beirut, Lebanon1963). Al-Zahabi wrote: "Ahmad bin 'Abdullãh al-Hãfiz Abu Na'ïm al-Asfahãni was no doubt one of the greatest scholars and a truthful narrator, and people have unanimously accepted his station of Imam, (spiritual leader).

It appears that Imam Abu' Fadhl al-'Asqalãni (d. 1464 C.E.) in his book *Lisãn al-Mïzãn* (The Utterings of the Scale) also confirmed the same opinion. Al-'Asqalãni's book was first published in Hyderabad, India, [currently a state in Pakistan], in 1941, and a second printing was published in Beirut, Lebanon, in 1971.

Al-<u>K</u>hatïb al-Baghdadi said: "Among the shaikhs and teachers of our time, including my own shaikhs, no one is better than Abu Na'ïm al-A<u>s</u>fahãni and Abi <u>H</u>ãzim al-A'raj in knowing the Qur'an.

In his famous book *Wafiyyãt al-A'yãn wa Anbã Abnã' al-Zamãn* (The Accolade of the High Ranking Scholars, and the Chronicle of the People of the Time), Ibn <u>K</u>halkãn (608-681 A.H./1220-1293 C.E.), wrote: "Abu Na'ïm al-A<u>s</u>fahãni is a noteworthy and a trustworthy *<u>H</u>ãfiz* (i.e., one who memorizes the entire Qur'an by heart), and he was a beacons among the teachers and a great orator of his time. He learned at the hands of the most famous scholars and shaykhs of his time, and later on, several of them benefited from his work. His book *al-<u>H</u>ilya* (Regalia of the Righteous) is one of the best reference books, and he also known for his books *Ma'rifat us-<u>S</u>ahãba* (Knowing the Companions of God's Prophet ﷺ), and *Tãri<u>k</u>h I<u>s</u>fahãn* (History of Isfahãn). His ancestral line goes back to Mihrãn Aslam, who was the first man in his family to embrace Islam, and he was a companion-servant (*mawla*) of 'Abdullãh bin Mu'ãwiya, son of 'Abdullãh bin Ja'far, son of Abi <u>T</u>ãlib, God be pleased with him."

Al-Zirkly, in his book *al-A'lãm* (Famous People, vol. I, p. 157), indicated that the book *Ma'rifat us-<u>S</u>ahãba* (Knowing the Companions of God's Prophet ﷺ) is a large manuscript in two volumes, a copy of which is catalogued in the Library of Ahmad III in Istanbul, Turkey, under the number #497, and is signed by a scribe who copied the original manuscript in 551 A.H.; Al-Zirkly also mentions three other manuscripts preserved at the same library, namely *Dalã'il al-Nubuwwa* (The Signs of Prophethood), *Akhbãr Isfahãn* (The Chronicles of Isfahan), and the book of *al-Shu'ara* (The poets), all three manuscripts were written by Abu Na'ïm. *(Cf. Muzakkarãt al-Maimani*; Treatises of al-Maimani).

Imam al-A<u>s</u>fahãni was also mentioned in the book *<u>T</u>abaqãt al-Shãfi'iyya* (The Ranks of Shafi'i Scholars), volume I, by Muhammad Taqiyyuddin al-Dimashqi (779-851 A.H./1377- 1448 C.E.). He wrote: "Abu Na'ïm was born 336 A.H. in the month of Mu<u>h</u>arram (the first month of the Islamic Lunar year), and he died in the month of Mu<u>h</u>arram of the year 430 A.H./1038 C.E.). His name was also mentioned in the *Raw<u>d</u>ha* (at the Prophet's mosque in Medina) during the writing of *Kitãb al-Qa<u>d</u>hã* (The Book of Religious Jurisprudence), wherein it says 'that it is sometimes permissible for an accredited scholar (*mujãz*) to abridge the text and the reference of the chain of narrators as generally accepted by the savants."

The original book *<u>H</u>ilyatul Awliya wa <u>T</u>abaqãt al-A<u>s</u>fiya* of Imam al-A<u>s</u>fahãni, comprises eighteen volumes, all catalogued at Al-Asad, Central Library of Damascus, Syria. The present book 'The Beauty of the Righteous, and Ranks of the Elite' is a translation of one of the manuscripts, catalogue number #13493, 230 pp, and it begins with the Arabic text: "*Al-<u>H</u>amdu Lillãhi Mu<u>h</u>dithil Akwãn wal A'yãn* ..."

Imam al-<u>H</u>ãfiz Abu Na'ïm al-A<u>s</u>fahãni, God bless his soul, died in the month of Muharram, the year 430 A.H. / 1028 C.E., leaving a most precious heritage, and a unique depth of spiritual understanding which is greatly cherished by all the seekers on God's path.

# The Beauty of The Righteous & Ranks of the Elite

*In the Name of Allah, The Most Merciful & Compassionate Lord*

# I

# THE BEAUTY OF THE RIGHTEOUS & RANKS OF THE ELITE

All praises be to Allah. May He grant success to His servant. In seeking His help, I have compiled this book which contains the names and sayings of a special group of people who are known for their faith and piety, who have attained a unique spiritual integrity that was recognized by their contemporaries, and who are revered to this day by every true seeker on the path of God Almighty, Allah, the Lord and Cherisher of the universes, blessed be His Name.

This book comprises selected narrations of some of the early companions of God's messenger ﷺ, upon whom be peace, and their status and signs.

From the numerous prophetic sayings and those of the blessed companions of God's messenger ﷺ, I quoted in this book, the reader will acknowledge that it is only by the grace of Allah that such blessed beings have recognized the signs of their Lord, and only through His guidance that they have forsaken the common to seek the uncommon, and intelligibly, they have departed from the ephemeral to pursue the eternal. In fact, these most blessed human beings have renounced the company of the affected, the indolent and the ostentatious ones, and they longed for the company of their Lord and His blessings in the thither life[1] to come (Arb. *Ākhira*).

'Abdullāh bin Mas'oud narrated that God's messenger ﷺ once said to his companions: "What will you do when a calamity will strike at you and people come to adopt innovations, claiming them to be prophetic traditions, — innovations the young will grow to

[1] Arb. *Ākhira*: The conclusion of life in this world and proceeding to the predestined life thereafter. The *hereafter* is the commonly used term in modern English to describe the end of life in this world, and the beginning of a permanent existence thereafter.

practice as (though if they were prophetic traditions) sunna, and the elders will die satisfied to have pietistically held unto them, — and should one default in any of them, it will be said that he breached the sunna?" The people inquired: "O messenger of Allah, when will that come to happen?" He replied: "This will take place when your Qur'an readers increase in number, and your truly learned ones decrease; when the number of your leaders and princes (*umarã'*) increases, and when your trustworthy ones turn few; when worldly gains are sought via deeds which are supposed to be done for the sake of the hereafter, and when people solicit to acquire religious knowledge for worldly status and not for God's sake!" 'Abdullãh then added: "This is how you have turned out." (*Cf. account 280; pp. 123*)

In this book, the reader will also recognize our plain and lucid approach to this most sensitive subject, and he will recognize the argument of scholars in this regard. Once the essence is understood, then these unique prophetic sayings and traditions of the blessed companions will stand clearly to refute the heretical trends of the innovators, and they will adamantly reject the utter confusion of the incarnationists (*hulüliyün*) who adhere to the doctrine of the divine "indwelling" in the human being, or the doctrine of the anarchist freethinkers (*mubahiyün*), among other types of atheists. However, their lies and denials cannot affect the truth, and their vehement attacks against it do not alter its purity, or influence the attainment of the pious ones. To the contrary, they will prove themselves wrong and their argument hollow, while the truth is clear and its adherents are exalted and pure. If the believers do not expose the trends of the innovators who clearly lack true knowledge, and mostly use the weak minded ones for their personal gains, heedlessness will continue to be the immediate cause of destruction, and the ultimate cause of eternal damnation in hell-fire.

As for the religious advocates who argue against the authenticity of spiritual experiences and its people, they prove nothing, except their lack of trueness or true knowledge, not to mention their weakness and attachment to temporary comforts and satisfaction with worldly ranks. Our predecessors have struggled against the shallowness of those trying and desiring worldly status and personal gain, and their attempts to frustrate the efforts of the students on this path — their attempts to keep this religion on an intellectual platform only in order to tighten their grip, domineer, and widen their control over God's creation.

As for those who have experienced the divine benevolence, their endowment cannot be measured, and the entire wealth of this world cannot weigh even an atom in comparison to the bliss their Lord showed them. Although from a religious standpoint, our purpose in this work is not to expose the ill intentions of those who deny such divine gifts, however, it is our duty to disclose their schemes in order to distinguish truth from falsehood. In fact, by the grace of Allah, our predecessors on this path have published famous studies in this field, and through their efforts, God Almighty revived the names and works of several spiritual masters at whose hands many seekers discovered true spiritual comfort.

Furthermore, how can we permit the unjust attacks against God's deputies and blessed ones when their assailants are warned of a divine war.

**1-** On this subject, Abu Huraira narrated that God's messenger ﷺ said: "God Almighty said: 'Whosoever harms any of My deputies, I shall declare war on him. The striving of My servant to please Me does not receive a reward greater than that of fulfilling what I have commanded him to do. My servant volunteers in his perseverance, offering supererogatory devotion to please Me and to earn My love. Once I cast My love upon him, I become his hearing with which he hears, his sight with which he sees, his hand with which he exacts justice, and his foot that carries him. Should My servant then pray for something, I will answer his prayers, and should he seek refuge in Me, I will protect him. Indeed, there is nothing I have decreed, and which I hesitate to do for the sake of a believer except causing him to experience death. He dislikes it, and I hate to displease him, but I have thus ordained."

**2-** Omar bin al-Khattāb once found Mu'āth bin Jabal, God be pleased with both of them, sitting and crying near the grave of God's messenger ﷺ. He asked him: "Why are you crying?" Mu'āth replied: "I have remembered something God's messenger ﷺ said: "The slightest ostentatiousness is polytheism, and whosoever harms any of God's deputies has surely earned God's wrath."

God's deputies have clear signs and known virtues. The righteous and wise people will seek their company, and their stations are enviable even by the martyrs and the prophets.

**3-** Omar bin al-Khattãb, God be pleased with him, narrated that God's messenger ﷺ said: "Some of Allah's blessed servants are neither prophets nor martyrs; they are special people who on the Day of Reckoning, the prophets and the martyrs will envy them for their ranks and nearness to their Lord." Someone asked: "O messenger of Allah, who are they, and what type of deeds do they perform, so that we may love them as well?" God's messenger ﷺ replied: "They are people who love one another in Allah, even though they have no consanguineous ties, money to exchange, or worldly business to barter with. I swear by God, that on the Day of Reckoning, their faces will be like effulgent lights, and they will be raised on pulpits of light. They will not be subject to fear when the creation is seized by the awesomeness of the Day of Resurrection, nor will they be subject to sorrow when the rest of the creation will be seized by it." He then recited: ﴾ Surely, God's deputies are not subject to fear nor shall they grieve.﴿ (*Qur'an 10:62*)

Among their signs is that the seekers of their circles will inherit the delight of God's blessings and be encompassed with His bounty.

**4-** Asmã' bint Zaid narrated that God's messenger ﷺ said: "Shall I tell you about your most exalted ones?" The companions replied: "Indeed." He then said: "Such are the ones that when one sees them, one remembers God Almighty."

Such blessed beings are also protected against trials and are shielded from suffering during tribulations.

**5-** 'Abdullãh bin Omar, God be pleased with him, reported that God's messenger ﷺ said: "God Almighty has created a flock He nurtures with His mercy. He grants them a life of purity from His own, and when they return to their Lord, He permits them into His paradise. Such blessed ones are among those who endure stupendous adversities and issue in safety."

Also among their signs is poverty in this world and scarcity of their food and clothing, though their shares reach them without much effort on their part.

**6-** Abu Huraira, God be pleased with him, reported that God's messenger ﷺ said: "Perhaps there is amongst you a disheveled person wearing a couple of rags; when people see him they turn their faces the other way, and yet, should he call upon God Almighty, He will answer his prayer."

Indeed, it is by their certitude that mountains are rent-asunder, and the seas parted.

**7-** On this subject, Abu Huraira, God be pleased with him, said: "I witnessed three magnificent signs in Al'alã bin al-Hadhrami, each one of them is greater and more confounding than the other. We once drove in a campaign until we reached the two Arabian seas (in the North-East.) Al'alã commanded us to charge through as he took the lead in driving his own horse across the water, and we followed him. The water came up to our horses' knees. When Ibn Muka'bar, Kisra's army commander, saw that, he screamed in shock: 'Nay, by God, I will not face such a people,' and he immediately mounted his ship and ordered his soldiers to sail back to Persia."

**8-** Sahm bin Minjãb reported a similar miraculous event, saying: "We once drove under the command of Al'alã bin al-Hadhrami. When we reached the vicinity of the town of Dãrën in Persia, there was a sea separating us from our enemy. Al'alã bin al-Hadhrami then prayed: 'O Omniscient Lord! We call upon Thee, O Most-Forbearing, Most-Exalted, and Magnificent Lord. We are Thy servants, and we have mounted this campaign for Thy sake. Lord! Grant us access to Thy enemy.' " Sahm bin Minjãb added: Immediately and miraculously the sea parted before our very eyes and its waters became shallow as we drove through it to win victory over the enemy," — by God's leave.

**9-** 'Abdullãh bnu 'Amr narrated that God's messenger ﷺ described God's deputies, saying: "Every century unveils forerunners amidst my followers," and indeed, they are the forerunners in faith, certitude and determination. The rain falls and the barren land becomes fertile by the sincerity and trueness of their prayers.

**10-** 'Abdullãh bnu 'Amr narrated that God's messenger ﷺ said: "The best ones among my followers in every century are five hundred, and the deputies are forty. Their number does not decrease. Neither the five hundred nor the forty diminish in number. When any one among the forty deputies dies, God Almighty replaces him with one of the five hundred." 'Abdullãh bnu 'Amr added: "We asked, 'O Messenger of Allah, tell us about their signs.' He replied, 'They pardon their oppressor, they show kindness to the unjust ones, and they share God's blessing with others.' "

**11-** On another occasion, God's messenger ﷺ said: "God Almighty has created three hundred people whose hearts are like that of Adam, upon whom be peace, and He created forty people whose hearts are like that of Moses, upon whom be peace. He also created seven people whose hearts are like that of Abraham, upon whom be peace, and He created five people with a heart like that of Gabriel, upon whom be peace, three people with a heart like that of Mikã'ïl, upon whom be peace, and only one person with a heart like that of Isrãfïl, upon whom be peace. When such a person dies, God Almighty will replace him with one of the three. When one of such three dies, He will replace him with one of the five. When one of the seven dies, God Almighty will replace him with one of the forty, then when one of the forty dies, He will replace him with one of the three hundred, and when one of the three hundred elite dies, God Almighty will replace him with someone He chooses from the pious masses. Such a person will live among the people, and through his prayers, by God's leave, life and death, rain and prosperity will come, and calamity will be averted."

'Abdullãh bin Mas'oud was asked: "How does such a person bring life and cause death?" He replied: "When he prays to Allah to expand the creation, the Almighty Lord fulfills his prayers, and when he prays that the tyrants be put to their knees, they will be destroyed. When he prays for rain, it will fall, when he prays for a barren land, its harvest will grow in abundance, and when he prays to God Almighty to lift a calamity, by God's leave, it will be lifted."

**12-** Speaking to Huthaifa bnul Yammãn, God's messenger ﷺ once said: "O Huthaifa, in every community among my followers there are such matted and unkempt people. In truth, they ask only for me, they only follow me, and they live strictly by God's Book. They issue from me and I am one of them, even if they have never seen me."

**13-** In another prophetic Hadīth, 'Aisha, God be pleased with her reported that God's messenger ﷺ said: "Whosoever inquires about me — or who is elated to look at me, then let him look at any unkempt, emaciated and a pale, though a hard-working person who has never laid a brick or built a hut. A banner was raised before him, and he raced toward it without hesitation. Today he is unknown, and tomorrow he is a winner, and the ultimate attainment in such race is either heaven or hell."

Such people look carefully at the ephemeral and reject it. They examine the pleasures and glitters of this world and they turn them down.

**14-** On this subject, Wahab Ibn Munbih reported that the disciples asked Jesus, son of Mary, upon both of whom be peace: "It is said that God's deputies are not subject to fear nor shall they grieve; tell us something about them, who are they?" Jesus, replied: "They are those who look deep into the earth when others look at the surface. They observe what is hidden when others are attracted to the passing pleasures, and they focus on the consequences of this world, when others seek its immediate profits. They let die in them what may shame them, and they renounce what will ultimately leave them. They are satisfied with little and the bare necessities from this world, and they do not even waste their time in discussing what is ephemeral. What they receive from this world becomes a burden and a cause of their sorrow, and they are adamant in refusing to look at other attractions therein. What comes to them as lawful they renounce, and the success that may cross their path they turn down. When their dwellings fall apart, they do not rebuild them, and when their desire for this world dies in their hearts, they do not renew it. They use their determination and will to sustain their true comfort in the abode of the hereafter instead. They have sold the pleasure and comfort of this world for the price of their comfort in the hereafter. They sold what is ephemeral, and for such a meager price, they bought what is eternal, and subsequently, they became the truly happy ones. They look at the people who love this world and see them as dead and toiling in-between one calamity after another. They recall death and renounce the idea of occupying themselves with this life. They truly love Almighty Allah. They love to speak of Him, and to constantly invoke His remembrance. They walk by His light, and they invite and allow others to walk by it as well. In fact, they are a true wonder, and they know the True Wonder. Allah's glorious Book is proclaimed through them, they establish it, and live by it. The magnificent revealed Book speaks through them, and with it they speak. Through them the glorious Book becomes known and they will live by it. They consider their trials as a vehicle for advancement despite the extreme sufferings they may endure. They find no peace except in what they seek, and they fear nothing except what should concern them most."

Such are the true believers, and such are God's deputies (*awliyã*). They are protected from looking at this abject world with arrogance, and they observe the work of their Beloved with contemplation and heedfulness.

**15-** On this subject, Ibn 'Abbãs, God be pleased with him, once said: "When God Almighty commissioned Moses and Aaron to go to Pharaoh, He said to them: 'Be not deceived by the garment with which I dressed him, for I control his destiny, and he cannot utter a word or blink without My will. Be not deceived by the comfort and pleasures of the world he dwells in, for these are the lot of the ornate and the luxury of the opulent ones. If it were My will, I can surely dress you with ornaments from the world, and which Pharaoh will certainly recognize his inability to muster. It is not because you are not worthy of it, rather it is because I have dressed you with your share of honor and exaltedness besides which the world becomes insignificant. I protect My deputies in this world just like a shepherd drives his flock away from dangerous fields. I drive them away from its pleasures just like a shepherd prevents his flock from eating contaminated or poisonous grass. I want thus to illuminate their stations, and cleanse their hearts. The countenance of My deputy carries his signs and the reason for his true happiness. You also must know that whosoever persecutes any of my deputies or causes them fear, has indeed declared war on Me, and he shall meet with My ultimate wrath on the Day of Resurrection.' "

**16-** Wahab bin Munbih in his narration of the same Sacred Tradition (*H̲adīth Qudsi*), added that God Almighty also said to Moses and Aaron: "You also must know that My servants cannot wear a garment which has more significance than the garment of asceticism and renouncing the world, for it is the cloak of the pious ones. By it, their peacefulness and piety can be identified. The marks of their prostration show on their faces. Such are My true servants. If you encounter them, lower your wings to them, and speak humbly to them. You also must know that whosoever persecutes any of my deputies or causes them fear, has indeed declared war on Me, and thus, he has invited Me to bring about his destruction, for I hasten first to help My deputies, and I have assigned such responsibility to no one but Me."

**17-** Ismā'īl Ibn 'Isa in relating the above Sacred Tradition also reported another section of the divine address whereby, Allah further said: "O Moses! You must know that My servants maintain vigilant hearts and constant fear of Me. Such state manifests in their physical condition and in their striving in the world, and it is the immediate cause of their winning My blessings in the hereafter. I am their sole hope by which they call upon Me, and thus, if you meet them, humble yourself to them."

Indeed, such special beings are the light that dispels the darkness. They are people who have filled their hearts with constant awareness of God Almighty, and with recognition of His divine majesty. In fact, they are God's proof on earth and His witnesses. He dresses them with the effulgent light of His love, and raises before their eyes the banners of His guidance so that they may seek it. He endows them with patience to protect them against resisting His will. He makes them the champions and models of those consenting to His will. He purifies their bodies with the constant alertness of observing and contemplating Him. He anoints them with the perfume of His intimate ones. He dresses them with cloaks that are woven with the threads of His kindness, and crowns them with the light of His pleasure and blessings. He then fills their hearts with the vestige of the innermost secrets of His being, so that they become attracted to Him, and their hearts attached solely to Him. Thus, their zeal and ardor rise only towards Him. Their inner eyes constantly observe Him, and He stations them at the gate of gazing at Him. He then makes them the gnostics, the physicians of the hearts, and the wise sages to serve the needs of the seekers of His path. He then says to them, 'If a needy one comes to you asking for the medicine of My nearness, nurse his needs. Treat kindly the one who is sick and emaciated because of his separation from Me. Comfort the heart of the one who is fearful of Me. Warn he who is not mindful of Me. Congratulate the one who yearns for My continuous presence. Provide the provisions for a seeker journeying toward Me. Encourage a coward to come forward and to barter with Me. Promise a good reward for the one who is in despair of My munificence. Give the glad tidings of My generosity to one who is hoping for Me to favorably consider his condition. Open your doors to the one who thinks well of Me. Maintain strong ties with the one who loves Me. Honor those who honor Me. Guide those who are seeking My path. Inquire about the one who fails to regularly join your circles. Be patient with someone's burdens if he unloads them before you. Bear up any accusations any one may cast upon you. Do not reprimand someone who fails in observing My rights upon him. Gently advise one who is committing wrongdoing. Visit the sick among My deputies. Comfort someone who is struck with grief, and shelter someone who desperately seeks you."

"O My deputies, for your sake I reprimand, and keeping you in My presence is My will. I ask for nothing from you except loyalty and gratitude. To comfort you, I have chosen and elected the best of people to serve you. I have chosen you to serve Me, for I do not like to employ tyrants or arrogant people. I do not cultivate the confused ones for My company, nor do I answer the inquisitions of the fraudulent ones. I do not bring nigh unto Me the ostentatious or the pretentious ones. I do not like to sit with the lazy ones, nor do I favor the company of the gluttonous ones."

"O My deputies! I shall reward you with the best reward, and I shall endow you with the choicest of gifts. I have conferred upon you My bounty. My favor upon you is the most generous, and My dealing with you is the best of commerce. However, what I ask of you is most demanding. I am the expert collector and connoisseur of hearts, I am the best judge of their quality, and I know what they hide. I am the observer of every move, and not a single blink of an eye can escape My knowledge. I oversee all thoughts, and I know best the range of each mind. Be ye My harbingers. Let no authority bewilder you, and fear only Me. Whosoever threatens you, I shall come to your rescue, and I will declare war on him. Whosoever befriends you, I shall befriend him. Whosoever harms you, I shall destroy him. Whosoever recognizes you as My servants, I shall reward him, and whosoever forsakes you, I will let him suffer confusion, regret, and loneliness."

Such are God's deputies. He is their only delight. His subtle presence and kindness is their only solace. He safeguards their covenant, and they are answerable solely to Him.

**18-** On this subject, 'Aisha, God be pleased with her, reported that God's messenger ﷺ once said: "Moses, upon whom be peace, once asked God Almighty, 'My Lord, tell me about Your most exalted people.' God Almighty responded, 'They are the ones who hasten to do what I want first, just like an eagle glides with precision towards what it desires. They are the servants of My creation who hasten to serve the guests like a young servant does in the house of his master. They feel offended if any of My injunctions are violated, just like an angry tiger does, for an angry tiger attacks with impunity no matter how many people it faces.' "

Hence, among Allah's creation, there is an elite He blessed, and a choice He made. They are servants who take off the shoes of comfort, put on their best effort, and dislike honor and status in this world. The admonitions and warnings of the glorious Qur'an deprive their eyes from resting at night; and understanding the words of the benevolent King humbles to submission their body, mind, and gaze.

Such are the ones who have made their foreheads a constant pillow for their prostrations, and the rough grounds of the earth a comfort for their sides. Such people embody the Qur'an to the degree that they may even renounce the comfort of resting with a wife, and instead, they may choose to stand up all night in prayers, and they embrace the Qur'an instead. Hence, their hearts open, their understanding expands, and their determination to comply with its demands is stirred to the degree of intensifying their striving. Thus, the Qur'an becomes the candlelight of their nights, the seat and bosom of their rest, the guiding light of their life, and the confounding proof against their own mind. They grieve while people seem happy, they are awake when others are asleep, they fast when others are eating, they are bewildered while others seem at peace. Thus, they are in constant fear and reverence of their Lord, and they are cautious about any changes that might affect the conclusion of their life. Hence, they are mostly fainthearted, anxious, woeful, and absorbed in their struggle. They venture onward to meet their destiny. They free themselves from any entanglements before it is too late, and they prepare themselves to meet their death. Their audaciousness in pursuing the inevitable seems unimportant alongside their greater fear of the promised punishment for failure and the dangers that engulf the attainment of a most sought reward. They conduct their lives by the dictates of the magnificent Qur'an. They liberate themselves by making sincere offerings and true sacrifices. They pursue the guiding light of the Merciful Lord and are impassioned in their pursuit until the divine utterance of the Qur'an is fulfilled, its promises are satisfied, and its promised comfort and joy for the believers become lawful to them. In fact, its comfort and light shelter them, and its warnings spare them. Through it, they satisfy their wishes, embrace their beloved, and in living by the Qur'an, they escape adversities, and live a heedful and a vigilant life in this world. This is because they readily and willingly bid farewell to the glitters of this world with contempt, and they focus their gaze on the effulgent light of the hereafter with confident expectations. Hence, they become truly content, for they have bartered the comforts of what is ephemeral for that which is everlasting.

Indeed, blessed is their commerce, and winsome is their barter, for such true human beings have truly won both, benefited from the best of both, earned God's blessings in both, and achieved what is most praiseworthy in both. Such true believers attain their exalted and elevated stations as a reward for their brief endurance, determination, and a few short hours of patience. They live through the ephemeral days of this passing world satisfied with little, and cautious of a forthcoming distressful Day of Reckoning. They intensify their struggle when calm entices others to slow down, and they are mindful of the unexpected surprises of the hour.

They do not live their days indulging in heedlessness or in the pleasures of this world, rather they engulf themselves in striving and walking through hardships in order to build what is praiseworthy and everlasting. Exhaustion emaciates their bodies and weakens their physical strength, while standing up during long nights in prayers makes them look pale, remembering a blazing fire and praying to be spared from its sufferings.

Such blessed ones hasten to do good and to abstain from distractions, and they are free from affectation and obscenities. They are silent but eloquent, blind but seeing, and in fact, no description can do them justice. For the sake of their trueness calamities are dispelled, and upon them God's blessings are showered, for they have the best of manners and the sweetest of tastes, and they are most true to their promise. They are like a saddle that carries the rider, and they are the minarets of the land, the light in the darkness, the substance of mercy and compassion, the prime of wisdom, and the backbone of the believers. Their sides disdain from resting and they would rather stand up in prayers, and they are most forgiving of others' pitfalls, they are most pardoning of those who repent, and they are most generous in their gifts.

They aspire for God's gifts with awe, watchful awareness, and praiseworthy deeds. They dismount the saddle of this world, brake the reins of their hopes in it, and their fear of displeasing their Lord does not leave them a nickel to feed their hunger, to secure their next meal, or to upgrade their shelter. They solicit nothing of the treasures of this world, nor do they accept to relax in the comfort of its furs. They are not attracted by the ease of its vehicles, nor is their focus ever distracted by the glitters of its monumental palaces. Nay! They instead see everything in its reality through the guidance of Almighty Allah, and by His inspiration to their hearts, they live with what they have, and they move onward with constancy, perseverance, and patience, consenting to few short days of hard labor.

They wrap their bodies with the essential rags, they guard them against the impermissible, and they renounce the enjoyment of savorous foods. They retreat to themselves to avoid possible wrongdoing, and they seek the safest passageway and the wisest course. They walk the road of wisdom and righteousness, and they share the blessings of the hereafter with their companions in this world. Their guarding themselves against true losses is their precaution against suffering when death comes, and they fear death, its pangs, agony, distress and shock. They contemplate the grave and its tightness, and they often think about the questioning angels in the grave, and how will they initiate the questioning, their scorning of the sinners, and probing of the believers. They also fear the day when they will stand before their Lord, blessed is His name and holy are His attributes.

Such servants of God Almighty are the light that dispels the darkness, and indeed they are the fountainhead of wisdom, righteousness, and balance. God Almighty endows them with unique and unparalleled virtues, He cleanses them from affectation and replaces it with purity, trueness and sincerity.

**19-** 'Abdullãh bin Omar, God bless both of them, narrated that Omar once walked by Mu'ãth bin Jabal, God be pleased with him, who was crying with great chagrin. Omar asked him: "O Mu'ãth, why are you crying?" He replied: "I just remembered God's messenger's ﷺ saying, 'Among His servants, Allah loves most the pious and the anonymous. If such a servant is not seen, no one will miss him, and if he is present, no one will notice him. Such true and pious ones are the pillars of guidance, and the minarets of knowledge.' "

**20-** Recalling another prophetic tradition, Thãbit bin Thawbãn narrated that God's messenger ﷺ said: "Blessed are the sincere ones, for they are the lights of guidance that dispels darkness and adversities in this world."

Such true human beings attain their exalted stations by holding fast to the rope of Allah, by spending freely and generously from what God Almighty favors them with, and by upholding justice.

**21-** Imam Ahmad Ibn Hanbal reported that the mother of the believers, 'Aisha, God be pleased with her, narrated that God's messenger ﷺ said: "Do you know who wins sanctuary under God's Throne on the Day of Judgment?" People replied: "Allah and His Messenger know best!" He explained: "Those are the ones who graciously accept what is just when it is offered, they generously give when they are asked, and they judge between people by the same criterion they seek for themselves. They are cheerful outwardly but ever anxious inwardly. The spirit of elation comes from their contentment, satisfaction, and constant yearning for their beloved, and their fear of losing their struggle, or even the mere thought of separation from Him, bewilders and distresses them."

**22-** Also on this subject, 'Iyādh bin Ghanam narrated that God's messenger ﷺ said: "I was informed by the heavenly hosts of angels that the most dignified among my followers are people who rejoice in public when they ponder the vastness of Allah's all-encompassing mercy and compassion, and they weep privately when they contemplate the rigorous punishment He reserved for the sinners and the deniers of the truth. They sit in His blessed mosques morning and evening worshipping Him and celebrating His praises inwardly, and they implore Him with their tongues outwardly with reverence and awe. They pray to Him with their hands raised as well as lowered, and they yearn for Him unceasingly. They take little from people, and yet, it bears heavily on their hearts. They walk barefooted, humble, unpretentious, and unnoticed, just like ants, without finery; and they are free of self-adulation. They walk with dignity and serenity, and they rise to the nearness of their Lord through their link to His Messenger (ﷺ). They wear the garment of good conduct and follow the clear proof. They read the Qur'an regularly, take their daily guidance from it, and they happily make the necessary personal sacrifices to meet its requirements. Almighty Allah has surrounded them with distinguished witnessing angels, and faithful guardians, and He has illumined their faces with effulgence as a sign of His blessings upon them and as a demonstration of His satisfaction with them. When they look at His servants, they anticipate promising signs. They often contemplate the vastness of Allah's creation. Their bodies dwell on earth, and their eyes are anchored upon the heavens. Their feet stand on earth, and their hearts dwell in the heavens. They breathe on earth, and yet, their spirits are connected to the divine Throne. Their souls live in this world, and their thoughts are focused on the hereafter. They only worry about what may come. Their graves are in this world, and their ranks are exalted in Allah's sight." God's messenger ﷺ then recited: ﴾ Such is the reward of one who reveres My Majesty, and fears My warning. ﴿" (*Qur'an 14:14*)

Such true believers hasten to pay what they owe without delay, and they do not procrastinate or take lightly when it comes to fulfilling their religious obligations.

**23-** Jãbir, God be pleased with him, narrated that God's messenger ﷺ said: "God's servant has three main duties: 1) If he recognizes one of God's rights upon him, he does not postpone complying with it to a day he does not know whether he will live to see; 2) he practices privately the same righteousness he offers in public; and 3) he places his hope in Allah's mercy and acceptance of his deeds." God's messenger ' then added, 'Such is Allah's deputy,' as he pointed with his hand thrice."

**24-** Al-Barã' bin 'Ãzib narrated that God's messenger ﷺ said: "God Almighty has selected an elite among His servants. He reserved for them the highest of heavens, for they are the wisest of people." Al-Barã' added: "We asked: 'O Messenger of Allah, in what way they are the wisest?" He ﷺ replied: "They mainly endeavor to please their Lord, and they renounce curiosity, aspiration for leadership, and comfort in this world, hence, the trials of the world are light and easy in their eyes, knowing that their exercise of patience in this world for a short while will help them attain permanent peace in their permanent life thereafter."

# II
## ASCETICISM AND VIRTUES

In the previous chapter, we described some of the virtues of God's deputies (*awliyã*) and the ranks of the elite (*asfiyã*). Pursuing the prophetic example, the adherents to the path of inner traditions, sometime use allegories (*ishãrãt*) to describe a phenomenon, though at other times they may depict the nature of sainthood, or viceregency (*wilãya*) as a blessing which is conferred upon one who lives by the dictates of the divine command revealed in the magnificent Qur'an, and who emulates the *sunna* traditions of God's messenger ﷺ upon whom be peace. The diversity of expressions (*'ibãrãt*) they used throughout the ages are clear signs to those whose hearts are awakened.

Primarily, God's deputies emphásize the virtues of the early companions of God's messenger ﷺ, their piety, ascetic detachment, devotion, sincerity, deeds, faith, certitude, and determination. The complexity of spiritual and intellectual levels of their audience sometimes influence the outcome and the depth of their speeches. Since all the creation that surround the human being are testimonies to the oneness and sovereignty of God Almighty, which creations constantly celebrate His praises and obey His commands, the most blessed companions of God's messenger ﷺ commenced by noticing such phenomena, and they pointed at such attributes. Thus, they were satisfied to draw on such parables that relate to the human nature. What is innate and common, they explored, and what is unique, they emphasized. The early companions of God's messenger ﷺ who are the beacons of purity, piety, and devotion also used such similes, as described by Sa'ad bin Abi Waqqãss, God be pleased with him, in his saying, 'Whatever we had was common to all, as when a ewe delivers a baby lamb, it becomes common to all.'

A true believer is content with what he has. He is grateful for it, and he shares its blessings with others. A true believer is also protected against excess comfort or indulgence in this world. He uses a meager portion of his share in it to sustain his short journey toward his Lord, and therefore, he becomes one of the numerous pillars of trueness and guiding lights to the seekers in this world. He refrains from abominable actions and strives for deeds that bring him closer to his Lord. He dedicates every minute he spends in this life to exercising more devotion to guard himself against the unexpected, and thus, he escapes from sufferings and trials as he embarks on the straight path and takes the road to safety.

**25-** 'Ali bin Abi Ṯālib, God bless his countenance, said: "God's messenger ﷺ once said to me, 'O 'Ali, when you see people striving for the nearness of their Lord through the avenues of being true unto Him, you should strive toward His nearness through the avenues of reason (*'aql*). In such a way, you will rise to a higher station than the others, and you will reach closer to Him in this world as well as in the hereafter.' "

**26-** Abu Tharr al-Ghafāri said: "I once asked God's messenger ﷺ, 'O Messenger of Allah, what are the records that were revealed to Abraham, upon whom be peace?' He replied: 'They were mostly parables and allegories. They included sayings such as: "A servant who is not deprived of reason, and who is not overwhelmed by material concerns must balance his time. At one time, he should converse with his Lord, then he should question himself, then contemplate God's work, and furthermore, he must also nurture his body with its needs of food and water.' "

Hence, like the wool that covers the back of a sheep and protects it from changing weather, a true believer also has such a coat that cloaks his needs and suffices him from needing other than his Lord. He accepts no substitute for it, nor does he let go of it as long as he can.

**27-** On this subject, Anas bin Mālik narrated that God's messenger ﷺ said: "When Abraham saw the fire (which Nemrod ignited to cast him in), he exclaimed, 'God is sufficient, and He is the best of guardians.' "

**28-** Abu Huraira narrated that God's messenger ﷺ said: "When Abraham was thrown into the fire, he prayed, 'Surely thou art are the only Lord in the heavens, and I am the only one who worships Thee on earth.' "

**29-** Nawf al-Bakāli reported the above prophetic hadīth adding: "Upon hearing Abraham's prayers, God Almighty commanded three thousand angels to descend on earth, and Abraham led them in prayers uninterruptedly for three consecutive nights and days."

**30-** Pursuing the same account, Bakr bin 'Abdullāh al-Mazīni narrated: "When Abraham was brought to be thrown into the fire of Nemrod, the entire creation in the heavens prayed solemnly and fervently to their Lord, imploring Him: 'Lord! Thy bosom friend is going to be thrown into the blazing fire. Lord, grant us permission to extinguish it.' God Almighty replied, 'He is my bosom friend, and I have no other bosom friend on earth besides him today. Surely, I am his only Lord and Sustainer, and he has no other Lord or Sustainer except Me. However, if he asks for your help, then help him, otherwise, leave him alone.' The angel of rain then came and asked God Almighty. He said, 'Lord! Thy bosom friend is going to be thrown into the blazing fire. O Lord, grant me permission to extinguish it.' Again, God Almighty replied, 'He is my bosom friend, I have no bosom friend on earth besides him today. Surely, I am his only Lord and Sustainer, and he has no other Lord and Sustainer except Me. Yet, if asks for your help then help him, otherwise, leave him alone.' As Abraham was being thrown into the fire, he called upon his Lord directly, praying, 'Sufficient is Allah, and He is the best of guardians.' Immediately God Almighty commanded the fire, saying, ‹ O fire, cool down and do not harm Abraham. › "

It is reported that on that day, the weather changed suddenly, and strong winds struck the entire globe from the East to the West, and had God Almighty not stressed for the fire not to cause Abraham harm, and instead He commanded it to bring about his comfort, Abraham would have frozen to death.

**31-** Also on this subject, Muqātil reported: "When Abraham was brought before the fire, and as soon as the guards took off his shirt and tied him to a scaffold to throw him into it, the heavens cried out, and so did the earth, the mountain, the sun, the moon, the divine throne, the divine seat, the clouds, the winds, they all cried, and all the angels cried out: 'Lord! Thy servant Abraham is going to be thrown into the blazing fire. Lord! Grant us permission to come to help him.' The fire itself then cried out, saying: 'My Lord! Thou created me and subjugated me to be subservient to the needs of the children of Adam, and now, Thy servant Abraham is going to be thrusted into me to be consumed by me.' God Almighty then spoke to all of them by inspiration and said: 'My servant worships Me, and he is being chastised by others for My sake. If he calls upon Me, I will surely answer him, and if he asks for your help, then you may help him.' "

"As soon as the scaffold was brought closer to the blazing fire, the archangel Gabriel descended and stood between Abraham and the fire, and he said: 'Peace be upon thee O Abraham, I am Gabriel, would you need my help?' Abraham replied: 'As for your help, nay, I do not need it, I only need my Lord.' "

"When the scaffold released him to the fire, Allah then ordered the archangel Isrãfil to envelop Abraham and to protect him from the blazes with his own cloak. God Almighty then commanded the fire: ❮ O fire, cool down and do not harm Abraham. ❯' " (*Qur'an 21:96*)

**32-** Al-Manhal bin Khãlid said: "I was told that Abraham remained in the fire for maybe forty or fifty days, and later on, he used to say: 'My nights and days were the most blessed therein. If it were up to me, I would have preferred to remain all my life therein, (in God's nearness, blessings and guardianship.)' "

The modest woolen cloak God's deputies wrap around themselves helps to make their life simple. The absence of trims also benefit their concentration upon their real goal as a shield against the material distractions and glitters of this world. Such modest cloak also brakes the arrogance of the mind and eliminates any feeling of haughtiness or of being special. It keeps the mind enthralled, feeling unimportant, and it keeps its urges under control. Moreover, simplicity drives one's carnality to contentment and satisfaction with little.

**33-** Imam Abu Na'ïm al-As̲fahãni narrated that Imam Ja'far al-S̲ãdiq, God be pleased with him said: "Whosoever emulates the living sunna traditions (*z̲ãhir*) of God's messenger ﷺ, upon whom be peace, is a sunni, and whosoever seeks to emulate the innermost being (*bãt̲in*) of God's messenger ﷺ, upon whom be peace, is a sufi."

What Imam Ja'far al-Sãdiq, God be pleased with him, meant by emulating the 'innermost being' (*bãt̲in*) of God's messenger ﷺ, is to strive and embrace the prophet's most exalted chaste character and love for his Lord, and to pursue his choice and preference for the company of His Lord in the hereafter, and that is the correct way of the sufis.

Thus, to prefer what God's messenger ﷺ preferred, to desire what he desired, to practice the type of devotion he practiced, and to discard what he discarded, will unfailingly cleanse and purify one's heart, and it will make him true to his Lord. Such a person will be guarded against adversities, and he will be saved from any harm others may try to inflict upon him. Otherwise, to waiver from such a path and to fail in such pursuit, to grant oneself and one's deeds high esteem, and to indulge in satiating one's desire and hunger in this world earns the human being nothing but growing torpor, ignorance, heedlessness, and they block his cognizance from realizing the dangers it faces in this world as well as in the hereafter.

**34-** Suwayd bin Ghafla reported that Abu Bakr al-Siddïq once asked God's messenger ﷺ: "O Messenger of Allah, what were you sent with?" He replied: "I was sent with 'Reason' (*'aql*)." Abu Bakr further asked: "How can we receive that?" God's messenger ﷺ replied: "There is no way to fully encompass Reason (*'aql*), although if one adheres to what Allah made lawful and abstains from what He qualified as unlawful, such a person will be called intelligent and sagacious (*'ãqil*). Should he strive further, he will be called a true worshipper (*'ãbid*), and should he strive further yet, he will be called generous and cognizant of his Lord (muhsin). On the other hand, if one simply strives to merely comply with what God Almighty has ordained, though incorrectly and without the needed luck, or without having true reason to guide him to do what is good, and to dissuade him from pursuing what God Almighty has forbidden, he becomes one of those ›Whose efforts have been wasted in this life, and yet, they hold their deeds to be valuable.› ' "(*Qur'an 18:104*)

**35-** Abu Sa'ïd al-Khidri reported that God's messenger ﷺ saying: "Allah has divided reason (*'aql*) into three parts. Whosoever has them, his judgment is mature and perfect, and whosoever does not have them, he has no brains. They comprise: 1) having true cognizance of one's Lord; 2) offering true obedience to His commands; and, 3) exercising true patience toward what Almighty Allah has ordained."

Thus, how can one be called a true ascetic if when he is challenged about his true cognizance of his Lord, he grows ambivalent and confused, and sometimes he even becomes choleric, and when he is asked to subscribe to God's commands, he falters and becomes confounded, and moreover, when he is tried with a passing challenge requiring him to exercise patience, he fails and becomes angry.

The learned shaikhs spoke frequently about the inner spiritual realms, and they expounded upon their meanings, boundaries, characteristics, and foundations. Furthermore, the attained shaikhs have described true asceticism to have ten meanings: 1) To restrain one's partaking from his share in this world rather than unleashing his desire for it; 2) to train one's heart to depend solely on God Almighty and to grow from quietude to absolute acceptance; 3) to desire submission, adding willingness in volunteering one's servitude; 4) to exercise patience toward the loss of comfort in this world, and to refrain from asking or complaining about it; 5) to be selective when nursing one's needs if the object is adequately available; 6) to occupy oneself exclusively in God Almighty; 7) to constantly celebrate His praises more inwardly than outwardly; 8) to develop true sincerity that is free from suspicion; 9) to have certainty when doubt emerges; and finally, 10) to resort to absolute peace in God Almighty by dispelling and controlling any disturbance or bewilderment. Whosoever has such qualities is a true ascetic, a sufi, otherwise he is a fraud and a hypocrite.

If one asks: 'What is asceticism (Arb. *zuhd*)?' The answer is: Asceticism is a raiment which God Almighty confers upon the elite among His devout creation. If they are inspired to be grateful for it, then it will be well deserved, otherwise, they become subject to His reprimand and they will engulf themselves in ongoing trials and tribulations. In fact, to dispel evil conduct and to harbor every exalted quality is the nature of a true ascetic. When he speaks, he unfailingly expresses the truth, and when he is silent, he asserts his ascetic detachment. The truth is that asceticism is an attribute, the meaning of which is hidden to the majority of people aside from the unique achievers, and they are most rare.

Ascetic detachment means to cleanse and purify one's heart and to keep it exclusively for the Lord of the unseen, hence, an ascetic is a true Gnostic. On the other hand, the bosom of a true gnostic (*'ārif*) is exposed, his heart is wounded, and his body is waning. A true gnostic is one who truly knows God Almighty, who has understood God's purpose, who acts upon what God commands, abstains from what He forbids, and who calls God's creation to answer the call of their Lord and Creator. A true gnostic is one whose heart is pure and who follows the path of God's chosen Messenger ﷺ and the seal of His prophets. He casts away the world behind him, and feeds his passion the taste of desolation and bitterness. He truly knows God's glory and recognizes His compassion toward His creation. If there is a preferable expression, a true gnostic is then one who is free from despondency and confusion. He is abounding with contemplation and purpose, and in his eyes gold and dirt are equal.

To pursue such life, one has to imbibe good character, and such good character will bring one to meet with good people. To do so, one must sacrifice his carnality, expose his own wantonness and put it to shame, upset his adversary, and lend people good advice. He must be concerned at all times. He must teach by example, and hold the reins of his own expectations. He must not pretend to notice others' pitfalls. He should first acknowledge his own faults, be ready to correct his own defects to begin with, and easily and willingly apologize for them. Such a servant of God Almighty must embrace sorrow as his trade, and he must make contentment the foundation of his life.

A gnostic truly knows his Lord, he remains continuously at His doorsteps, and he forsakes any supplemental company. His trueness raises him in station, his kindness is the tree that nurtures him, and he faithfully guards his covenant like a shepherd guards his sheep.

The learned shaikhs have expounded on a variety of complex questions concerning asceticism, and they used distinct expressions. Each one of their answers reflects the spiritual state of the speaker, as well as the prevailing level of perception and understanding of his audience. Altogether, the explanations of the learned shaikhs consist of three categories: 1) first and foremost, they speak of God's Oneness; 2) they speak of the goal of the seeker and the different stations of his attainment; 3) and thirdly, they speak of the seeker himself and his plight. Each one of these three categories involves numerous issues and branches. The first is cognition (*'irfãn*), which knowledge must be followed by one's adherence to the code of service and ardor.

**36-** On this subject, Ibn 'Abbãs, God be pleased with him, narrated that when God's messenger ﷺ sent Mu'ãth to teach in Yemen, he said to him: "You will be going to live among some of the people of the book. Call them first to worship Allah alone, and to associate no one with Him. If they acknowledge, then inform them that Allah has enjoined upon them five times prayers for each day and night. If they comply, then apprise them that Allah has decreed a tithe that will be exacted from their rich and turned over to their poor."

**37-** 'Abdullãh bin al-Musawwar narrated that a man once came to God's messenger ﷺ and asked: "O messenger of Allah, teach me about the mystical knowledge." God's messenger ﷺ replied: "What have you done with the elementary knowledge to prepare yourself to inquire about the extraordinary knowledge?" The man asked: "What is the elementary knowledge?" God's messenger ﷺ replied: "Do you know God?" The man replied: "Yes, I do." God's messenger ﷺ then asked: "What have you done with His rights upon you?" The man replied: "Whatever God willed." God's messenger ﷺ asked: "Do you recognize death?" The man replied: "Yes, I do." God's messenger ﷺ then asked: "What have you prepared for it?" The man replied: "Whatever God willed." God's messenger ﷺ then said: "Go and perfect that section in your life, and then come back to me so I may teach you about the mystical knowledge."

Thus, true gnosis is to attain a perfect state which is based on knowing God Almighty, His holy Names, eternal Attributes, and divine Actions. A seeker on this path also must understand the characteristics of the carnal self (*nafs*), its evil and stimulants. He also must know the nature of such an avowed enemy, its entrapments and deceptions. He also must understand the nature of the world, its arrogance, allurements, and colors; how to guard oneself from its dangers and hazards, and how to control it and then renounce it. Once he recognizes that all of these elements belong to one category, he will carry a struggle of endurance by waging a rigorous battle against it while observing the mandated prayers, marshaling supererogatory devotion, disregarding personal comfort, and savoring the cultivated delights which will be unveiled gradually and exclusively before such true servants, and then, he must labor to guard such divine gifts and blessings as long as Allah wills. During the process of such elevation, a true dependant and servant of Allah does not refrain from serving his community and abiding by the law, nor is he ever satisfied with conjecture or speculation. What he seeks is true and binding, and what he disallows are obstructions that can prevent his progress. All his concerns are one. He emulates the exalted traditions of the blessed companions from among the Meccan émigrés (*muhājireen*) as well as the Medinite partisans (*ansār*). He discards wealth and renounces fame, and instead, he favors striving and giving preference to the needs of others. He escapes with his body to the farthest points in the mountains and wilderness, and he raises it healthy and safe from the disdains of the jealous eyes. At the beginning, he safeguards himself from people's meddling with his name, in fear that they may hamper his progress or envy his inner peace and joy, then once his reserved station is conferred upon him by God Almighty, and once it is attained, only then that he will rest in its bliss and effulgent light, and later on, God willing, he may return to serve people's needs.

Such are the pious ones, the unknown, the strangers, the travellers, and the true ones. When their faith become true, their innermost being becomes clear and pure.

**38-** On this subject, Sa'ad bin Abi Waqqāss narrated that God's messenger ﷺ said: "Allah loves a servant who is pious, content, and unknown."

**39-** In another prophetic saying reported by 'Abdullāh bin 'Amr, God's messenger ﷺ said: "Allah loves the strangers most." Someone asked: "Who are the strangers?" He replied: "Those who escape with their faith to protect it. On the Day of Judgment, God Almighty will resurrect them in the company of Jesus, the son of Mary, upon both of whom be peace."

**40-** Ibn Mas'oud reported that God's messenger ﷺ said: "There will come a day when everyone's religion will be in danger, except for someone who escapes with his faith from village to village, from mountain to mountain, and who hides inside an abandoned den after another."

**41-** Abi Imāma reported that God's messenger ﷺ said: "Among my followers, I love most a believer who controls his emotions, who gives prayers and fasting a good share in his life, who is known to worship his Lord, and who obeys Him in secret. No one recognizes him, and he arouses no curiosities. He subsists on meager sustenance, and exercises patience. His Lord awaits to bring him to stand before Him, few will know of his death, and fewer are his heirs."

Inwardly, such blessed servants enjoy illustrious ranks, and outwardly, they exhibit a noble character and magnanimity, along with a gentle disposition, and hence, their ranks are sublime, and their humor is most touching.

## Glorifying The Supreme Divine Omnipresence (*Salātu Tasābīh*)

**42-** On this subject, Ibn 'Abbās, God be pleased with him and with his father, reported that God's messenger ﷺ once encountered him as a young boy, and he said to him: "Child, would you like me to express my love for you? Child, should I make you a present? Should I give you a gift?" Ibn 'Abbās replied gratifyingly: "Yes, indeed, O messenger of Allah, for you are to me as dear as my own father and my own mother. Please do so." Ibn 'Abbās continued: "I thought that God's messenger ﷺ was going to give me some money, or perhaps give me a share in a property." God's messenger ﷺ then said: "Pray four groupings of supererogatory obeisance (*rak'āt*) each day and night. In the first grouping and following the intention and the initial article of thanā', praising Almighty Allah, recite fifteen times, 'Glory be to Allah and all praises are due to Him; surely there is no god except Allah.' Proceed to recite the opening chapter of the Qur'an plus another chapter, and then, while still standing up, recite the same formula ten times. Recite this prayer ten times when you bow in ruku, and again, recite it ten times when you stand up again, ten times when you prostrate, ten times when you sit back (*julūs*), and ten times when you prostrate yourself for the second time, and do the same in the remaining three groupings of prayers. When you complete the last article of your prayers, and before the final greetings, say, 'Lord, I ask Thee to grant me the success of Thy guided ones, the deeds of the pious ones, the consent of the penitent ones, the determination of the vigilant ones, and the gratitude of the learned ones, so that I may fear Thee and hold Thee in utmost reverence. Lord, make me revere Thee so that I may never disobey Thee, and help me to follow and obey Thy command so that my deeds would merit Thy blessings. Make me fear wrongdoing so that I can offer true and sincere repentance, and help me give others the good advice purely for the love of Thee. Lord, grant me to think well of Thee so that I may depend solely on Thee. Indeed Thou art the glorious Lord and the effulgent light.' God's messenger ﷺ then continued: ' If you keep up this practice, God Almighty will forgive you all your sins, the minor and the major ones, the old and the new ones, the private and the public ones, and the intentional and the unintentional ones.'"

God's ambassadors to His creation, His intimate and beloved ones are bewildered by any form of separation, and they are constantly perturbed should they be demoted for any failure.

**43-** On this subject, Mu'āth bin Jabal reported that God's messenger ﷺ said to him: "O Mu'āth, a believer in this world is like a prisoner. He knows well that he is watched. He acknowledges that his hearing, sight, tongue, hand, foot, stomach and sexual organ are under constant scrutiny. Even his glimpses and glances or whatever he gazes upon is recorded — even should he be looking at the droppings of a bird, or beautifying his eyelids with kohl. Every minute of striving he endures is closely watched. A true believer cannot trust the constancy of his own heart. There is nothing that can calm his ultimate concerns, and even then, he does expect to meet his death at any moment. Thus, his own piety becomes his observer, the Qur'an his guide, fear of wrongdoing his proof, nobility his trade, caution his companion, awe his mark, prayers his cavern, fasting his shield of protection, charity his relief, truthfulness his attendant, chastity his commander, and behind all of that stands the glory of his Lord to watch over his performance. O Mu'ãth, knowing the revealed Qur'an has subdued the believer's desires and wants, and by God's leave, the Qur'ãn stands to save him from his possible demise. O Mu'ãth, I love for you what I love for myself, and I have conveyed to you what the archangel Gabriel, upon whom be peace, has told me. If you recognize that, I do not know of anyone who will be happier than you when you meet me on the Day of Resurrection and enjoy the excellence God Almighty has brought out of you."

# III
# The Righteous Caliphs

We solicit Allah's guidance and mercy, and we commence this chapter by citing few of the numerous virtues of some of the blessed elite, the righteous companions of God's messenger ﷺ, the witnesses of the divine revelation, and later on his successors. Each one of them was known for his distinct virtues and uprightness; their own contemporaries as well as believers of all times will always learn from their excellence, trace their deeds, analyze their thoughts, and try to emulate their traits. These dear companions of God's messenger ﷺ, upon whom be peace, were guarded against languor and procrastination, their ultimate prize was outlined to them during their lifetime, and none of them was ever victim to weariness or listlessness.

In the previous chapters, we learned how spirituality is an overwhelming state that focuses the true heart of the believer upon his most urgent needs, and helps him to recognize his real goal. By virtue of one's sincere striving, spirituality becomes a new nature through which the seeker's character, conduct, and clarity become refined. Hence, when one seeks and allows reality to come to the surface, such innate unique essence will capture the entirety of the human being: his mind, soul and body. The attainment of such station is then recognized through one's recognition of his Lord, ardent devotion, absence of doubt, constancy of servitude, purity of intention, clarity of thoughts, acuteness of judgment, confident anticipations, and exact knowledge and control of one's moods, tempers, and traits. Such realization also eases the seeker's struggle against carnal urges, confrontations with falsehood, and attachments to worldly ranks or material effects. He clearly realizes the difference between truth and falsehood, and he lucidly discriminates between the ephemeral and the eternal, true existence and nullity.

Such a blessed forerunner never ceases to ponder the miracle of his Maker, and he constantly contemplates the divine work of his Beloved. The more his realization expands, the more his devotion increases, and his detachment from the ephemeral world becomes easier. His *zikr* (remembrance) of Allah is constant in his heart and on his tongue, and modesty and meekness become his trade, while he constantly battles against procrastination and neglect of his duties. Only a profligate will take lightly the status of such exalted beings, and only a wimp will falsely claim to have attained their station. On the other hand, only a most intelligent person will follow in their footsteps, and only a yearning soul for its Lord seeks their company.

Our ambition is to lay eye on them, we take their covenant as our covenant, we vow to walk in their footsteps, and we pledge to remain thus until the day we meet with them before the glorious and most magnificent presence of our Lord.

Among such most pious prominent *muhãjireen* (émigrés) from Mecca to Madina, we begin herein by citing few of the awe-inspiring accounts of the first righteous caliph Abu Bakr al-Siddïq, may God's blessings shower upon him eternally, the most loyal and sincere companion of God's messenger ﷺ, upon whom be peace.

## 1- Abu Bakr Al-Siddïq

Abu Bakr, God be pleased with him, is one of the foremost believers who had accepted God's message which called people to Islam, and to believe in His Messenger ﷺ upon whom be peace. Abu Bakr was called *al-Siddïq* (one who never fails to testify to the truth), because of his unquestionable faith in what God's messenger ﷺ brought from his Lord, and he never had any doubt about the supreme authority of the One Who revealed it. Abu Bakr was also called *al-'Atïq* (the ancient), for he was one of few believers who embraced Islam as soon as they heard about the divine revealed message.

Abu Bakr al-Siddïq, God be pleased with him, was granted an unequivocal victory from the heavens. He was the bosom companion of God's messenger ﷺ during his residence and travels, and he shared with him a magnificent fellowship filled with love, compassion, and sharing under all circumstances. Lastly, he was laid to rest within the same chamber where God's messenger ﷺ was laid to rest, in the realms of peace and beauty of the Prophet's Mosque, in the splendor of the garden of paradise which radiates with the effulgent lights of the message, the chosen Messenger, and the Seal of God's prophets, and the host of heavenly angels who continuously and up to the Day of Resurrection will continue to descend upon his resting place. This is the garden which housed the revelation of the holy scripture and witnessed the birth of the city of God's messenger ﷺ and his school of divine truth.

Abu Bakr al-S̲iddïq is also the blessed companion who is cited in the holy Qur'an in the most honoring reference: ﴾ One of the two companions who were in the cave. ﴿ *(Qur'an 9:40)* His name resonated with honor throughout the ages, and no one among the greatest achievers has ever attained his faith, nobility and grandeur. Again, in the holy Qur'an, the Lord of the unseen describes his generosity, saying: ﴾ Those who spent freely and who had fought (to defend the truth) before the victory are not of the same rank as those who did so later, the earlier ones are surely better ﴿ (*Qur'an 57:10*).

Abu Bakr al-S̲iddïq accepted God's guidance and believed in His Oneness, and his guidance to Islam was Allah's choice. When Abu Bakr, God be pleased with him, heard the call of God's messenger ﷺ, he immediately accepted it and attested to its truth. He then renounced the comforts of this world, and dedicated all his entire wealth to serve God's message. Abu Bakr became the harbinger of God's messenger ﷺ, and consequently, he was a prime target of persecution, abuse, and sufferings. His heart was filled with God Almighty, he took shelter in his Lord, and he cared little about what the world had to offer.

**44-** Ibn 'Abbās, God be pleased with him, reported that after the death of God's messenger ﷺ, Abu Bakr arrived in Madina when Omar was delivering a speech. Abu Bakr gently said to Omar: "Sit down, O Omar!" Omar discounted the advice and he pursued his speech. At once, Abu Bakr reiterated with an imposing voice: "O Omar sit down!" Abu Bakr then stood before the crowd, and he testified to the oneness of Allah, and to the apostleship of His Messenger ﷺ, and he then said: "O ye people! He who amongst you worships Muhammad, indeed Muhammad has died, and he who amongst you worships Allah, then surely Allah is ever living and He does not die." Abu Bakr then recited a verse from the holy Qur'an: ﴾ Muhammad is but a Messenger, many apostles like whom have passed away before him. Will it be then when he dies or is slain, that you will turn back on your heels? Surely, he who turns back on his heels does no hurt to Allah; and Allah will generously reward the thankful ﴿" (*Qur'an 3:144*)

Ibn 'Abbãs continued: "I swear to Allah, that it was as if the people had never heard this verse until Abu Bakr recited it."

**45-** Sa'ïd bin al-Musayyib also narrated that Omar, God be pleased with him, said: "By God, as soon as I heard Abu Bakr recite this verse, I sat down, and my feet could not support me. I nearly fell in a swoon when I heard him say that God's messenger ﷺ had died."

The purity of Abu Bakr's allegiance to Allah and to His blessed messenger ﷺ, helped him to reach the highest moral standard. Such piety can only develop from one's longing to remain in the presence of his Lord, the unique and only Sustainer of the universes.

**46-** On this subject, 'Urwa bin al-Zubair reported that Abu Bakr's blessed daughter, the mother of the believers, 'Aisha, God be pleased with her, said: '(In Mecca), when the tribe of Quraish gained influence over the property of Ibn al-Dughna, they stirred him to demand from Abu Bakr, his neighbor, to refrain from tormenting their feelings by reading the Qur'an aloud, and instead to read it and to worship in the privacy of his own house as much as he wants. Abu Bakr complied with their request, and later on he even built a prayer niche inside his courtyard. Therein, he performed his prayers and read the Qur'an in privacy. The neighboring women and children of Quraish kept on harassing him and prying at his house from their roofs. Abu Bakr was lachrymose and particularly given easily to crying when reading the Qur'an. Such faith alarmed the highborn of The tribe of Quraish, and they further incited Ibn al-Dughnah who went again to Abu Bakr and said: "You recognize well what we have convened. Either you curtail your act, or give me back my property for I do not like the Arabs to say that I cringed or failed to demand compliance with an agreement." Abu Bakr replied: "Then I will give you back your property and solicit shelter in Allah and in the company of His Apostle."

Abu Bakr used to easily and readily discard his ephemeral interests in this world, and he solicited the everlasting delights of the hereafter. It was as though he had divorced the world and was unyielding to its allurements.

**47-** Zaid bin al-Arqam, God be pleased with him, said: "We were visiting Abu Bakr, God be pleased with him, and he asked for a drink. Someone in his household brought a pitcher of fresh honey sweetened water. As soon as they handed him a cup to drink from, Abu Bakr gazed at it and recognized what it is, he immediately wept. We remained silent, but as soon as he regained his calm, he looked at it, and he again burst out crying and no one dared to inquire from him. When he finally regained his poise, we asked, 'What is it that upset you to cry thus?' He replied: 'I was once with God's messenger ﷺ, and he suddenly became annoyed and he kept on saying: 'Get away from me, get off my back!' I said, 'O messenger of Allah! What's happening? I see you warding off something, though I can see no one near you!' He replied, 'The whole world (*dunya*) appeared before me adorned with its ornaments, and I told it to leave me alone. The world then said to me, 'By God, if you do turn your back to me, then no one after you will ever escape me.' Abu Bakr added: 'When I saw the honey sweetened water, I became afraid that perhaps the world is now coming after me, and that made me cry.' "

Abu Bakr, God be pleased with him, was mostly sober and abstemious. He struck a balance of the rightly guided ones, and he never hedged on his limits. He was serious in every endeavor in his pursuit to please Almighty Allah, the King of all kings.

**48-** On this subject, it is narrated that Abu Bakr had a male servant who used to bring him what he collected daily of businesses and supplies. One day the servant brought home a little food with him, and Abu Bakr was somehow hungry, and he hastened and took a bite from it. The servant was astonished and asked: "You usually inquire where do I get the food from! What happened to you tonight, you did not ask?" Abu Bakr replied: "I was hungry, but anyhow, where from did you acquire this food?" The servant replied: "Sometime ago, I was passing by a gathering of Quraishi people, and I helped them. They were so pleased with my courtesy, and they promised me a reward. Today, I happen to pass by them again, and they were having a wedding. When they saw me, they remembered me, and they offered me some food." Abu Bakr shook and said: "You have nearly killed me!" He immediately tried to induce vomiting but without success. Abu Bakr was then told that water would help, so he drank some and kept on attempting to induce vomiting until his stomach was cleared. Someone said to him: "May Allah have mercy on you. You did all of that because of a single small bite?" Abu Bakr replied: "Even should my soul leave my body with it, I would have carried out that undertaking. I once heard God's messenger ﷺ say: 'Any body that grows on a forbidden substance, hell will be its final abode.' Thus, I feared should any cell of my body feed on this small bite.' "

Abu Bakr would even risk danger if the outcome were beneficial. In fact, to tolerate the heat of adversities is a virtue only a loyal seeker will endure in longing for his beloved.

**49-** On this subject, Asmã', daughter of Abu Bakr, reported that her father was at home when he heard a loud commotion inside his house. Someone then ran to him and cried out: "Hurry up, hurry up and help your friend!" Abu Bakr quickly took off toward the sacred Mosque, and he saw a group of unbelievers from the tribe of Quraish heckling God's messenger ﷺ. Abu Bakr cried out: 'Woe unto you! Would you kill a man for saying 'God is my Lord,' and who has brought you clear signs from your Lord?' " The people got distracted from their earlier purpose and they lashed mercilessly at Abu Bakr. Asmã', God be pleased with her, continued: "Later on, Abu Bakr was carried home shaken by the confrontation. We all hastened to nurse him, and whatever tresses of hair he touched came out with his own hand as he kept on reciting: 'Blessed be Thou art, the Lord of majesty and glory, blessed be Thou art, the Lord of majesty and glory.' " As soon as Abu Bakr woke up from his shock, he anxiously asked: "What happened to God's messenger?" And he was told that he was safe back in his house.

In fact, Abu Bakr, God be pleased with him, sacrificed the insignificant to secure himself the ultimate in significance. He sat his focus correctly and guided his intention wholly towards the Lord of the undiminishing grace.

**50-** On this subject, Zaid bin al-Arqam narrated that God's messenger ﷺ once asked everyone to give money in charity. It happened that Omar had some money to offer, so he said to himself: "If I ever have the opportunity to outdo Abu Bakr, it will be today." Thus, he brought half of his money and presented it to God's messenger ﷺ who asked him: "What did you keep for your family?" Omar replied: "An equal balance." Later on that day, Abu Bakr arrived with everything he had, and he presented it to God's messenger ﷺ who asked him: "What did you keep for your family?" Abu Bakr replied: "I left them God and His Messenger." Omar then said: "O Abu Bakr, I shall never attempt to vie with you again."

In deed, Abu Bakr, God be pleased with him, was true in his devotion, and he was overflowing in his brotherly love. He exhausted every possibility for the sake of his beloved, God's messenger ﷺ, and he attended to every meticulous detail to make the heart of his beloved comfortable.

**51-** On this subject, Anas bin Mālik reported that when God's Messenger ﷺ and Abu Bakr withdrew to the cave of *hirā'*, during their flight from the persecution of the Meccans, and on their way to Madina, it was nighttime, and Abu Bakr said: "O messenger of Allah, allow me to enter the cave before you do, for should there be a snake or another unforeseen danger, it will strike me first." God's messenger ﷺ consented: "Enter it." There, inside the cave was extremely dark, and as soon as Abu Bakr entered it, he kept on combing its floor and feeling every single stone. He then tore a piece of his garment and cushioned each stone with a piece of it. He did so with each stone and pebble until only one stone was left, and which he sat on before he invited God's Messenger ﷺ, upon whom be peace, to enter the cave. In the morning, God's

Messenger ﷺ saw Abu Bakr's condition, and he lifted his blessed hands to the heavens and prayed: "Lord, I beseech Thee to grant Abu Bakr to be with me in my station on the Day of Resurrection," and God Almighty granted his prayer.

**52-** Abi Sãlih reported that during the caliphate of Abu Bakr, a delegation from Yemen arrived to Madina, and when they heard a recitation from the Qur'an, they wept. Abu Bakr remarked: "We were like that in the beginning, but since then, our hearts have hardened." In this sense, he meant that the companions' faith helped their hearts grow stronger in the comfort of knowing God Almighty.

**53-** Imam Ahmad Ibn Hanbal reported that when Abu Bakr fell ill, people visited him and asked whether he had called a physician. He replied: "He already saw me." They asked: "What was his prognosis? " Abu Bakr replied: "He said: 'I do whatever I want.' "

**54-** Imam Ahmad Ibn Hanbal narrated that 'Abdu-Rahmãn bin 'Awf said: "I visited Abu Bakr, God be pleased with him, during the illness of which he died. I paid my regards of peace and I sat near him. Abu Bakr turned to me and said, 'I saw the world (*dunya*) come before me and it knelt down, but it refrained from coming closer. Surely a day will come, when people will adorn themselves with silk and fineries, and they will contemn woolen garments. I swear to Almighty Allah that it will be more advantageous for one to be unjustly beheaded than to wallow in the throes of this world.' "

**55-** Yahya bin Abi Kathïr reported that sometimes during his Friday sermon, Abu Bakr used to say : "Where are the bright ones, the handsome-looking ones, and where are those who took pride in their youthfulness, where have they gone? Where are the great kings who built cities and castles and fortified them with towering walls? What happened to the lionhearted valorous ones who made their enemy suffer humiliation in the battlefields? Time waned under their feet and they ended inside dark graves. Think of it and take heed. They have gone far far away." Abu Bakr would then cry out perturbedly: "Help, help!"

**56-** Quoting from another sermon, 'Abdullãh bin 'Akïm

reported that Abu Bakr after praising God Almighty said: "O ye people, I advise you to heed God's warning, to fear Him and to revere Him. Celebrate His Holy Name with praises that are consistent with His majesty and glory. Mix your yearning for Him with awe and reverence to please Him. Persist in beseeching Him, for Almighty Allah praised the devotion of His servant Zakaraya and his household, saying: ﴿ Lo! They vied with each other in good deeds, and they cried to Us in longing, fear, and submission .﴾ (*Qur'an 21:90*) O ye people. You must know that Almighty Allah has entrusted you with His rights, and He has taken firm covenants from you in this regard. He also has accepted the little ephemeral deeds you offer, and He promised you bounty and lasting comforts for your reward. Here you have the Book of Allah, the wonders of which cannot be fully compassed, and the light of which cannot be extinguished. So believe in His words, pay heed to them, and make His Book your guiding light the day you become prisoner of a dark grave. Almighty Allah has created you to worship Him, and He delegated honorable angels to record your actions and to watch over you. O God's servants, you must know that whatever you do is destined for a purpose that is sometimes hidden from your immediate perception. Thus, if you can hold to a course of serving Him when you meet your death, then do so, though you can only do that if God wills. Thus, vie in such pursuit before your term expires and before you become answerable for your failures. I warn you not to follow the example of the less fortunate people who made their striving the reward of others, while they forgot about their own reckoning. Think about it and take heed. They have gone far far away." Abu Bakr would then cry out: "Help, help! O ye people, death is a persevering caller who is haunting you, and it is swift and unyielding."

**57-** 'Amru bnu Dinar quoted from another sermon in which Abu Bakr, God be pleased with him, said: "O people! I exhort you to beware of the day when you become poor and needy, to fear your Lord, to hail His holy Name with praises that befit His majesty and glory, and to pray for forgiveness, for He is most forgiving."

**58-** 'Abdullāh bin 'Akīm reported another segment of this sermon, quoting Abu Bakr, God be pleased with him, to have said:

"O ye people! You must know that when you serve God Almighty sincerely, you will have obeyed your Lord, as well as you will have protected your rights. Pay your alms taxes and what you owe before you are asked and pressured to do so, and on a day you have no means to do so. Pay them even in advance when you are comfortable, and make them work for you, those will be regarded as your supererogatory offerings. Only if you do so, that you may receive a refund, and particularly when you are poor and need it most. O servants of Allah, think for a moment about your predecessors. Where were they yesterday, and where are they today! Where are the great kings who aroused the land and raised its cities? They are forgotten, and no one even remembers them. Today, they are like nothing, ❮ Now their dwellings are desolate ruins because of their sins. ❯ (*Qur'an 27:52*) laying dead in dark graves ❮ Can you find a single one of them alive, or can you hear as much as a whisper from them? ❯ (*Qur'an 19:98*) O ye people, tell me, where are your other friends and brethren? They are now reaping the fruit of their earlier work in this world. Today, they are either happy or aggrieved. God Almighty does not have a kinship with anyone in His creation, and therefore, He does not grant anyone special status, favors, or exemptions, except with regards to obeying His command and abstaining from what He forbids. In fact, there is no benefit in any so-called good deed that drives its author to hell-fire, and there is no evil deed after which repentance leads its author to paradise. Indeed, there is no benefit in any speech that does not solicit God's acceptance, nor in a deed that is not done for His pleasure, and surely there is no benefit in a wealth which is not spent freely for Allah's sake. In fact, one's deeds are of no worth whatsoever if his ignorance exceeds his forbearance. Surely there is no righteousness or virtue in one who disdains to speak the truth in fear of people's criticism regarding God's rights. Thus, I conclude my sermon, and I ask for Allah's forgiveness for myself and for you."

**59-** 'Abdu-Ra<u>h</u>mãn Ibn 'Abdullãh Ibn Sãbi<u>t</u> narrated that during Abu Bakr's last illness, he called for Omar bin al-<u>K</u>hat<u>t</u>ãb, God be pleased with him, and said: "O Omar fear Allah and realize that He has enjoined upon us duties which we must fulfill during the day, and He will not accredit them if we fulfill them at night. He also enjoined upon us duties He decreed that we must fulfill them during the night, and therefore, He will not accept them should we comply with them during the daytime. In fact, Allah, blessed is His Name, does not accept a votive deed unless one offers the obligatory ones first. In the hereafter, the balance of people's good deeds only tilt the balance in their favor because they had accepted and followed His command in this world, hence, their recognition of their Lord keeps them heedful during this life. If such truth is placed in the balance tomorrow, it will definitely weigh heavy in their favor. On the other hand, the good deeds of the unlucky ones are worthless and they will weigh nothing on the Day of Reckoning, and that is because they follow naught but conjecture and falsehood in this world, and therefore, it will be just and equitable for the balance on the Day of Judgment to compute their deeds as inconsequential. Whenever Allah, blessed is His Name, mentioned the dwellers of paradise, He described them according to their good deeds, and He discounted their pitfalls. Whenever I remembered such verses in the Qur'an, I worried about myself should I not to be in their company. Moreover, whenever Allah, blessed is His Name, mentioned the dwellers of hell-fire in the Qur'an, He described them by their evil deeds, and He refused to accept their good ones for they were not done for His sake, and hence, whenever I remembered such people, I always prayed not to be in their group. Thus, Allah's servant must be constantly yearning and uneasy at the same time. He should not consider his devotion as valuable, nor should he despair of God's favor and mercy. If you accept my admonition, then await the apace arrival of no distant visitor more than you await the angel of death, and it will surely come, and should you not heed my admonition, then hate nothing more the sure arrival of a distant visitor more than the angel of death, and yet, you cannot frustrate him."

**60-** 'Urwa bin Al-Zubair reported that 'Aisha, God be pleased with her, said: "I once wore a new robe and I kept on admiring it. Abu Bakr saw me and said: 'What are you looking at? Do you not know that right now Allah is not looking at you?' I replied: 'Why is that?' Abu Bakr answered: 'When a servant admires the glitters of the world, God Almighty detests him until the servant comes out of it.' 'Aisha immediately took off her new robe and gave it away in charity. When Abu Bakr learned about what his daughter did, he commented: "Perhaps this will be your atonement."

**61-** Habīb bin Dhumra reported: "One of Abu Bakr's sons fell ill and was nearing his death. On his deathbed, the young boy kept on anxiously looking towards a pillow on his side. When he died, someone said to Abu Bakr, 'Before he died, your son often gazed ponderously at this pillow!' Thus, when they raised his head and pulled out the pillow they discovered five Dinars hidden under it. Abu Bakr became extremely upset and he clapped one hand over the other, reiterating, 'To Allah we belong, and to Him we return.' He then looked at his deceased son with tears in his eyes, and said: 'My dear son, I never thought that your tender skin is capable of bearing such a weight!' "

**62-** Sa'īd bin Omar narrated that Bilāl al-Habashi was under torture, and he was buried alive under heavy stones when Abu Bakr came and bought his freedom for five measures of gold. After accepting the deal, the Quraishi headman remarked to Abu Bakr: "I would have sold him to you even if you had insisted and bargained on a single measure of gold!" Abu Bakr replied: "Should you even had insisted on asking one hundred measures of gold for his freedom, I would have paid them."

## 2- Omar Bin Al-Khattāb

The next sire of the people is Omar bin al-Khattāb, God be forever pleased with him. His rank was decreed in the heavens and then it was established on earth as the harbinger of the truthful messenger of Allah and the seal of His prophets ﷺ. Omar bin al-Khattāb, God be forever pleased with him, was the voice of the truth, and he judged by the criterion of God's Book. His wisdom and forbearance are forever his banners, and through him, God Almighty strengthened His message and supported His Messenger ﷺ. When Omar embraced Islam, its banners rose high, for he was the answer to the prayers of God's messenger ﷺ. Since that day, God's message became populace, and its foundation took firm roots. Through his God given magnanimity, the Muslims turn of fortune became obvious, and the voice of the believers was heard after being clandestine. When Omar embraced Islam, the spirit of the believers was uplifted, and he brought about a new clarity and determination to defend the divine revealed message of Allah, the Lord of majesty and glory, blessed is His Name. From that day on, the perfidy of the unbelievers and their ruses were heavily shaken, the weight of their numbers no longer influenced the balance of power, and their villainous stratagem was openly challenged and was doomed to failure.

Omar had a remarkable strong faith. His determination to put an end to the schemes of those who challenged Allah's message, compelled the unbelievers to rethink their modus operandi. He challenged them publicly through his unquestionable trust and irreproachable reliance on the supreme power and help of the Creator of all existence, the Sustainer of all lives, and the Guide of all souls, Allah, the supreme and only Lord of the universe, the Lord of majesty and glory no associate has He. Omar also shared in the hardships and the sufferings of the believers in anticipation of seeing God's promise fulfilled, His religion established, and to serve His supreme will on earth. Omar's equanimity spoke even when he was silent; his immanence transcended his strength; his ascetic detachment stated his intention, and his poised words were near prophetic, and in fact, they were supported by divine revelations several times. Allah loved Omar and made his words resonate with truth and justice, and Omar loved the Lord of the universes, and feared none besides Him.

It is said that attainment is the surfacing of hidden worth and the assertion of clear signs. When what is hidden is valuable then what will manifest is right.

**63-** On this subject, Ibn 'Abbās once asked Omar bin al-Khattāb: "Why were you nicknamed al-Fārouq?" Omar replied: "Hamza accepted Islam three days before I did, then Almighty Allah opened my heart to it, and I exclaimed: 'Surely there is no God except Allah, the Lord of the munificent divine Attributes.' Suddenly, no one was more beloved to my heart than God's messenger ﷺ. I went to my sister and asked her: 'Where is God's messenger ﷺ?' She replied: 'He is meeting with the believers at the house of al-Arqam bin al-

Arqam near the hill of Safa.' Immediately I took off and went there. At that time, Hamza and several other companions were meeting with God's messenger ﷺ then. As I knocked on the door, the people took guard and Hamza asked: 'What is the matter?' They replied: 'Omar is at the door.' God's messenger ﷺ then said to them: 'Stand back!' He then came out to the door, and he shook me and said: 'O Omar, when are you going to cease your act?' I replied: 'I came here to bear witness that there is no God other than Allah, no associate has He, and that Muhammad is His servant and Messenger.' Upon hearing that, the believers exclaimed: '*Allahu Akbar*!' And their loud voices resonated with joy as they were heard by those living in the vicinity of the sacred Ka'ba.' "

Upon entering the house of al-Arqam and hearkening to God's messenger ﷺ, Omar asked: "O Messenger of Allah, if we openly proclaim our faith, would we not be right, regardless whether we live or die?" God's messenger ﷺ replied: 'Indeed, I swear by Him in Whose omnipresence my soul stands that you are right whether you live or die.' Omar then added: "Why hide then? I swear by Him Who sent you with the message of truth that this must be declared openly.'

Omar added: "We then walked out of the House of al-Arqam in two rows, and God's messenger ﷺ walked steadily between Hamza and myself in the front row until we reached the sacred mosque. The people of Quraish shook and became distressed as they saw us, and on that day, God's Messenger named me al-Fãrouq."

Thus, by guiding Omar to Islam, Allah, blessed is His Name, raised a new banner in the battle between truth and falsehood, light and darkness, and with it, He reconfirmed the criterion that separates them.

Omar, God be pleased with him, was gifted with serenity, quietude, a presaging impact, and clarity of speech. His thoughts were balanced and concise, and his verdicts were just. He accepted what Allah revealed, and he disagreed with the personal opinions of His creation.

**64-** On this subject, 'Ali bin Abi Tãlib once said: "We used to say that there is an angel that speaks with Omar's tongue."

**65-** Abi Juhaifa narrated that 'Ali bin Abi Tālib also said: "It never occurred to us that Omar was not encompassed with the heavenly quiescence and awareness of the divine presence (*sakīna*). In fact, we always believed that it spoke with his tongue."

**66-** Abu Huraira narrated that God's messenger ﷺ, upon whom be peace, said: "Allah placed truth and justice on the tongue and in the heart of Omar."

Omar, God be pleased with him, was gifted with strong determination and will, and several times the divine revelations supported his insight. He remained mostly in the company of God's messenger ﷺ, and he witnessed his guided approach to most of the circumstances that surrounded the advent of God's message. Omar controlled his thoughts, and he focused on acquiring knowledge and emulating the character of God's messenger ﷺ, and he was a model believer and a pattern of a true follower.

**67-** Sulaimān bin Ahmad narrated that when Omar was on his deathbed, his son, Ibn Omar came to his father and said: "I heard people talking about you, and I promised myself to convey to you what they said. They claim that you are not going to appoint a successor, and yet, if you employ a shepherd, and should he leave the flock grazing in the field and come to see you for consultation without leaving an attendant, you would certainly consider him disloyal; surely caring for the people is a more serious duty than shepherding."

Omar heard what his son had to say and he pondered for a while then remarked: "My dear son, if I do not appoint a successor, it would be because God's messenger ﷺ did not appoint one, and if I do, it would be because Abu Bakr did appoint a vice regent."

Ibn Omar added: "By God, as soon as he mentioned God's messenger ﷺ and Abu Bakr, I realized that no one can overrate the traditions of God's messenger ﷺ, and that my father is not going to appoint a caliph after him."

**68-** Abi Salma narrated that Omar, God be pleased with him, once wore a new shirt, and he called his son 'Abdullāh and said to him: "Son, take this blade and trim these long sleeves for me. Place your forefingers across the edge of my knuckles and trim the balance." The son, Ibn Omar, clipped the two sleeves with the blade accordingly, but the cut looked somehow sloppy, and the fabric began unraveling. Ibn Omar then said: 'Father, let me adjust the trim with a pair of scissors instead, and then I will hem them for you?' Omar insisted: 'It is all right son, leave them like that. I saw God's messenger ﷺ wear it this way.' "

'Abdullãh bin Omar continued: "Hence, Omar kept on wearing his shirt as is, and shortly after that, many a times, I kept on noticing the fallen threads hanging over his garment and feet until the shirt wore out."

Omar, God be forever pleased with him, was a great devotee. He was extremely thankful to his Lord, and he was most grateful for His favors. He swerved away from falsehood, and he was disinclined to mixing with its people. In his personal life, he eliminated any pattern that could possibly distract his focus. Although sometimes, he himself may have versified a momentous elation, nevertheless, Omar disliked poets because they would laud or defame someone for a fee, fame, or praise. Omar's genuineness made him free from polytheism or arrogance, and he was known for the purity of his intention, his kindness and interest in others' welfare. In fact, Omar's innate virtues strengthened his faith and made him unyielding in his pursuit of the divine goal. Thus, he sustained an unobstructed and ever progressing spiritual state that made him evermore ready to perceive the divine guidance, and consequently, his clarity was the prize of his humility before his Lord, which clarity manifested by his renouncing of personal comfort or any indulgence in mundane pleasures, and he did so by finding such strength solely in Allah, the Lord of majesty and glory. Hence, Omar, God be pleased with him, rose above worldly ranks to receive the glad tidings of his Lord's blessings during his lifetime.

**69-** On this subject, T̲ãriq bin S̲hahãb narrated that one his way to Syria, a miry track crossed Omar traveling path, so he descended his camel, took off his shoes and walked through the track. Abu 'Ubaida, who also was traveling with him commented: "Today, you have done something that is most outrageous in the eyes of the people of the world!" Omar shook inside and said: "Oh! I wish someone else had said that O Abu 'Ubaida! You were the most undignified people on earth and Allah has honored you with His Messenger ﷺ. From now on, whenever you seek honor in anything else, God Almighty will humiliate you."

**70-** Muhammad bin Shibl narrated that when Omar arrived in Syria, some people welcomed him at the outskirts of the city and said to him: "O Prince and Commander of the Believers, I wish that you would only ride on a ceremonial horse or a jade, surely some of the highborn of the town are coming out to welcome you!" Omar replied simply: "I do not agree with you here," and then he pointed toward the firmament and said: "The truth resides there," adding, "Make way for my camel."

**71-** Al-Awza'i narrated that Omar, God be forever pleased with him, used to walk out of his house covertly at night. One night Talha saw that, and he followed him. Talha saw Omar going to one house, and in a while he came out and proceeded to another house before he returned to his own house. In the morning, Talha went to the house he saw Omar entering at night. He knocked on the door to find a blind old woman who was infirm. He asked her: "Who is the man that visited you last night?" She replied: "He has been taking care of me for such a long time now. He brings me whatever I need, and then he removes the adverse." Talha excused himself and left, adding: "I damned myself, and I said to myself, 'May your mother mourn you and be bereaved of you O Talha, are you spying on Omar and questioning his deeds?' "

**72-** Al-Hassan narrated that Omar was once walking along with some of his companions when they passed by a trash dump. Omar stood there for a moment pondering, and his act disturbed his fellows. When he noticed that they were offended by the stench, he commented: "this is the world you care so much to hoard, and this is the outcome of you trust most and rely upon for your needs!"

Omar, God be pleased with him, was a true ascetic. He withheld and limited his intake of the ephemeral comfort, he opted for hardships over convenience, and he uncompromisingly sought the everlasting solace of the hereafter.

**73-** On this subject, Thãbit bin Anas narrated that during an arid year known as 'The Year of Ashes', Omar vowed not to eat ghee for such a time until the calamity is lifted. Omar was once extremely hungry, and his stomach was rumbling. Thãbit saw him tapping on his venter with his index finger, saying: "It does not matter whether you rumble or not! You will only receive oil when life returns to normal."

**74-** Sa'ad bin Abi Waqqãss narrated that during the caliphate of Omar, God be pleased with him, Hafsa, his daughter, once said to her father: "O Prince and Commander of the Believers! I wish you would wear a garment less coarse than what you have, and accept to eat food less plain than what you eat, for God has increased our revenues, and His favors are plenty now!" Omar replied: "I will let your own reasoning rebuff your idea. Now tell me, do you not remember how God's messenger ﷺ and his companions lived, and how scarce was their personal comfort?" Reminiscing and yearning for his company, Hafsa burst into tears, and the thought of extra personal comfort was no longer an issue. Omar added: "By God, I said to myself, if I can share with them some of their hardships in the world, perhaps I could share with them some of their comfort in the hereafter."

**75-** Also on this subject, al-Hassan narrated that Omar, God be pleased with him, once said: "Surely I do have the means to wear the finest of clothing, to eat the best of food, and to live a most comfortable life. I swear to God Almighty, that if this was the idea of comfort, then I do have the means to do so. I am not ignorant of how to dress a camel's hump to make it more comfortable, or how to build myself a rich reception hall, acquire impressive commodities, or make competitive choices in this world, but I have heard God Almighty reprimanding some people for doing so, and quoting the Holy Qur'an, Omar read: ❮ You have wallowed in your satisfaction during your life in the world and sought comfort therein.❯ (*Qur'an 46:20*)

**76-** Sãlim bin 'Abdullãh narrated that Omar said: "By God, we do not care much for the pleasures of this world. We ask for the most inferior of goats to be prepared for food when we are hungry, and we ask for wheat husk and oats' pith to be grounded for our bread, and we prefer raisins to make our vinegar. We want to save our pleasures and comfort for the hereafter, for we have heard God

Almighty say: ﴾ You have wallowed in your satisfaction during your life in the world and sought comfort therein. ﴿ (*Qur'an 46:20*)

**77-** 'Amru bin al-Hãrith narrated that Omar, God be pleased with him, also gave the same analogy when he went to Iraq and when he saw how Iraqis and some of those who migrated from the Arabian Peninsula to Iraq served luxuriant banquets and took great pride in doing so. He said: "Listen to me O people of Iraq! If I wished to indulge in gentry like you do, I surely have the means to do so, but we (the companions) have renounced the comfort of this world for the sake of that of the hereafter. Have you not heard Allah's saying (such people who love the world): ﴾ You have wallowed in your satisfaction during your life in the world and sought comfort therein. ﴿ (*Qur'an 46:20*)

**78-** At one time during Omar's stay in Iraq, some people visited him, and he offered them a little bread and oil to eat. The visitors felt shy from him, and they politely took only little of what he offered. Omar noticed that, and he quietly commented: "I do realize that you are used to nibbling on fancy food! What do you want me to offer you, a banquet of sweet and sour food together with hot and cold drinks, or otherwise you would not stuff your bellies?"

**79-** Khalaf bin Hawshab narrated that Omar, God be pleased with him, once said: "I pondered upon this subject and realized that if I desired comfort in this world, I would harm my lasting comfort in the hereafter, and if I desired the hereafter, I must renounce comfort in this world, and hence, I decided to give up the ephemeral. Therefore, if you find the same, then it is surely better for you to endure a little discomfort in this life."

**80-** Sa'ïd bin Abi Burda narrated that Omar once wrote a letter to his deputy in the North, Abu Müsa al-Ash'ari, God be pleased with them both, and in closing, Omar said: "... Therefore, the happiest of governors (on the Day of Judgment) is one whose subjects were happy with him (in this world), and on that day, the most wretched of governors is one whose subjects have suffered under him in this world. Beware never to procrastinate or fail to serve the people. Otherwise, your deeds will fritter away and you will be like a cow, once it sees green pasture, it hasten to chomp on it to grow fatter, not realizing that once it becomes fat, it will be fit for slaughter."

**81-** In another letter he sent to Abu Müsa al-Ash'ari, Omar wrote: "...When one's intention is sincere, God Almighty will suffice his needs, protect him, and guide him in his dealings with the people. However, if one adorns himself to please the people in this world, only God knows what end awaits him in the hereafter. In this example, tell me, what destiny do you expect God Almighty to grant such a person in his immediate life, and what bounty He will reserve for him in the hereafter? I bid you peace."

## His Words of Piety and Wisdom

One's words reflect the state of his heart. Omar's words of wisdom are a truthful mirror of a true believer who has submitted and dedicated his body, mind and soul to the privilege of serving his Lord.

**82-** On this subject, Mujãhid narrated that Omar, God be pleased with him, said: "Patience is the healthiest ingredient of our life."

**83-** In one of his sermons, Omar was quoted to have said: "You must know that greed means poverty, and despair means wealth. When a man gives up hope in having something, it means that he no longer needs it, and hence, abundance connotes absence of need."

**84-** Describing Omar's spiritual state in his own words, 'Ãmer al-Sha'bi quoted him to have said: "My heart was mellowed in Allah to the degree that it became softer than butter, and it was steeled in Allah to the degree that it became harder than a rock."

**85-** Ibn 'Utba also quoted Omar's saying: "Mix with those who have patience, for their hearts are the softest."

**86-** Sufyãn bin 'Uyaina narrated that Omar, God be pleased with him, once admonished the believers in a sermon to hold unto God's path, wherein he said: "Become the bearers of God's Book and the fountainhead of knowledge, and ask Almighty Allah for your food one day at a time."

**87-** Al-A'amash narrated that Omar, God be pleased with him, once heard a man praying loud: "My Lord, I hereby dedicate my property and soul to Thy path." Omer then commented: "Why wouldn't one of you acquiesces to privacy regarding his circumstantialities. When he is tried with adversities, he should exercise patience, and when he is well, he must increase his gratitude!"

**88-** Yahya bin Ja'da narrated that Omar, God be pleased with him, once said: "I would love to have already met my Lord had it not been for three blessings in this world — that is: 1) to prostrate my forehead on the ground before Him; 2) to sit in gatherings that favor the good word, which is like opting for the better of dates on a platter; and finally, 3) for the opportunity to fight in His cause, to proclaim His Word, and to establish His religion on earth."

**89-** As for his love to worship his Lord, Abi 'Uthmān al-Nahdi quoted Omar, God be pleased with him, to have said: "Wintertime is an auspicious opportunity for worshippers."

**90-** 'Abdullāh bin 'Isa described Omar's piety and reverence of the Almighty Allah, saying: "Omar had two dark lachrymal lines, marking the effect of his frequent crying in fear of his Lord."

**91-** Hishām Ibn al-Hassan said: "When Omar read a Qur'ānic verse admonishing the people, he would suppress his emotions and gasp for breath, and he often erupted sobbing until he was nearly choked by his own tears, and sometimes, he even fell unconscious. When Omar recouped, he would constrain himself to the confines of his house for some days. People would think that he was ill, and they would go to visit with him and inquire about his health."

**92-** Mālik bin Dinar narrated that al-Hassan saw Omar bin al-Khattāb during his caliphate delivering a sermon and wearing a cloak patched in some twelve places.

**93-** Dāwoud Bin 'Ali narrated that Omar, God be pleased with him, was extremely sensitive about his responsibilities, and he quoted him to have said: "Even should a lost goat die at *Shat al-'Arab*,[1] I tend to think that Allah, the most exalted, will question me about it on the Day of Judgment."

**94-** Yahya Ibn Kathīr narrated that Omar, God be pleased with him, said: "If a harbinger from the skies cries out: 'O ye people, you shall all enter paradise except one!' I would fear that it could be me, and if he proclaims: 'O ye people, you shall all enter hell-fire except one of you!' I would hope it will be me."

[1] Shat al-'Arab: North-Easte of Arabian Peninsula.

**95-** Ibn 'Akïm reported that God's messenger ﷺ once said to Omar: "Pray 'Lord, make my innermost being better than my outer look, and make my outer look true and pleasing to You.' "

**96-** On the day Omar became the Caliph, he stood on the pulpit, and after praising Almighty Allah and thanking Him for His countless favors, Omar said: "O ye people, I am going to pray to God Almighty, so endorse my supplications: 'Lord! I am gruff, so please soften me. I am stingy, so please make me generous. Lord, I am weak, so please make me strong.' " The whole congregation then solemnly assented: "Amen."

**97-** Ibn Omar, may Allah be bless him and be forever pleased with him, once spoke of his beloved father, saying: "Whenever I prayed behind Omar, I could hear his moaning even from behind three rows."

**98-** Thãbit bin al-Hajjãj narrated that he heard Omar, God be pleased with him, admonishing the people in a sermon, saying: "Weigh your actions before they are weighed, and reckon yourselves before you are reckoned, this will make it easier for you tomorrow. Adorn yourselves for the grand exhibition: ﴾ On that Day, you will be displayed for judgment, and all your secrets will be brought to light ﴿ (*Qur'an 69:18*).

**99-** Omar, God be pleased with him, sometimes expressed much regret to have been a human being who is not infallible, and who has to face awesome trials in this world. On this subject, Abu Mu'ãwiya narrated that Omar once said: "I wish I was a ram that people fatten for food. When someone they love visits them, they slaughter it, broil some to serve their guest, and then hang the leftover to dry. When they are hungry they eat from it, and further discard me as feces, this would surely have been better for me than to be human in the flesh in this world!"

**100-** Omar knew of his destiny, for he was foretold by God's messenger ﷺ of his martyrdom. On this subject, Zaid bin Aslam narrated that his father once heard Omar pray during his prostration: "Lord, Thy will be done, I pray that Thou will not let my murder be at the hand of a servant who prostrated himself even once before Thee, so that his prostration will not be in his favor on the Day of Judgment."

**101-** Zaid bin Aslam narrated that Omar's daughter Hafsa heard her father pray: "Lord, let me be killed for Thy sake, and let me die in the city of Thy Prophet." Hafsa became upset and emotional, and she said to her father: "How could this prayer be answered?" Omar gently replied: "If Allah wills, He will make it happen thus."

**102-** Sa'ïd bin al-Musayyib narrated that Omar once built a pile of sand in the open, he placed his cloak over it, and he laid on his back facing the skies. He then lifted his hands to the heavens and prayed: "Lord, I have become old, my strength have waned, and my subjects have spread all over the land. Lord, take me unto Thee undesecrated and let my devotion not be in waste."

**103-** Salim bin Hanzala narrated that Omar, God be pleased with him, used to pray: "My Lord, I seek refuge in You from a sudden and unexpected death; I implore You not to let me be incognizant of You for even a moment, or to gather me on the Day of Reckoning among the heedless ones."

Omar died from a lethal wound he suffered from the poisoned dagger of a traitorous Magian who stood behind him during a congregational prayer, and pretended to be a believer.

**104-** On this subject, 'Āsim bin 'Ubaidullāh narrated that in his last breath, Omar's head was laying on the lap of his son, and Omar said to him with a waning voice: "Son, put my head down on the floor!" Ibn Omar replied grievingly: "And what difference does it make whether it is on my lap or on the floor?" Omar insisted, and when the son complied with his father's wish, and as soon as his head hit the floor, Omar bursted out with tears, as he prayed with tears in his eyes: "Woe to me and to my mother should my lord not show His mercy to me today!"

**105-** Ibn 'Abbās visited Omar during his last days, in his deathbed, and said to him: "Rejoice O Prince of the Believers with the glad tidings of your achievements, for during your regency, God's message triumphed in distant lands, and through you, God Almighty cleansed the land from hypocrisy, and He endowed every one in this land with prosperity." Omar replied: "O Ibn 'Abbās, are you lauding me regarding what Allah allotted, and concerning the responsibility associated with administering it?" Ibn 'Abbās realized that Omar did not want to take credit for such, and he hastened to add: "As well as for your countless virtues!" Omar replied: "I swear by Him in Whose presence my soul stands, I wish that I could have left this world as on the day I was born into it, having no deeds and carrying no burdens."

**106-** After Omar passing, al-'Abbās bin 'Abdul Muttalib once said: "I was a neighbor of Omar bin al-Khattāb, God be pleased with him, I highly valued such a privilege, and I never thought that there is anyone better than him. His nights were spent in prayers, and during his days he fasted and served the people. After Omar's death, I prayed to Allah to allow me to see him in a dream, and last night, I saw him in a dream, walking the marketplace of Madina, and he was wearing a very nice shawl. I bid him peace, and he reciprocated. I then asked him, 'How are you doing?' He replied, 'Well.' I asked, 'What did you find?' Omar replied, 'My reckoning was just concluded. During its consideration, my stance was just about to be rent asunder had I not met a Merciful Lord.' "

**107-** Muhammad bin Shahāb narrated that Omar, God be pleased with him, said: "Do not censure something which has no immediate link to your interest. Forsake your enemies, and beware of your close companions, except for the trustworthy ones, for nothing equals the worth of a trustworthy companion. Do not mix with an insolent person lest he influences you with his contumelies. Never trust such a person with your secret, and solicit advice only from the God-fearing people."

**108-** Abi al-Zubair reported that Omar, God be pleased with him, once said: "God Almighty has blessed servants who abolish evil by renouncing it, and who enliven the truth by remembering it. What they yearn for shook them, and what they fear most drives them to forsake all comforts. They are seized by awe, and their fear cannot be appeased. They recognize in seeing death what they have not yet experienced, and they mix such fear with everything they renounce. Their fear renders their sincerity true and helps them to renounce what will eventually leave for the sake of what will certainly come. Life for them is a blessing, and death is an honor. Such are the ones who are betrothed to heavenly chaste brides, and who are served by eternally blessed celestial children."

## 3- 'Uthmān Ibn 'Affān

The next sire of the people, is the humble before his Lord, the chaste and truly devoted to his Lord, the bearer of the two lights, the most revering of his Lord, who prayed toward the two *Qibla,* the Sacred House in Mecca and the Furthest Mosque in Jerusalem, and who enjoyed the privilege and blessings of migration twice, that is 'Uthmān Ibn 'Affān, God be forever pleased with him, the blessed caliph of God's messenger ﷺ, upon whom be peace.

'Uthmān, may Allah shower him with His utmost blessings, prayed and invoked the divine favors between the two pinnacles of the night. He rose regularly at night to offer extended supererogatory prayers and to prostrate himself before his Creator, Cherisher, and Lord. He prayed for God's mercy to embrace him in this life and in the next, and he feared His displeasure and castigation. 'Uthmān was generous and most shy, and he was vigilant, reverent, and fearful of his Lord. His fortune during the day consisted of goodness of character, fasting and prayers, and during the night, his fortune was made of supererogatory devotion, reading the Qur'ānic revelation, contemplation, and prayers.

**109-** 'Uthmān was a hard-working and a persevering devoted worshiper. On this subject, and after the passing of 'Uthmān, God be pleased with him, al-H̲assan bin 'Ali, God be pleased with him and with his father, was once sitting in a group of believers, and they were reminiscing the virtues of 'Uthmān, God be pleased with him. Al-H̲assan, referring to his father, and in anticipation that he will further illumine this subject, said, 'The Prince of the Believers will soon arrive.' When 'Ali, God bless his countenance, arrived, he reanimated the subject of 'Uthmān, commenting: "Indeed, 'Uthmān was among those about whom God Almighty said: ﴾ Those who believe in Allah and do righteousness deeds, who guard themselves against evil, and who have faith, thence, and as long as they are God-fearing and do good deeds, surely Allah loves the charitable ones. ﴿ (*Qur'an 5:93*)

**110-** Abu Bakr bin Müsa narrated that 'Abdullāh bin Omar, God be pleased with him, once explained that the Qur'ānic verse: ﴾ He who worships devoutly during the hours of the night, prostrating himself or standing up (in devotion), who heeds the call of the hereafter, and hopes to win the mercy of his Lord,﴿ (*Qur'an 39:9*) refers to 'Uthmãn, God be forever pleased with him.

**111-** Sulaimãn bin Ahmad narrated that Ibn Omar narrated that God's messenger ﷺ said: "The most humble and unassuming person among my followers is 'Uthmãn Ibn 'Affãn."

**112-** On this subject, Ahmad Ibn Hanbal reported that al-Hassan spoke of 'Uthmãn's regard to modesty, saying: "Even when he was in the privacy of his house, and his doors were locked, 'Uthmãn would not take off his robe when he poured water to wash himself, he would sit down while taking a bath, and his modesty prevented him from standing up naked before the all-Seeing Omnipresent Lord."

**113-** 'Abdullãh bin Omar once said: "Three men from the tribe Quraish are the most cheerful, the most modest, and they have the best of character. They are truthful when they speak, and they are not suspicious of others' truthfulness. They are Abu Bakr al-Siddïq, 'Uthmãn Ibn 'Affãn, and 'Ubaida al-Jarrãh."

**114-** Imam Muhammad Ibn Seerïn narrated that when the assailants besieged 'Uthmãn's house, and in moment of distress, his beleaguered wife bursted out in tears as she cried out: "Whether you kill him or not, he is used to recite the entire Qur'an throughout the night during a single *rak'a* of his prayers."

**115-** Abi Ja'far narrated that Masrouq saw al-Ashtar, a member of the mob that murdered 'Uthmãn, God be pleased with him. Masrouq inquired: "Did you kill 'Uthmãn?" Al-Ashtar boastfully and conceitedly replied: "Yes we did." Masrouq pondered in dismay for a moment and then said: "By God, you have murdered a man who has fasted all his life and prayed all his nights."

'Uthmãn, God be forever pleased with him, was given the glad tidings of the adversities he had to meet, and his heart was guarded against anxiety or complaints in that regard. 'Uthmãn met anxiety with patience, and he traveled through afflictions with thankfulness to his Lord. He sipped the bitter taste of his trials and tribulations in this world to savor the everlasting sweetness and solace of salvation in the hereafter.

**116-** On this subject, Abu Müsa al-Ash'ari narrated that he was once together with God's messenger ﷺ inside a garden when someone came to the gate and sought permission to enter. God's messenger ﷺ said: "Open the gate and give him the glad tidings of paradise and of an atrocious last trial in this world." When Abu Mūsa opened the gate, he found 'Uthmān, God be pleased with him, standing at the door, and when I told him the news, he came in thanking Allah for His favors, and he sat down quietly next to God's messenger ﷺ.

**117-** Abi Hāzim narrated that when 'Uthmān was besieged inside his house, he said: "I have made a solemn promise to God's messenger ﷺ, and I must endure its consequences with patience."

**118-** Ahmad bin Sanān narrated that 'Uthmān earned two distinct badges of honor that added to his prominence, and neither Abu Bakr nor Omar had them: (1) 'Uthmān was unjustly murdered, and (2) he compiled the Qur'an.

Among his other traits, 'Uthmān spent freely his entire wealth on God's path, he sought the pleasure of his Lord, and he provided comfort to His servants. 'Uthmān took little for himself, he wore ordinary cloaks, ate plain food, and sought the highest of achievements, and finally, by the mercy of his Lord, he was crowned with the highest of honors.

**119-** Abu Huraira, God be pleased with him, narrated: " 'Uthmān bought paradise from God's messenger ﷺ, upon whom be peace, twice: 1) Once in a business transaction when he bought the well of *rūmah* (from the disbelievers), and which he made a public property for all Muslims, and 2) he bought it a second time when he fully financed and equipped the Army of Hardship (*Jaish al-'Usra*)."

**120-** Also on this subject, 'Abdu-Rahmān Ibn Abi Habab al-Salmi narrated that prior to the Battle of Badr, God's messenger ﷺ delivered a sermon concerning the Army of Hardship, and he admonished the people to support it. Initially, 'Uthmān pledged to equip one hundred men. When God's messenger ﷺ further invited the people to share in this responsibility, 'Uthmān made an additional pledge to equip another hundred. God's messenger ﷺ spoke again on their behalf, and 'Uthmān again added a pledge to equip another hundred. God's messenger ﷺ then said: " 'Uthmān does no longer need a deed of righteousness (i.e., to please Allah) after this."

**121-** 'Abdullãh bin Omar narrated that when God's messenger ﷺ saw 'Uthmãn going back and forth to equip the Army of Hardship (Arb. *jaish al-'usra*) before the Battle of Badr took place, God's messenger ﷺ prayed: "O Allah, forgive 'Uthmãn for every step he takes back and forth, for every deed he hides and every deed he displays, and forgive him for whatever thoughts he conceals and whatever words he utters."

**122-** Al-Hassan, son of 'Ali, once said: "I saw 'Uthmãn resting inside the mosque covered with an ordinary blanket, and he had no personal guards when he was the Muslim State's Calif and commander of the believers. When he woke up in the morning, the marks of stones showed on his side, and the people would point out, saying: "This is *Amir ul-Mu'mineen*."' (the commander of the believers).

**123-** Ja'far bin Muhammad bin al-Fadhl narrated that 'Uthmãn used to feed the people the best of food, and later on, he would enter his house to partake a modest meal of some bread which he dipped in a little oil and vinegar.

**124-** Sulaimãn bin Müsa narrated that during his caliphate, 'Uthmãn was called upon once to reprove a group of people who engaged in an iniquitous act. When he came out of his house, the people had dispersed, 'Uthmãn praised God Almighty for sparing him from such encounter, and on that day, he bought the freedom of a slave as an expression of his deep gratitude to his Lord."

**125-** Maimoun bin Mihrãn narrated that al-Hamadãni told him: "I once saw 'Uthmãn, during the appogé of his caliphate, riding on a mule and his servant Nã'il riding behind him."

**126-** 'Abdullãh bin al-Rümi narrated that 'Uthmãn once said: "If I was given a choice between going to heaven or hell, and not knowing to which of the two I will ultimately be taken, I would rather be turned into ashes before I know my final destination."

**127-** 'Abdullãh bin 'Amir bin Rabi'a was once visiting with 'Uthmãn and he heard him say: "Let Allah be my witness, that I have never committed adultery in my life, whether during the period of *jãhiliyya* (Arab paganism), or later on in Islam, and I became more reserved since the religion Islam was established."

**128-** 'Abdullāh al-Madīni narrated that 'Uthmān's servant Hāni said: "Whenever 'Uthmān visited a grave, he sobbed until his beard was soaking in tears."

**129-** Abi Masja'a narrated: "We once went along with 'Uthmān to visit a dying person, and 'Uthmān instructed him to utter the testimony, *'Lā ilāha il Allah'* (Surely there is no god except Allah). When the person did what he was told, 'Uthmān immediately commented, 'I swear by Him in Whose presence my soul stands, with this testimony which he has just cast upon his sins, he has wiped them out altogether.' The people inquired with a degree of wonder, 'Is this something that you are personally testifying to, or did you hear this statement from God's messenger ﷺ ?' 'Uthmān replied, 'Indeed, I have heard it from God's messenger ﷺ.' Someone then asked, 'If uttering this testament proves thus for a dying person, then what effects would it have on a healthy person when he testifies to it?' 'Uthmān replied, 'Much much stronger.' "

## 4- 'Ali Bin Abi Tālib

The fourth sire of the people, is the beloved of God Almighty and of His faithful creation, the gate of the city of knowledge, the commanding orator, the master of reason and intellect, the explainer of allegories, the pure blessing, the moral authority, the instinct of certitude, the fathomer of truth, the dean of piety, the beauty of knowledge, the truthful explainer whose heart is full of wisdom, whose tongue is most inquisitive, and whose ears are most conscious; the chieftain of the pious ones, the mirror of sages, the righteous judge, the most forbearing sire and the righteous caliph, 'Ali bin Abi Tālib, God bless his countenance.

**130-** Abu Huraira narrated that on the eve of the Battle of Khyber, God's messenger ﷺ said: "Allah will grant us victory tomorrow at the hand of a man to whom I will hand this flag. He loves Allah and His Messenger, and Allah and His Messenger love him." That night, the people retired wondering who of them will receive and carry the flag. In the morning, God's messenger ﷺ inquired: "Where is 'Ali?" People replied: "He is suffering from conjunctivitis." God's messenger ﷺ said: "Call him up." Thus, when 'Ali, God bless his countenance, came, God's messenger ﷺ placed a touch of his blessed saliva over 'Ali's eye, prayed for its recovery, and by God's leave, miraculously 'Ali's eyes became healthy again, and God's messenger ﷺ handed him the flag. 'Ali asked: "O messenger of Allah, should I fight them until they become like us?" He replied: "Be patient first and until you reach them. Kindly invite them to accept God's message of Islam, and explain to them about God's rights therein, for I swear by Allah, that should He guide even a single man through you to His path, it will be better for you than owning the ever largest herd of red camels in all the land."

**131-** Sa'ad narrated that God's messenger ﷺ said to 'Ali, God bless his countenance: "You are unto me what Aaron was to Moses."

**132-** Sa'ad also narrated that God's messenger ﷺ once said to 'Ali, God bless his countenance: "You are from me and I am from you."

**133-** Omar, God be pleased with him, said about 'Ali, God bless his countenance: "Before God's messenger ﷺ died, he was pleased with 'Ali."

## The Epitome of Islam!

**134-** Muqãtil bin Qatãda narrated[1] that a man from the Tribe of Khazã'a once came and asked 'Ali, God bless his countenance: "Have you ever heard God's messenger ﷺ, upon whom be peace, epitomizes the religion of Islam?" 'Ali replied: "Yes indeed, I have heard God's messenger ﷺ say, 'Islam is based on four pillars: 1) patience; 2) certitude; 3) struggle (*jihãd*); and 4) justice. From patience evolve four branches, 1) yearning; 2) compassion; ascetic detachment; and 4) contemplation. Therefore, whosoever yearns for the heavenly paradise must control his passion, and whosoever fears burning in hell-fire must step away from what is forbidden, and whosoever develops ascetic detachment from this world must regard his adversities as negligent, and whosoever awaits death must hasten to do good. On the other hand, from certitude branches four shoots; 1) An intelligent insight; 2) wisdom in interpreting the events; 3) cognizance and taking heed of the past and present lessons of life;

[1] Khalãs bin 'Amru also reported this tradition, re 'Ali, describing the epithet of *Islam* (acceptance of God's message), while other narrators also reported this tradition, re al-Isba' bin Nabãta, re 'Ali, depicting *Imãn* (faith).

and finally, 4) pursuing the prophetic traditions. Therefore, whosoever develops an intelligent insight, he will be able to interpret the past and current events with wisdom, and he will recognize and take heed of the lessons of life. Whosoever develops such true knowledge and wisdom, he will unavoidably pursue the prophetic traditions, and finally, whosoever pursues the prophetic traditions, he will be assembled among the earlier (*al-awwaleen*) and the most blessed cluster of believers. As for the branch of struggle (*jihād*), it also has four branches, 1) to command what is good and beneficial; 2) to forbid what is evil and loathsome; 2) to speak the truth in its proper place; and 4) to forsake the company of evil people. Therefore, whosoever commands what is good and beneficial, he would have become the backbone of the believer, and whosoever forbids what is evil and loathsome, he would have compelled the spite of a hypocrite to yield to the truth, whosoever always speaks the truth, he would have paid his dues and proved the truthfulness his religious adherence, and whosoever forsakes the company of evil people, he would have spared himself the wrath of Allah, and finally, whosoever becomes angry for the sake of Allah, then Almighty Allah will defend him imperiously. Finally, the branch of justice also has four shoots, 1) depth in one's understanding; 2) fruition of his knowledge; 3) unswerving adherence to the divine jurisprudence; and 4) resting in the gardens of forbearance. Therefore, one who fathoms the depth of matters can explain the beauty of knowledge; one who guards the fruit of knowledge will recognize and adhere to the divine jurisprudence; and one who recognizes the boundaries of the divine jurisprudence will be able to enter and enjoy the gardens of forbearance, and finally, one who enjoys the gardens of forbearance will be shielded against the bitterness of trials and visitations, and will he live among people who will delight in his company."

It is also said that spiritual purity means to exclusively and happily seek one's beloved for all of one's needs.

**135-** On this subject, Abu Bakr bin Khallād narrated that Fātima, the blessed daughter of God's messenger ﷺ, God be pleased with her, went to her father one evening, with a request to find her a maid to help her through her ever growing daily chores. When she got there, she shied from asking him, and when he inquired about what's worrying her, she quietly replied, 'I have only come to pay my respect to you.' When Fāṯima, God be pleased with her, returned to her house, 'Ali, God bless his countenance, asked her, 'What happened?' She replied, 'I couldn't ask him for anything!'

**136-** Also in reference to the above tradition, 'Amru bnu Murra narrated that 'Ali, God bless his countenance, expounded: "...On the third evening, we were in bed when God's messenger ﷺ came to us. I wanted to get up and leave my bed, but he quickly and firmly said, 'Stay where you are!' God's messenger ﷺ then sat down between us, and when his feet touched our bed, I felt their coolness in my chest. God's messenger ﷺ then said, 'Let me teach you something which will prove to be more beneficial for both of you than what you have asked of me! When you retire to your bed, say, '*Allahu Akbar*' thirty-four times, '*Subhan Allah*' thirty-three times, and '*al-Hamdu Lillah*' thirty-three times, and that will be much better for you than a servant.' "

'Ali continued: "I have never departed from that practice since then."

'Ali, God bless his countenance, upheld the course of his established daily routine invocations *awrād*, including his regular reading of the holy Qur'an, and in combination with his regular required prayers, and yet, he loved to excel. 'Ali accepted God's will pietistically, he submitted his own will and strength to his Lord, and he made his religious life a total dedication to the will of Almighty Allah by unfailingly and happily accepting His decree.

**137-** On this subject, al-H̲ussain son of 'Ali, narrated that his father once said: "One evening, we had gone to bed when God's messenger ﷺ visited us late at night. When I opened the door, he entered our chamber and said: 'Do you not pray at night?' I evasively replied: 'O messenger of Allah, our souls are in Allah's Hand, and if He wills, He will wake them up.' God's messenger ﷺ left immediately without reply, and walking away, he tapped over his side with his hand and recited the verse: ﴿ Surely, humans are exceedingly contentious ﴾ (*Qur'an 18:54*).

**138-** Abi Sālih̲ al-H̲anafi narrated that 'Ali, God bless his countenance, once asked God's messenger ﷺ to advise him, he replied: "Say, 'God is my Lord,' and then hold fast to the criterion of the straight path." 'Ali repeated the prayer, then added, 'Allah is my Lord. My success can only come from God. In Him I trust, and towards Him I look.' God's messenger ﷺ then said, 'O Aba al-Hassan! May your knowledge be blessed. Indeed you have received knowledge from its fountainhead, and you have earned your share of it with uttermost devotion.' "

**139-** Also on this subject, Ibn Mas'oud said: "The Qur'an was revealed in seven local dialects. Each letter of it has an outer and an inner meaning, and 'Ali has the knowledge of both."

**140-** Habïrah bin Barïm narrated that al-Hassan, son of 'Ali, God be pleased with both of them, once gave a sermon after his father's martyrdom, and during his speech, he said: "The man who has just departed yesterday, no one in the past could have ever rivalled his knowledge, nor will anyone in the future be able to do that."

**141-** Ibn 'Abbās narrated that Omar, God be pleased with him, used to say: " 'Ali is the most equitable judge among us, and Ubiyyu is our most learned Qur'an reader."

**142-** Mu'āth bin Jabal narrated that God's messenger ﷺ said: "O 'Ali, I vie you with the prophethood, and there will be no prophet after me, and yet you vie people in seven virtues, no one among the Quraish tribe can deny them: (1) You were their first to believe in Allah; (2) you are their most true to your promise; (3) you are their most discerning with regards to God's commands; (4) you are their most just, (5) the most compassionate toward the people; (6) the most enlightened in understanding matters; and finally, (7) you have the most advantage before God Almighty on the Day of Judgment."

**143-** Also on this subject, 'Abd Khair narrated that 'Ali once said: "When God's messenger ﷺ passed away, I vowed not to put a cloak over my shoulders (or cross over the threshold of my door) until I had memorized the entire Qur'an from cover to cover by heart, and thus I did."

**144-** Abi Sa'ïd al-Khidri narrated: "We were once walking with God's messenger ﷺ when his shoe strap broke. 'Ali hastened and immediately mended it for him, and then, he went back to his other duties. As we proceeded, God's messenger ﷺ spoke: 'O people, some among you will be fought for their interpretation of the Qur'an as fiercely as I was fought by those who denied its revelation.' "

Abi Sa'ïd al-Khidri continued: "I sought 'Ali to tell him about the *hadïth* (prophetic saying) of God's messenger ﷺ, but when he heard it, he did not comment nor did he show any emotion, and as though he had heard it from before."

**145-** Sulaimãn al-Ahmasi narrated that 'Ali, God be pleased with him, said: "I swear by Allah that whenever a verse was revealed, I knew who it concerned and where it was revealed, for my Lord has gifted me with a conscious heart and an inquiring tongue."

**146-** Abi al-Bakhtari narrated that 'Ali was once asked about himself, and he replied: "I was always given whatever I prayed for, and whenever I refrained from asking, I was presented with a greater divine generosity, I had no choice but to accept."

When in tight circumstances, 'Ali, God be pleased with him, engaged in hard labor to earn his daily bread, he used common sense, and he stood above mundane motives.

**147-** On this subject, Mujãhid narrated that 'Ali, God bless his countenance, said: "One morning in Madina, I was extremely hungry, and on that day, I took off from my home and sought to find some work in the upper outskirts of the city. On my way, I found a bedouine woman who had raised a small hump of dates on the ground intending to wash them. I went to her and offered to clear off the dates from their spadix and to wash them for the price of a single date, and the woman agreed. Thus I worked until my hand broke out with boils. When I completed the job, I washed my hands with some water, and I went to her with my hands stretched out to receive my wage. The woman graciously placed therein sixteen dates (instead of one). Immediately, and before eating any of them, I walked all the way back to God's messenger ﷺ, and I told him about what happened, and he smiled and shared some dates with me."

'Ali, God bless his countenance, was adorned with the garment of true devotion, trueness, and ascetic detachment.

**148-** On this subject, 'Ammār bin Yasār narrated that God's messenger ﷺ, upon whom be peace, once addressed 'Ali, God bless his countenance, saying: "O 'Ali, surely Allah has adorned you with a cloak there is no other raiment He likes better, and that is the cloak of the *abrār* (the true ones to their Lord). He inspired you to renounce the comfort of the world, and neither you nor will the world cause one another any losses. He made you love the meek, He made you happy in their company, and He made them love your leadership."

**149-** Also on this subject, 'Ali, son of al-Hussain, God be pleased with both of them, narrated that his grandfather 'Ali bin Abi Tālib said: "On the Day of Judgment, this *dunya* (world) will come before its Lord adorned with its best regalia and it will say, 'Lord, make me a gift to some of your deputies.' Almighty Allah will say: 'Go away, you are naught. You are too flimsy and unworthy of any of My deputies.' The world will then be folded like a piece of fabric, and it will be cast to burn eternally in hell-fire."

When 'Ali renounced any attachment to the world, his ascetic detachment removed many veils, and thus his blindness was lifted, and he was guided with the inner light of *basīra*.

**150-** Al-Hussain bin 'Ali narrated, re 'Ali bin Abi Tālib, God bless his countenance, that God's messenger ﷺ said: "One who renounces the world, Allah will endow him with knowledge without him seeking education, He will endue him with inner guidance beyond guidance, and He will open his inner sight (*basīra*) and remove his blindness."

'Ali was indeed an indisputable gnostic who truly knew the Lord of the universe (*'ārif -billāh*). He fathomed the divine essence, and his heart was filled with gratitude and reverence for his Lord. Consequently, 'Ali was able to recognize the veils of separation before they were lifted.

**151-** Ibn 'Abbās narrated that 'Ali, God bless his countenance, once commissioned him to go to Zaid bin Sawhān. In his reply, Ibn 'Abbās said: "O Prince and Commander of the Believers, I have only known you as one who has fathomed the divine essence, and in whose heart God is greatly revered..."

## Know Your Lord

**152-** Also on this subject, al-Nu'mãn bin Sa'ad said: "I was in the city of Küfa, visiting the Prince and Commander of the Believers, 'Ali bin Abi Ṯālib, when Nawf bin 'Abdullāh came to see him and said: 'O *Amir al-Mu'mineen,* there are forty Jews at the door requesting to see you.' 'Ali replied: 'Let them in.' When the visitors stood before him, their spokesman said: 'O 'Ali, describe to us your Lord who is in the heavens, how is that, how was He before, when was He; and what is He.?' 'Ali immediately straightened up his sitting posture, and he replied, 'Hearken to me and do not worry! You need not to ask anyone else beside me about this subject.' 'Ali then added: 'My Lord was there first, and nothing ever existed besides Him. He did not commence from what or was intermingled with what! His attributes cannot be fixed or limited. He is not an apparition that can be pursued or delimited, nor is He veiled to be contained. He did not issue from what was not, and thus He is not an occurrence. Exalted and most glorious is the Creator and Maker of everything, Lord of the universe, Whose divine majesty is most awesome and beyond having to explicate His essence to His creation, and instead, we say (as He described Himself, *Qur'an 57:3*) that He was there from the beginningless beginning, and He is the eternal without end. He is not subject to changes, nor is He affected by what He causes to change. How can He be described by an occurrence He created, and how can His divine being be limited to the best fathom of the greatest rhetoricians of all times. He did not emerge from something else that can lead one to assume His manifestation, nor did He emanate from anything else that brought Him into being. He is without how, and He is closer than one's jugular vein, and yet, He is beyond description in the widest perceivable realms. Not a single glaring of anyone of His entire creation combined is ever hidden to Him, nor the sequence of any uttering or a sound is ever veiled to Him or is unperceived by Him, and neither is a single progression of any toddler is obscure to His divine knowledge, and nor is the stretch of the tiniest step taken by any of His creation in a dark gloomy night, or at any depth or layer of this world is not visible by Him. The brilliant moon in its fullness does not veil His magnificent effulgent presence, nor can the radiant sun and the full gamut of its rays brighten and make His presence more luminous. The orderly changing stretches of the nights and what they bring, and the prolongation and shortening of the daylight hours are within His knowledge, for He alone has the knowledge of what He wills to exist, and the wisdom behind their alterations. He is the omniscient Lord Who is full of knowledge of every space, time, sequence, duration and term. The time allotted for the existence of His creation is predetermined solely by Him, and boundaries are not His attributes. He did not create things from preexisting matters nor from elements that were known before Him; rather, He created everything from inception, He made their nature perfect for their respective needs, and He fashioned everything and rendered it its best complementary form. Exalted is He in His glory, for there is nothing that can prevent or limit His reach, nor can anything interfere in His will. He does not benefit from the obedience of His creation, and He is swift in answering their prayers. The countless myriads of angels in the heavens as well as the two earths are subservient to Him. His knowledge of the annihilated beings and past souls is as intricate as His knowledge of the ever-expanding universe and changing lives. His knowledge encompasses everything in the highest heavens and what is in the deepest layers of the earth. He knows everything. He distinguishes the multitude of sounds He created, and each of them stands distinct from the others before Him. Languages do not preoccupy Him. He is the All-Hearing Lord and without the extremities of a body, and He alone manages the entire universe, and He is the All-Seeing Lord, the Living, and the sole Sustaining power behind the entire existence. Glory be to Him, He spoke to Moses with words without the need for limbs or tools, nor lips nor through the vibration of a uvular sound. Exalted is He beyond ascription of mechanical attributes. He who alleges that our Lord is limited is indeed ignorant of the Creator who is worshipped in the heavens and on earth. The one that imagines Him contained within boundaries will live his life confused and mixed up. Instead, it is God Almighty, Allah, who encompasses everything. Therefore, if you are troubled, and if you have gone to the extend of asking questions to describe the Merciful Lord, seeking an explanation beyond what He already revealed about

Himself, inquiring in excess of the manifest proof of His sovereignty, then describe to me the archangels Gabriel, Michael, or Isrãfil. How can you? Thus, if you are incapable of describing the created (angels), then how can you describe the Creator? What you can understand is limited to recognizing the attributes and the essence of perceived matters, but when it comes to describing the One Whom no slumber nor sleep can seize Him, you will surely fail. To Him belongs what the two earths, the heavens and all what they embody, and He is the Lord of the magnificent throne." (*Also narrated by al-Nu'mãn and Is<u>h</u>ãq*)

**153-** Also on this subject, A<u>h</u>mad bin Abi al-<u>H</u>awwãri narrated that 'Ali bin Abi <u>T</u>ãlib, God bless his countenance, said: "I would not be happy if I had died as an infant, and if I entered paradise without experiencing this life and growing up to know my Lord."

**154-** 'Ali bin al-<u>H</u>ussain narrated that his grandfather 'Ali, God be pleased with both of them, said: "Among people, the most true in their advice, and the unsurpassed in their knowledge of who is God, are those who have the most love and reverence for the people of *Lã ilãha il Allah* (Surely there is no god other than Allah)."

**155-** Ya<u>h</u>ya Ibn Abi Kathïr narrated that the companions once asked 'Ali, God bless his countenance: "Should we guard you?" He replied: "One is best guarded by his own destiny."

## His Allegories & Symbolism

The sayings of 'Ali, God bless his countenance, were quoted by his immediate companions, although later on, and after his passing, many more sayings surfaced, some of which may be regarded as apocryphal. However, the selected accounts compiled in this book are held as authentic, and the original manuscript of Imam al-A<u>s</u>fahãni, *<u>H</u>ilyat'ul Awliya Wa <u>T</u>abaqãt'ul A<u>s</u>fiyã*, among other sources, tally the chain of their narrators:

**156-** Sa'ïd bin al-Musayyib narrated that 'Ali, God bless his countenance, said: "True blessings are not children or wealth, rather they are knowledge, forbearance and an ever increasing devotion to one's Lord. When you do good, praise God Almighty, and when you fail, then ask for His forgiveness. Surely there are no benefits in this world except for two types of people, 1) Someone who commits a wrongdoing then amends it with repentance; and 2) someone who hastens to do good while he does not neglect to perform his required religious duties, hence, how can his deeds then diminish when goodness is blessed."

**157-** 'Akrama bin Khālid narrated that 'Ali bin Abi Tālib, God bless his countenance, once said: "Learn five things from me, — although, even if you were to ride on the speediest racing camels to attain them, your camels will fall exhausted before you can ever arrive at fully accomplishing them; 1) Let a servant implore no one beside his Lord; 2) let a servant fear nothing greater than the consequences of his own sin; 3) let an unlearned person not shy to inquire about what he does not understand; and finally, 4) let no scholar, when asked about something he does not know, shy to say, 'I do not know the answer to that question, surely Allah knows best.' You also must know that patience to one's faith is like the head in relationship to one's body."

**158-** Muhājir bin 'Āmir narrated that 'Ali, God bless his countenance, said: "Attachment to obeying one's passions and cravings, and overextending one's hope are what I fear most. As for the disadvantages of attachment to obeying one's passions and cravings, they prevent the servant from recognizing his Lord, on the other hand, overextending one's hope makes one oblivious of the hereafter. Surely the world is set and ready for departure, and most certainly the hereafter is set and ready to come. Each one of them has children, therefore, strive to be the children of the hereafter and not the children of this world. Today you are required to do deeds where reckoning is deferred, and tomorrow you will face reckoning where the reward for deeds mirrors the past."

**159-** Al-Hassan son of 'Ali, God be pleased with them both, narrated that his father said: "Blessed is the unknown and despised worshipper who knows and understands the people. The people give no regards to him, nor do they recognize him, and yet, he knows Allah through His divine benevolence and blessings. Such are the beacons of guidance. God Almighty will safeguard them from every gloomy ordeal in this world, and later on, in the hereafter, He will encompass them with His divine mercy. Such blessed ones do not spread hearsay, and they are neither ostentatious nor hollow."

**160-** 'Ãsim bin Dhumra narrated that 'Ali, God bless his countenance, said: "A true gnostic is one who does not let people despair of God's mercy, and he does not license or make it easy for them to do wrong. A scholar is one who does not forsake the Qur'an by craving other readings, besides that, there are no benefits in an act of worship which is void of knowledge, nor are there benefits in knowledge without understanding, and surely there are no benefits in reading without inference."

**161-** 'Amru bnu Murra narrated that 'Ali, God bless his countenance, once said: "Be the fountainhead of knowledge and the candlelight of the night, and even if you were raggedly clothed, always have renewed hearts. This will make you distinguished in the heavens, and you will always be remembered on earth."

**162-** Bakr bin Khalifa narrated that 'Ali, God bless his countenance, once said: "O ye people, I swear by God Almighty, that even if you were to crave the yearnings of the grief-stricken despondents, or pray constantly like cooing pigeons, or feel upset and cry out like a discontented monk who feels forgotten and unlucky despite his constant prayers, or even if you were to offer God Almighty all your wealth and children in charity, soliciting His nearness, hoping to rise in station, or to have a sin recorded by His lofty angels to be erased, all of that will be little of the blessings I would have wished for you. Instead, be more fearful of His painful chastisements for the sinners. I swear by God Almighty, and in His Name I swear and I swear, that even if your eyes were to melt down from crying in fear of Him and in yearning for Him, and even if you were to live in this world as long as it will last, making constant offerings combined with every type of worship in thankfulness towards His magnificent and countless blessings upon you, it would not be sufficient as a demonstration of gratitude for His guiding you to Islam, and regardless of whether you merit such a blessing or not. In fact, on their own merit, there is no way that any of your deeds can constitute a sufficient ground to receive the magnificent reward of His paradise, although it will be through His divine mercy and compassion that ye will finally be encompassed, and to His paradise will the righteous ones among you be led. May Allah grant us and you to be among the true penitents, and to be gathered on the Day of Reckoning among His true and righteous worshipers."

**163-** Ja'far narrated that after a funeral prayer in which 'Ali, God bless his countenance, officiated, and when the procession reached the grave site, 'Ali, descended the grave along with a helper, and upon laying the deceased in his sepulcher (Arb. *lahd*), his family broke out in mourning. Hearing that, 'Ali turned to his companion and he soberly commented: "Why are they crying thus? I swear by God Almighty, that if they were to taste what their deceased person is experiencing right now, their cognizance will lead them to forget about their departed companion, and they will surely think about nothing but their own individual conclusion in this world. Nevertheless, they will certainly come back to this cemetery, time after time, and until none of them is left in this world."

After the burial, 'Ali, God bless his countenance, stood up and delivered a short sermon, wherein he said: "O servants of Allah, I admonish you to persevere in piety before the Lord of majesty and glory, Who teaches you through parables, and Who has fixed your life-term in this world. He gave you ears to listen with and brains to perceive the meaning of what you hear, and He gave you eyes through which you must see, and consequently, wash off any stupor. He gave you hearts that understand fate, and He gave you a form and existence. Surely Almighty Allah did not create you in vain, nor did He deprive you of hearing His admonitions and revelations. Instead, He blessed you with countless favors, bestowed generous benedictions upon you, provided for you all what you need in this life, and He promised you every exalted reward for every moment of elation or adversity you experience in this world. Therefore, O dependents of Allah, strive hard, and further your pursuit of good deeds as long as the opportunity of this life is present. Do as much as you can, before the destroyer of pleasures in this world arrives. Surely, the comfort of this life will not last, and no one is secure from its bereavements. This world is the ground of a dying arrogance, and a disappearing shadow, and it is a mutable stand which yields pride at first, and then it lies down motionless to be carried on its back for its burial in its own grave. The price of what it desires is surely exuberant, and its pretension of humility is most deceiving. O servants of God Almighty, hearken to these allegories, and heed the signs and the traces left for you to ponder upon. Repel potential calamities with votive offerings, and try to benefit from the admonitions of human's past history. In reality, it seems as though the claws of death have gotten hold of you, and that a house of dirt is dug for you, and it looks as though the trumpet of the Resurrection has interrupted your worldly pursuit, followed by the scattering of the graves, the exposure of cadavers, the resurrection of the dead who will then be driven to the land of the great gathering, and where they will stand up for as long as Allah wills, and await their final reckoning. All these events are controlled solely by the divine power of the magnificent Lord. Each soul is driven to its destined location by its own guide. Each soul is accompanied with its witnessing angels who will testify to its deeds, and then, thereat, ‹ The earth will resplend with the glorious light of its Lord, the book of records will lay open, the prophets and the witnesses will be brought forward; and all shall be judged by the divine and just criterion, and they will not be treated unjustly. › (*Qur'an 39:69*)"

"On that day, all the cities will be rent asunder, and the harbinger will call, for it is the convened promised day for the grand gathering. On that day, the shin shall be laid barren, the sun will be eclipsed, the beasts grouped, the gathering land laid flat, the secrets exposed, the evil ones destroyed, the hearts shaken, and the dwellers of hell-fire will receive a most humiliating blow, and a most painful and lasting punishment for their sins. Hell will be brought forth, and along with it will come its dog and tumult, uproar and thunder, rage and sanctions. Its fire will be blazed, its waters boiling, and its poisons biting. Its eternally doomed dwellers never die, their sorrows and pain do not end, and their shackles and fetters do not brake. Next to them will also stand angels who will announce to them the coming ‹ Entertainment of a scalding water, and an ever burning in hell-fire. › (*Qur'an 56:93-94*) ‹ On that Day (of Resurrection), they shall be veiled from the Light of their Lord. › (*Qur'an 83:15*). They will be set apart from His blessed ones and His deputies, and they will be bound to hell. O servants of God Almighty! Fear your Lord with the piety of the one who understands the truth and humbles himself before his Lord. Fear Him with the piety of the one who is terrified by the possibility of meeting such consequences, and who struggles to escape from any such associations that could drive him to be in such company. Fear your Lord with the piety of one who has seen with his own eyes what has just been described, and the one who holds back himself at once to protect it against such dreadful fall. By pondering such a sight, he is prompted to speed up his efforts, to accelerate his steps, and to escape from such potential horrific end. Instead, he chooses to counter it with heeding God's admonition, carrying worthy deeds, and sufficient is God for a reward. Allah is indeed the All-Hearing, the All-Seeing Lord, and sufficient is one's own records as a challenger of arrogance, and a proof guilt. Sufficient is the heavenly paradise as a reward for the believers, and hell as a curse and as an eternal punishment for the unbelievers. In conclusion, I pray to Almighty Allah to forgive me and to forgive all of you."

## His Advice to Kamīl Bin Ziyād

**164-** 'Abdu-Rah̲mān bin Jandab narrated that Kamīl bin Ziyād told him: " 'Ali held my hand once, and he walked with me in the direction of the cemetery. When we reached the open desert, he soughed a deep breath before he said to me, 'O Kamīl son of Ziyād, hearts are like vessels, the best are exceptionally conscious and vast. Learn from what I am going to tell you. There are three types of people: (1) A godly scholar, (2) a student who is seeking salvation, and (3) a ferocious follower of every howler and his own type. The third type of people are biased, and they float with the currents. They neither seek enlightenment through knowledge, nor do they take refuge in a safe recess during a storm. You must understand that knowledge is better than money, for knowledge will guard you, while you have to be the guard of your money. Deeds are more exalted than knowledge, while money needs someone to spent it justly in order to render it pure. To love a man of knowledge and to learn at his hand is a debt one can never repay. Knowledge earns its owner respect during his lifetime and praiseworthy remembrance after his death, while what money can do expires once it is spent. The keeper of a safe dies and what he guards and the treasures remain, however, a men of knowledge lives throughout the ages.

Their distinct form may no longer be seen, but their findings are preserved in people's hearts. Although knowledge is preserved in the hearts, yet, if it is acted upon, it will carry its bearer, otherwise when merely memorized, knowledge remains vulnerable. A person may use his religious knowledge for worldly gains. He may add his personal commentaries regarding God's revelations to gain status in this world, and he may use God's favors upon him to take advantage of His creation. He alleges to hold fast to the path of the righteous ones, although his superfluousness shows that he has no insight. Whenever he faces a question he does not recognize its answer, doubt and suspicion quickly overtake him. He indulges in mundane pleasures, he is easily driven and allured to satisfy his passion and lust, he is deceived by hoarding money, and he is not a caller to God. The closest similitude to such a character is a freely grazing cattle. Like that, knowledge dies away when its carrier dies."

"However, the earth will never remain devoid of someone who carries the proof of God's sovereignty, and the testimony of His messenger ﷺ, otherwise, God's revelations and clear signs will be abrogated. Such true human beings are the rare few, although they are the most exalted in God's sight. Through them, Almighty Allah guards His message, and He will not take them back unto Himself until they have delivered the same to their coequals. These people endeavor to plant such seeds in hearts akin to their own. Hence, knowledge gushes forth from their hearts, and they take from it the terrain the opulent ones judge as rugged and what the ignorant ones deem as reprehensible. In fact, God's people live in this world with bodies who's souls are captivated by the Upper Observer of all. Such are God's vice-regents on earth, and such are the callers to His religion. Ah, ah! I yearn to meet them, and I ask for God's forgiveness for me and for you. Now if you wish we may go back."

## His Asceticism and Devotion

'Ali, God bless his countenance, accepted the little in this world, and he renounced most of what the world can offer. When possible, and outside his public duties, 'Ali was reclusive, ponderous, and he mostly spent his personal time in offering supererogatory devotion to his Lord. He solicited delight in other than treasuring this world, and in order for him to rise to his ultimate goal.

**165-** On this subject, Ahmad Ibn Hanbal narrated that 'Ali bin Rabī'a al-Walibi reported that one day Ibn al-Nabbāj came and said to 'Ali, God bless his countenance: "O *Amīr al-Mu'mineen* (Prince of the believers), the Treasury House of the Muslims is filled to capacity with every kind of yellow and white." Hearing that, 'Ali exclaimed: "*Allahu Akbar* (Surely Allah is the greatest)," and he walked out of his house leaning on Ibn al-Nabbāj until they reached the Treasury House. 'Ali then called for the people of the city of Kūfa to come, and he kept on handing out everything therein until not a single Dinar or Dirham remained, while saying: "O yellow, O white, go and deceive someone else."

Once the Treasury House was empty, he ordered it to be washed, and he performed his prayers therein before he returned to his house.

**166-** Abu Hayyān al-Teemi narrated that from time to time, 'Ali, God bless his countenance, used to personally sweep and wash the floors of the Treasury House, and that he often used it as a prayer ground, in the hope that it will testify in his favor on the Day of Judgment.

**167-** Abu Bakr bin Khalād narrated that 'Ali, God bless his countenance, once during a sermon said: "I swear by Allah, Whom there is no god except He, that I have deprived myself from everything you collect except this..." 'Ali then pulled out from under his sleeves a small empty glass bottle and added: "My companion Dahqān gave it to me as a gift."

**168-** Imam Ahmad bin Hanbal, God bless his soul, narrated that someone brought 'Ali, God bless his countenance, a plate of sweet made of flour and honey, called *fālūthaj*, and the man placed it before 'Ali on the floor. 'Ali looked at it, and he spoke to the sweet, saying: "Surely your smell is most appetizing, your color is appealing, and certainly you are tasty, but I hate to retrain my nature (*nafs*) to eat something I have not taught it before," and 'Ali did not eat from it.

**169-** Imam Ahmad bin Hanbal, God bless his soul, narrated that 'Ali once brought a dish of jellylike mixed food, and he placed it before his guests who happily ate from it. 'Ali then commented: "Surely Islam is not a strayed youth, but the people of Quraish saw this much amenity, and they fought against one another to keep it."

**170-** Al-Hussain bin 'Ali narrated that his father, may Allah be pleased with both of them, said: "The most difficult things for a man to do are three, 1) To pay what he owes willingly; 2) to remember Allah under all circumstances; and 3), to help his brother when he needs money."

**171-** Ahmad bin Ja'far narrated, re Hãroon bin 'Antara, that his father 'Antara said: "I once visited 'Ali bin Abi Tãlib at Khawranq, and he was shivering from the winter cold, wrapped to warm himself up under a piece of a worn out rag, and I said to him, 'O Prince and Commander of the believers, surely Allah has made an allowance for you and for your family from the revenues of the Treasury House, and here I see you doing this to yourself!' 'Ali replied, 'Let Allah be my witness that I did not deprive of any of your properties. This is my own velvet shawl which I brought with me when I left Madina!' "

**172-** Zaid bin Wahab narrated that a delegation from the City of Basra once visited 'Ali, and among them came a man from the dissenters (*khawãrij*) called al-Ja'ad bin Na'jah who reproached 'Ali for the way he dresses. 'Ali replied, 'What business do you have to do with my personal clothing. Surely my garb is far from pretension or haughtiness, and it is surely better for any Muslim to follow my example.'"

**173-** 'Amru bnu Qays narrated that someone asked 'Ali, God bless his countenance: "What do you use to patch your shirt?" He replied: "I patch it with piety, and a true believer will surely follow such example."

**174-** Muhammad bin Ka'ab narrated that 'Ali, God bless his countenance, said: "During the time of God's messenger ﷺ, I used to tie a small rock around my stomach to control my hunger, and today, by contrast, my charity amounts to Forty-Thousand Dinar per year.

# IV
## Virtues of The Blessed Companions

Those who developed such virtues and attained such stations were innately inclined to seeking the depth of every matter. Their faith was strong, their words were decisive, their verdicts were just, their hearts overflowed with knowledge, and wisdom permeated their soul as well as every cell of their body. Comfort in this world bewildered them, and the silence and stillness of the night attracted them to pursue and intensify their devotion. They were close to the people, they loved the meek, they were expeditious in satisfying his needs, and they were well respected in the community. The weak people never despaired of their justice, and the strong ones always carefully considered and respected their righteousness. Little did they smile, and yet, their faces were ever glowing like a radiant full moon. They sought unity among the believers, and they showed true understanding and extreme compassion towards others.

The blessed companions of God's messenger ﷺ were gifted with understanding, wisdom and inner knowledge. Often, their lips were dry. They discarded the comfort of this world, and forsook the company of its advocates, and they mostly rested over their own forearms. They labored hard and renounced most of the so-called worldly pleasures, and in fact, they truly emulated the lives of God's prophets and messengers, their deputies and the blessed ones who abide in the safety and nearness of their Lord. Furthermore, the blessed companions of God's messenger ﷺ, upon whom be peace, gave away everything they had, and the material wealth was the cheapest offering they happily distributed to comfort the need of others. To their wisdom and perception, material comfort was a burden that they had to constantly unload. The journey of this life bewildered them, and their grief was incessant, just like that of a bereaved mother whose child was slaughtered in her own lap, her tears never cease to flow, and her crying for God's mercy and compassion is constant. Seldom did they sleep, and so little did they eat.

## 1- TALHA BIN 'UBAIDULLÃH

Among such example we find Talha bin 'Ubaidullãh, may God bless his soul and be eternally pleased with him. He was generous, magnanimous, and a radiant star among the blessed companions who distanced themselves from personal satisfaction with their own deeds, and thus lightened their burdens.

**175-** 'Abdullãh bin Ja'far narrated that 'Aisha, God be pleased with her, used to say: "Whenever the day of the Battle of Mount Uhud was mentioned, Abu Bakr referred to it as 'The day of Talha bin 'Ubaid-Allah'."

**176-** Abu Bakr, God be pleased with him, once said: "On the day of Uhud, Abi 'Ubaida al-Jarrãh and myself took shelter in the shade near God's messenger ﷺ who turned to us and said: 'Hasten to your friend!' He meant Talha bin 'Ubaid-Allah, who was bleeding profusely, but we first took care of God's messenger's condition, and then we sought Talha who was lying wounded in one of the groves. When we found him, he had sustained near seventy wounds and blows, and he had lost his fingers during the battle, hence, we attended to him and nursed him the best we could."

"After the battle, when God's messenger ﷺ returned to Madina, he stood upon the pulpit, praised God Almighty and thanked Him for His countless blessings, and he then recited: ❴ Among the believers are men who have been true to their covenant with Allah. Some have fulfilled their vows, while others await their end, yielding to no changes. ❵ (*Qur'an 33:23*) Someone stood up and said, 'O Messenger of Allah, who are such people?'"

Abu Bakr continued: "At that moment, Talha had just arrived to the mosque, and he was wearing a green robe under a green cloak, when God's messenger ﷺ saw him, he said, 'O questioner, here is one of them.' "

**177-** Muhammad bin 'Imrãn narrated that Sa'dah, daughter of 'Awf, and the wife of Talha, said: "In one day, Talha distributed one hundred thousand Dirham in charity. Some money was still left in the house, so I tied it up in his robe, and he carried it to the mosque where he distributed it in charity."

**178-** Al-Hassan, God be pleased with him, narrated that Talha once sold a piece of land he owned for seven hundred thousand Dirham. Talha kept the money in his house for a long sleepless night, and at sunrise, he distributed everything in charity."

## 2- Al-Zubair bin Al-'Awwãm

The peer and companion of Talha bin 'Ubaid-Allah was al-Zubair bin al-'Awwãm, God be pleased with both of them. Beside his spiritual distinctions, al-Zubair was a stern challenger, as well as resolute and prudent warrior, however, he was submissive to his Master, and he was totally dependent on Him. Al-Zubair was loyal, steadfast, oft-forgiving, generous, and he was his earnest possible. At the age of sixteen, when he embraced Islam, his uncle used to tie him up to a metal pole and kindle a fire around him, nearly suffocating him with its smoke, and his uncle used to scream at him: "Renounce your faith," and al-Zubair would keep on avowing: "I will never ever go back to denying the truth."

**179-** 'Ali bin Zaid reported that those who were close to al-Zubair narrated that his chest was filled with open cuts that looked like open eyes from wounds he sustained while defending God's messenger ﷺ. The poet Hassãn bin Thãbit once lauded al-Zubair bin al-'Awwãm, saying: *"He unsheathed his sword during scores of stressful moments to defend God's chosen Messenger, and God surely gives His munificent blessings to whomever He wills. In his time, no one matched his courage, nor before that did anyone meet his caliber. Moreover, time will pass and no one can come even near his uprightness. To praise you, O lion of the jungle, is surely better than many immaculate deeds, and yet, O son of al-Hashimiyya, your actions are a much greater deed."*

**180-** Al-Walïd bin Muslim narrated that Sa'ïd bin 'Abdul 'Aziz said: "At one time, al-Zubair bin al-'Awwãm was extremely rich, and he had one thousand servants who collected his daily revenues from a variety of businesses and properties he owned. Each night he divided the entire income they brought him, and he distribute the same in full before he entered his house."

**181-** The same was confirmed in the narration of Mughïth bin Sama, who said: "Al-'Awwãm had one thousand workers who collected his land revenues, and not a Dirham (i.e., a dime) of that money ever entered his house."

**182-** Abi Salma narrated that upon the revelation of the Qur'anic verse: ﴾ Then, on the Day of Resurrection, you will settle your disputes in the presence of your Lord, ﴿ (*Qur'an 39:31*) al-Zubair asked: "O Messenger of Allah, will we have ﷺ to face each others again and reenact the arguments we had in this world?" God's messenger ﷺ replied: "Indeed you will surely do that." Al-Zubair pondered for a moment and then said: "I swear by Almighty Allah that this is a most serious matter."

**183-** 'Abdullãh bin Al-Zubair also narrated that on the day of the Battle of the Camel, his father al-Zubair instructed him concerning his debts, and he added: "My dear son, when sometimes you find it difficult to manage, then call for the help of my Master."

'Abdullãh added: "I did not understand what he meant by 'My Master' until I once asked him, 'Father! Who is your master?' He replied, 'Allah.' Later on, 'Abdullãh said, 'By God, whenever I felt any anxiety about his business, I prayed, 'O Master of al-Zubair, satisfy his debt,' and surely Allah fulfilled his wish."

**184-** Hishãm bin 'Urwa narrated, that upon his martyrdom, al-Zubair bin al-'Awwãm did not leave a single Dinar or Dirham in cash, except for two estates and some houses he owned. He incurred his debts from his practice of not accepting to keep anything on consignment, for during the pilgrimage season, and whenever a traveling merchant brought him his remaining goods to sell for him and to keep the money until the next season, al-Zubair bin al-'Awwãm would reply: "I do not accept anything on consignment, but I will take the goods as a loan, for I fear to mix them with other merchandise."

Later on, after he died, and when his son counted his debts, they added up to two million. To satisfy his father's debts, 'Abdullãh bin al-Zubair used to attend the pilgrimage season annually, and he called the pilgrims to come forward to claim the monies they loaned to his father. 'Abdullãh did that for four consecutive years and until everything was repaid. Only after the four years passed that 'Abdullãh divided the remaining balance between the heirs. Al-Zubair had four wives, and each one of them inherited one million and two hundred thousand Dirhams.

## 3- Sa'ad bin Abi Waqqãss

Sa'ad bin Abi Waqqãss also was among the early believers since the dawn of Islam in Mecca. He defended God's messenger ﷺ, and he suffered persecution and hardships at the hand of the unbelievers, and then he became segregated from his family and tribe. Sa'ad relinquished all comforts and wealth to earn God's pleasure and blessings in the company of His Messenger ﷺ. Sa'ad's particular blessing was that no matter what he prayed for, his prayer received a favorable answer from God Almighty. Sa'ad also was tried with the office of leadership, and he proved to be a great leader. God Almighty opened vast lands and spread His message at his hands, and He granted him a blessed progeny. At the later stage of his life, Sa'ad, God be pleased with him, renounced his worldly status, and he sought seclusion from his worldly responsibilities and their associated trials to satisfy his spiritual quest and to redeem the balance of his life. Sa'ad became a model of piety and particularly after the countless permutations he survived, and he became a pillar of faith, and a proof of wisdom and knowledge.

**185-** Sa'ïd bin al-Musayyib narrated that Sa'ad bin Abi Waqqãss once said: "When I became Muslim, no one else besides me embraced God's religion on that day. Hence, and for the following seven days, I counted as one third of the congregating new believers."

**186-** Qayss bin Abi Hãzim narrated that Sa'ad said: "At one time, we were with God's messenger ﷺ in isolation in the outskirts (*Hirãb*) of Mecca, and as a result of the prohibition of commerce imposed against us by the tribe of Quraish, we had nothing to eat but the leaves of shrubs and wild plants, and our women gave birth in the open like a ewe."

**187-** Qayss bin Abi Hãzim also narrated that Sa'ad said: "God's messenger ﷺ prayed for me and said, 'Lord, make his arrows hit their target, and fulfill his prayers.' "

**188-** Mus'ab son of Sa'ad told of his father's narration that during the early years of hardships in Mecca and the persecution of Muslims, God's messenger ﷺ once said: "Today, we are experiencing the easy trials, and I am more concerned for you about the adversities that will come. Should you have to face them, endure that with patience and perseverance, for comfort in this world appears sweet and tempting."

According to Islamic law, one is only permitted to will up to one third of his property, the balance is divided according to the divine decree, which is detailed in the holy Qur'an.

**189-** On this subject, Imam Ahmad Ibn Hanbal, God bless his soul, narrated, re Sa'ad, that his father, Abi Waqqãss, was in Mecca when he fell ill. At that time he only had one daughter. When God's messenger ﷺ visited him, he asked him: "O Messenger of Allah, should I will everything I have to her?" God's messenger ﷺ replied: "Nay! Only the third, and even that is too much. Perhaps God will grant you recovery, and you will live, whereby, through you, He will bring forth a progeny that will benefit some people and afflict others with trials."

**190-** Abu Bakr bin Khallãd narrated, re Sa'ad bin Abi Waqqãss, re his father, that God's messenger ﷺ said: "Allah loves a servant who is free from want, who is discreet and pious, and whose wealth comes from his satisfaction with what he has."

**191-** Imam Muhammad Ibn Seerïn narrated that someone said to Sa'ad bin Abi Waqqãss, God be pleased with him: "Why don't you fight the dissenters, for surely you are a man of council (*ahlu shura*), and you have more rights to speak than others." Sa'ad replied: "Bring me a sword that has two eyes, a tongue, and a pair of lips, and that can discern between a believer and a disbeliever, and only then I will enter this battle, for I have endured real *jihãd*, and I surely know what it means in a true sense."

**192-** Tãriq bin Shahãb narrated that a difference in opinion once took place between Khãlid bin al-Walïd and Sa'ad bin Abi Waqqãss, God be pleased with both of them. Someone tried to take advantage of the situation, and he went to Sa'ad to report what Khãlid said, but Sa'ad stopped him, saying: "Say nothing, for what is between me and my brother does not affect our unity and religious brotherhood, and it has no bearing on the truth of our religion."

## 4- Sa'īd bin Ziyād

As for Sa'īd bin Zaid bin 'Amru bnu Nafīl, he also was one of the blessed companions who spoke the truth, who spent his wealth on God's path, controlled his passions, and who restrained his want. He feared no censure or reproach when it came to God's rights. His prayers were answered, and he embraced Islam prior to Omar bin al-Khattāb, God be pleased with them both. Sa'īd bin Zaid had no inclinations for leadership, and instead he engaged in serving the community. He tamed his mind, and he kept away from personal conflicts and competition.

**193-** Rabāh bin al-Hārith narrated, re Sa'īd bin Zaid, that God's messenger ﷺ named ten of his companions who were given the glad tidings of paradise in the hereafter during their lifetime in this world, and the list included: Abu Bakr, Omar, 'Uthmān, 'Ali, Talha, al-Zubair, Sa'ad bin Mālik, and Sa'īd bin Zaid.

**194-** Sulaimān bin Ahmad narrated Arwa, daughter of Uways once accused Sa'īd bin Zaid of annexing a piece of her land. When Mawrān bin al-Hakam brought the subject before Sa'īd, he replied: "I would never annex even a span of land from someone else since I heard God's messenger ﷺ, upon whom be peace, say, 'Whosoever annexes even a span of someone else's property, he will be confined into the abyss of the seven layers of the two earths.' "

**195-** Also in reference to the above subject, Abu 'Amru bnu Hamdān narrated that in his reply to Marwān, Sa'īd bin Ziyād also lifted his hand up and prayed: "O my Lord, this woman has falsely accused me of being unjust to her, and that I have stolen a piece of her land. So, if she is lying, then blind her, and throw her in a deep well; my Lord, and exonerate my name with a miraculous light of Yours that will show the Muslims that I was never unjust to her."

Abu 'Amru bnu Hamdān continued: " 'Amru bnu Hazm narrated that immediately upon completing his prayer, a tumultuous rainstorm with thunder and lightening that has never been seen before took place, and the valley of 'Aqīq became flooded. By the end of the day, the water receded again, and the people saw the line of Sa'ïd's property which was clearly marked, and thus, Sa'ïd was vindicated. A month later, the woman, Arwa, daughter of Uways became blind, and one day, while strolling through her farmland, she fell into a well where she died."

## 5- 'Abdu-Rahmãn bin 'Awf

'Abdu-Rahmãn bin 'Awf was a most trustworthy, wealthy and a generous companion. He spent his wealth on God's path in gratitude for His countless favors and blessings. 'Abdu-Rahmãn bin 'Awf constantly sought God's guidance and help against temptation or any sense self-righteousness. He was most sensitive and lachrymose, and he shed his tears easily in reverence and fear of his Lord. 'Abdu-Rahmãn was a model of how a rich Muslim should conduct his life, and he had a soft and a most compassionate heart towards the poor and needy.

**196-** Anas bin Mãlik narrated that 'Aisha, God be forever pleased with her, was at home when she heard a constant tumultuous blasting sound, the whole city of Madina shook from its intensity. 'Aisha, the mother of the believers, God be pleased with her, then had partially lost her sight to cataract, and when she inquired about the sound she heard, she was told that a large herd of seven hundred camels loaded with goods belonging to 'Abdu-Rahmãn bin 'Awf had just arrived from Syria. 'Aisha quietly commented: "Indeed, I heard God's messenger ﷺ say, 'I saw 'Abdu-Rahmãn bin 'Awf entering paradise crawling on his knees and elbows.' "

Later on, when her comments reached 'Abdu-Rahmãn bin 'Awf, and before he entered his house, he hasten to her house inquiring, and when she confirmed the prophetic saying. 'Abdu-Rahmãn immediately avouched: "I call upon you to witness that from this moment on, this entire caravan and all the goods it carries are an offering for God's pleasure, and they belong to the treasury of Muslims to distribute them to the poor and needy."

**197-** Al-Musawwar bin Makhrama narrated that 'Abdu-Rahmãn bin 'Awf owned a piece of land he had bought from 'Uthmãn, and he sold it for forty-thousand Dinar, and then, he divided its entire revenues between the tribe of Bani Zahra, the needy people of Madina, and the mothers of the believers. Al-Musawwar added: "I personally carried 'Aisha's share to her, and she commented: 'I once heard God's messenger ﷺ say, 'Only the righteous people (*sālihеen*) will show compassion on you after me.' "

**198-** 'Abdullāh bnu Abi 'Awfa narrated that God's messenger ﷺ once called for 'Abdu-Rahmān bin 'Awf who had arrived late, and God's messenger ﷺ asked him: "What delayed you?" He replied: "Taking care of my accounts held me back, for I do have a large business. I have one hundred camels that has just arrived from Egypt, and I hereby offer them with all the goods they carry in charity for the widows of Madina."

**199-** Also on this subject, Ibrāhīm, son of 'Abdu-Rahmān bin 'Awf narrated that God's messenger ﷺ once said to his father 'Abdu-Rahmān: "O son of 'Awf, you are one of the richest people of this town, and being thus rich, I think that you can only enter paradise crawling on your elbows and knees, so lend Allah a good loan so that He may unbind your feet." Ibn 'Awf replied: "What should I lend Allah?" God's messenger ﷺ replied: "Exonerate yourself in the evening from what you have achieved during the day." Ibn 'Awf replied: "Would distributing something every night purify my earnings?." He replied: "Indeed." Immediately Ibn 'Awf hastened to do so. The archangel Gabriel, upon whom peace, soon descended upon God's messenger ﷺ and said: "Order Ibn 'Awf to open his house for guests, to regularly feed the hungry and the needy, and to financially help people when they seek him. If he does so, this will be atonement for his concerns."

**200-** Nawfal bin Iyās al-Hathli narrated that 'Abdu-Rahmān bin 'Awf used to frequent his circle. One day, after sitting with him and with his guests for a while, 'Abdu-Rahmān excused himself for a short while, he went to his house, took his ablution and when he returned, he brought back with him a large tray of bread and meat. When the tray was placed in the middle, 'Abdu-Rahmān cried in great chagrin, so the people asked him: "O Abu Muhammad, why are you crying like this?" He replied: "A thought came to me, and I suddenly remembered that God's messenger ﷺ died having not satisfied his basic hunger or that of his family, not even in eating just barley bread, and I do not think that God Almighty has kept us alive after him for better times than the days of His messenger ﷺ."

**201-** Also on this subject, Shu'ba narrated that a group of companions once sat to partake a meal, and 'Abdu-Rahmãn bin 'Awf was in their midst but he did not eat, so the people assumed that he was fasting for that day. 'Abdu-Rahmãn then commented: "When Hamza was killed, we did not have a piece of cloth to shroud him, and he is better than me. Also, when Mus'ab bin 'Umair was killed, we did not have a piece of cloth to shroud him, and he is better than me, and here we are enjoying the comfort and delight of this world. I am afraid that perhaps our share in the hereafter is instead given to us in this world." Shu'ba added: "I am not sure whether 'Abdu-Rahmãn ate with us on that day or not."

**202-** Al-Hadhrami narrated that someone once read from the Qur'an before God's messenger ﷺ during an assembly, and his reading touched everyone's heart. On that day, everyone's eyes were overflowing with tears except 'Abdu-Rahmãn bin 'Awf, and God's messenger ﷺ commented: " 'Abdu-Rahmãn bin 'Awf's eyes were not overflowing with tears, but his heart did."

**203-** Sulaimãn bin Ahmad narrated that 'Abdu-Rahmãn bin 'Awf, God be pleased with him, said: "When we were tried with adversities, we endured that with patience, but when we were tried with comfort, we surely failed to exercise patience."

## 6- Abu 'Ubaida bin Al-Jarrãh

Among the blessed companions also rises the star of the trustworthy and righteous, the tributary and humble servant and ascetic, the loyal and faithful to his trust, Abu 'Ubaida bin al-Jarrãh, God be pleased with him. He limited his needs to little, and he was patient until the time when he met his Lord, and when he began the second and final segment of his journey.

It was in reference to Abu 'Ubaida bin al-Jarrãh, God be pleased with him, that God Almighty spoke to His blessed messenger ﷺ, revealing: ❮ Thou will not find among the people who believe in Allah and in the Last Day, someone who loves those who resist Allah and His apostle, and even if they were their fathers, their sons, their brothers, or their nearest kindred. Allah has inscribed faith in their hearts, and He strengthened them with a spirit of His own. He will admit them to gardens beneath which rivers flow, wherein they will dwell for ever. Allah will be well pleased with them, and they with Him. They are the party of Allah. Truly it is the party of Allah that will achieve (true) felicity. ﴿ (*Qur'an 58:22*)

**204-** Omar bin al-Khattāb, May God be pleased with him forever, narrated that God's messenger ﷺ said: "Every nation (*umma*) has a loyal trustee, and Abu 'Ubaida bin al-Jarrāh is the trustee of this nation."

**205-** Mu'ammar narrated that when Omar bin al-Khattāb arrived to Syria, the masses welcomed him along with some of the most distinguished people of the land. Omar looked around him in surprise, and he asked: "Where is my brother?" They replied: "Who do you mean?" Omar said: "I mean Abu 'Ubaida." They replied: "He will come before you immediately." When Abu 'Ubaida arrived, Omar descended his ride and embraced him, and he went with him to his house. Upon entering, Omar noticed that Abu 'Abaida's modest house only had his sword, a shield, a lance and a horse saddle."

**206-** Bishr bin Müsa narrated that Omar bin al-Khattāb was sitting with a group of his companions and he asked: "Let each one make a wish!" Someone said: "I wish if this house was filled with gold and which I would happily spend it on God's path." Omar asked the people again: "Make a wish!" Someone else said: "I wish that this house was filled with pearls, chrysolites, and with every kind of precious gems that I would most happily spend in charity on God's path." Omar asked again: "Make a wish!" They replied: "O Prince of the Believers, we truly do not know what to wish for!" Omar then said: "I wish that this house was filled with men like Abu 'Ubaida bin al-Jarrah."

**207-** 'Imrān bin Mujammar narrated that Abu 'Ubaida bin al-Jarrah once lead a campaign, and he addressed the soldiers saying: "Perhaps there is a man among you who washes his clothes clean, and who sullys his religion, or someone who exalts himself when in fact he is disgracing it. Ward off your old sins by replacing them with new worthy deeds. Should one's sins fill between the heavens and the earth, and should he then do even one worthy deed, his single good deed will surely prevail over them and until it abolishes all of them."

**208-** K̲hãlid bin Ma'dãn narrated that Abu 'Ubaida bin al-Jarrah̲ once said: "The parable of a believer's heart is like that of a bird, it alights and then soar again and again so many times each day."

## 7- 'UTHMĀN BIN MAZ'ŪN

Among the early companions and peers also glimmers the name of the ascetic, the humble and the pious companion 'Uthmãn bin Maz'ün, God be pleased with him. He was among the early followers of God's messenger ﷺ, and he migrated twice from his homeland, — once to Abyssinia to escape the persecution of the tribe of Quraish, and in the second time, he migrated to the blessed City of Light, Madina, to join God's messenger ﷺ and his blessed companions.

Ibn Maz'ün's rank was most exalted and revered among the blessed companions of God's messenger ﷺ. He was a tireless worshipper, and he was a blessed servant who was truly touched by the love of God Almighty, and he devoted his entire life to please his Lord, and to serve His will.

Ibn Maz'ün also was grief-stricken, and he lost one of his eyes while defending Allah's Holy Name. The comfort of this world could not distract his focus, and his Islam turned into trials he had to endure for the sake of his Beloved. Hence, his comfort in God's pleasure increased his longing for Him, and it opened his heart to greater realities he cherished greatly.

During the pre-Islamic era, the Arabs of Quraish enjoyed Abyssinia as their neighboring marketplace. There, they sought their supplementary needs and found security and ample supplies all year around. In the early days of the divine message, and for several years thereafter, the believers were instructed to hold off their defenses. When the persecution reached its peak and the physically weak ones could no longer bear the atrocities inflicted upon them by the unbelievers of the Tribe of Quraish, God's messenger ﷺ instructed some of his followers to take temporary shelter in the East African kingdom of Abyssinia. 'Uthmãn bin Maz'ün was appointed then as their *Amir* (leader), and he remained with them therein until *Sūra al-Najim* was revealed. Later on, he returned to Mecca, although he needed tribal protection which he received from one of his uncles and neighbor in Mecca, al-Walid bin al-Mughira.

**209-** On this subject, 'Abdu-Rahmān bin 'Awf narrated that when 'Uthmān bin Maz'ūn reflected upon the comfort and peace he was enjoying in the protection of his polytheist neighbor al-Walid bin al-Mughira, while the companions of God's messenger ﷺ were suffering the pounding of destiny at the hands of the unbelievers all over the Arabian peninsula, and when he saw the persecution of Muslims intensify, he said to himself: "By God, it makes me feel depressed to hold unto comfort and illusionary tranquillity in the company and protection of a polytheist while my companions and the people of the faith are suffering persecution and atrocities at the hands of the disbelievers!"

Upon realizing that, 'Abdu-Rahmān bin 'Awf then went to al-Walid bin al-Mughira, his influential uncle, and said to him: "O Aba 'Abd Shams,[1] your decency of a neighbor has come to its conclusion. I have decided to forgo your protection." Al-Walid replied: "O my dear nephew, why would you want to do that? Perhaps someone among my people has offended you or grieved you!" Ibn Maz'ūn replied: "Nay, no one did, but I would rather seek the protection of Almighty Allah, and I do not wish for anyone else's favor or dominance." Al-Walid answered: "Then lets go to the Ka'ba and give it to me in public as I pledged my protection for you in public."

Thus, they both went to the Ka'ba and al-Walid announced: "Ibn Maz'ūn has decided to waive away my neighboring tribal protection." Ibn Maz'ūn immediately stood and said: "He spoke the truth, and I have found him loyal to his promise and a generous neighbor. However, I have pledged to seek no protection besides that of Almighty Allah, and that is why I decided to forgo al-Walid's protection."

On his way out of Mecca, and as 'Uthmān bin Maz'ūn was leaving, there was a poet called Lubaid bin Rabi'a al-Qaysi, who

[1] That was his firstborn son's name, 'Abd Shams, i.e., the sun worshiper, by which name he was patronymed.

was sitting near God's House, the Ka'ba, reciting his poetry before a group of fans from the Tribe of Quraish. Ibn Maz'ūn decided to sit down with them for a while, and to hear what Lubaid had to say as he chanted:

*Everything other than Allah is false,*

'Uthmān commented loudly: "This is the truth."

The poet looked towards Ibn Maz'ūn in surprised, he pondered for a moment before he continued:

*And every comfort will unfailingly perish.*

'Uthmān commented: "What you said is not true, for the bliss and comfort of the heavenly paradise is everlasting."

The pagan poet Lubaid became extremely upset for the interruption of his recital, and he turned to the people and said: "O ye people of Quraish, it was not common that your guests be humiliated in your presence!" Someone in the crowd leaped out and said: "Do not feel prejudiced with regards to what he said, for he is only an impudent apostate who, with a group of a likewise people, have defected the religion of our fathers for the sake of a new one."

'Uthmān became distraught by the comment and his reply to the man was evenly injurious. A fist fight then started between the two men, and during that fight, 'Uthmān lost one of his eyes. Al-Walīd was close by, and as he witnessed what happened to 'Uthmān, he approached him and commented: "O my nephew, by God, your eye did not need this injury!" 'Uthmān replied: "Nay, O Aba 'Abd Shams! It is my other eye that needs what happened to its sister eye in defending the truth. Now I do stand right here in the neighboring divine protection of someone Who is mightier than you!"

**210**- Ibn Shahāb narrated that God's messenger ﷺ was sitting with some companions when 'Uthmān entered the Mosque wearing a torn rag he patched with a piece of a camel's hide. God's messenger's heart felt for him, and the companions felt for the compassion of God's messenger ﷺ who commented: "O ye people, what would you say when a day comes, when you will wear a garment in the morning then put another one in the evening, and when you will sit at tables offering you one variety of food after another, and when you will decorate your homes like you adorn the Ka'ba?" The people replied: "We certainly would like that O messenger of Allah, so we can enjoy a comfortable life." He replied: "This will take place, but you are better off today than those who will come after you and live such a life."

**211-** 'Abd Rabbo bin Sa'ïd al-Madani narrated that when 'Uthmān died, God's messenger entered his room, kissed his forehead and said: "May God's mercy be upon you O 'Uthmān, you have held true to your faith. You have taken nothing from this world, nor did the world succeed at taking anything from you."

**212-** Zaid bin Aslam reported that when 'Uthmān bin Maz'ūn was laid in his grave, his wife commented: "Be blessed in God's paradise O Aba Sā'ib!" God's messenger ﷺ turned to her and said: "How do you know that?" She replied: "O Messenger of Allah, he fasted every day of his life, and he stood up all his nights in prayers." God's messenger ﷺ then commented: "It is more reverend and felicitous if you had said that he truly loved Allah and His messenger."

## 8- Mus'ab bin 'Umair al-Dāri

He is Mus'ab bin 'Umair of the Tribe of Bani Dār. He was one of the early callers to God's path and a pious believer. Mus'ab bin 'Umair God be pleased with him, memorized the entire holy Qur'an by heart, and he was sent by God's messenger ﷺ to teach it to the Muslim partisans (*ansār*) in Madina prior to God's messenger ﷺ migrating to it. Mus'ab renounced the comfort of this world, he lived a modest life, and he found comfort and exhilaration in the meadows of the Holy Qur'an. Mus'ab bin 'Umair was known as the Qur'an reciter, and he won his martyrdom during the Battle of Mount Uhud, near the City of Madina.

**213-** 'Urwa bin al-Zubair narrated that when the Medinites heard the words of God's messenger ﷺ, upon whom be peace, their hearts opened to Islam, and they hearkened to God's message, Who entrenched acceptance, faith and certitude in their hearts, and He made them the pioneers of His last message. The Medinites pledged to return the following year to Mecca, during the pilgrimage season, to hear the divine revelation, and to hearken to God's messenger teachings. After fulfilling their pledge, when this group of early believers returned to Madina, they spoke of their encounter with God's messenger ﷺ, and their people dispatched an emissary to Mecca, requesting God's messenger ﷺ to send them someone to instruct them in their religion. God's messenger ﷺ responded by sending Mus'ab bin 'Umair who stayed in Madina at the house of As'ad bin Zirara, and later on, he moved to become the guest of Sa'ad bin Mu'ãth. People gathered regularly around Mus'ab and they hearkened to his teachings and recitation of the Holy Qur'an until nearly every house in Madina had someone who embraced Islam at his hand. Hence, they proclaimed God's oneness, broke all status of deities their forefathers worshipped, and they rebutted polytheism. Mus'ab, God be pleased with him, played a major role in gathering the Muslims, instructing them, and in organizing them as a community in Madina some years before the blessed migration of God's messenger ﷺ and his arrival to Madina.

**214-** 'Ubaid bin 'Umair narrated that when the Battle of Uhud ended, God's messenger ﷺ passed by the body of Mus'ab bin 'Umair and recited: ﴾ Among the believers are men who have been true to their covenant with Allah. Some have fulfilled their vow, while others are awaiting their end, yielding to no change. ﴿ (*Qur'an 33:23*) God's messenger ﷺ then turned toward the scattered bodies of the martyrs of Uhud and said: "I bear witness that you are alive in the presence of Allah." He then turned to his companions and said: "O ye people, visit them and pay your regards of peace to them. I swear by Him Who governs my soul, that whenever you greet them, they will reply to your greetings, and this will be thus until the Day of Resurrection."

**215-** Omar bin al-Khattãb narrated that God's messenger ﷺ once saw Mus'ab bin 'Umair coming to the mosque wearing a sheep skin, and God's messenger ﷺ commented: "Look at this man whose heart God has enlightened. I saw him sitting before two compassionate authors like parents, who were nourishing him with the best of food and drinks. Surely his love for Almighty Allah and for His Messenger (ﷺ) have raised him to what you see."

## 9- Abdullãh bin Jahsh

His mother, Umaimah bint 'Abdul-Muttalib, was the paternal aunt of God's messenger ﷺ, and his sister, Zainab bint Jahsh, was the wife of God's messenger ﷺ and the mother of the believers. 'Abdullãh bin Jahsh was the first companion behind whose leadership the Muslims stood united, and he was among the early émigrés to Abyssinia. Later on, he returned to the Arabian peninsula and fought in both the Battle of Badr and that of Uhud. In his spiritual struggle, he used every permissible mean to reach his exalted station, and he was a great sire among the believers.

## 10- 'Ãmir bin Fahïrah

It is said that spirituality also means to love to die for the sake of one's beloved.

**216-** On this subject, Hishãm bin 'Urwa narrated that on their way to Madina, God's messenger ﷺ and Abu Bakr took temporary shelter for three nights in the cave of *Hirã'* in the mountain of Thawr. A shepherd called 'Ãmir bin Fahïrah, who had secretly embraced Islam, concealed knowledge of their whereabouts. Every morning, when the Arab shepherds drove their flock to their grazing land, 'Ãmir tarried in their company, but in the evening, as the shepherds returned to their homes in Mecca, 'Ãmir, inconspicuously slowed down and went to the cave of *Hirã'* to attend to God's messenger ﷺ and Abu Bakr's needs. Later on, when God's permission came for them to continue their journey, 'Ãmir bin Fahïrah was their guide and companion in their migratory journey to Madina, which later on became known as the City of God's messenger ﷺ and as the City of Light.

'Ãmir bin Fahïrah's faith kept him strong, and his heart was free from jealousy or envy. His consciousness, values, and moral standards were high, and his trueness to his Lord reserved him a most exalted place in Allah's sight. He loved Allah and His Messenger ﷺ, and he defended His message with his heart, soul, and body. 'Ãmir bin Fahïrah willingly and with peerless courage drove into the most dangerous adversities, and by God's leave, came out victorious.

**217-** 'Aisha, God be pleased with her, the mother of the believers, narrated that "God's messenger ﷺ, Abu Bakr and 'Ãmir arrived together to Madina."

**218-** Ka'ab bin Mãlik narrated that God's messenger ﷺ sent seventy of his best learned men and distinguished companions to the Tribe of Banu Sulaym of the Mountains of Najd to teach them Islam as per their request. A betrayal on the part of the host tribe of Najd ended in a battle near the well of Ma'unah.

**219-** Also on this subject, 'Ãmir bin Tufayl narrated that when 'Ãmir bin Fahïrah was killed, they saw his body rising in the air.

**220-** Hishãm bin 'Urwa narrated that during the Battle of the well of Ma'unah, 'Ãmir bin al-Tufayl asked 'Amru bnu Umayya about a martyr whose body was lifted up in the air, he replied: "This is 'Ãmir bin Fahïrah's body." He later on added: "I saw him raised between the heavens and the earth," and all the companions agreed that his body was washed by the heavenly angles who also buried him away from people's sight and knowledge.

## 11- 'Ãsim bin Thãbit

Faith in Almighty Allah also means to discard what is clearly false, and to humbly pursue what is distinctly true. In his life time, 'Ãsim bin Thãbit, God be pleased with him, was true to his Lord. He guarded his covenant with his Lord, and he pledged never to accept the promise of a polytheist.

**221-** Buraida bin Sulaimãn al-Aslami narrated that on the day of his martyrdom, 'Ãsim prayed: "My Lord, today I am defending Your faith and religion, so defend and protect my body from mutilation."

Hence, 'Ãsim, God be pleased with him, understood that comfort in this life is transient, while it is permanent in the hereafter for the believers. He also realized that whatever God Almighty has decreed will take place, and that one's eventual return will ultimately be to his Creator and Lord.

**222-** 'Ãsim bin 'Amr narrated that God's messenger ﷺ once sent six of his companions, including Murthid Ibn Abi Murthid, 'Ãsim bin Thãbit, and Khãlid bin al-Bakïr in a mission to the tribe of Bani Luhyān. On their way back to Madina, the tribe of Bani Huthayl betrayed the convoy of believers, and they launched a vicious attack them. During the battle, the believers were offered amnesty if they would surrender, but at that point, 'Āsim made a covenant with his Lord never to trust the pact of a polytheist, and he had earlier vowed never to touch a polytheist or let a polytheist touch him. it is then that 'Āsim prayed: "Lord, today I am defending your faith and religion, so defend and protect my body from mutilation". He then charged against his enemy and fought until he was martyred along with all of his companions in that battle.

When the tribe of Bani Huthayl learned of 'Āsim's death, they wanted to behead him and to sell his skull to Sulāfa, the daughter of Sa'ad bin Shahi'd, who had vowed when her two sons were killed during the Battle of Uhud at the hand of 'Āsim, that if she could put her hand on him, she will drink wine in his skull. Thus, when the men of Bani Huthayl went to seek his head, they could not near his body because of a swarm of wasps that had gathered around him. Seeing the present danger, the men of Bani Huthayl drew back, and they decided to wait until the nightfall, hopping that by night, the wasps would have left. At night, when they arrived, they could not find his body. When Omar bin al-Khattāb heard of 'Āsim's destiny, and how the wasps prevented his enemy from reaching his body, he commented: "God has accepted the vow of His true servant, and surely He has fulfilled his prayers."

## 12- KHUBAIB BIN 'UDAI

Among the blessed companions of God's messenger ﷺ also towers the name of Khubaib bin 'Udai, God be pleased with him. He was blessed in martyrdom, and he endured great sufferings at the hands of his torturers who crucified him because of his love for his Beloved. Khubaib concealed his sufferings, and he endured his crucifixion with great courage and faith in an unparalleled demonstration of endurance to raise the flag of God's message. When the incredulous confederates plotted to kill him, they stirred the tribes to execute him, then they made him a cross, and they celebrated his execution by inviting women and children to witness, but Allah took away his anxiety, replaced it with peacefulness in a manifestation of His presence (Arb. *sakïna*), and He strengthened him with faith and endurance.

**223-** Ibn Ishãq narrated that before his execution, the tribes gave Khubaib a choice between renouncing his faith in Allah and returning to believe in their dieties, or facing death. His tears flew profusely as he did not hesitate to embrace and defend God's call. Before his death he said: "Why would I fear death when it will eventually seize me no doubt, and when what I truly fear is to become fuel for hell-fire. Hence, as long as I die as a believer, it does not matter to me how it happens."

**224-** Also on this subject, Abu Huraira, God be pleased with him, narrated that God's messenger ﷺ once sent a brigade of ten people on a mission, and he appointed 'Ãsim bin Thãbit al-Ansãri from Madina, as their leader. When the brigade reached between the town of 'Asfãn and city of Mecca, someone discovered them and reported what he saw to the tribe of Bani Huthayl who immediately dispatched one hundred strong men to search for them. During their chase, they found tracks of some date pits from Madina that led them to 'Ãsim and to his men. When 'Ãsim bin Thãbit realized that he was being pursued, he directed his men to a high desert plateau, however, it was too late then, for the clan of Bani Huthayl had already surrounded them.

The leader of Bani Huthayl then called out: "Come down and give yourselves up as war prisoners, and you have my solemn word that if you do surrender, none of you will be killed!" 'Ãsim bin Thãbit, the leader of the Muslim men then proclaimed: "I swear by Allah that I do not trust the covenant of a disbeliever. O my Lord, inform Thy prophet about what happened to us." 'Ãsim then charged against the enemy and he was martyred along with six of his companions. The other three men including Khubaib bin 'Udai, were forced to surrender. When the clan of Bani Huthayl captured them, the clan negated its promise not to kill its prisoners, and they tied them up and dragged them to sell them as slaves in Mecca. On their way, one of the three men realized what happened, and he proclaimed: "By God, this is a flagrant betrayal, and I shall not follow you." As he resisted, the men of Bani Huthayl killed him, and then they continued on their way to Mecca with the remaining two Muslims.

In Mecca, the son of al-Hãrith bin 'Ãmir bought Khubaib bin 'Udai who had killed his father during the Battle of Badr. One day, the son of al-Hãrith bin 'Ãmir decided to kill Khubaib, and Marya the servant of Hujair bin Abi Ahãb who later became Muslim narrated: "I walked into the room where Khubaib was imprisoned, and I found the son of al-Hãrith holding a sharpened dagger against the neck of his tied-up prisoner. I screamed and Khubaib understood why. The son of al-Hãrith then said to me, 'Are you afraid that I may kill him?' I replied, 'By God, I have never seen a prisoner who is more blessed than Khubaib. I found him one day in his chains eating from a cluster of fresh grapes when the entirety of Mecca did not have a single fruit!' "

Later on, Marya used to say: "Surely it was a miracle, — a blessed food the All-Compassionate, Almighty Allah gave to Khubaib."

**225-** Ibn Ishãq narrated: "When the disbelievers brought Khubaib out of the area of the sacred Haram to kill him, Khubaib asked permission to pray two *Rak'ãt,* and his executioners granted his wish. After completing his prayers, Khubaib said to his murderers: "I swear to Allah that I did not wish to prolong my prayers lest you think I am afraid of death."

"As they tied him up to a cross and raised it to execute him, Khubaib prayed, 'My Lord, we have delivered Thy message to the people. Lord, inform Thy Prophet about the sufferings they put us through."

## 13- Ja'far bin Abi Tãlib

Also among the blessed companions there shines the name of the blessed Ja'far bin Abi Tãlib, God be pleased with him. As a pious caller to God Almighty, Ja'far bin Abi Tãlib was a forthright, honorable, and a courageous speaker, he was a benevolent and a generous host who opened his house to both rich and poor people. Ja'far migrated twice, once to Abyssinia, and then to Madina. He often deserted the company of people to contemplate the work of his Creator, for often intimately associating with people for mere socializing could cause ambiguity in one's action, and it can affect the purity of one's thoughts.

**226-** Sulaimãn bin Ahmad narrated that Burda said: "God's messenger ﷺ commanded us to migrate under the leadership of Ja'far bin Abi T̲ãlib to the land of al-Najãshi in Abyssinia. When the tribe of Quraish heard of our exodus, they immediately dispatched a delegation made of 'Amru Bnul-'Ãss̲ and 'Ammãra bin al-Walïd to meet with the leaders of Abyssinia. Upon arriving before the Abyssinian king al-Najãshi, they prostrated themselves before him, and they offered him precious gifts they collected from the wealthy people of Quraish. When the king inquired about the purpose of their journey, they replied, 'Some people from our land have renounced our religion and sought refuge in your land.' The king inquired: 'In my land?' They answered in the affirmative."

Burda continued: "Prior to our arrival, 'Amru Bnul-'Ã<u>ss</u> also had said to the king al-Najãshi, 'O great king, they will even refuse to prostrate before your majesty or pay obeisance to you!' Hence, when the king al-Najãshi summoned us, and before leaving our dwellings, some of our people became distraught, and they engaged in a quiet debate. Someone asked, 'What would you say to the king? Someone else replied, 'By God, we will tell him what we know, and what our prophet taught us, then let whatever happened happen!' "

"On our way to the palace, our leader, Ja'far bin Abi T̲ãlib, said, 'Let no one among you speak before him, I am your spokesman today!' Hence, when we arrived before al-Najãshi, there we found the Quraishi delegation, consisting of 'Amru Bnul-'Ã<u>ss</u> sitting by the al-Najãshi's right side and 'Ammãra bin al-Walïd by his left side. The court priests were also gathered, and they were sitting in the royal meeting hall in twin rows, facing one another. Earlier, when we entered the palace, the priest in charge of royal protocols instructed us: 'When you come before the king, you must prostrate yourselves to him.' However, we did not heed his instruction, and thus, when we stood before al-Najãshi, one of the priests rebuked us stridently, 'Prostrate yourselves before the king!'

Ja'far then replied: "We only prostrate to Allah, the Lord of majesty and glory."

Al-Najãshi impetuously said: "And who is he?"

Ja'far replied: "O king, Allah, the Lord of the universe, the most exalted, has sent us a Messenger who was foretold by Jesus, upon whom be peace, when He said to His apostles: 'A Messenger will come after me called Ahmad.' Hence, God's messenger ﷺ commanded us to worship Allah, the most exalted, and to associate no one with Him, and he commanded us to establish regular prayers, to give charity, to do good, and to abstain from evil."

Al-Najãshi then asked: "What is this new religion of yours that led you to forsake the ways of your people? Why did you not enter my religion or the known religions of the world?"

Ja'far replied: "O king! We were a pagan people who lived in ignorance. We worshipped idols, ate dead flesh, and committed abominable sins. We used to forsake our blood relations, mistreat our neighbors, and the strong among us took advantage of the weak. We remained thus until God Almighty send us a Messenger from among ourselves, of whom we know his lineage, truthfulness, trustworthiness, and purity. He called us to Almighty Allah, to worship only Him, and to glorify His Oneness. He also commanded us to refrain from the pagan worship of stone idols, and he commanded us to be truthful, trustworthy, caring for one's consanguineous relations, to abstain from what is forbidden, to protect the property of orphans, to abstain from mendaciousness, and to desist from committing blasphemy against chaste women. He also commanded us to worship God Almighty alone, and to associate no partner to Him, to offer regular prayers, to pay charity, and to fast."

Ja'far, having thus enumerated all aspects of Islam and its pillars, he added: "We accepted God's message, we followed His messenger ﷺ, and we prescribed to what God Almighty ordained, that is, to do what is lawful and to abstain from the unlawful. Seeing that, our people persecuted the weak among us, they oppressed us and restrained our conditions to force us to renounce our faith. When God's messenger ﷺ saw our fit, he told us to come to your country, and he apprised us that you are a just king. Thus, we made the choice to migrate to your land over other choices, soliciting your good neighboring reputation, and hoping that we will not be unjustly treated."

Al-Najãshi replied: "Can you recall any of the revelations he brought from God Almighty?"

Ja'far replied: "Indeed," and he recited the beginning of the chapter 'Mary' from the holy Qur'an (*chapter 19*), in which revelation Almighty Allah says:

(*In the Name of Allah, the Merciful and Compassionate.*)

﴾ Kaf, ha, ya, 'ain, sãd. This is the account of your Lord's mercy upon His servant Zacharia. When he cried to his Lord in secret, saying: "My Lord, my bones are enfeebled and my head glows with gray hair, and yet my Lord, I have never prayed to You in vain. Now I fear when my kinsmen will succeed me, and my wife is barren. Grant me O Lord a son to be my heir and to inherit the house of Jacob, and bless him, O Lord." — (Allah said:) "Rejoice O Zacharia, We are granting your prayer with a son that shall be called Yahya (*John*), and on no one before him did we confer such distinction (or name)." He said: "Lord! How (is it possible that I) can have a son when my wife is barren, and I am well advanced in age?" He replied: "Thus will it be, you Lord said. It is easy for Me, for I have created you, and you were nothing before." "Lord," said Zacharia, "Give me a sign." He answered: "Your sign is that you will be bereft of speech for three days and nights." Thus, Zacharia came out from his niche and exhorted his people in sign language to glorify their Lord morning and evening. (To his son came the command): "O Yahya! Have resolve in observing the scripture;" and We bestowed upon him wisdom while yet a child. We also endowed him with compassion for all creatures from Our own, and with grace and purity he grew up to be a righteous man; honoring his parents, and he was neither arrogant nor rebellious. So peace be upon him the day he was born, the day that he dies, and the day he will be raised to life again." ﴿ (*Qur'an 19:1-15*)

'Al-Najãshi liked what he heard as did his priests, but when 'Amru Bnul-'Ãss noticed that, he quickly said: 'May God guide your majesty. They differ with your faith utterly in the subject of the son of Mary!' Al-Najãshi then turned to Ja'far and asked him: 'What does your companion say about the son of Mary?' Ja'far replied: 'He says what God Almighty says about him. He is a soul from Allah and His Word. He came forth from the virgin and chaste Mary whom no human has ever touched, and no one ever claimed his fatherhood;' and Ja'far then recited from the same Chapter:

﴾ Also narrated in the Book is the story of Mary: how she withdrew from her people and betook herself to a solitary Eastern chamber, and she drew a screen between herself and them. We sent to her Our spirit who appeared before her as a perfect human being. When she saw him, she exclaimed: "I seek refuge in the Merciful Lord to defend me from you! If you fear the Lord, do not come near me!" He replied: "I am only the messenger of your Lord, and have come to grant you a holy son." She said: "How can I bear a son when no human has ever touched me, nor was I ever unchaste?" He replied: "Such is the will of your Lord. He said, 'It is easy for Me, and We shall make him a sign to humanity, and a mercy from Us, and thus it was a matter which We had decreed.'" ﴿ (*Qur'an 19:16-21*)

Hearing that, al-Najāshi wept until his beard became wet, and all the priests wept as well until the scriptures they spread before them also became wet with their tears. Meanwhile, back in Mecca, a revelation concerning the people of the Book who recognize Allah's message descended upon God's messenger ﷺ, saying: ﴾ When they listen to that which was revealed to the Apostle, you will see their eyes filled with tears as they recognize its truth. They say: 'Lord, we believe. Count us among Your witnesses. Why should we not believe in Allah and in the truth that has come down to us? And for their words Allah has rewarded them with gardens beneath which rivers flow, and there they shall dwell forever. Such is the recompense of the righteous, but those that disbelieve and deny Our revelations shall be the heirs of hell-fire. ﴿ (*Qur'an 5:83*)

Al-Najāshi, with his scepter, then drew a line on the floor and said: "O assembly of priests! What these people have attributed to your faith weighs no more than this line regarding what they voiced concerning the son of Mary." He then added: "What was just rehearsed before you and what Moses brought surely comes from the same niche."

Al-Najāshi then addressed Ja'far and his companions saying: "By God, I shall not extradite you or surrender you to them, and how could I? I welcome you in this land, and I welcome the one who sent you. I too bear witness that he is God's messenger who was foretold by the son of Mary, upon whom be peace. If it were not for my pressing duties, I would go in person to him and kiss his foot. As for now, you may stay in this land as long as you wish. Go and you shall be safe in my land. Whoever harms you shall be punished." The king repeated this warning three times.

Al-Najãshi then added: "I would hate to have even a mountain of gold should any of you be hurt. He then addressed the priests saying: "Give these people their gifts back to them. God did not take a bribe as an offering from me when He returned my kingdom back to me! He it is that made people obey me and I will obey Him in their subject."

The king then ordered that a periodic measure of food and other supplies be assigned to us along with the needed clothing, and he kept us in a house near his palace."

'Amru Bin al-'Ãss and 'Ammãrah bin al-Walïd left the court dismayed. 'Ammãra bin al-Walïd was killed by adverse circumstances before returning to Mecca, while 'Amru Bnul-'Ãss returned empty handed to face humiliation and the rebuke of his peers in Mecca.

**227-** Abu Huraira, God be pleased with him, said: " Ja'far bin Abi Tãlib used to love the poor and the meek. He used to sit with them and to engaged in extensive amicable discussions, until God's messenger ﷺ called him 'Father of the meek.' "

**228-** 'Abdullãh bin al-Zubair narrated that his foster father told him: "By God, it is still a vivid image in my mind, when I saw Ja'far charging on his blond horse against the enemy on the day of the Battle of Mu'tah. He then dismounted and slaughtered his horse before he walked to fight on foot, chanting a poem: '*Welcome to paradise and its nearness, Welcome to the eternally blessed abode and the cool drink.*' 'Abdullãh bin al-Zubair fought on foot until he was martyred."

**229-** Ibn Omar, God be pleased with him, said: "We missed Ja'far the day of the Battle of Mu'tah, and we sought him among the martyrs to find him decorated with over ninety wounds."

## 14- 'ABDULLĀH BIN RUWĀHA AL-ANSĀRI

Among the marks of true faith is to contemplate the signs of one's Lord, and to persevere with patience and endurance under the pangs of one's trials. 'Abdullāh bin Ruwāha, God be pleased with him, was more than willing to cross any barrier, even if it were of burning coal, to reach the abode of comfort in the nearness of his Lord and to receive His blessings. 'Abdullāh had little attachment to this world, and without failing, he sought the infallible meeting with his Lord, and he was amiable, ascetic, and a humble man.

**230-** On this subject, 'Urwa bin al-Zubair narrated that when 'Abdullāh bin Ruwāha was preparing to join the campaign of Mu'tah in Syria, his family and companions in Madina came to bid him farewell. 'Abdullāh cried and everyone became emotional and cried with him. His family and companions asked him: "Why are you crying?" 'Abdullāh replied: "By God, I have no attachment to this world, nor do I have any longing to remain with you, it is rather a verse I heard from God's messenger ﷺ that is making me cry." He then recited: ❮ None of you but shall pass the confines of hell: such is the irrevocable decree of your Lord. ❯ *(Qur'an 19:71)* 'Abdullāh continued: "I understand the notion of passing through its confines, but I do not know how to proceed and step out of it after that! I realize that I have to go through it, but I do not know whether I will be able to come out of it or not." He then added: "However, I ask the Merciful Lord for His forgiveness, and to grant me a single fatal blow in this battle, so that when people pass by my body, they will say: 'Allah has surely guided you.' "

This expedition to the north was a punitive action against the governors of the Byzantines, and the Roman empire they represented then. It took place when an emissary of God's messenger ﷺ was murdered in the name of Hiraclius, the Byzantine monarch of Syria then, as the emissary carried a letter from God's messenger ﷺ to the governor Hiraclius.

When the Muslim expedition arrived to Ma'ān, in Syria, they learned that the Byzantine's governor had mobilized over one hundred thousand strong men who were joined by another one hundred thousand Arabised men from various tribes in the north.

The Byzantine army was led by Theodorus, Hiraclius's brother. When the Muslim army of three thousand men, lead by Zaid bin H̱āritha, God be pleased with him, learned about that, they debated for two days and nights, and someone in the council suggested to send someone back to God's messenger ﷺ asking for support and further orders. During their debate, 'Abdullāh bin Ruwāẖa, God be pleased with him, rose and said: "O people! By God, what you are afraid to happen is precisely what you have come here to meet, — namely, martyrdom. We do not fight either with number, physical strength, or equipment. Our strength comes only from this religion we were blessed to receive from God Almighty. Thus, rise to battle, and it will be only one of two blessings you may receive: either victory or martyrdom." 'Abdullāh's convictions and faith inspired the people, while his brave and sincere counsel united their hearts. Later on, at some point during the battle, 'Abdullāh bin Ruwāẖa felt some indecisiveness on his part. He then looked up and saw his companions Zaid and Ja'far fighting valiantly, and he recited: "O my soul, if you are not killed here, death is eventually your ultimate confine. Here comes the messenger of death. Indeed, what you have wished for has come! Here is your chance to meet your Lord if you follow their footsteps."

During that battle, one of the companions also heard 'Abdullāh reciting : "O my soul, I have sworn that you will fight in battle deliberately, or that I shall force you to fight. Now that people have assembled for the battle, why then do you not persevere and charge with them? Do you hate to enter paradise?"

'Abdullāh fought in that battle until he met the countenance of his Lord while defending the banner of God's messenger ﷺ, upon whom be peace.

**231-** Sa'īd bin al-Musayyib narrated that following that battle, God's messenger ﷺ said: "Last night, in a vision, I saw them in paradise gathered under a dome made of pearl. Each one of them was comfortably reclining on a couch, and I saw Zaid and Ibn Ruwāẖa, and their neck had some distress, although that was not the case for Ja'far. I asked about them, and I was told that when they encountered death, they hesitated for a moment."

## 15- Anas bin Al-Nadhr

**232-** Anas bin Mãlik, the nephew Anas bin al-Nadhr, God be pleased with them both, narrated that his paternal uncle "Anas bin al-Nadhr was unable to participate in the Battle of Badr. When he arrived after the battle he vowed: 'I was unavailable to partake in the first battle in which God's messenger ﷺ fought the polytheists, and should Almighty Allah allow me to live and witness another battle, He will surely behold what I will do!"

On the day of the Battle of Uhud, when the confederates' army of polytheists became visible, Anas bin al-Nadhr exclaimed: "My Lord, bear witness that I disavow and refute what these polytheists claim, and I apologize for what the Muslims have done." He then charged on foot toward the enemy. On his way he met Sa'ad bin Mu'ãth, God be pleased with him, and said to him: "O Sa'ad, I smell the fragrance of paradise, O Sa'ad, what a sweet aroma it has!" After the Battle of Uhud, Sa'ad bin Mu'ãth reported what he saw to God's messenger ﷺ saying: "O Messenger of Allah, I could not have fought the way he did!"

Anas bin Mãlik continued: "When we searched for his body, we found it laying amidst the martyrs having sustained over eighty wounds between the blows of swords, lances, and arrows. After they killed him, the unbelievers mutilated him, and only his sister was able to recognize him from his garment."

Later on, Anas bin Mãlik, God be pleased with, also said: "When we used to recite the Qur'anic verse: ❮ Among the believers are men who have been true to their covenant with Allah. Some have fulfilled their vow, and others are still awaiting their end, yielding to no changes, ❯ (*Qur'an 33:23*) we used to think that it was revealed referring to Anas bin al-Nadhr and his companions the martyrs of Uhud."

## 16- 'Abdullãh Thul-Bajãdain Al-Mazini

Among the companions we also treasure the blessed and pious Qur'an reciter 'Abdullãh Thul-Bajãdain al-Mazini of Madina, who was free from pretentiousness, pride, or superciliousness. He fraternized with Omar bin al-Khattãb, God be pleased with both of them. 'Abdullãh was martyrized during the Battle of Tabouk, and it was God's messenger ﷺ that laid him to rest in his grave, and shed his blessed tears of love over him.

**233-** 'Atã bin Abi 'Abbãs reported that God's messenger ﷺ buried 'Abdullãh Thul-Bajãdain at night, he lit a fire by the grave, and then descended the grave first, before he said to his two blessed companions Omar and Abu Bakr: "You may now lower down your brother." God's messenger ﷺ then laid him in his charnel (*lahd*) facing the *Qibla*, and after straightened the grave with the remaining of the companions, they all performed the funeral prayer on him at the grave site. Before leaving, God's messenger ﷺ looked at the grave of 'Abdullãh, and he addressed him saying: "God bless your soul O 'Abdullãh, for you were indeed a true penitent oft-pondering your Lord, and you recited the Qur'an regularly and methodically." Facing the Ka'ba, God's messenger ﷺ then lifted up his hands and prayed: "My Lord, as of the fall of this night, I am pleased with him, so may Thou be pleased with him, and bless him as well."

'Abdullãh, the son of Omar, also was present that night, and when he heard God's messenger ﷺ recite this exalted prayer, he said to himself: "By God! I wish I was in his place. He received such exalted blessings even though I had embraced Islam fifteen years earlier than he did."

## 17- 'Abdullãh bin Mas'oud

Among the early Muslim émigrés (*muhãjireen*) who were also known for their immaculate purity, devotion, and ascetic detachment (*zuhud*), we also list herein the honorable companion 'Abdullãh bin Mas'oud, God be pleased with him. He enjoyed a long life of servitude to Almighty Allah, he devoted his life to studying and reading the holy Qur'an from an early age, and he taught the same to the other companions. In fact, 'Abdullãh bin Mas'oud was one of the best readers of the Qur'an and an excellent tutor. Although he began teaching at a young age, yet, he proved to be a great teacher, and later on in his life, he became a versed canonist and an distinguished commentator. 'Abdullãh bin Mas'oud was a sincere and a loyal companion who was true to his covenant, and he was one who honors his promises. He was one of the foremost devoted followers and a wise man whose intercession was most respected, and his prayers were always subject to Allah's favorable answer.

**234-** 'Ãsim narrated that 'Abdullãh bin Mas'oud told him: "I learned and memorized seventy *Süra* (chapters of the holy Qur'an) directly from God's messenger ﷺ while Zaid bin Thãbit was still a lad playing with the boys with a tress of hair hanging over his shoulders."

**235-** 'Alqama narrated that a man once came to Omar bin al-Khattãb and said: "I have just visited a man who speaks with the Qur'an. Omar shook and looked upset, and he commented: "O man! Watch what you say! I am only telling the truth." The man replied. Omar asked: "Who are you talking about?" 'Abdullãh bin Mas'oud," the man replied.

Omar immediately regained his poise and calmly said: "I know of no one who is more worthy of such virtue besides him."

Omar then added: "Let me tell you a story about him. One night, God's messenger ﷺ and myself stayed late at Abu Bakr's house. When we left, Abu Bakr and myself walked God's messenger ﷺ back to his house, and he walked between the two of us. The night was opaque, and the streets were extremely dark. As we reached near the mosque, we perceived the shadow of a man who was reciting the Qur'an. God's messenger ﷺ immediately stopped to listen, and he signaled me out to keep quite. When the man finished reading, he bowed and then prostrated himself before he sat back praying and invoking *zikr* of the divine attributes. God's messenger ﷺ then softly and gently said: "Ask and you shall be given." He then turned to us and added: "Whosoever wishes to read the Qur'an afresh as it was revealed, then let him read it like Ibn Um 'Ubãda." My companion and I immediately knew that he was speaking of 'Abdullãh bin Mas'oud (whose mother was known as Um 'Ubãda). In the morning, I hastened to carry the glad tidings to him, and to my surprise, he replied: 'Abu Bakr was here earlier.' I pondered for a moment praising the Almighty Allah, and surely whenever I hastened to do a good deed, I always discovered that Abu Bakr was leading everyone in such virtues."

**236-** Sa'ïd bin al-Musayyib narrated that 'Abdullãh bin Mas'oud was praying at the Mosque in the middle of a dark night when God's messenger ﷺ, Abu Bakr and Omar passed by, and they heard him pray: "Lord, I ask Thee to grant me faith that never ceases growing, blessings that never end, and comfort in Thy presence that will never be veiled again." Hearing that, God's messenger ﷺ quietly said: "Ask and you shall be given."

On his way back home, Abu Bakr went straight to 'Abdullãh to bring him the glad tidings, and he asked him: "Teach me the supplication you recited earlier!" Upon receiving the tidings, 'Abdullãh praised God Almighty, glorified Him, and he then prayed: "My Lord! Truly there is no God besides Thee. Thy promise is true, and meeting Thee is true. Verily, paradise is true, and hell is true, Thy messengers are true, Thy Book is true, Thy prophets are true, and Muhammad ﷺ is true."

**237-** Sa'ïd bin al-Musayyib narrated that God's messenger ﷺ once said: "Hold fast to the covenant of 'Abdullãh bin Mas'oud."

**238-** Abu Dãwoud narrated that 'Abdullãh bin Mas'oud said: "I was a young boy herding the sheep of 'Uqba bin Abi Ma'ïṯ when God's messenger ﷺ and Abu Bakr walked by me, and after greeting me, Abu Bakr asked: "Young boy, do you have some extra milk to give us for drinking?"

"I only work here, and I have no authority to let you have what I am entrusted to guard." 'Abdullãh replied.

God's messenger ﷺ then asked: "Is there a lamb here that no ram has yet mounted?"

'Abdullãh continued: "When I brought him what he asked for, Abu Bakr held the lamb while God's messenger ﷺ took hold of its udder and prayed before the udder miraculously became lactescent. He then drew some milk, and after they drank to satisfaction, he commanded the udder to shrink back to its original size, and it did, by God's leave. When I saw that, I was amazed, and I immediately went to him and said: 'Teach me such good words!' God's messenger ﷺ replied: 'You are indeed blessed, and you are surely a well taught youngster.'

'Abdullãh further continued: "Later on, when I migrated to

Madina, I memorized seventy *süra* directly from him, no one can evidence otherwise."

In Madina, 'Abdullãh became very close to God's messenger ﷺ, and he often carried his personal pillow, cloak, *miswãk,* and sandals.

**239-** 'Alqama narrated that he once traveled to Syria, and there he visited Abu Ddardã' who asked him: "Where do you come from?" "From Küfa," 'Alqama replied. Abu Ddardã' then eagerly inquired with great anticipation: "Is the carrier of the pillow and the *miswãk* among you today?"

**240-** Also on this subject, Abi Wã'il narrated that 'Abdu-Rahmãn bin Yazïd once inquired from Huthaifa: "Point out to us someone who is nearest in guidance and manners to God's messenger ﷺ so we may solicit his company, emulate his character, and learn from him!" Huthaifa replied: "I know of no such person alive today besides his companion Ibn Um 'Ubãda." He then added: "The blessed companions of God's messenger ﷺ know well that on the Day of Judgment, the intercession of 'Abdullãh bin Mas'oud is nearest to acceptance."

**241-** 'Ali, God bless his countenance, narrated that God's messenger ﷺ said: "Each prophet was given seven compassionate, true and trustworthy companions, and I was given fourteen; Hamza, Ja'far, 'Ali, al-Hassan, al-Hussain, Abu Bakr, Omar, 'Abdullãh bin Mas'oud, Abu Tharr, al-Miqdãd, Huthaifa, 'Ammãr, Salmãn and Bilãl."

**242-** Imam Ahmad Ibn Hanbal, God bless his soul, narrated that when 'Abdullãh bin Mas'oud died, Abi al-Ahwas was at his funeral and he heard Abu Müsa al-Ash'ari say to Abu Mas'oud: "I wonder if there is anyone left of his caliber?" Aba Mas'oud replied: "If you say so! Surely he was given access to the inner circles of God's messenger ﷺ when such access was not everyone's privilege, and he was in the forefront defending God's message when we were absent."

**243-** Abi al-Bakhtari narrated that someone asked 'Ali, God bless his countenance, about 'Abdullãh bin Mas'oud, 'Ali replied: "He read the Qur'an and it answered every question he had. He learned the Qur'an and the prophetic traditions (*sunna*) and he stopped there, for sufficient is such knowledge."

**244-** Referring to 'Abdullãh bin Mas'ouḍ's knowledge and understanding of Islam, Abu Müsa al-Ash'ari once said: "Ask us no questions as long as this true luminary (*h̲ibr*) lives amidst you!"

## The Qur'an Reader

'Abdullãh bin Mas'oud guarded himself against adversities with his unwavering dependence on the guidance of the divine source of reference (i.e., *the holy Qur'an*), and the lucid example of prophetic traditions (*sunna*) of his great companion, God's messenger ﷺ, upon whom be peace. In essence, his spiritual struggle was based upon improving one's own trait to balance his stance.

**245-** On this subject, 'Abdullãh, the son of Imam Ah̲mad bin H̲anbal, narrated that 'Abdullãh bin Mas'oud, God be pleased with him, once described the Qur'an reader, saying: "You recognize the Qur'an reader when he stays up worshipping at night while others remain asleep, and he observes voluntary fast during the day, when others feast. He is mostly heavyhearted, while others blithely celebrate the attractions of this ephemeral world. He cries when others laugh, he is silent when others mix truth with falsehood, and he is humble and meek when others walk around exhibiting haughtiness, disdain, and arrogance. In fact, one who reads the Qur'an is contemplative and despondent, he is wise, forbearing, knowledgeable and mostly quiet. Such one is neither coarse nor slumberous, and he is not boisterous, vociferous or argumentative."

**246-** Al-Musayyib bin Rãfi' narrated that 'Abdullãh bin Mas'oud said: "I hate to see a man who is hollow. He is neither successful in managing the business of this world, nor that of the hereafter."

**247-** K̲haithama narrated that 'Abdullãh bin Mas'oud said: "Let me not find any of you like a *qurt̲ub,* a dead corpse during the night, and sprightly and bright like a firefly during the day."

**248-** Imam Ah̲mad bin H̲anbal, narrated that Ibn 'Uyaina said: "A *qurt̲ub* is someone who sits one hour with one type of people, and in the next hour, he sits with their opposites, trying to be pleasing to both."

**249-** Expounding on the virtues of prayers (*salāt*), Bishr bin Müsa narrated that 'Abdullāh bin Mas'oud used to say: "As long as you are in prayers, you are knocking at the door of the King, and if you knock at the door of the King, it will surely open. If you can, be the interlocutor who listens to what is being said. If you hear God Almighty say: ❮ O ye who believe, ❯ then hearken to His call, for such call is an admonition that will either bear benefits He ordains, or warns against an evil He forbids."

**250-** Ishāq bin Ibrāhīm narrated that 'Abdullāh bin Mas'oud also used to say: "This Qur'an is the banquet of Allah. If one can learn something from it, then let him do so, for the poorest of homes, and which tenants are most sick, is one that has nothing of it. In fact, a household that does not memorize the Qur'an and live by its dictates is like an abandoned ruin, and Satan will never abide in a house that regularly recites (the chapter) *al-Baqara.*"

**251-** Elaborating on the subject of the Qur'an and knowledge, 'Abdu-Rahmān bin al-Aswad narrated that Ibn Mas'oud used to say: "These hearts are vessels. Fill them up with the Qur'an and occupy them with nothing else."

**252-** Khālid bin 'Aoun narrated that Ibn Mas'oud once said to him: "True knowledge is not measured in relationship to how much you memorize and then narrate, but rather, true knowledge is an expression of piety."

**253-** 'Alqama narrated that 'Abdullāh bin Mas'oud said: "Study and act upon what you learn."

**254-** 'Adiyyi bnu 'Ubiyyi quoted Ibn Mas'oud to have said: "Woe to the ignorant one, although it had been God's will, He would have granted him knowledge, and woe to the one who knows and does not act upon his knowledge." Ibn Mas'oud reiterated that statement seven times.

**255-** 'Abdullāh bin 'Akīm narrated that he heard Ibn Mas'oud speak in the mosque. Ibn Mas'oud commenced by addressing the people sitting on his right side and said: "None of you but shall be brought before his Lord for a private hearing, just as one of you stands alone to gaze at the full moon. His Lord will say to him: 'O son of Adam, what is it that deceived you about Me? O son of Adam, what did you answer My messengers? O son of Adam, what have you done with what you learned?' "

**256-** Bakr bin Bakkãr narrated that he heard Ibn Mas'oud say: "I think that one forgets his knowledge, and his memory fails him because of his sins."

Ibn Mas'oud guarded his heart against attachment to worldly comforts, family and child. He cared little about his personal needs and hardly did the material world take any prominence in his life. Finally, he was extremely grateful to his Lord for granting him faith and guidance, and he continuously prayed to God Almighty to grant him His choiciest blessings. Ibn Mas'oud taught and trained his soul to seek such excellence, and thus, he rose above fear and doubt. In the latter part of his life, Ibn Mas'oud reminisced the blessed fellowship of God's messenger ﷺ and his righteous companions, and nothing could replace the blessings contained in the early days of the divine revelation in his heart.

**257-** On this subject, Abu Ju<u>h</u>aifa narrated that Ibn Mas'oud said: "The splendor of this world has gone, and gloominess is what remains — making death the greatest blessing for every Muslim to win."

**258-** Abu Bakr bin Shayba narrated that Ibn Mas'oud said: "This world is like a small pond at the top of a mountain that collects rain water, much of the water has expired, and what remains is brakish and begrimed with dirt."

**259-** Qays bin <u>H</u>abtar narrated that Ibn Mas'oud said: "Better are the disfavored constrainers, death and poverty, — I do not care whichever trial befalls me in this lifetime, because it can either be richness or poverty! Should my luck attract richness, it embodies compassion, and should my luck invite poverty, it necessitates the blessing of exercising patience!"

**260-** 'Abdu-Ra<u>h</u>mãn bin Yazïd narrated that 'Abdullãh bin Mas'oud revealed to him that God's messenger ﷺ once told him: "I give you permission to sometimes lift off the (spiritual) veil and to hearken to the favorites until I order you otherwise."

**261-** 'Abdullãh, the son of A<u>h</u>mad bin <u>H</u>anbal, God bless his soul, narrated that 'Abdullãh bin Mas'oud said: "A servant of Allah does not attain true faith unless he recognizes the ultimate, and he will not perceive the ultimate unless he comes to favors poverty over richness, meekness over honor and pride, and until he deems praises and blames as equal." Ibn Mas'oud's companions interpreted that to mean that he would prefer to be poor rather than to earn unlawful money, and to humbly obey his Lord rather than breach His covenant for the sake of material gain, honor or pride.

**262-** Abu Muhammad bin Hayyãn narrated that Ibn Mas'oud said: "I swear by Allah Who alone is God, it does not matter what adversities one may encounter during the day as long as he rises up in the morning in a state of Islam, and winds up his day in the evening in a state of Islam, accepting and submitting to his Lord."

**263-** Al-Hãrith bin Suwayd narrated that Ibn Mas'oud once spoke to himself, saying: "I swear by Allah, Who alone is God, Ibn Mas'oud's family woke up today having no means to bring themselves good or to repel evil, except that God Almighty knows that 'Abdullãh associates no one with his Lord."

**264-** 'Ãmir bin Masrouq narrated that a man visiting 'Abdullãh Ibn Mas'oud said during the course of a conversation: "Surely I do not wish to be resurrected among the companions of the right, but I would rather be among the near ones." Hearing that statement, 'Abdullãh commented: "However, perhaps there is someone here who would rather not be resurrected after he dies!" — Meaning himself.

**265-** Al-Hãrith bin Suwayd narrated that 'Abdullãh Ibn Mas'oud once said: "If you knew what I know, you would bury me alive."

## His teachings and admonitions

**266-** 'Abdu-Rahmãn Ibn Hujaira, father of 'Abdullãh al-Khawlãni, once Egypt's supreme justice, quoted from his father's narration that during a study circle (*halaqatu ta'leem*), 'Abdullãh Ibn Mas'oud said: "O people, as the night and the day go by, your residency in this world becomes shorter, your actions are recorded, and your death will be sudden. One who sows good will soon harvest his heart's wishes, and one who sows evil will soon harvest regret.

Every farmer will harvest what he plants. An unhurried person cannot forerun or accelerate his luck, and a sharp-witted person cannot exceed his bounds. Thus, if one receives any benefits, it is Allah the most exalted Who allotted them to him, and if one is shielded from evil, Almighty Allah is the one Who protected him from their danger. Surely the pious ones are the sires in this world, and the scholars and canonists are the heirs and leaders, whosoever sits in their company will definitely reap benefits."

**267-** Al-Dhahhãk bin Muzãhim narrated that 'Abdullãh bin Mas'oud said: "You are only guests in this world, and you own is only a borrowed trust. Eventually the guest will depart, and the borrowed trust must be returned to its rightful Owner."

**268-** 'Abdu-Rahmãn, son of 'Abdullãh bin Mas'oud, narrated that someone asked his father: "O father of 'Abdu-Rahmãn, teach me few words that are all-encompassing and beneficial, so that I will need no further elaboration!" Ibn Mas'oud replied: "Worship Allah and associate nothing with Him. Live by the dictates of the Qur'an and pursue its guidance. Accept truth and justice even if they come from a stranger you do not recognize, or even from someone you regard as despicable, and refute falsehood even if it comes from a sibling you love."

**269-** Müsa bin 'Ubaida narrated that 'Abdullãh bin Mas'oud said: "The truth is heavy and bitter, and falsehood is light but infected. How often desires inherit their author attenuated agony!"

**270-** Bishr bin Müsa narrated that 'Abdullãh bin Mas'oud said: "By Allah Who alone is God, nothing on this earth requires extended incarceration more than one's tongue."

**271-** Bishr bin Müsa narrated that 'Abdullãh Ibn Mas'oud also used to say: "One's heart sometimes feels a strong yearning and responsiveness, and yet, at other times, it feels waning and disengaged. Take advantage of its responsiveness when inviting, and disregard what is offered when your heart feels despondent."

**272-** Imam Ahmad Ibn Hanbal, God bless his soul, narrated that 'Abdullãh bin Mas'oud, God be pleased with him, said: "Follow the coherence of your heart, beware of anything towards which it feels despondent, and disregard what it declines to concur with."

**273-** 'Abdullãh bin Muhammad al-'Absi narrated that 'Abdullãh bin Mas'oud, God be pleased with him, said: "If you can protect your property against woodworms and thieves, then do so, for often one's heart is attached to his property."

**274-** 'Atreess bin 'Arqoub al-Shaibãni once came to 'Abdullãh bin Mas'oud and said: "What an awful end awaits someone who does not command good and forbid evil!" 'Abdullãh bin Mas'oud replied: "You should rather say, 'what an awful end awaits someone whose heart does not recognize truth, and who refuses to acknowledge what is false when it is evidenced before him."

**275-** Abu Yahya al-Rãzi narrated that 'Abdullãh bin Mas'oud, God be pleased with him, said: "In this world, you will find that a disbeliever sometimes has a healthy body, and yet his heart is most sick, while when you look at a believer, you will discover that his heart is most healthy, and yet his body maybe emaciated. I swear to Allah, that if you allow your hearts to grow up diseased while steering your focus to build healthy bodies, then you will certainly become an easier target of the divine retribution than a dung beetle who is unable to get away from its food source."

**276-** Abi al-Aswad quoted 'Abdullãh bin Mas'oud to have said: "Our righteous predecessors have departed, and those who remained are people of suspicious nature. They do not accept the truth, nor do they repudiate falsehood."

**277-** 'Amru bnu Hafs narrated that 'Abdullãh bin Mas'oud once admonished someone who asked for advise: "Be content with what you have, be satisfied with your dwelling space to accommodate your enterprise, restrain your tongue, and shed the tears of regret regarding past sins you committed knowingly, and those you do not recognize."

**278-** 'Abdu-Rahmãn bin Yazïd narrated that 'Abdullãh bin Mas'oud once said to his companions: "You fast, pray and study more than the companions of God's messenger ﷺ, yet, they are better than you!" Someone in the gathering replied: "O Abu 'Abdu-Rahmãn, why is that?" He replied: "Because they were less attached to this world than you do, and they were more desirous of the hereafter than you do."

**279-** Al-'Alã bin al-Musayyib narrated that 'Abdullãh bin Mas'oud once said: "A believer finds no comfort except in meeting his Lord, thus, should he experience such comfort, it means that he has attained his goal."

**280-** 'Alqama narrated, re 'Abdullãh bin Mas'oud, that God's messenger ﷺ once said to his companions: ""What will you do when a calamity will strike at you and people come to adopt innovations, claiming them to be prophetic traditions, — innovations the young will grow to practice as (though if they were prophetic traditions) *sunna,* and the elders will die satisfied to have pietistically held unto them, — and should one default in any of them, it will be said that he breached the *sunna?*" The people inquired: "O messenger of Allah, when will that come to happen?" He replied: "This will take place when your Qur'an readers increase in number, and your truly learned ones decrease; when the number of your leaders and princes (*umarã'*) increases, and when your trustworthy ones turn few; when worldly gains are sought via deeds which are supposed to be done for the sake of the hereafter, and when people solicit to acquire religious knowledge for worldly status and not for God's sake!" 'Abdullãh then added: "This is how you have turned out."

**281-** Abi H̲as̲een narrated that 'Abdullãh bin Mas'oud said: "Should one of you wake up fasting, then let him also abstain from causing harm to others; if you hand out a charity with your right hand, then let your left hand not see it; and, when you offer voluntary supererogatory prayers (*nafl*), do so in private."

**282-** Abi al-Ah̲was̲ narrated that 'Abdullãh bin Mas'oud said: "Entrust your faith to no man, for should one believe, the other will follow, and should one deny, the other will conform. However, if you find it necessary to emulate a good example, then take heed and contemplate the dead, for a living person is not infallible to straying."

**283-** 'Abdu-Rah̲mãn bin Yazïd narrated that 'Abdullãh bin Mas'oud once said to a gathering of his companions: "Do not become opportunists!" Someone asked: "What is an opportunist?" Ibn Mas'oud replied: "It is someone who says: 'I am with the majority, should they be right, then I will be right as well, and should they go wrong, then I accept to suffer the consequences with them as well.' " Ibn Mas'oud then added: "Thus, make a covenant with yourselves, and train your souls to resist apostasy (*kufur*) when the majority of people stray away from their religious covenant."

**284-** 'Amru bnu Hafs narrated that 'Abdullāh bin Mas'oud said: "Do not become opportunists!" People asked: "What is an opportunist?" He replied: "That is to say, I follow the masses, if they follow the true guidance, I win, and if they go astray, that will be my fate as well. Therefore, promise yourselves, and train your souls to resist apostasy (*kufur*) when the masses deny the truth or renege on their religious covenant."

**285-** Abi Ishāq narrated that Ibn Mas'oud said: "Three things I testify to their authenticity, and the fourth, should I swear by it, it will prove my trueness to my Lord! 1) Allah does not grant equal footing to one who is committed to His religion of Islam and one who does not; 2) One who depends on other than Allah in this world, He will assign his care to someone else in the hereafter; 3) One who loves the fellowship of a particular group of people in this world will be gathered in their company in the hereafter; and 4) the fourth oath that will prove my trueness to my Lord is that whenever Allah chooses to veil the shortcomings of His servant in this world, He will also veil them for him in the hereafter."

**286-** Abi al-Ahwas narrated that 'Abdullāh bin Mas'oud said: "Let no man make his religious covenant dependent on another man's performance and model. Should the second believe in something, he conforms to the same conviction, and should the second man refute something, he rebuts it as well. However, if one must follow a model, then let him seek and contemplate the dead, for a living being is not immune to temptation, and he is not infallible to going astray."

**287-** Abi Wā'il narrated that 'Abdullāh bin Mas'oud said: "On the Day of Judgment, none of you but will wish that he ate mere leaves of shrubs to satisfy his hunger in this world. No matter what condition a believer finds himself in when he wakes up in the morning, or when he retires in the evening, as long as he does not have rancor. Surely it will be better for you to chew on a live coal until it is smothered inside your own mouth, rather than objecting to God's will, or to say about something which Almighty Allah ordained, 'I wish it did not happen this way!' "

**288-** 'Ubaidullah narrated that 'Abdullãh bin Mas'oud said: "Your Lord knows no darkness of night or daylight. The light of the heavens and the earth emanate from the effulgent light (*Noor*) of His divine countenance. He created your days of perpetual twelve hours, and the deeds of your preceding night are presented before Him for His consideration in the first part of the following day, and He views them during the first three hours. During the next three hours, the carriers of the divine Throne and its pavilions, the cherubs (*al-karrubiyyoun*) among His most exalted angels, besides the remaining hosts of celestial angels and the myriads of heavenly angels celebrate the praises of the Merciful Lord (*Yã Rahmãn*), until the divine luminesce permeate all of them with divine Mercy, and then, the archangel Isrãfil blows once through the trumpet of the creation, and no one in the entire universes can avoid hearing that (subliminal) sound. This makes it six hours of your days. The wombs are then brought before Him, and He looks into their needs for the next three hours. That is the meaning of the revelation, ❬ He it is that fashions you in the wombs of your mothers as He chooses. He allots whichever womb He wants males, and He allots whichever womb He wants females, or He may create twins, male and female, and He makes whichever womb He wants barren ❭ (*Qur'an 3:6*). Thus pass nine hours (of your days). During the next three hours, your daily sustenance, and that of the entire creation, is then brought before Him to apportion, and that is the meaning of the revelation, ❬ He expands and restricts the portions of whosoever He wants, He surely knows everything ❭ (*Qur'an 42:12*) – ❬ Everyone in the heavens and on earth asks Him, and every day He manifests distinct bounties ❭ (*Qur'an 55:29*). 'Abdullãh bin Mas'oud then added: "This is (how) your daily hours are implemented in relationship to the work of your Lord."

**289-** 'Amru Bnu Thãbit narrated that 'Abdullãh bin Mas'oud said in one of his sermons: "Surely the most truthful speech is that of the Qur'an, the Book of God Almighty; and the best of covenants and bonds are an expression of piety; the best of persuasions is that of Abraham, and the best of traditions are those of Muhammad ﷺ, upon whom be peace; the most noble and exalted of speeches and conversations is to talk about God Almighty; the best and most truthful of stories are told in the Qur'an; the worth of a good deed will show at the end, and the most evil of deeds are innovations; to have less of what satisfies one's needs is better that to have aplenty one cannot compass or control; the worst self-blaming (*nafsu lawwāma*) is sorrow when death comes to seize the person, and the worst grief is to have regret on the Day of Judgment; the worst aberration is to stray from God's path after receiving His guidance; true prosperity is to have satisfaction and contentment; the best provision for the hereafter is piety; the best grasp to capture one's heart is certitude and assurance of the hereafter; suspicion is a branch of apostasy; the worst blindness is that of the heart; wine is the source of every evil; the temptation about women is the rope of Satan; teenage heralds the growing up of arrogance and folly; mourning losses is a pagan act; some people come late to the Friday's congregational prayers, dragging their feet, and they speak of God Almighty illusively. In fact, to lie is the greatest sin; to insult a believer is an act of insolence; and to fight a believer is apostasy. The sanctity of the property of a believer is as sacred as his life; one who pardons the sins of others, Allah will forgive him his sins, and one who swallows his anger, Allah will reward him; one who forgives others, Allah will forgive him, and one who bears his adversity, Allah will reward him aplenty. The most evil of earnings is money made of usury and accumulation of interest; the worst of food is to eat up the inheritance of the orphan. The luckiest of people is one who takes heed of the reason behind others misfortunes; and the unlucky is thus conceived in the womb of his mother. Sufficient for you is what satisfies your basic needs; surely the lag of one's journey will culminate in a grave six linear feet long; one's real goal will eventually be seen at the end, — and truth will surely manifest at the end. The results of one's action will expose his initial intention; the worst story is a lie; the best death is that of a martyr; one who knows the value of adversities will bear them, and one who does not understand that will question the reason behind them. Almighty Allah will surely bring an arrogant person to humiliation. Whosoever vies to capture the world will reach a dead end, and whosoever obeys Satan would have disobeyed God Almighty; and finally, whosoever disobeys Almighty Allah will be punished in hell-fire."

## 18- 'Ammãr Bin Yãsir

Here we must cite the name of another blessed champion among our peers, who was also one of the prominent companions of God's messenger ﷺ, upon whom be peace. His name is 'Ammãr Bin Yãsir, and he was patronymed Abu'l Yaqzãn. 'Ammãr, God be pleased with him, was abounding with faith and sincerity, he was heedful of the hereafter with assurance and clarity, and he was best enduring and serene during trials and adversity. He bore with great patience the sufferings and physical torture to which his persecutors had subjected him to endure, besides the emotional agonies of humiliation, shame and disgrace they inflicted on him as they leached their anger against his father and mother.

'Ammãr Bin Yãsir, God be pleased with him, was among the early cluster of young believers, and he was a pillar among the blessed companions, a vanguard among the foremost believers in God's message, and a loyal supporter of His messenger ﷺ, upon whom be peace. 'Ammãr Bin Yãsir fought most courageously alongside God's messenger ﷺ against the tyranny and oppression of the incredulous clans of disbelievers, and he continued his struggle against the aggressors and the unjust ones in defense of the divine message in the times of the Trustworthy and Guided Successors (*al-Khulafã al-Rãshideen*).

Whenever 'Ammãr Bin Yãsir, God be pleased with him, sought permission to visit God's messenger ﷺ, upon whom be peace, he received him with cheerfulness, auspiciousness, and welcome. God's messenger ﷺ comforted him as well, offered him the glad tidings of paradise, and he imbued his spirit with blessings and solace.

'Ammãr Bin Yãsir renounced worldly comforts, and he gave no attention to possessing any of its fineries. He was a humble companion who censured any personal feelings of pride, and he curbed his mind against assuming any superciliousness or high-mindedness. He exalted and honored the proponents of faith and the followers of God Almighty's religion, and he resolutely and sincerely followed with utmost loyalty the example and guidance of God's messenger ﷺ, the leader of the universal order of peace, who was sent by his Lord, to invite humanity to receive eternal spiritual comfort, and true knowledge of their Lord.

'Ammãr Bin Yãsir fought in the Battle of Badr.[1] Later on, during the caliphate of Omar bin al-Khattãb, 'Ammãr was appointed as the *amir* (governor) of Küfa, in Iraq. In his letter to the people of Küfa, Omar commended him, saying: "He was a true companion of God's messenger ﷺ. In fact, 'Ammãr Bin Yãsir was one of the four companions paradise yearned to welcome. He labored hard on its roads, and he always longed to attain it, and until he finally met his beloveds, Muhammad ﷺ and his companions.

A shaikh once said: "Attaining perfect spiritual clarity is like trying to climb the unsurmountable high walls of the Garden of Eden with the intention of betrothing one of the *houri* virgins of paradise."

**290-** On this subject, Abi Ishãq narrated that Hãni' bin Hãni' said: "We were visiting with 'Ali, God bless his countenance, when 'Ammãr Bin Yãsir entered the mosque, and 'Ali welcomed him saying, 'Welcome to the good and blessed companion.' 'Ali then added, 'I heard God's messenger ﷺ say that 'Ammãr is filled with faith down to his bone marrow.' "

**291-** Sa'ïd bin Jubair narrated, re Ibn 'Abbãs, God be pleased with him, that God's messenger ﷺ, upon whom be peace, said: " 'Ammãr is filled with faith from head to toe."

**292-** Salïm bin Abi al-Ja'ad narrated that 'Uthmãn bin 'Affãn said: "I was treading in the plains of Mecca when God's messenger ﷺ saw me, and he came and took me by the hand, and we walked until we came by a group of Quraishi leaders torturing 'Ammãr and his mother. God's messenger ﷺ exclaimed, 'O family of Yãsir, endure what you are subjected to with patience, for surely paradise is your ultimate destiny.' "

**293-** Mujãhid reported that the first group of believers who

[1] i.e., the Well of Badr, the first battle of the believers against the Quraish unbelievers, near the city of Medina

challenged the Quraishi ban on proclaiming faith in God's oneness, and who declared their Islam (submission and acceptance to God's message) in public, were originally seven people, namely: God's messenger ﷺ, Abu Bakr, Khabãb, Suhayb, Bilãl, 'Ammãr bin Yãsir, and Sumayyah, his mother. As to God's messenger ﷺ, it was his uncle Abu Tãlib who warned him against the consequences of openly declaring his message. Abu Bakr, and because of his high social rank in the community, he was merely contested by his clan, while the other five people were subjected to awesome torture. Frequently, the Quraishi disbelievers placed the blessed companions from among their slaves in the open desert, and they fitted them naked with tight armatures made of iron, and to intensify their agony, they were first placed for a long day under the sun, exposed to the torrid heat of the desert and until their skin blistered because of the sun-heated iron armature, and before they were subjected to physical cruelties, in an attempt to force them to renounce their faith in God Almighty. On that day, and shortly before sunset, Abu Jahl, God's curse be upon him, came carrying a spear with which he poked his prisoners, rebuked them, and insulted them angrily because of their belief in the oneness of God Almighty."

**294-** Abi 'Ubaida Ibn Muhammad, grandson of 'Ammãr, said: "The polytheist pagans of Quraish took 'Ammãr, and they subjected him to awesome torture until they forced him to renege on his faith, and they further forced him to insult the name of God's messenger ﷺ, and to praise their deities. The Quraishis then released 'Ammãr, but when 'Ammãr went back to God's messenger ﷺ, he was troubled, and God's messenger ﷺ asked him, 'What happened?' He replied with tears in his eyes, 'An evil has touched me! O messenger of Allah, they did not cease torturing me until I spoke ill of you, and I had to praise their deities.' God's messenger ﷺ replied, 'How did you find your heart then?' 'Ammãr replied, 'At peace with Almighty Allah, and filled with faith and trust in Him.' God's messenger ﷺ replied, 'If they force you again, do what you have to do, and do not worry.' "

**295-** Abi Umãma narrated that some friends of 'Ammãr bin Yãsir asked him: "O Abu'l Yaqzãn, tell us about the three virtues you have, and about which God's messenger ﷺ foretold of their exalted merit, adding that 'Whoever has them, he has indeed perfected his faith?' " 'Ammār replied: "Indeed, I heard him naming them, (1) 'To spend generously in charity even when you have little; (2) to be just even if it were against your personal interest; and (3) to greet all people with Allah's peace.' "[1]

**296-** 'Abdullāh bin Salma narrated that 'Ali, God bless his countenance, once met two people who had anointed themselves with scented oils, as they were leaving a building after taking a bath. 'Ali asked them: "Who are you?" They said: "Two emigrants (to Allah from Mecca)," 'Ali replied: "That is not true, the only true emigrant (to Allah) that I know of in this town is 'Ammār bin Yāsir."

**297-** Maisara narrated that on the day of the Battle of Siffeen, 'Ammār bin Yāsir asked for a drink of milk. After drinking it, he stood up and said: "I had heard God's messenger ﷺ during his last illness say, 'This is the last drink I take from this world.' 'Ammār then hastened towards the battlefield, and fought bravely and gallantly against the pagans until he earned his martyrdom.

**298-** In another narration, the companion of God's messenger ﷺ, Abi Sinān al-Du'li said: "On the day of the Battle of Siffeen, 'Ammār bin Yāsir asked for a cup of milk, he drank some of it, and then said, 'God and His messenger ﷺ spoke the truth. Today I shall meet the beloveds, Muhammad and his companions.' He then added, 'I heard God's messenger ﷺ during his last illness say, 'This is the last drink I take from this world.' 'Ammār bin Yāsir then exclaimed, 'I swear by God Almighty, even if they were to defeat us, and pursue us down to the outskirts of Mecca, we will always know that we are following the truth, and that they are following falsity.' "

**299-** Abi Maleeh al-Ansāri reported that 'Ali bin Abi Tālib said: "I once mentioned 'Ammār before God's messenger ﷺ who commented, 'He will be with you when he will witness and meet awesome events that will receive magnificent rewards from Almighty Allah. People will always speak about these events with great reverence, and their praiseworthiness will evermore speak for themselves.'"

---

[1] i.e., To spread peace everywhere by greeting all people with *As-Salaamu 'Alaykum.*

**300-** 'Abdullãh, the son of Omar bin al-Khattãb, said: "I know of no one who had left his home solely for the sake of Allah's pleasure and seeking the abode of the hereafter to attain the nearness of his Lord besides 'Ammãr."

**301-** Anas bin Mãlik narrated that God's messenger ﷺ, upon whom be peace, said: "Paradise yearns to meet four people: 'Ammãr, 'Ali, Salmãn, and al-Miqdãd."

**302-** Al-Hãrith bin Suwayd narrated that a man reported some damaging news about 'Ammãr Ibn Yãsir to the caliph Omar bin al-Khattãb, God be pleased with him. When the news reached 'Ammãr, he prayed: "My Lord, if this man is lying about me, then inflict him with humiliation and inferiority and allow him access to wealth and temptation in this world."

**303-** Khãlid bin Numair once described 'Ammãr, saying: "He was most quiet and self-absorbed. 'Ammãr spoke little, and often appeared grieved and distressed because of his long physical sufferings. Whenever he spoke, he mostly beseeched Almighty Allah to safeguard him against temptation in this world."

**304-** 'Abdullãh bin Abi'l-Huthayl narrated that when 'Abdullãh bin Mas'oud built a new home, he met 'Ammãr Ibn Yãsir and said to him: "Come with me, let me show you what I built!" When 'Ammãr saw the new house, he commented: "Indeed, you have erected a solid foundation, but you have overextended your confidence and hope to attain a permanent future, and yet, your venture does not reflect how short is one's domicile in this world, and how soon will one die!"

## 19- Khabãb Bnul Art

Among the early striving believers in Allah's oneness and uniqueness, and the Lord, Creator, Cherisher and Sustainer of the entire universe, and everything it embodies, we also must learn about the faith and deeds of Khabãb Bnul Art, God be pleased with him, patronymed Abu 'Abdullãh. He was a *maoulã*, a captured slave by the tribe of Bani Zahra, and he was blessed with confronting crucial trials. Khabãb suffered harrowing torture and persecution at the hands of the Meccan polytheists, the pagans who worshipped multi deities they invented, and they did so until polytheism was abolished from the Arabian peninsula by God's leave.

Khabāb Bnul Art, God be pleased with him, accepted Islam readily, and his Islam was true and sincere. Upon his release from bondage, he migrated from Mecca to Madina in obedience to God's messenger's orders, and he spent his entire life supporting the struggle to defend God's message and His blessed messenger ﷺ, upon whom be peace.

Khabāb was most lachrymose, and he was often seen alone, mourning and grieving with endless crying because of the accumulated physical pain he suffered as a result of the lasting cuts and burns inflicted on his body by his merciless torturers.

Khabāb was among the early believers and émigrés who were forced out of their homes because of their belief in Almighty Allah. Khabāb was a close and an honored companion of God's messenger ﷺ, and he attended the believers' regular gatherings and study circles at the prophet's mosque, which gatherings were led by the best of teachers, God's messenger ﷺ, and the seal of His messengers and prophets, upon all of whom be peace.

Khabāb was often seen sitting alone, and he solicited solace in reading the revealed Qur'an, and in celebrating God's praises (*zikr*) at the mosque.

**305-** Muhammad bin Fudhayl narrated that Kardous al-Ghatfāni said: "Khabāb was the sixth person to embraced Islam, and he was one of the early companions who memorized the entire Qur'an by heart."

**306-** Also on this subject, Sulaimān bin Ahmad narrated that Ma'adi Karb said: "We went to 'Abdullāh bin Mas'oud, God be pleased with him, and we asked him to teach us *Süra t'ul Shu'arā* (Qur'an, Chapter XXVI), he replied, 'I have not memorized it yet, go to the one who learned it directly from God's messenger ﷺ, go to Abu 'Abdullāh, Khabāb Bnul Art.

**307-** Al-Sha'bi narrated that Omar bin al-Khattāb, God be pleased with him, once asked Bilāl bin Rabāh to tell him about the types of physical torture he was subjected to at the hands of the Meccan polytheists during the early days of the message. When

Bilãl did so, Khabãb looked at Omar and said, 'O Prince and Commander of the Believers, look here and see the lasting marks on my back!' When Omar saw that, he commented, 'I have never seen such inhumane thing until this day!' Khabãb then said, 'They lit a fire, and nothing could smother it better than the fat collected under my skin.'

**308-** 'Abdullãh bin Ja'far narrated that Khabãb Bnul Art, God be pleased with him, once said: "We went to God's messenger ﷺ,[1] and we found him laying in the shade of the sacred Ka'ba, covered with a cloak (Arb. *burdah*), and we pleaded, 'O messenger of Allah, why wouldn't you pray to Almighty Allah on our behalf, why wouldn't you ask Him to help us?' God's messenger ﷺ, immediately sat up, his face turned red, he pondered for a moment, and said, 'Why are you so impetuous? I swear by God Almighty that in past times, a man of faith would be brought by his torturers to a public square, and they will apply a saw to split him in half in slow motion, from his head down to his fundament, to force him to renege his faith, and nothing will dissuade him or force him to refute the truth or deny his knowledge of Allah. Others, also in former times, were subjected to a more afflictive form of torture, where their skin was carded by a machine with rollers covered with peercing iron spikes, moving to incise their skin from their nerves, in an effort by the unbelievers to force them to deny God Almighty and to renege their faith, and yet, they stood firm by their faith, consenting to the will of Allah. However, Almighty Allah will surely evidence His supreme sovereignty, He will surely establish His message in the land, and when such time comes, a traveler can walk on foot from the city of San'a to the city of Hadramout in perfect safety, fearing no one besides God Almighty, and guarding his sheep against a chasing wolf, — and yet, in comparison to earlier times, today, you seem to want things done right away.'"

**309-** Abi Ishãq narrated that Hãritha bin Mudhrab said: "One time, after the passing of God's messenger ﷺ, we visited Khabãb Bnul Art on a day he was cauterized in seven areas of his body to treat some festering wounds he had suffered earlier at the hands

[1] Referring to the Meccan period during the early days of Islam, and prior to the Muslim's *Hijra*, migration to Medina.

of his torturers. When we inquired how he felt, he replied, 'Had God's messenger ﷺ not forbade us to wish for death, I would have wished for it right away!' Someone asked Khabãb , 'Tell us something about the early days in Islam, about your fellowship with God's messenger ﷺ, upon whom be peace, and how was it like to visit with him?' "

In the course of his talk, Khabãb, God be pleased with him, said: "... I know of no one who was subjected to unbearably painful and harrowing physical torture, yielding permanent injury, such as those I sustained." Furthermore, during slavery, I was so poor and there was a time when I did not even have a decent rag to put on me to go to see him, and by contrast, here I am today, sitting on forty thousand Dirham, laying somewhere in this house."

Khabãb then asked for his burial shroud, and when he saw it and held it in his hand, he embraced it and wept over it. When he recouped, Khabãb resumed: "When Hamza was killed, we couldn't find more than a begrimed scanty piece of an old cloak to shroud him with, and which when we pulled up to cover his head, it became short of covering his feet, and when we stretch it down to his fee, it exposed his head. Finally, we laid it down as it was to cover his head, and we then covered his feet with some branches of Meccan ginger grass." (Arb. *Athkhar*)

**310-** Shaqïq bin Salma narrated that during another call to cauterization, Khabãb once pointed out to a coffer that laid in a corner of his room, and he said to his guests: "There are eighty thousand Dirhams in that coffer,[1] I have never locked it, and I have never tied them up, or prevented anyone who asks for money from taking anything he needed." Shaqïq bin Salma then said: "Khabãb pondered for a moment and he wept, and we all wept with him. When we inquired about what made him weep, he replied, 'My companions have all gone, and they have missed nothing in this world. Meanwhile, here we are after them, and despite all what we have collected in this world, we will find nothing but dirt to cover this wherewithal. — I wish this was a herd of cattle, or some other consumable provisions.' "

[1] Arb. *tãboot;* E. casket, coffin.

**311-** In another narration of this episode, Qays bin Muslim narrated that Khabãb said: "Some good people have left this world before us, and they took nothing of it with them, and here we remained after them, having collected some vain wherewithal we do not know what to do with except burying it. You must know that a Muslim will be rewarded for everything he spends during his lifetime on God's path, except for what he leaves behind him to his heirs."

**312-** Qays bin Muslim also narrated that Tãriq bin Shahãb said: "Some of the remaining companions of God's messenger ﷺ visited Khabãb during his last illness, and when they found him suffering the pangs of his last agony of death, one of the visitors said, 'Cheer O Abu 'Abdullãh, here are your friends, and tomorrow you will be reunited with your beloved brothers!' Khabãb immediately wept and commented, 'I am not afraid of death. You have just reminded me of my early companions, and you have named some people you called them my brothers! The people you have mentioned have left this world, and they have already received their reward. I am only afraid that our dividend be as little as the comfort they struggled to leave for us, and which we have enjoyed in this world since they departed.' "

**313-** Abi Sa'ïd al-Azdi narrated that Khabãb Bnul Art, God be pleased with him, once spoke about the early days of Islam,[1] in Madina, and said: "One time, a group of highborn Meccan Arabs from among the unbelievers, including al-Aqra'a bnu Hãbis al-Tamïmi and 'Uyaina bnu Husn al-Farãzi, came to meet with God's messenger ﷺ to inquire about his message. When they found him sitting with a group of poor and defenseless Muslims, among some of the slaves they earlier owned, including, 'Ammãr, Suhayb, Bilãl, and my self. The Meccans showed disdain towards us, for they saw people they considered of a lower class, and in their mind, they did not consider the blessed companions suitable to sit in their social gatherings. The Meccans scorned us, rebuked us, and pointed out that we should leave immediately. Eventually, the believers gave way, and we moved to a remote corner of the mosque, in order to permit the desired private meeting to take place, and to avoid greater

[1] Cf. *Ahlu Suffa*, Chapter V.

repercussions. One of the Meccans then spoke arrogantly to God's messenger ﷺ, he said: "You see, we would like to sit down and talk with you, but as you know, some delegations of reputable Arab tribes and their leaders also come to meet with you, and we somehow feel shame if they should find us sitting together with these slaves. Therefore, we want you to ask these slaves for some leave when we come to see you."

God's messenger ﷺ quietly replied: "Let it be so!" Immediately, when the Meccans thought that their demand maybe attainable, they further demanded: "Then write a pact to that effect between us and you." Hence, in his prophetic wisdom,[1] God's messenger ﷺ asked 'Ali, God bless his countenance, to bring some paper to write on.

Khabāb continued: "While we were sitting withdrawn, the archangel Gabriel descended upon God's messenger ﷺ with the Qur'anic revelation, ❮ Do not dismiss those who call upon their Lord morning and evening, seeking His presence. You are not accountable for their actions, nor are they accountable for your actions. Therefore, should you censure them, you would have committed a wrongdoing. In such a way, We try some with (uneasiness towards) others, that they may say (skeptically), 'Are these the people whom Allah chose to favor over us?' Alas, is Allah not aware of those who are truly thankful?` Therefore, when those who believe in our revelation come to see you, say: "Peace be on you, your Lord has made mercy His benevolent act. Thus, whoever commits a wrongdoing in ignorance, and then repents, and amends his conduct, or makes reparation, then surely your Lord is oft-forgiving, and most Merciful. ❯" (*Qur'an 6:52-54*).

"Upon receiving this revelation, God's messenger ﷺ immediately threw away the paper, and he called for us. When we arrived and sat by his side, he welcomed us cheerfully with the blessed greeting, 'Peace be upon you, Peace be upon you.' Thus, we happily drew up closer and nestled by him, and we blithesomely sat so tightly close to him to the point that our knees touched his

[1] God's messenger ﷺ, upon whom be peace, as the most noble and perfect teacher, perceived a chain of events that will become a lucid lesson for every believer, hence, his reply evolved thus.

knees. From that day on, God's messenger ﷺ regularly joined our circles, and when he needed to attend to his other duties, he left us.

Later on, God Almighty revealed His further guidance to His messenger ﷺ, upon whom be peace, saying: ❴ Apply yourself with patience to remain in the company of those who call upon their Lord morning and evening, seeking (to be in) His presence. Keep them continuously under your constant watch, and do not let your focus dither beyond their circle, or solicit (the company of those who seek) the pump and glitter of this lower life (form); Nor obey anyone whose heart We have veiled and caused to forget to remember Us. Those who follow their own whims and desires, and whose condition has degenerated to the point that it can only bring about their ultimate loss, and whose case is already proscribed... ❵ (*Qur'an 18:28*);"

Khabãb Bnul Art continued, 'Since that day, whenever God's messenger ﷺ sat with us at the mosque, he did not leave us, and when we recognized the time he usually attended to his other duties, we asked for leave. Otherwise, he would remain indefinitely patient until the last one of us have left."

**314-** Al-A'amash narrated that Zaid bin Wahab said: "We were with 'Ali, God bless his countenance, on his way back from the Battle of Siffeen, and when we reached the gates of the city of Kūfa, he passed by seven graves. 'Ali inquired, 'Who do these graves belong to?' We replied, 'O Prince of the Believers, Khabãb died after you have left to Siffeen, and he had previously asked to be buried in the outskirts of Kūfa.' 'Ali, God bless his countenance, commented, 'May God's mercy be upon Khabãb, for he willingly and readily embraced Islam. He migrated in obedience to God's messenger's orders, he lived to defend the truth, and his body sustained insufferable torture because of his faith. Surely Allah will not dismiss the efforts of those who do righteous deeds.' 'Ali then added, 'Blessed is he who constantly remembers the Promised Hour, who recognizes that his commerce is bound for reckoning, and whose work is consecrated accordingly, who is content with the basic necessities, and who is pleased with his Lord.' "

## 20- Bilãl Bin Rabãh

Also among the blessed companions was we must cite the name of Bilãl bin Rabãh, the devout and oft-forgiving sire, who was free from abstractness or illusion about this world. Born to a woman in bondage called Rabãh, Bilãl became free from slavery at the hand of Abu Bakr al-Siddïq, God be pleased with him, the truthful and benevolent, the trustworthy and blessed bosom friend of God's messenger ﷺ, upon whom be peace.

Bilãl had an exceptional noble character. He taught the believers who suffered at the hands of the pagans great lessons in faith and piety through his endurance and steadfastness. In fact, throughout his life, and even to this day, Bilãl always remains a school of piety and a great source of inspiration and spirituality for all Muslims, Bilãl was a pioneer among the early believers, and he was a tender-hearted loving man of Allah, and he placed his entire trust in Almighty Allah, depended solely on Him for all his needs, and finally, he was most trusted by God's messenger ﷺ, upon whom be peace.

**315-** Abu Bakr al-Talhi narrated that Omar bin al-Khattãb, God be pleased with him, said: "Abu Bakr is our sire, and he freed our second sire from bondage."[1]

**316-** Zaid bin al-Arqam narrated that God's messenger ﷺ said: "Bilãl is a most blessed man, and he is the sire of the callers to prayers."

**317-** Hishãm bin 'Urwa, the son of al-Zubair, narrated that Waraqa bin Nawfal once passed by Bilãl during his bondage while he was being tortured. When Waraqa saw the bitter torture dispensed to Bilãl, he became alarmed, and he went to Umayya bin Khalaf, Bilãl's master then, and addressed him, saying: "I swear by Almighty Allah, should he die because of your torture, I will make his case a reason for my relentless wrath upon you all."

**318-** Hishãm bin 'Urwa continued: "One day, Abu Bakr al-Siddïq, God be pleased with him, passed by Umayya bin Khalaf and his ring as they were torturing Bilãl to force him to renege his faith. With every blow he received, Bilãl, gasped for air as he cried loud from his harrowing pain: ***"Ahadun Ahad! Ahadun Ahad!"*** (There

[1] i.e., meaning Bilãl bin Rabãh, God be forever pleased with him.

is only one God, and only He is Allah!) When Abu Bakr saw that, he addressed Umayya bin Khalaf, saying: "Why wouldn't you try to be smarter and guard yourself against the wrath of Almighty Allah? For how long will you keep subjecting this poor man to such unbearable torture, don't you fear God Almighty?" Umayya replied angrily: "You are the cause that turned this salve rotten, and now, redeem him if you can afford it!"[1] Abu Bakr replied: "I will. Listen, I have a slave who is stronger and wieldier than he, and he follows your religion as well. If you want, I will trade him for this man." Umayya instantly answered: "I accept."

Hence, Abu Bakr traded his salve for Bilãl, and he freed Bilãl from bondage. It is also narrated that prior to his migration from Mecca to Madina, Abu Bakr also bought additional six slaves who had secretly embraced Islam, and he freed them from bondage, and Bilãl was their seventh.

**319-** Muhammad Bin Ishãq narrated that Bilãl was born to a slave woman belonging to the Arab Tribe of Bani Jamh, a woman prisoner (Arb. *mawãli*) they captured during a tribal feud, and they turned her into a slave. Her name was Rabãh, and she begot a son whom she named Bilãl, and a highborn from among the Meccans named Umayya bin Khalaf, bought Bilãl.

In Mecca, Bilãl knew God's messenger ﷺ, upon whom be peace, and he became Muslim from the early days of hearing about the divine message, and his Islam proved to be true and sincere. Bilãl had a pure heart and noble qualities, he readily accepted God's message, proclaiming the divine Oneness, and he wholeheartedly followed the guidance of His messenger ﷺ upon whom be peace. When Umayya learned that his slave had embraced Islam, he became outraged, and he inflicted upon him all kinds of torture, including, exposing him unclothed to the heat of the midday desert sun, and then placing a giant sun-heated rock on his chest. Other slaves would carry out Bilãl's torture to force him to renege his faith. Bilãl would be gasping for air, as he cried loud from his agonizing pain: ***"Ahadun Ahad! Ahadun Ahad!"*** (There is only one God, and only He is God!). Every day, Umayya, in his exasperation, would personally administer

[1] *Cf. Sirat Ibn Hisham.*

the castigation of his slave, and seeing Bilãl suffering in agony under the giant sun-heated rock, Umayya would scourge him, saying: "You will keep suffering until either you die, or you refute what Muhammad brought and return to worship our idols *Lãt* and *Uzzah*!"

Despite his ordeal and harrowing pain, Bilãl, who had testified that lordship belongs solely to God Almighty, would keep on crying loud: ***"Ahadun Ahad! Ahadun Ahad!"*** (There is only one God, and only He is Al!ah!)

**320-** 'Ãsim narrated that 'Abdullãh said: "The first people to declare their Islam in public were seven, and their Islam was immediately challenged, and ferociously fought by their clan. These were, God's messenger, upon whom be peace, Abu Bakr, 'Ammãr, his mother Sumayyah, Suhayb, Bilãl, and al-Miqdãd. Some of them and mostly the slaves among others who were considered of lower class, suffered immense cruelties and harrowing physical torture because of their faith in the Oneness of God Almighty. God's messenger ﷺ was admonished by his uncle Abu Tãlib who warned him against declaring his message in public, and he asked him to hide his knowledge of God Almighty. Also Abu Bakr was warned vehemently by his clan, and as for the other five, they were picked up by the polytheists, their patrons then, and they were fitted daily with tight armatures made of iron, with nothing under them, as they were placed under the scorching heat of the sun, exposed all day long to the torrid heat of the desert, and until the metal armatures became extremely hot and their skin blistered with sores before they lashed them with every kind of torture, to force them to renege their faith.

Under torture, many who were not killed during their ordeal were forced to confessed to what the pagans and polytheists wanted, except for Bilãl. He deemed his life to be of meager worth besides the reality of God Almighty, and he regarded his sacrifices to be of no worth in comparison with meeting God's pleasure by holding to his faith and knowledge of His Oneness. As a last recourse, the polytheist pagans of Mecca gave up on Bilãl, and they delivered him to the hands of their teenage boys, among some other mutant youth, who tied him, beat him up, abused him, and dragged him half naked through the plains of Mecca, before they lashed their frustration at him, and took pleasure in beating and stoning him, while Bilãl kept on exclaiming, *'Ahadun Ahad! Ahadun Ahad!"* (There is One and only God, and only He is Allah!)

**321-** 'Abdullãh al-Howzani narrated: "I once met Bilãl and asked him, 'Tel me about God's messenger's spending habits!" Bilãl replied, 'He had nothing! I was the keeper of his expenditure from the time Almighty Allah sent him and until he passed. For example, when he found someone in need of clothing, he would ask me to take care of him, and I would go out and borrow some money to cloth him and to feed him.' "

**322-** Abu Bakr bin Khallãd narrated, re 'Abdullãh, that God's messenger ﷺ, upon whom be peace, once visited the house of Bilãl, and he found there a cluster of dried dates hanging down from the ceiling. God's messenger then turned to Bilãl with astonishment and said: "O Bilãl! What is this?" Bilãl humbly replied: "O messenger of Allah, I have only kept them to welcome you should you ever visit me!" God's messenger ﷺ then said: "Are you not afraid to grumble against me in hell fire? Spend O Bilãl, spend generously, and do not fear any restrictions to your needs, nor limit the generosity of the sole Provider, the Lord of the divine Throne."

**323-** Abi Sa'ïd al-Khidri reported that God's messenger ﷺ, upon whom be peace once said to Bilãl, 'O Bilãl, strive to die poor, and do not die rich." Bilãl became perplexed as he replied: "O Messenger of Allah, how do I do that?" God's messenger ﷺ answered: "Do not store away for later what comes, and never refuse to give when asked." Bilãl became more puzzled as he further inquired: "O messenger of Allah, tell me, how can I do that?" God's messenger ﷺ, upon whom be peace, then replied, "Do what I say, or it will be hell."

**324-** Anas bin Mãlik narrated that God's messenger ﷺ, upon whom be peace, said: "I was persecuted in Allah to a degree that caused me great fear which no one has ever suffered, and I was injured on Allah's path to a degree that no one has ever experienced. At one time, I endured thirty nights and days where neither me nor Bilãl had anything to eat except a tiny scrap of food that could have been hidden under Bilãl's armpit."

**325-** Jābir narrated that God's messenger ﷺ, upon whom be peace, said: "I saw myself entering paradise, and suddenly I heard the sound of some steps preceding me, and yet, I could not perceive no one there. I asked, 'O Gabriel, who is that?' He replied, 'It is Bilāl!' "

**326-** Abu Huraira, God be pleased with him, narrated that God's messenger ﷺ, upon whom be peace, said: "While visiting paradise, I heard the sound of steps preceding me. I inquired about it, and I was told, 'It is Bilāl. Tell him.' "

After narrating this story to his companions, God's messenger ﷺ asked Bilāl: "Tell me how did you arrive at entering paradise before me?" Bilāl pondered for a moment, and he replied: "O messenger of Allah, perhaps it is because I mostly remain abluted. Whenever I become aware of losing the state of ritual purity, I immediately renew my ablution, and when I do, I always feel that as an expression of gratitude, I must offer Almighty Allah, the most Exalted, a thanksgiving prayer of two *rak'āt*."

**327-** Abu Mu'āwiya narrated that Qayss said: "Abu Bakr bought Bilāl's freedom, and he paid Umayya bin Khalaf, Bilāl's former master, five okes of gold.[1] As soon as Bilāl came out of slavery from under Umayya, he said to Abu Bakr, 'If you have released me from bondage for God's pleasure, then set me free to serve Him, but if you have bought me as a slave, then let me serve you?' Abu Bakr immediately wept and said, 'Indeed, I have bought you to free you from bondage. You are a free man. Go and serve Allah, the most exalted.' "

**328-** Ibn al-Mubārak narrated that Sa'īd Ibn al-Musayyib said: "During the caliphate of Abu Bakr, God be pleased with him, Bilāl prepared himself to join a campaign headed for Syria. When Abu Bakr saw him equipped and geared for departure; and in his gentle heart and soft nature, he said to Bilāl, 'O Bilāl! I did not think that you would leave us under such circumstances. I wish you would stay here with us, and help us during these difficult times!'

Bilāl replied: "If you had released me from bondage for the pleasure of Allah the most exalted, then let me go to Him, but if you had bought me for your own needs, then keep me."

---

[1] Arb. *Oqā* > E. Oke: an ancient weight measure of approx. 2 and 3/4 lb.

Abu Bakr immediately gave Bilãl permission to leave, and hence, Bilãl joined the campaign to Syria, where he then lived the balance of his life."

Bilãl died in Damascus, and he was buried near the central mosque, nowadays known as the Omayyad mosque.

## 21- SUHAYB BIN SANÃN BIN MÃLIK

Among our peers also comes the name of one of the leading believers called Suhayb Bin Sanãn Bin Mãlik, God be pleased with him. He joined the early group of émigrés from Mecca to Abyssinia, in East Africa, and he was a successful merchant as well. Suhayb spent his wealth generously on God's path, while he limited his personal indulgences in worldly comforts, and observed a firm restraint regarding his own comfort and satisfaction. Suhayb, God be pleased with him, was a most generous man, and he happily, and without any hesitation, fed whoever he could invite to share his meals. He also understood the meaning of the divine message with wisdom, he observed his religious duties with clarity, and in fact, his entire being was engrossed in the knowledge revealed by Almighty Allah, and with God's help and guidance, Suhayb hastened from early on to answer the call of God's messenger ﷺ, upon whom be peace, and to defend the divine revealed truth.

It is said that spiritual clarity means to track the source, to search thoroughly, and to investigate one's path before taking any steps forward. Spiritual clarity also means to abstain from prying, to make an effort, and to take the necessary steps to attain one's sublime goal of dwelling eternally in the august abode of nearness to one's Lord and Creator.

**329-** Muhammad bin Hassan al-Makhzoumi narrated that Suhayb once described the fidelity of his fellowship with God's messenger ﷺ, saying: "I never abstained from a spectacle of chivalry and martyrdom whenever God's messenger ﷺ, upon whom be peace, was there; and I was always present whenever someone accepted Islam with him. I never missed a campaign he led, and I was always at his right and left sides whenever the enemy charged against the believers. In the battlefield, whenever the first lines of believers became bewildered with the awesomeness of the battle, I was there to lead them back to the front lines, and I encouraged them to stand firm in the face of their enemy. On the other hand, whenever their back lines were struck with hesitation or inaction, I stood behind them to encourage them to go forward. Also in the battlefield, I mostly achieved to fight in the front line, in-between God's messenger ﷺ, upon whom be peace, and the enemy, and I remained thus until he passed."

**330-** Sa'ïd bin al-Musayyib narrated that when Suhayb Bin Sanãn Bin Mãlik migrated from Mecca to Madina to join God's messenger ﷺ, upon whom be peace, a band of Quraishi people concocted a foul play, and they chased him in an effort to challenge his purpose, and to prevent him from joining the ever-growing number of believers, who were gathering in the North, in Madina. When Suhayb found out that he was pursued, and as he recognized their intent, he turned towards them, and he descended his horse, pulled out an arrow, and stretched his bow and aimed at them, and with a loud voice, Suhayb shouted with a fierce voice: "O gang of Quraishi people! You know well that I am the most accurate archer among you. Let Allah be my witness that should you advance any further towards me, I will not let you come a step closer until I have emptied my quiver off its arrows to let you lie where my arrows hit you, and whoever survives them, I will unsheath my sword and fight whoever can sustain its blows."

Suhayb then added: "Listen to me! Do what you think is best. If you wish to let me continue on my way, I will tell you where did I hide my monies and personal belongings back in Mecca." When the Quraishi people consented to his second proposal, Suhayb told them whereabouts he hid his belongings, and they left him to pursue his journey.

As soon as Suhayb arrived to Madina, he told the story to God's messenger ﷺ, who rejoiced and exclaimed: "You won the barter O Abu Yahya, you won the barter O Abu Yahya!"

Following that episode, God Almighty praised His servant Suhayb, among others, when He revealed the Qur'anic verse, saying: ﴾ And among the people are those who purchase the freedom of their souls for the sake of God's pleasure ﴿ (*Qur'an 2:207*).

**331-** According to the narration of Haseen bin Huthaifa, Suhayb also told his story to some companions, adding: "When I reached Madina, God's messenger ﷺ was still praying at the mosque of Qiba, and when he completed his prayers and upon seeing me, he greeted me with a smile, saying, 'O Abu Yahya, you have won the barter, you have won the barter!' I became amazed as I said, 'O messenger of Allah, no one could have reached here before me to tell you what happened! Surely, only the arch angel Gabriel, upon whom be peace, could have descended upon you, and told you what happened.' "

**332-** According to the narration of Ziyãd bin Safiyy bin Suhayb, he said that when Suhayb arrived at the mosque of Qiba, Abu Bakr came out to greet him, and he announced to him the Qur'anic revelation, saying: ❮ Among the people are those who purchase (the freedom of) their souls for the sake of God's pleasure ❯ (*Qur'an 2:207*). Abu Bakr then took Suhayb by the hand, and brought him to God's messenger ﷺ, who greeted him saying: "O Abu Yahya, you have won the barter, you have surely won the barter!"

Suhayb was a most generous man, and he fed anyone he could invite to his table.

**333-** On this subject, 'Abdullãh bin Omar narrated that Suhayb, God be pleased with both of them, quoted God's messenger ﷺ during one of his sermons, to have said: "Paradise can only be entered by someone who generously spends his money right and left on God's path."

**334-** 'Abdullãh bin Muhammad bin 'Aqĩl narrated that prior to birth of Suhayb's first son Hamza, Omar bin al-Khattãb, God be pleased with him, said to him: "O Suhayb! You call yourself *Abu Yahya* (the father of Yahya), although you do not have a son; and you call yourself an Arab, although you have come to us from among the Romans." Suhayb replied: "O Prince of the Believers, as to my surname Abu Yahya, it was God's messenger ﷺ who called me thus; and as to my ancestral roots, I was born to an Arab man called al-Nimr bin Qãsit. During my childhood, I lived in Mosul, Iraq, and one day, I was taken as a prisoner of war, and then, I was sold as a slave, but today, I do know my roots."

**335-** The same account is also narrated by Zuhair, re 'Abdullãh bin Muhammad, son of 'Aqĩl, who described Suhayb, God be pleased with him, saying: "He was most generous, and he increasingly sought and invited guests to share his food, and moreover, he used to regularly distribute food to the poor and the needy, as well as he was a great host, and he honored his guests and presented them with elaborate meals.

Omar bin al-Khattāb, God be pleased with him, once said to Suhayb: "O Suhayb, you spend a lot of money on food, and such spending may be called *isrāf* (wasting money)?" Suhayb replied: "God's messenger ﷺ used to say, 'The best among you are those who share their food, and who return the salutation when greeted,' and in pursuing that *sunna* tradition, I distribute my money and share my food."

**336-** In another narration of the above incident, although somehow different, Yahya bin 'Abdu-Rahmān bin Hātib narrated that Omar bin al-Khattāb once said to Suhayb, God be pleased with both of them: "I have only observed three comments about your Islam: 1) You call yourself *Abu Yahya*, although Almighty Allah have said concerning His prophet Yahya, the son of God's prophet Zacharia, ‹ We gave that name to no one before him › (*Qur'an 19:7*); 2) you get hold of nothing that you do not give away without hesitation; and 3) your father's name is al-Nimr bin Qāsit, although you belong to the early group of émigrés, whom Allah blessed."

Suhayb replied: "As to my patronym Abu Yahya, indeed, it was God's messenger ﷺ who surnamed me thus; as to my habit of happily distributing whatever I get hold of without hesitation, indeed Almighty Allah have said, ‹ Whatever you spend, He replaces it for you, and surely Allah is the best of providers › (*Qur'an 34:39*); and finally, as to my lineage, you know that the Arabs use to sell whosoever they captured as a prisoner of war as slaves. One day, during a tribal feud, I was a young boy when an Arab tribe captured me, and they sold me as a slave in the countryside of Küfa, Iraq, and I grew up speaking their tongue. Therefore, no matter who is my father, I will always be called by his name."

**337-** Abi al-Salīl narrated that Suhayb, God be pleased with him, said: "I once prepared some food and intended to invite God's messenger ﷺ to partake from it. When I went to invite him, I found him sitting in the mosque talking to a group of people, so I went over and sat close to him, and I discretely signaled out my intention, inviting him to eat. God's messenger ﷺ looked at me, and in turn, he made a gesture, signaling, 'And those people!' I further communicated, 'No!' When God's messenger ﷺ remained silent, I stood up to leave, and when our eyes met again, I made another gesture inviting him to eat, but he further made another sign, meaning, 'And what about those people!' Hence, our eye-to-eye verbatim lasted for a short while, and finally, on the third time, I consented, 'And those people of course.' In fact, it was only a little food I had prepared for him, but when they came, they all ate their fill, and miraculously, when they left, there remained some leftover food we kept for later."

**338-** S̲uhayb Bin Sanãn narrated that he heard God's messenger ﷺ say: "If a man marries a woman and promises to give her a fixed dower, although he has no intention to fulfill his prenuptial agreement, thus, he would have deceived her by using an oath in the Name of God Almighty, and he would have falsely claimed her as his lawful wife, and he would not have complied with the laws governing the consummation of the sacrament of marriage, and therefore, on the Day of Reckoning, when he stands before his Lord for judgment, he will be found guilty of adultery. Likewise, if a man borrows some money and promises to repay it, although he has no such intention, he would have used the Name of Allah to deceived the lender, and he would have taken for lawful what does not belong to him, and therefore, when he stands for judgment before Almighty Allah on the Day of Reckoning, he will be found guilty of theft."

**339-** S̲uhayb Bin Sanãn, God be pleased with him, narrated that God's messenger ﷺ, upon whom be peace, once recited the Qur'anic verse ❮ Those who perform well, their good deeds will receive a reward of a better recognition, and more... ❯ (*Qur'an 10:26*), and he commented: "When the dwellers of paradise enter it, a caller will announce, 'O people of paradise, there remains a promise, your Lord wants to fulfill!' The people will reply with astonishment, 'What else is there? Has He not cleared our reputation, brightened our faces, increased the weight of our deeds in the records, and permitted us into paradise?' The callers will reiterate their announcement thrice, and then, Almighty Allah will manifest His divine presence, and the dwellers of paradise will gaze upon His divine countenance, and His glorious presence will be more magnificent and satisfying than everything they received."

**340-** Suhayb Bin Sanãn, God be pleased with, narrated that God's messenger ﷺ, upon whom be peace, once prayed: "Lord, Thou art not a god who is produced by our imagination, nor a lord we invented. Indeed, there has never been a god that we solicited besides Thee, nor do we ever neglected to call upon Thee, and surely no one has ever helped Thee to create us so that we would claim him as Thy associate. Blessed Thou art, and most exalted is Thy Holy Name."

**341-** 'Amru bnul Haseen narrated that Ka'ab-ul Ahbãr, God be pleased with him, also had narrated the above tradition, adding: "God's prophet David, upon whom be peace, also called upon God Almighty with the same prayer." *ibid.*

**342-** 'Amru Bnu Mãlik al-Rãsibi quoted the above prophetic prayer as follows: "Lord, Thou art not a god whom our imagination had produced, nor a lord we invented. Indeed, Thou art the Lord Whose remembrance cannot be abolished, and there has never been a god that we solicited or implored besides Thee, nor did we ever neglect to call upon Thee. Surely no one had ever helped Thee to create us so that we would develop doubt about Thee. Blessed Thou art, and most exalted is Thy Holy Name."

**343-** 'Abdu-Rahmãn bin Abi Laila narrated that Suhayb, God be pleased with him, said: "We once prayed behind God's messenger ﷺ, upon whom be peace, and when he concluded the prayers, he turned towards us with a smile, and he said, 'Why wouldn't you ask me about the reason behind my smiling?' The people humbly replied, 'Surely Allah and His messenger know best!' He continued, 'I pondered with wonderment upon Allah's judgment towards the Muslims amongst His creation, and it made me extremely happy to realize that no matter what godsend fate awaits a Muslim, it would ultimately prove to be most beneficial, while the just fate of no one else ever measures up to the reward that await one who accepts Allah's message of Islam, — (*i.e.*, a Muslim.)' "

**344-** Al-Haseen Bin Huthaifa narrated, that God's messenger ﷺ, upon whom be peace, said: "The émigrés are the forerunners, and they are the intercessors whose mediation is most accepted by Almighty Allah. They are the harbingers and the preachers who invite the creation to recognize its Lord. I swear by Him Who holds the destiny of my soul, that they will rise on the Day of Reckoning, having only their weapons to carry, and when they knock on the door of paradise, its custodians will inquire, 'Who are you?' They will reply, 'The émigrés.' The custodians of paradise will further inquire, 'Did you pass through your judgment?' Immediately, the émigrés will kneel down and scatter into the open the contents of their quivers, and they will turn towards Almighty Allah, and raise their hands, praying, and imploring Him, 'Lord, would Thou judge us regarding what we are carrying? Thou knowest best that we have renounced the comfort of our monies, families, and homes solely for Thy sake!' "

"As soon as they complete their prayer, Almighty Allah will provide them with golden wings studded with chrysolites and sapphires, and they will use them to soar towards paradise."

God's messenger ﷺ continued: "That is the meaning of their prayer, ❴ All praises be to Allah, Who dispelled our sorrow and grief. Surely our Lord is oft-forgiving, and He is the most bountiful. He, out of His mercy and favor upon us, has lodged us in eternal mansions of comfort, wherein, neither toil nor weariness can affect us ❵ (*Qur'an 35:34-35*)."

**345-** Suhayb Bin Sanãn, God be pleased with him, narrated that God's messenger ﷺ, upon whom be peace, also spoke in reference to above prophetic tradition, adding: "They will recognize their assigned dwellings and stations in the heavenly paradise better than those they had in this world."

## 22- Abu Tharr Al-Ghafãri

Among our peers, there is also the devoted ascetic, the oft-imploring at night, the one who lived a monastic life, who was the fourth to embrace Islam, and who refused to concede to the arts of divination, or the practices of occult science, even before the laws and rules of Islam were revealed. His name is Abu Tharr Al-Ghafãri, God be pleased with him.

Abu Tharr knew the monotheistic life of Islam some years before the message was revealed. He spent few years in devotion and prayers to Almighty Allah, he worshiped no man-made god, and he never associated any partner with God Almighty. Abu Tharr also was the first to greet God's messenger ﷺ with the regards of Islam, saying, *As-Salaamu 'Alaikum* (Peace be upon you), even before this formula was ordained by God Almighty as the greeting of Muslims among themselves.

Abu Tharr was not a man to be dissuaded from speaking the truth even if that would bring blame and censure upon him, and he never feared the tyranny of an unjust ruler, or was he ever discouraged by such encounters.

Abu Tharr was the first to speak about the knowledge of eternal life and the quality and purpose behind one's permanent being in the life to come. In the process of defending his earlier beliefs, and later on his faith, and even before accepting the divine message of Islam, Abu Tharr suffered awesome trials, persecution and adversities, and later on as well, he held to an unyielding resoluteness to his promise and covenant with God's messenger ﷺ, upon whom be peace. He bore his calamities and losses with unequaled patience, and later on, near the end of his life, Abu Tharr, God be pleased with him, withdrew from the society until he was seized by the eventual and inevitable common destiny of all the creation.

Abu Tharr, God be pleased with him, lived in a modest house close to God's messenger ﷺ and he often personally served him. He also learned from him the correct protocols of thinking and of conducting one's life in this world, how to reform one's character in a way that pleases Almighty Allah, and he also learned from him how to eliminate impertinent curiosity and prying on other's business.

**346-** 'Abdullãh bin al-Sãmit narrated that his uncle Abu Tharr Al-Ghafãri once said to him: "My dear nephew, I observed the regular daily prayers for nearly four years before Islam was proclaimed." 'Abdullãh inquired: "Who did you worship?" He replied: "The Lord of the heavens!" 'Abdullãh asked: "To what direction did you turn to pray?" Abu Tharr replied: "I turned to whichever direction Almighty Allah disposed me."

**347-** In another narration of the above account, Sulaimãn bin al-Mughïra narrated that Abu Tharr told his nephew 'Abdullãh bin al-S̲ãmit̲: "My dear nephew, I prayed regularly for over three years even before I met God's messenger ﷺ, upon whom be peace." 'Abdullãh asked: "You prayed to whom?" Abu Tharr replied: "To Almighty Allah of course!" 'Abdullãh further inquired: "To what direction did you turn to pray?" Abu Tharr replied: "Wherever Almighty Allah directed me. I regularly prayed the nightly *Isha* prayer, and then, I stayed up praying until *suh̲ur*, before dawn, and mostly, I found it necessary to remain in prayers until I was blanketed with the sunlight, and until I had to take cover in the shade."

**348-** Abu Laila al-Ash'ari narrated that Abu Tharr al-Ghafãri, God be pleased with him, said: "We once suffered a couple of years of drought that affected our living conditions badly; hence, my mother felt it necessary to travel with me and my brother Anees to visit her brother and some of our in-laws who lived in the northern plateau of Najd. There we stayed as their guests, and my uncle was extremely happy to have us, and he treated us most generously. One day, someone went to my uncle and claimed that my younger brother Anees is flirting with one of the girls in his family. My uncle felt extremely hurt and he withdrew to himself that day. When I came from herding the family sheep, I sought my uncle, and I found him sitting alone, sad, and crying. I asked him: "My dear uncle, what is hurting you?" And when he told me what he heard, I realized that these were false charges prompted by a jealous person, and I said to him: "O my dear uncle, God forbid that we commit such inequity. We are people who guard their chastity and honor, and had we not suffered adverse circumstances, we would not have left our homes and traveled this far."

**349-** According to the narration of Sulaimãn bin al-Mughïra, Abu Tharr continued: "Following that incident, I took my mother and younger brother, and we traveled back south to Mecca. When we reached the outskirts of the city, we heard that there was a puerile idiotic man who is possibly bewitched , and who is causing much pother and commotion in town. When I reached the city, I met a group of teenagers, and I inquired from them, 'Where is this strange man everyone is talking about?' Hence, they pointed me to God's messenger ﷺ, upon whom be peace, and they said, 'There is your man!' As soon as I took the first step in his direction, I felt a shower of stones and discarded bones descend on me, and every one in that band of polytheists jumped at me, and they pounded me until they smeared me with my own blood, and until I fell unconscious. When the evening cool breeze touched my face, I woke up, and I painstakingly dragged myself away from that place and went to God's House (the *Ka'ba*), where I hid in-between the *sitra* (covering cloth) and the stone building. Hence, I stayed at the *Ka'ba*, for thirty days, and thirty days, I had nothing to eat, except for the water I drank from the well of Zamzam. By that time, I felt as though the walls of my stomach began to crack, and I couldn't even recognize my own feebleness or hunger. It was during that period, when one evening I saw God's messenger ﷺ, upon whom be peace, at God's House. He came and circumambulated the Holy Ka'ba, and he prayed behind the Station of Abraham. I observed him in his devotion, and I went to him, and I greeted him with the regards and salutation of Islam, '*As-Salaamu 'Alaikum*' (peace be upon you). He replied, '*Wa 'alaika wa Rahmatullah*' (and upon you peace and the mercy of Allah).' Hence, I was the first to use the greeting of Islam."

**350-** In another narration attributed to Abu Laila al-Ash'ari, referring to the abovementioned account, he quoted Abu Tharr, God be pleased with him, to have said: "Later on, when I went to see God's messenger ﷺ, upon whom be peace, to declare my Islam, Abu Bakr, God be pleased with him, took me by the hand, and he treaded few steps along with me and gently asked me, 'O Abu Tharr.' I replied, 'Order me O Abu Bakr!' He said, 'Did you worship the sole sovereign Lord before Islam?' I replied, 'Indeed I did. Didn't you me waking up at dawn, when I remained in prayers until the rays of the sun drove me to seek a shade.' Abu Bakr, God be pleased with him, said, 'Indeed I did, but tell me, to what direction did you turn to pray prior to your Islam?' I replied, 'Wherever Almighty Allah directed me, and I did so until Almighty Allah guided me and blessed me to know the correct way of Islam.' "

**351-** Ibn 'Abbãs narrated that Abu Tharr, God be pleased with them both, said: "I stayed in Mecca with God's messenger ﷺ, upon whom be peace, and he taught me the religion of Islam, and I also memorized some Qur'anic verses I heard directly from him. One day, I said, O messenger of Allah ﷺ, I wish to declare my Islam in public.' He replied, 'I fear for your life.' I then said, 'Death is something no one can escape, so what if I am killed!' God's messenger ﷺ, upon whom be peace, kept quiet. When I left him, I passed by some Quraishi people sitting in a circle talking near the mosque, and when they saw me, I looked in their eyes and I declared with a loud voice, 'I bear witness that there no god except Allah, and I bear witness that Muhammad is His messenger.' The whole crowd became extremely upset, and they jumped at me, and they lashed their anger and frustration upon me, as they punched me and pounded me to the point that I fell unconscious. Seeing that, made them think that I was dead. When I woke up, and as soon as I gathered my strength, I went back to God's messenger ﷺ, upon whom be peace, and when he saw me in that state, he looked sad, and he said to me, 'Didn't I forbid you?' I replied, 'O messenger of Allah, it was something in my heart I wanted to verify and substantiate.' Hence, I stayed with God's messenger ﷺ, upon whom be peace, for sometime, and one day, he said to me, 'Go back to your clan, and when you hear my proclamation, come back and join me.' "

**352-** Ibn 'Abbãs also told a group of believers the story of how Abu Tharr entered Islam, he said: "Abu Tharr once came to God's messenger ﷺ, upon whom be peace, and said, 'O messenger of Allah, order me, and I will obey.' God's messenger ﷺ replied, 'Go back and stay with your clan, and when you hear my proclamation, come back and join me.' Abu Tharr said, 'I swear by God Almighty, I will not go back to my clan until I defy the polytheists' curfew on the believers and proclaim my acceptance of Islam as my religion.' "

Ibn 'Abbãs continued: "Before leaving town, Abu Tharr went to the Holy Ka'ba, and he exclaimed in public, 'I bear witness that there no god except Allah, and I bear witness that Muhammad is His servant and messenger.' When the pagans who were their heard him, they shouted, 'Surely this man is gone mad, the man is possessed.' Immediately, they all jumped at him, and they beat him so severely and mercilessly until he fainted."

Just at that moment al-'Abbās, God be pleased with him, the uncle of God's messenger ﷺ, upon whom be peace, passed by, and in an effort to stop the polytheist pagans from finally killing Abu Tharr, he reasoned with them, saying, 'O people of Quraish, you are merchants, and your caravans pass regularly through the highways of the tribe of Ghafār, the Tribe of Abu Tharr al-Ghafāri. Do you want them to avenge their man by regularly looting your caravans, and by cutting you off your trading pipeline?' Hearing that, the assailants reflected upon the economic consequences, and the Quraishi left Abu Tharr smeared in his own blood, and they went back to their homes. Al-'Abbās, who also was a highborn from the tribe of Quraish itself, immediately descended his horse, and he attended to Abu Tharr.

**353-** 'Abdullāh bin al-Sāmit narrated that Abu Tharr, God be pleased with him, once said: "My bosom friend, God's messenger ﷺ, upon whom be peace, advised me to love the meek, and that should I have to look people's fortune in this world, to look at those who have less luck than me, and he advised me to avoid looking at those who have better luck than I do. He advised me to speak the truth even if it tasted bitter, and to fear no tyranny or censorship of an unjust ruler when it comes to defending the truth of God Almighty."

**354-** Hamīd bin Hilāl narrated that 'Abdullāh bin al-Sāmit said: "I once went along with my uncle Abu Tharr to visit the caliph 'Uthmān bin 'Affān, God be pleased with him. My uncle said to him, 'I seek permission to leave this town.' 'Uthmān replied, 'Yes, if you wish to do so, and we will endow you with a grant from the charity fund that will suffice you for a long time to come.' Abu Tharr replied, 'I have no need for that. Surely Abu Tharr is most content with his small herd of camels, Allah has entrusted him with.' "

**355-** 'Abdullāh bin al-Sāmit narrated: "We once visited 'Uthmān bin 'Affān, God be pleased with him, and it happened that Ka'ab, among others, was at his house dividing the inheritance of 'Abdu-Rahmān bin 'Awf for distribution. 'Uthmān asked Ka'ab, 'How would you judge a man who had amassed all this wealth, and who had spent his entire life distributing it to every needy person he knew, and to every charity he thought of, and who did such and such act...?' Ka'ab calmly replied, 'I wish him the best.' "

Hearing that conversation, Abu Tharr stood up to leave, and he addressed Ka'ab: "How do you know that? Perhaps, on the Day of Judgment, the owner of this money would rather have had scorpions constantly smarting at the deepest fold of his heart in this world, rather than having labored hard to gathered this wealth.' " As Abu Tharr was leaving the House of 'Uthmãn, God be pleased with him, he commented: "Define and resolve your worldly interests and concerns as you see fit, and leave us alone to our Lord and to our ways of life!"

**356-** Muhammad bin 'Abdullãh al-Hadhrami narrated that 'Abdullãh bin Khirãsh said: "I once saw Abu Tharr, God be pleased with him, at Rabtha, and he had nothing for himself and his family except for a bedouin black canopy that provided them with shade, and I found him sitting on a dry and lacerated traveler's bag filled with stones. Abu Tharr had a wife, an old woman of swarthy complexion, and they had no children. I said, 'O Abu Tharr, if you remain like this, you will die having no offspring!' He replied, 'Praise be to Him Who withholds them in this ephemeral abode, and Who grants them as eternal blessings in the hereafter.' I asked, 'O Abu Tharr, Why wouldn't you take a second wife along with this one?' He replied, 'Nay, I prefer to have a wife who humiliates and upsets me rather than a wife who honors and comforts me.' I said, 'Why wouldn't you replace this dry and lacerated bag and use something softer to sit on?' Abu Tharr prayed, 'O Lord forgive me,' and he then turned to me and said with a stern voice, 'Take whatever you want from under this tent and leave us alone.'"

**357-** Qatãda narrated that Abi Asmã al-Rahbi once visited Abu Tharr at his retreat in Rabtha, and he noted that Abu Tharr's wife, Umm Tharr, did not cover her hair, nor was she courteous towards him or towards his guests. When Abu Tharr, God be pleased with him, looked into Abi Asmã's eyes, and recognized his perception, he commented jestingly, 'Look at what this swarthy woman is ordering me to do? She is always aspiring for worldly comfort, and she wants me to move to Iraq, but I am afraid that if I do so, they, the Iraqis, will present me with worldly comforts. I also remembered that my bosom friend, God's messenger ﷺ, upon whom be peace, advised me that for those who love comfort in this world, there is an inescapable track beneath the *sirāt* (Bridge of the Day of Judgment) that leads straight to hell-fire, and which track will earn its travellers nothing but despise and humiliation. When we come upon that junction, the lesser the burdens we carry, and the less vulnerable we are, the better are our chances to escape from hell-fire.' "

**358-** Imam Ahmad bin Hanbal, God be pleased with him, narrated that Abi Bakr bin al-Munkadir said: "Habib bin Maslama, the governor of Syria, once sent a gift of three hundred dinars to Abu Tharr with the message, 'Use them according to your needs.' Abu Tharr, God be pleased with him, replied to the carrier, 'Take them back to him, and tell him, couldn't he find someone else who is less guarded and more ready to be deceived be this money? Sufficient for us the blessings of a shade over our heads, a handful of sheep that grazes around us, and moreover, a free woman who, as a courteous wife, is doing us the favor of serving our daily needs, and even then, I am afraid that such blessings could be too much for people like us.'"

**359-** Imam Muhammad Ibn Seerīn narrated that the Al-Hārith once heard from someone who visited Syria, that Abu Tharr was living in substandard conditions. Hearing that, al-Hārith sent him a gift of three hundred dinars. Abu Tharr, God be pleased with him, returned the gift and said to the carrier: "Can't he find a servant who more gullible for him to favor than me? I have heard God's messenger ﷺ, upon whom be peace, say, 'Whosoever has forty coins, and yet begs for help, he is indeed an opportunist.' "

Abu Tharr, God be pleased with him, continued: "When I heard that, I said to myself, 'Surely the clan of Abu Tharr owns more than forty Dirhams. They own forty sheep along with other accessories and related traps."

**360-** 'Abdullāh, son of Imam Ahmad bin Hanbal, God be pleased with him, narrated that Abu Tharr, God be pleased with him once said to some of his contemporaries: "On the Day of

Judgment, I will be closer to God's messenger ﷺ, upon whom be peace, than any of you in this room. This is because I heard God's messenger ﷺ say, 'Among you, the closest to me on the Day of Judgment are those who depart from this world having the same look I saw them last.' " Abu Tharr continued, "I swear by God Almighty, that in one way or another, and except for me, all of you somehow look entangled in the ropes of this world."

**361-** 'Abdullãh, son of Imam Ahmad bin Hanbal, God be pleased with him, narrated that someone once said to Abu Tharr: "Why wouldn't you buy a farm as so and so did, among others?" Abu Tharr replied: "What benefits do I get by becoming a landlord. I only need a drink of water a day, and a *cafiz*[1] of wheat per week."

**362-** Sufyãn al-Thawri narrated that Abu Tharr, God be pleased with both of them, said: "I never needed more than a single *sã'a* (measure) of wheat which is sufficient to sustain my physical strength, and I will not add anything to it until I meet Allah, the Lord of majesty and glory."

**363-** 'Abdullãh, son of Imam Ahmad bin Hanbal, God be pleased with him, narrated that Abu Tharr al-Ghafãri, God be pleased with him, said: "I was once standing next to God's messenger ﷺ, upon whom be peace, when he turned to me and said, 'O Abu Tharr! You are a righteous man indeed, and you will suffer adversities after I leave this world.' I inquired, 'Adversities in Allah?' He replied, 'In Allah.' Hearing that, I said, 'I welcome and salute Allah's commands.' "

**364-** Sufyãn bin 'Uyaina narrated that Abu Tharr, God be pleased with him, said: "The clan of Bnu Umayya is threatening me with poverty and murder. Surely I prefer to be in the belly of this earth rather than to be walking on it, and I surely prefer poverty over wealth."

**365-** Abu Bakr bin Mãlik narrated that someone asked Abu Tharr, God be pleased with him: "O Abu Tharr, why do people leave your company upset every time they visit with you?" He replied: "They leave upset because I admonish them against hoarding the treasures of this world."

[1] Cafez: a weight measure; a small bag.

**366-** 'Abdullãh bin al-Sãmit narrated that his uncle Abu Tharr Al-Ghafãri, God be pleased with him, once said: "My bosom friend, God's messenger ﷺ, upon whom be peace, entrusted me with the admonition that any gold or silver one ties up with a thong to save for an austere day will become a charring coal in hell-fire, unless one spends it on God's path before he dies."

**367-** Abu Muhammad bin Hayyãn narrated that Abu Tharr, God be pleased with him, once described the people of the world, saying: "They breed what will they will ultimately bury, they build what will eventually be destroyed, they hold firm to what is ephemeral, and they forsake what is everlasting. Hence, blessed are the two cries[1] people abominate most: death and poverty."

**368-** On the same subject, Sulaimãn Bnu 'Amru Bnu Maimoun narrated that Abu Tharr al-Ghafãri, God be pleased with him, said: "One's money plays three possible roles in his life: 1) It may affect his own destiny; 2) it may influence the character of his heirs; or 3) it may bring about his eventual disgrace. As for his destiny, it urges him to spend it away until it exhausts both its own benefits and harm, or until one dies. As to one's heirs, they await his death to put their hands on it and to spin what they inherit into their own wheel of destiny, and finally comes the eventual humiliation and disgrace on the Day of Judgment. Therefore, if you can avoid being the most disadvantaged, then do so, for Almighty Allah says: ❮ You will not receive the benefits of trueness (to your Lord) until you spend out of what you love most ❯ (Qur'an 3:92)."

Recalling that revelation, Abu Tharr then suddenly looked around and saw a camel he owned, and he obligingly pointed at it and said: "Indeed my Lord, I do love this camel as my most cherished possession, and I wish to use it for my ultimate advantage." Abu Tharr then gave away the camel in charity.

**369-** Abi Shu'ba narrated that a man came to Abu Tharr al-Ghafãri, God be pleased with him, and upon seeing his living condition, the man proposed to offer Abu Tharr full maintenance (Arb. *nafaqa*). Abu Tharr replied: "My dear brother, by the grace of Almighty Allah, we do have here everything we need, we have

[1] Arb. *Mootãn*, the two malign conditions people hate most.

goats from which we draw our needed milk, we have donkeys to carry our burdens, we have a freed slave, and as a wife who serves us willingly, and we do have a cloak to cover our regular robe, so what else do we need? Yet, having this much in our possession, I am even afraid to be questioned on the Day of Judgment about any excesses."

**370-** Abu Muhammad bin H̲ayyãn narrated that Abu Tharr al-Ghafãri once said: "There will come a day in your world, when a man will be envied for the speed of his traveling vehicle, to which fascination he too will take pride, and which possession he will cherish, and such condition is similar today to the envy people may have towards someone who begets ten male children."

**371-** 'Abdullãh, son of Imam Ahmad bin H̲anbal, God be pleased with him, narrated that Abu Tharr, God be pleased with him, said: "On the Day of Judgment, the one who possessed two dirhams in this world will meet with a more rigorous accountability than the one who possessed one dirham."

**372-** Al-A'amash narrated that Abu Tharr, God be pleased with him, said: "I swear by Almighty Allah, that if you only knew what I have learned from God's messenger ﷺ you would not hasten to enjoy your women in bed, nor would you eventually lie impounded in exhaustion and depleted like an empty bottle in your beds. By God, I wish Almighty Allah had created me a tree which fruits are harvested for needed food, and which trunk is cut down for needed wood."

**373-** Abu Bakr bin Mãlik narrated that Abu Tharr, God be pleased with him, said: "One who desires to enter the heavenly paradise, must have constancy of purpose."

**374-** 'Abdullãh, son of Imam Ahmad bin H̲anbal, God be pleased with him, narrated that Abu Tharr, God be pleased with him, said: "Trueness to one's Lord requires the least supererogatory prayers to receive Allah's favorable answers, and as much as a pinch of salt one may need for his food."

**375-** Qurra bnu K̲h̲ãlid narrated that Abu Tharr, God be pleased with him, once said to someone: "You see how vast is humanity, and yet, it carries no benefits, except for the pious and the penitent."

**376-** Muhammad bin Wãsi' narrated that when Abu Tharr al-Ghafãri died, a man traveled to meet his wife, Um Tharr, and he inquired from her about the nature of her husband's worship. She replied: "He spent his entire days, mostly silent, pondering and meditating on Allah's work."

## His Admonitions

**377-** Sufyãn al-Thawri narrated that Abu Tharr al-Ghafãri, God be pleased with him, once stood by the Ka'ba, and he cried out: "O ye people, I am Jandab'ul Ghafãri. Come here and hearken to the good advise of your compassionate older brother." Immediately, people hastened and stood around him to hear what he had to say. Abu Tharr then said: "Do you see, when one of you plans to travel, doesn't he prepare himself and takes with him the needed provisions that will suffice him until he reaches his destination?" The people replied: "Indeed, he does." Abu Tharr continued: "In this regard, the road to the Day of Reckoning is the furthest of your ultimate destinations. Take with you what benefit you most." The people asked: "And what do you consider as most beneficial for such a journey?" Abu Tharr replied: "1) Make a pilgrimage to Mecca for your dire needs; 2) fast in the hottest day in contemplation of the horrific age-old standing of the Day of Resurrection; 3) pray two *rak'ãt* in the darkness of the night in contemplation of one's bewilderment, loneliness, and darkness of his grave; 4) either say something good, or remain silent pondering an awesome age-long standing in the grim silence of the Day of Resurrection; 5) spend your money in charity, so perhaps you can escape its trials, 6) make this world a setting for two types of conferences: One to seek the benefits of the hereafter, and the other to seek what is permissible. Should there be a third criteria of meetings, they will be of harm and of no benefit to you; and finally, 7) look at your money and divide it in two categories: One dirham you spend on your family, the second you spend for your own benefits in the hereafter, and should there be left a third dirham, it will be of harm and of no benefit to you." Abu Tharr then shouted at the top of his voice: "O ye people! Your craving to accumulate what is beyond your reach will surely destroy you."

**378-** 'Abdullãh, son of Imam Ahmad bin Hanbal, God be pleased with him, narrated that Abu Tharr al-Ghafãri said: "God's messenger ﷺ, upon whom be peace, said to me, 'O Abu Tharr, I know a Qur'anic verse which will satisfy people's needs, if only they comply with it!' He then recited: ‹ Whosoever guards himself against the wrath of Allah, his Lord will show him a way out of his difficulties, and He will provide for his needs from sources he does not anticipate › (*Qur'an 65:2*).' " Abu Tharr added: "God's messenger ﷺ, upon whom be peace, then kept on rehearsing this verse to me over and over."

## A Conversation With Rasul Allah ﷺ

**379-** Ahmad, son of Anas bin Mãlik narrated that Abu Tharr said: "I once entered the mosque and I saw God's messenger ﷺ, upon whom be peace, sitting there by himself, and I went and sat next to him. God's messenger ﷺ turned to me and said, 'O Abu Tharr, one must pay respect to a mosque when he enters it, and the greeting of a mosque is done by offering therein two *rak'ãt* of prayers.' I Immediately stood to the side and offered two *rak'ãt*, of prayers. When I returned and sat to his side, I asked him, 'O messenger of Allah, you ordered me to pray, what is prayer?' He said, 'Prayers are preordained blessings whether one offers them extensively or scarcely.' I asked, 'O messenger of Allah, what is the best of deeds?' He replied, 'To believe in Almighty Allah and to strive on His path.' I asked, 'O messenger of Allah, whose faith is most accomplished among the believers?' He replied, 'The best in character and conduct.' I asked, 'O messenger of Allah, whose Islam (submission to God's will) is most right among the believers?' He replied, 'The submission of a man the people are safe from the inequity of his hand and tongue.' I asked, 'O messenger of Allah, what is the best form of offering prayers?' He said, 'To prolong one's standing in imploring and supplications (Arb. *qunüt*) before God Almighty during *salãt*.' I asked, "O messenger of Allah, what is fasting?' He replied, 'Fasting is an obligatory pillar which is most rewarding by itself, and Allah will multiply its reward in the hereafter many folds.' I asked, "O messenger of Allah, what is the best of *jihad,* striving on God's path?' He replied, 'To sacrifice one's horse, and to be willing to shed one's blood in the battlefield to defend Allah's Words.' I asked, 'O messenger of Allah, what is the best charity?' He replied, 'To have meager means, and yet offer them to the needy.' I asked, "O messenger of Allah, which is the most glorious verse of Qur'an that Almighty Allah revealed to you?' He said, 'The verse of the Divine Seat (*Ãyat-ul Kursi - Qur'an 2:255*).' 'God's messenger ﷺ, upon whom be peace, further added, 'O Abu Tharr, the entire seven firmaments together with the divine Seat (*Kursi*) are not greater in size than a tiny small ring which is cast in the floor of a vast endless desert, and the superiority of the divine all-pervading, glorious, omnipotent, and all-encompassing Divine Throne (*'Arsh*), is similar to the superiority of the vastness of such a desert in size over that of the small tiny ring.' "

Abu Tharr continued: "I further asked, 'O messenger of Allah, how many prophets are there?' He replied, 'One hundred and twenty four thousand prophets.' I asked, 'How many messengers are there?' He replied, 'A large crowd of three hundred and thirteen messengers.' (Abu Tharr commented:) I said, 'Certainly, the more blessings there are, the better it is,' (and he further said), I asked again, 'O messenger of Allah, who was the first messenger of God Almighty?' God's messenger ﷺ replied, 'Adam was the first messenger.' I asked, 'O messenger of Allah, was Adam a sent prophet?' He replied, 'Yes indeed. Allah created him with his own Hand, and He blew a Breath from His own Soul into him. He placed him before Him, face to face, and He fashioned his form to perfection.' "

**380-** Imam Ahmad, son of Anas bin Mãlik, added in his narration of the above prophetic tradition that God's messenger ﷺ also said: "And He spoke to him face to face." God's messenger ﷺ, upon whom be peace, then added, 'O Abu Tharr, there are four messengers of Assyriac culture, and these are Adam, Seth, Enoch, and Idris who was the first to write with a pen, — and then came four messengers of Arab culture, and these are Hũd, Sãlih, Shu'aib, and your prophet.' Abu Tharr added, 'I asked, 'O messenger of Allah, how many Books did Almighty Allah reveal?' God's messenger ﷺ,

replied, 'One hundred and four Books. Fifty scrolls (Arb. *suhuf*) were revealed to Seth, then Enoch received thirty scrolls, Abraham received ten scrolls, and prior to the revelation of the Torah, Moses received ten scrolls, and after that, Almighty Allah revealed the Torah, the Injeel, the Zabour (the Psalms), and finally, He revealed the Qur'an.' "

Abu Tharr continued: "I asked, 'O messenger of Allah, what did the scriptures of Abraham deal with, and what were they like?' God's messenger ﷺ replied, 'They mostly contained parables and admonitions, such as when Almighty Allah's addressed a king, saying, 'O tyrant king whom I have placed on his throne, and who is self-deceived and arrogant. I did not create you to amass the world, nor to bring it together. I have ordained you and I sent you with a mission to answer the call of the beleaguered and the oppressed, and to be just towards him, on My behalf, for I am God, I do answer the call of the oppressed, and I hasten to his help when he calls upon Me, and that is even if he had previously denied Me.»'

God's messenger ﷺ, upon whom be peace, continued: "Different scriptures offered parables and wisdom, such as, 'Unless a wise person is faced with barring circumstances, he should balance his time. He should dedicate one hour to pondering his Lord, one hour to reckoning himself, one hour to contemplate the work and creation of God Almighty, and one hour to satisfy his personal needs of food and drink. A wise person must not allow himself to be distracted from his primal objectives, except for three reasons: 1) To gather the needed provisions for a journey, 2) to go to work and earn his livelihood, and 3) to solicit personal pleasure solely in what is made permissible. A wise person must recognize the era in which he lives, he must be vigilant of his surroundings, he must mind his own business, and he must guard his tongue. Hence, should one reckon his words as part of his deeds, he would speak little, except in reference to his personal needs.' "

Abu Tharr continued: "I asked, 'O messenger of Allah, then what did the other scrolls which Moses received speak of?' He replied, 'They were admonitions as well, such as, 'It makes Me wonder to see someone who recognizes death, and yet, finds a way to rejoice! It makes Me wonder to see someone who acknowledges the existence of hell-fire, and yet, finds a way to laugh! It makes Me wonder to see someone who recognizes fate, and yet, attempts to defy it! It makes Me wonder to see someone who witnesses how the world treats its children and turns them upside down, and yet, feels comfortable to relax therein! It makes Me wonder to see someone who claims to believe in the Day of Reckoning, and yet, he does nothing towards it!' "

Abu Tharr then asked: "O messenger of Allah, advise me." He replied: "I advise you to uphold piety towards God Almighty and make that your main focus." Abu Tharr added: "O messenger of Allah, advise me more!" He replied: "Read the Qur'an regularly, for it is your light on earth, and it promotes your name in the heavens." Abu Tharr further asked: "O messenger of Allah, tell me more." He replied: "Beware of laughing excessively, for excessive laughter kills the heart and darkens the face"

Abu Tharr asked again: "Tell me more, O messenger of Allah, tell me more." He replied: "Refrain from unnecessary talking, except when it fosters common benefits. This will protect you against satanic assaults, and it will rightlyguide your religious endeavors." Abu Tharr said: "Tell me more, O messenger of Allah." He replied: "Striving on God's path is the monasticism of my followers." Abu Tharr further said: "Tell me more, O messenger of Allah." He replied: "Always look at those who are less privileged than you, and do not look at those who are more privileged than you, for this will protect you against belittling and despising God's favors upon you." Abu Tharr asked: "Tell me more, O messenger of Allah." He replied: "Keep in touch with your relatives even if they cut off their ties with you." Abu Tharr asked again: "Tell me more, O messenger of Allah." He replied: "Fear no blame or censure by others when it comes to the truth of Almighty Allah."

Abu Tharr kept on asking: "Tell me more, O messenger of Allah." He replied: "Speak the truth even when it is bitter." Abu Tharr further inquired, and God's messenger ﷺ replied: "Knowing your own faults should prevent you from looking at others' faults. Do not criticize others for faults you still commit. In fact, it is most shameful, and it is a defect in his character for a man to know about others' faults more than he should know about his own, or to admonish them and not heed his own admonition."

Abu Tharr continued: "God's messenger ﷺ, upon whom be peace, then placed the palm of his hand over my chest and said, 'O Abu Tharr, know that there is no wisdom better than the proper management of one's life, there is no piety better than abstaining from wrongdoing, and there is no lineage better than having good character and conduct.'" [1]

**381-** 'Ubaid Bnu 'Umair narrated that Abu Tharr, God Be pleased with him, said: "I once entered the mosque where I found God's messenger ﷺ, upon whom be peace, sitting by himself. I took advantage of the moment, and I asked him, 'O messenger of Allah, does there remain in this world any of the texts of the old scriptures such as those revealed to Abraham or Moses?' He replied, 'O Abu Tharr, read the Qur'anic verse, ❬ Blessed is the success of one who purifies himself, and when he remembers the Name of his Lord, he engages in prayers. But (the majority of) you give preference to life in this world, although life in the hereafter is better and more lasting. This (knowledge also) was revealed earlier in the scrolls of Abraham and Moses ❭ (*Qur'an 87:14-19*).

Abu Tharr, God be pleased with him, was a close companion of God's messenger ﷺ, upon whom be peace. He regularly sat with him, and he eagerly cared to ask him as many questions as possible. He endeavored to draw from his wisdom, emulated his most exalted character, and he made great strides in applying the knowledge he learned from him in his personal life.

Abu Tharr asked God's messenger ﷺ, upon whom be peace, questions relating to the *uṣūl* (foundation of Islamic jurisprudence), as well as he asked him questions relating to the *furū'* (doctrine of branches and spirituality. He asked him questions about true faith and perfection of ethics). He asked him about seeing God Almighty. He asked him about the most cherished divine words, God Almighty loves. He asked him about the Night of Power, and whether its occurrence remain after God's prophet leave this world or not? In fact, Abu Tharr, God be pleased with him, asked God's messenger ﷺ, about every conceivable question.

**382-** On this subject, 'Abdu-Rahmān Bnu Laila narrated that

[1] The sequence of this narration is reported thus by al-Hassan bin Sufyān.

Abu Tharr, God be pleased with him, said: "I asked God's messenger ﷺ about every conceivable question, and down to desiring to scratch a skin sensation (during prayers to stop an irritation), to which question God's messenger ﷺ replied, 'You may scratch it once, if you wish to do so, or leave it alone.' "

Abu Tharr, God bless his soul, renounced the world; he rolled up his sleeves and embarked on a journey to meet the inescapable, and he embraced his adversities with contentment and gratitude, until he met his Lord.

## His Death

**383-** Muhammad bin Ishãq narrated that Al-Qarzi said: "Abu Tharr left the city Madina to a northern locality called Rabtha, where he met with his ultimate destiny. When Abu Tharr fell ill, he requested his wife, saying: "When I die, give me the initial ritual bath, shroud me, and then place me on the side of the road. When the first group of travelers come by, tell them, 'This is Abu Tharr, the companion of God's messenger ﷺ, upon whom be peace, please help us to wash him and to bury him."

Later on that day, it happened that 'Abdullãh bin Mas'oud, God be pleased with him, was traveling with a caravan from Iraq to Madina, and he recognized Abu Tharr, and he immediately hastened to help in his burial.

**384-** Ishãq al-Thaqfi narrated that Um Tharr, the wife of Abu Tharr al-Ghafãri said: "When Abu Tharr was dying, he saw me crying, and he asked me, 'Why are you crying?' I replied, 'I do not know what to do! I surely cannot wash your body and shroud you all by myself. I do not have a single robes that is big enough to shroud you, nor do we have in this entire place enough material to shroud your body with!' Abu Tharr said, 'Do not cry. Listen, I was once sitting in a group of people, and I heard God's messenger ﷺ, upon whom be peace, say to us, 'One of you will die in a desolated area, and near his death, a group of believers will pass by, and they will bury him and officiate his funeral prayer.' O Um Tharr, none of those who were sitting in that gathering is alive today except me, and each one of them have died in a town, or surrounded with a group of believers, and therefore, I believe that I am the one who will die in a desolated area as prophesied by God's messenger ﷺ, upon who be peace. I swear by Allah that I am not lying, nor did I ever disbelieve in what God's messenger ﷺ said. Go and look outside, perhaps you will see a group of travelers coming this way.'"

Um Tharr continued: "When I understood, I had no more excuses but to accept what I was told to do." Um Tharr then divided her attention between attending to her dying husband, and looking outdoor to find out about the traveling group of believers. One moment she stood near a dune looking in all directions, and the next moment she went back to nurse her dying husband. Suddenly, in the middle of her dilemma, there appeared in the horizon the shadows of travelers on their trotting horses, they floated smoothly across the desert, and the winds raised their overcoats to near their shoulders, making them appear from a distance like gliding kites. Um Tharr immediately waved her extra robe, signaling them to come to her rescue. When they arrived, they asked her: "What do you need O woman?" She replied: "There is dying Muslim in this dwelling, would you please help me in shrouding and burying him?" Someone asked: "Who is it?" She sobbingly replied: "Abu Tharr!" Hearing his name, the entire group cried out: "This is the beloved companion of God's messenger ﷺ, and by God, we will surely sacrifice and risk everything for his sake."

Immediately everyone jumped off their horses, and they gently pushed her aside, while they eagerly hastened to his bedside. Seeing them, Abu Tharr smiled and said to them: "Cheer ye good people. I was once sitting in a group of people, and I heard God's messenger ﷺ, upon whom be peace, say to us, 'One of you will die in a desolated area, and a group of believers will pass by near his death, and when he dies, they will bury him and officiate his funeral.' Since none of those who were sitting in that gathering is alive today except for me, and each one of them have died in a town surrounded by a group of believers, therefore, I believe that I am that one who was meant by God's messenger ﷺ, and who is destined to die in a desolated area.'"

Abu Tharr further continued: "O good people, did you hear what I said? I swear in the Name of Allah that if I had even a single overcoat which could cover me or my wife, I would certainly ask to be shrouded in it, and I would not have asked anyone for a piece of shroud. Do you hear me? I beg you in the Name of Allah and Islam, let no leader among you wash me or shroud me, nor should a corporal, a captain, or a courier among you do that, for no one among your elite but has committed what he admonishes others not to do. Furthermore, let no one who last night had sexual intercourse with his wife shroud me, except for a youth from Madina and who is here with you."

Immediately, a young man from the *ans̲ār* (partisans) of Madina said: "O uncle, I am not married, I will shroud you in my own coat, and I will use two extra coats, my mother have spun and weaved for me!" Abu Tharr replied: "You do that my son."

When Abu Tharr, God be pleased with him, died, the young man washed him and shrouded him as he promised, and a group of Medinites, including, H̲ajru Bnul Adbar, and Mālik Bnul Ashtar, among others from Yemen, officiated his funeral.

## 23- 'Utba Bnu Ghazwān

Also among our peers, we here note some of the virtues of the blessed companion Abu 'Abdullāh 'Utba Bnu Ghazwān, God be pleased with him, the blessed companion of God's messenger ﷺ, upon whom be peace. 'Utba Bnu Ghazwān renounced leadership and authority, and he relinquished the government of cities and countries. In the early days of the message, 'Utba Bnu Ghazwān was the seventh person to join the believers in their submission to the divine command, and who readily accepted the divine message of Islam. Later on, 'Utba Bnu Ghazwān was offered the seat of the governor of Basra, Iraq, where he went at first, and he built its central mosque, and established its pulpit. 'Utba is also well remembered for his inspiring sermon on *Governing The World and The Keenness Needed To Tie up Its Loose Ends, and What Changes of Colors One Should Expect To See In This World.*

**385-** K̲hālid bin 'Umair narrated that 'Utba Bnu Ghazwān, God be pleased with him, in one of his sermons, and after praising Almighty Allah, and invoking His blessings upon His messenger

ﷺ, upon whom be peace, 'Utba said: "O people! This world is most blatant about its harshness towards its children, while it is moving rapidly towards its inevitable demise. The most of what is left is as little as a meager couple sips of water one may find in the bottom of an empty pitcher. You also must realize and understand that you are presently moving from a temporary abode to the final and permanent one. Therefore, take with you the best of what you can find, and leave behind you what you do not need. I take refuge in Almighty Allah never to let me feel great in my own estimation while being insignificant in His sight. As for you, the time will come, and you will surely be tried with unjust rulers after I leave this world. History has taught us that whenever a prophet of Allah had left this world, its conditions deteriorated, and the government turned into a kingdom first, and then, it is ruled by tyrant dictators."

"In the early days of the message, there was a time when I was one of seven people who accepted God's message of Islam, and at that time we lived through the most austere conditions. We even had nothing to eat except the leaves of shrubs and trees, and yet, for a while, we had no choice but to eat them, and we did so until the corners of our mouths turned ulcerous. I once found a trashed cloak which I cut in two halves, one half I took for myself, and the other I gave to Sa'ad bin Mãlik. However, if you look for any of these seven people in this world today, and should he be alive, you would find him to be a most successful governor of a distant land."

"What a wonder a stone is! When it is thrown from the top of hell-fire, it takes seventy autumns to reach the bottom of it. Doesn't that make you wonder? On the other hand, it also takes forty years to cover the distance in-between the two posts of the gate of paradise, and yet, there will come a day when even that entrance will be crowded as well."

'Utba, God be pleased with him, died in the locality of Rabtha.

## 24- Al-Miqdãd Bin al-Aswad

Also among our peers, there comes al-Miqdãd bin al-Aswad, God be pleased with him, the son of 'Amru bnu Tha'laba, who was one of the early believers in God's message and in His messenger ﷺ, upon whom be peace. Al-Miqdãd was a chivalrous companion, and he had a most noble character. He declined an appointment to a government position, and he gave preference to the armed struggle to defend his faith and the family of believers. He coupled that with unquestionable devoutness and courage, and he solicited the guardianship of God Almighty to protect him against the temptations and the trials of this world.

**386-** 'Ãsim bin Zarr narrated that 'Abdullãh bin Mas'oud, God be pleased with him, said: "The first group of believers to defy the Quraishi ban on proclaiming faith in God's oneness, and who declared their Islam in public comprised seven people, namely: God's messenger ﷺ, Abu Bakr, 'Ammãr bin Yãsir and his mother Sumayyah, Suhayb, Bilãl, and al-Miqdãd."

"As to God's messenger ﷺ, upon whom be peace, it was his uncle Abu Tãlib who warned him against it. Next and because of his social rank, Abu Bakr was merely contested by his clan, and as for the others, they were subjected to awesome persecution and harrowing torture. At one time, they were fitted with tight iron armatures with no clothing under them, and they were laying in the open desert for a long day under the sun, exposing them to the torrid burning heat of the desert, and until their skin blistered under the sun-heated metal."

**387-** 'Abdullãh bin Buraida narrated that God's messenger ﷺ, upon whom be peace, once spoke to 'Ali, God bless his countenance, saying: "Almighty Allah ordered me to love four people He loves, and you are one of them O 'Ali, and along with you are al-Miqdãd, Abu Tharr (al-Ghafari), and Salmãn (al-Fãrisi)."

Prior to the Battle of Badr against the polytheist forces of the Tribe of Quraish, God's messenger ﷺ, upon whom be peace, came out and sought the advise of all people concerning facing an army of unbelievers four times larger in number than that of the believers, and which was better equipped.

**388-** On this subject, Muhammad bin Jurair narrated that 'Abdullãh bin Mas'oud, God be pleased with him, said: "I bore witness to the unique faith of al-Miqdãd bin al-Aswad at a most critical moment, and to have his perception and stamina is dearer to my heart than to own everything in this world. We all knew when God's messenger ﷺ, upon whom be peace, was upset when his cheeks turns red, expressing his displeasure with something. One day, at such a critical moment, al-Miqdãd bin al-Aswad arrived, and when he saw God's messenger ﷺ in that state, he said: "Cheer O messenger of Allah. I swear by Almighty Allah that we will not say to you what the children of Israel said to Moses when they said, ❬ Go with your Lord and fight (there), and we will sit here (and watch) ❭ (*Qur'an 5:24*), but we say, and we swear by Him Who has sent you with the message of truth, that we are all the way with you, and we will be in front of you, behind you, on your right side, and on your left side to defend you, and until the Almighty Allah grants you victory."

**389-** Also in reference to the above narration, Muhammad bin Is<u>h</u>ãq said: "When God's messenger ﷺ, upon whom be peace, came out and sought the advise of his companions, al-Miqdãd stood up and said, 'O messenger of Allah, go ahead and do what Almighty Allah commanded you to do, and you will find us with you. Cheer up O messenger of Allah, for I swear by Almighty Allah that we will not say to you what the children of Israel said to Moses, ❬ Go with your Lord and fight (there), and we will sit here (and watch) ❭ (*Qur'an 5:24*), but we say, "Go with your Lord, and we will fight on your side.' God's messenger ﷺ, upon whom be peace, then said, 'Blessed are these tidings,' and he prayed for al-Miqdãd."

**390-** 'Abdullãh, son of Imam Ahmad bin <u>H</u>anbal, God be pleased with him, narrated that al-Miqdãd bin al-Aswad said: "When we arrived to Madina, God's messenger ﷺ, upon whom be peace, assembled us in groups of ten in each house, and I was among the group of ten, where God's messenger ﷺ, upon whom be peace, stayed, and each ten people had a single goat to share its milk."

**391-** Bishr bin al-Mufad<u>dh</u>al narrated that al-Miqdãd bin al-Aswad, God be pleased with him, said: "God's messenger ﷺ, upon whom be peace, once appointed me to command an administrative post. When I completed my mission and returned to Madina, he said to me, 'How did you find leadership?' I replied, 'O messenger of Allah, when I occupied that post, I thought that everyone was my uncle. Let God be my witness that I will not accept any appointment from today on as long as I live in this world.' "

**392-** Also in reference to the above account, Anas Ibn Mālik, God be pleased with him, narrated that God's messenger ﷺ, upon whom be peace, once appointed al-Miqdād bin al-Aswad, God be pleased with him, to head an administrative post. When al-Miqdād completed his mission and returned to Madina, God's messenger ﷺ, upon whom be peace, asked him: "How did you find leadership?" Al-Miqdād replied: "I was treated like a monarch. Everything was brought before me, and the way was cleared for my needs, until, and for one moment, I though that I was somehow better than the others." God's messenger ﷺ, upon whom be peace, commented: "It is like that. Either you take it or leave it!" Al-Miqdād replied: "O messenger of Allah, I swear by Him Who sent you with the message of truth, I will never again accept to even command over two people."

**393-** 'Abdu-Rahmān bin Jubair, son of Nafīr narrated that he heard his father say: "A group of us once had some pressing concerns, and we invited al-Miqdād bin al-Aswad, God be pleased with him, to explain them for us. When he arrived we said, 'May Almighty Allah grant you continuous health and strength. Please sit down and let us present our case and express our concerns.'"

When al-Miqdād sat down, he said: "What a wonder! I once passed by some people who desired action, and craved trials. They claimed that should Allah had try them with adversities similar to those met by His messenger ﷺ, upon whom be peace, and by his companions, they would have faced them with courage! I swear by the guidance of Almighty Allah, which is the best of guidance, that I heard God's messenger ﷺ, upon whom be peace, say, 'Happy is the man who is allowed to avoid temptations.' God's messenger ﷺ repeated that thrice, and then he said, 'And when such a man meets with trials, he endures them wtth patience.' "

Al-Miqdād, God be pleased with him, further continued: "I swear by the guidance of Almighty Allah, which is the best of guidance, that I will not attest of anyone to be a dweller of the heavenly paradise unless I can see the conditions that surrounded his death. My conclusion is based on what God's messenger ﷺ, upon whom be peace, enunciated when he said, 'Indeed, the heart of the son of Adam can change its course faster than water when agitated by boiling.' "

**394-** 'Abdullāh bin al-Mubārak narrated that al-Nafīr, said: "We were one day sitting with al-Miqdād bin al-Aswad, God be pleased with him, when someone passed by and said to him, 'Blessed are these eyes that saw God's messenger ﷺ, upon whom be peace. I swear by Almighty Allah, that would have wished our eyes to have seen what you saw, and to have witnessed the events you witnessed!'

Al-Nafīr said, 'I heard what I heard, and I was amazed at what the man said, yet, I told myself, 'He just wanted to say something nice.' Al-Miqdād bin al-Aswad, God be pleased with him, turned to the man and said, 'What makes someone like you wish to have attended an event Allah has decreed him not to witness. Wishing for something far beyond his reach, and not knowing what stance would he have taken then! I swear by God Almighty that there were also some prominent people who witnessed God's messenger ﷺ, upon whom be peace, and yet, Almighty Allah decreed that they be humiliated, and He thrusted them, nose down, into hell-fire because they did not heed His call or believe in His messenger ﷺ. Why aren't you grateful enough to Almighty Allah to have granted you this life, to know no one besides your Lord, and to accept what your prophet ﷺ, upon whom be peace, brought you, and why wouldn't you be grateful to Allah for letting others meet such adversities and awesome trials in your stead?' I swear by God Almighty, that God's messenger ﷺ, upon whom be peace, was sent in dire circumstances, no other prophet has ever encountered. He came at the most difficult times, and after a long period following the last of God's messengers, (Jesus, the son of Mary, upon whom be peace). The people of Arabia were then immersed in an era of paganism and ignorance (Arb. *jāhiliyah*), and they had found pleasure in pursuing idol worship.'

'God's messenger ﷺ, upon whom be peace, came then with a criterion to help them differentiate between truth and falsehood. However, the truth was sometimes hard for them to bear, and initially, the criterion he brought from his Lord also had divided father and son in opinion and faith. In fact, when Almighty Allah unlocked one's heart and imparted faith to it, He also made it understand that those who reject the truth will culminate in unending torment and destruction in hell-fire. Hence, a man may have regarded his own father, his son, or his brother as an unbeliever, and he may have not liked to see his kin fall in such state, and therefore, he had little comfort when the thought of their possible destiny crossed his mind. Therefore, it is better for you to recall the prayer which Allah, the Almighty Lord of majesty, taught, ‹ Our Lord, grant us comfort in our spouses and offspring ›'(*Qur'an 25:74*)

## 25- Sãlem Mawla Abu Huthaifa

Also among our peers and the blessed companions of God's messenger ﷺ, upon whom be peace, is Sãlem, the companion and attendant (*mawla*) of Abu Huthaifa, God be pleased with both of them. He was an affluent and eloquent speaker and he memorized the entire Qur'an by heart. Later on, Sãlem became a renowned Imam who possessed clarity of faith, sincerity, and certitude, and his profound knowledge of the Holy Book gave brilliant depth and wisdom to his orations.

**395-** 'Abdullãh bin 'Amr, God be pleased with him, narrated that God's messenger ﷺ, upon whom be peace, said: "Learn the Qur'an from four people, Ibn Mas'oud, Sãlem mawla Abu Huthaifa, Ubiyyu Bnu Ka'ab, and Mu'ãth Bin Jabal." (May Allah be forever pleased with all of them).

**396-** Anas bin 'Iyãdh narrated that 'Abdullãh bnu Omar, God be pleased with them, said: "Prior to the arrival of God's messenger ﷺ, upon whom be peace, to the city of Madina, the first group of émigrés from Mecca used to gather to pray at a place called al-'Isba, near the mosque of Qabã, where Sãlem mawla Abu Huthaifa regularly led them in prayers, and he knew the Qur'an more of than the others, including Abu Bakr and Omar, God be pleased with both of them."

**397-** 'Ubãda bin Nasiy narrated, re Omar bin al-Khattãb, God be pleased with him, that God's messenger ﷺ, upon whom be peace, once spoke in reference to Sãlem mawla Abu Huthaifa, saying: "Indeed, Sãlem has intense heartily love for God Almighty, the Lord of majesty and Glory."

**398-** Muhammad bin Ishãq al-Thaqfi narrated that Omar bin al-Khattãb, God be pleased with him, said: "If I was to appoint Sãlem mawla Abu Huthaifa as my successor, and should my Lord question me about my reason for doing so, I would reply, 'Lord, I have heard Thy prophet ﷺ, upon whom be peace, say about Sãlem that he loved Almighty Allah with all his heart."

**399-** Mãlik bin Dinar narrated, re Sãlem mawla Abu Huthaifa, God be pleased with him, that God's messenger ﷺ, upon whom be peace, said: "On the Day of Reckoning, throngs of people will be brought in, carrying good deeds measuring as high as the Mountains of Tihãma.[1] When they stand before the Just Lord, He will cause their deeds to come to naught, and then He will order them to be thrown into hell-fire."

Sãlem asked: "O messenger of Allah, surely you are more dear to me than my own father and mother. I ask you by such station you hold in my heart to disclose them to us, so that we may come to know the truth about such people. I swear by Him Who sent you with the message of truth, that I too fear to be one of them!" God's messenger ﷺ, upon whom be peace, replied: "O Sãlem, such people do fast and pray regularly; and yet, whenever they encounter something unlawful, they wish for it, and when possible, they jump at the opportunity and grab it, and hence, Almighty Allah will render their deeds obsolete."

Mãlik bin Dinar commented on the abovementioned prophetic account saying: "This is what hypocrites are about."

## 26- 'Ãmer bin Rabĩ'a

Also among the blessed companions we must cite the name of Abu 'Abdullãh, 'Ãmer bin Rabĩ'a, God be pleased with him. He witnessed the Battle of Badr among others, and he was known to spend extended hours praying in mosques, standing up long nights celebrating the praises of God Almighty, pondering, contemplating,

[1] Tihãma: Coastal plains in the S.W. of the Arabian peninsula.

and invoking the remembrance of Allah, the Lord of majesty and glory. Ãmer bin Rabi'a, used his innate common sense to avoid many of the awesome trials and adversities that befell others in the community of his time. He renounced interest in gifts and grants, he lived with honor and dignity, and he died shielded and safe in the protection of God Almighty.

What drove 'Ãmer bin Rabi'a to such a remarkable level of ascetic detachment and made him prefer a life of poverty in this world over that of collecting riches, and furthermore, what invited 'Ãmer to become intoxicated with constant remembrance (*Zikr*) of his Lord, was a combination of his nearness to God's messenger ﷺ, upon whom be peace, the intensity of the missions he carried alongside God's messenger ﷺ and his blessed companions, the physical tension he endured throughout the campaigns, and the clarity and knowledge of the revelations he acquired directly from God's messenger ﷺ, upon whom be peace.

**400-** Yahya bin Ayoub narrated that Yahya bin Sa'ïd said: "I once heard 'Ãmer bin Rabi'a praying at the mosque when in the middle of the night the insurgence of a mutinous group against the caliph took place. In that night, 'Ãmer narrated that when went to rest, and in a dream, a voice said to him, 'Wake up to prayers and beseech Almighty Allah to protect you against trials as He protected His most favored servants.' 'Ãmer bin Rabi'a immediately woke up, and he stood up in prayers. Shortly after that vision 'Ãmer fell il, and he did not leave his house until his funeral."

**401-** 'Abdullãh, the son of 'Ãmer bin Rabi'a, said: "When the insurgence against the caliph 'Uthmãn, God be pleased with him, took place, my father woke up in the middle of the night, and he prayed, 'My Lord, I beseech Thee to deliver me from these trials and to protect me as Thou protected Thy most favored servants.' "

'Abdullãh continued: "Shortly after that, my father fell ill, and he did not leave the house until his funeral."

**402-** In another narration referring to the mutiny against the caliph, the vicegerent of God's messenger ﷺ, upon whom be peace, and the prince of the believers, 'Uthmãn bin 'Affãn, God be pleased with him, Muhammad bin al-Mutawakkil al-'Asqalãni, said: "When the insurgence against 'Uthmãn took place, a man became outraged, and he said to his family, 'Tie me up with solid chains for I have become insane, and I have no more control over my actions.' "

"Beholding his determination, the family chained the man inside his own house as he demanded, and later on, after the murder of 'Uthmãn, God be pleased with him, the man said to his family, 'You may release me now. To Allah belong all praises. I thank Him for curing me of my insanity, and for guarding me against having anything to do with the murder of 'Uthmãn.' "

**403-** Müsa bin 'Ubaida narrated that 'Ãmer bin Rabi'a, God be pleased with him, spoke of an Arab who once visited him, and whom 'Ãmer honored duly. Later on, 'Ãmer introduced his guest to God's messenger ﷺ, upon whom be peace, and he spoke of him with great esteem. After the guest had visited with God's messenger ﷺ, upon whom be peace, and prior to leaving the house, the Arab man said 'Ãmer bin Rabi'a: "I presented God's messenger ﷺ, upon whom be peace, with a gift of an estate I own, and I assure you that there is not a soil in the entire Arabian peninsula akin to its soil in fertility. Therefore, I want to offer you a gift of a piece land from that valley, and I am sure that it will suffice all your needs and those of your offspring for generations to come." 'Ãmer bin Rabi'a, God be pleased with him, replied to his parting guest, saying: "I surely have no need for such an estate. This mourning, Allah has revealed a verse which says, ‹ People's Day of Judgment has come closer, and yet, they are in oblivion of it, and they turn away when they hear its warnings ›(*Qur'an 21:1*)."

**404-** Abu Bakr bin Hafs narrated, re 'Abdullãh, that his father 'Ãmer bin Rabi'a, God be pleased with him, said: "Sometimes, God's messenger ﷺ, upon whom be peace, would send us on a mission, and the entire detachment will have a mere small bag of dried dates as its provisions. We use to divide the contents of the bag between us, a handful of dried dates for each person until we had nothing but a single dried date which we kept in the bag for later."

'Abdullãh became puzzled as he asked his father: "And what would a single dried date do for an entire detachment?" 'Ãmer replied: "My dear son, don't say that! Sometimes, when we were struck by extreme hunger, we even had to divide the last date among ourselves, and by God's grace, even a single date was sufficient."

**405-** 'Āsim bin 'Ubaidullāh narrated that 'Āmer bin Rabī'a, God be pleased with him, said: "We accompanied God's messenger ﷺ on a campaign, and at distant area from Madina, we were overcome by a dark night, hence, we stopped, and prior to lying down, each man went out and brought few stones to build a niche for prayers. When we walk up at dawn, we realized that we had prayed in a direction other than that of the Ka'ba, so we went to God's messenger ﷺ, upon whom be peace, and said: "O messenger of Allah, perhaps we prayed last night towards the wrong direction!" That morning, Allah, the Most Exalted, revealed the Qur'anic verse, ❮ Both the East and the West belong to Allah, and whichever way you turn, Allah's presence is surely there. Surely Allah is the All-Pervading, and the All-Knowing ❯ (*Qur'an 2:115*)."

**406-** 'Āsim bin 'Ubaidullāh narrated that 'Āmer bin Rabī'a, God be pleased with him, said: "One day, during a congregational prayer, a man standing immediately behind God's messenger ﷺ, upon whom be peace, sneezed, and he prayed in an audible voice, 'All praises are due to Allah, — indefinite, most fragrant, and blessed praises, so that they be pleasing to our Lord of majesty and glory. Praises that heighten and multiply for ever to meet the expediency of His infinite pleasure. Indeed, all praises are due to Allah for every condition He decrees.' After paying the concluding greetings due upon the closing of the prayers, God's messenger ﷺ, upon whom be peace, turned to the congregation and inquired, 'Who uttered these words?' The man immediately made himself known, and replied, 'That was me, O messenger of Allah. Surely, I only meant good!' God's messenger ﷺ, upon whom be peace, then said, 'I saw twelve angels stepping up, and soliciting who among themselves should write down this prayer to present it before the Lord of the Divine Throne.' "

**407-** 'Āmer bin Rabī'a, God be pleased with him, narrated that God's messenger ﷺ, upon whom be peace, said: "Whoever prays to Allah to bless me with *salawāt* once, Allah, the Most Exalted, will bless him ten folds. Therefore, it is up to you to solicit more or less of such auspicious and most favorable blessings."

**408-** Another segment of the above prophetic saying was narrated by Shu'uba, re 'Ãmer bin Rabi'a, God be pleased with him, that God's messenger ﷺ, upon whom be peace, said: "Whenever a servant invokes Allah's blessings (*salawāt*) upon me, the angels will pray to Allah to bless him as well, and to forgive his sins, and as long as he invokes such divine blessings, the angels will continue to do so. Therefore, it is up to the servant of Allah, Exalted be His Name, to solicit more or less of such most auspicious favors."

## 27- Thawbān Mawla Rasūl Allah ﷺ

Also among the blessed witnesses and companions comes Thawbān, the attending-companion (*mawla*) of God's messenger ﷺ, upon whom be peace. Thawbān was filled with contentment and gratitude, and he was most loyal, chaste, modest, charming, and graceful. He served the messenger of the Merciful Lord with utmost sincerity, and he was promised a guarantee of entering the heavenly paradise as long as he refrains from asking any one besides Almighty Allah for anything, or seeking the door of any one in authority in this world, which condition he fulfilled by the grace of Almighty Allah, as the following testimonies will attest:

**409-** 'Abdullāh bin 'Abdul Wahāb al-Hajbi narrated that Yusuf bin 'Abdul-Hamīd said: "I once passed by Thawbān, and he saw me wearing a luxury garment and a signature-engraved ring. He said to me, 'What are you doing with this outfit and this signature-engraved ring? Did you not know that signature-engraved rings belong to the kings of this world?' " Yusuf bin 'Abdul-Hamīd commented: "Hearing what Thawbān said, I never wore a ring since that day."

**410-** 'Amru bnu Hafs narrated, re Thawbān, that God's messenger ﷺ, upon whom be peace, was praying for his family (*Ãl al-Bait*), and he mentioned 'Ali and Fātima, among others. Thawbān, who served in God's messenger's house, asked, 'O messenger of Allah, am I not a member of your family (*Ãl al-Bait*)?' God's messenger ﷺ, upon whom be peace, replied, 'Indeed you are, and as long as you do not object to God's will when circumstances oppose your favored intentions, and as long as you do not seek someone in authority or ask him to supplement your needs.' "

**411-** Muhammad bin Qays narrated, re Thawbãn, that God's messenger ﷺ, upon whom be peace, said: "Whosoever accepts this single most pressing advice from me, I will personally welcome him into paradise." Thawbãn immediately jumped at the opportunity and said: "O messenger of Allah, I accept your advice." God's messenger ﷺ, upon whom be peace, then said: "Never ask any one in this world for anything."

Yazïd, son of Mu'ãwiya, commented on the above narration, saying: "For the balance of his life, and even should Thawbãn's leather scourge fall while riding his camel, he never asked any one to hand it to him, and he would descend his camel and pick it up by himself."

**412-** Ma'dãn bin Abi Talha narrated, re Thawbãn, that God's messenger ﷺ, upon whom be peace, said: "Whosoever asks anyone for something he does not really need, it will evince as a dark mark on his face on the Day of Resurrection."

**413-** Abu 'Ãmer narrated, re Thawbãn, God be pleased with him, that God's messenger ﷺ, upon whom be peace, said: "Any gold or silver, one leaves behind him when he dies, will be melted and rolled into sheets that will be used in the hereafter to brand him from the bottom of his feet and up to his chin."

Thawbãn, God be pleased with him, then said: "O Abu 'Ãmer, this prophetic statement may even apply to the leftover milk of one's she-goat, and therefore, you better find a way to dispense of any excess before it is too late."

**414-** Mubãrak bin Fadhãla narrated, re Thawbãn, God be pleased with him, that God's messenger ﷺ, upon whom be peace, said: "There will come a day, when nations will converge upon the Muslims from every direction, treading on the heels of each others, without mercy, just as hungry ravens voraciously attack and devour their meal." The peopled asked: "O messenger of Allah, is that because we will be fewer in number?" He replied: "To the contrary! At such a time, you will be in great number, and yet, you will be like the scum that washes on the surface of a torrent. The hearts of your enemies will be filled with contempt towards you, and they will be stripped of any regards or fear of you, while your hearts will be clogged by *wahn*, an attenuating disease." People asked: "Describe such an attenuating disease in the heart?" God's messenger ﷺ, upon whom be peace, replied: "Such disease affects hearts which are filled with love for the world, and which hate death."[1]

**415-** Sãlem bin Abi Ja'ad narrated that Thawbãn, God be pleased with him, said: "We were traveling with God's messenger ﷺ, upon whom be peace, and some people from among the Meccan émigrés were discussing the meaning of some Qur'anic verses dealing with Gold and silver, and they were wondering what type of money one should have? Omar bin al-Khattãb, God be pleased with him, overheard their conversation, and he said, 'If you wish, I will ask God's messenger ﷺ, upon whom be peace, about it?' The people consented, and I followed him, and I heard Omar as he asked God's messenger ﷺ, upon whom be peace, the question, 'What type of money should one keep, since the revelations spoke about the consequences of saving gold and silver?' God's messenger ﷺ, upon whom be peace, replied, 'The best property one should keep is a tongue which is constantly engaged in *zikr*, praising God Almighty, a heart which is filled with gratitude to its Lord, and a wife who believes in God Almighty, and who helps her husband reach his ultimate goal in the hereafter safely.' "

## 28- Rãfi' Mawla Rasũl Allah ﷺ

Among the blessed companions of God's messenger ﷺ, upon whom be peace, there also lived Rãfi' Abu al-Bahiy, God be pleased with him. He was known to despise what is lowly and ephemeral, and he loved what is exalted, pure, and everlasting.

**416-** 'Amru bnu Dinar narrated, re Muhammad, son of 'Amru bin Sa'ïd bin al-'Ãss, whose his family owned and freed all its slaves from bondage after the advent of Islam, except for one. This man went to God's messenger ﷺ, upon whom be peace, and asked for his intercession. When the owner, 'Amru bin Sa'ïd bin al-'Ãss, came to discuss the case with God's messenger ﷺ, upon whom be peace, he gave him to his care, and God's messenger ﷺ in turn told the man to go free. His name was Rãfi' Abu al-Bahiy, and he developed

[1] i.e., A dislike to meet one's Lord.

a great love and feelings of strong ties to God's messenger ﷺ, and he liked to often say about himself: "I am the *Mawla* (slave-attendant) of God's messenger ﷺ, upon whom be peace."

**417-** 'Abdullãh bin 'Amr narrated that someone asked God's messenger ﷺ: "Who is the best of people?" God's messenger ﷺ, upon whom be peace, replied: "A believer who possesses a tamed heart and a truthful tongue." The man asked: "What is a tamed heart?" God's messenger ﷺ replied: "A heart which is filled with piety towards Allah, the Lord of majesty and glory. That is a pious heart which is free of ills, transgression, cheating, jealousy, or envy."

The man further asked: "O messenger of Allah, who is next in character and praiseworthy qualities?" God's messenger ﷺ, upon whom be peace, replied: "A believer who despises status in the world, and who loves the hereafter." The people present then said: "We are only aware of Rãfi', the companion-attendant (*Mawla*) of God's messenger ﷺ to possess such quality; — and who is next in praiseworthiness?" God's messenger ﷺ replied: "A believer who possesses a noble character and conduct."

## 29- Aslam Abu Rãfi'

Aslam Abu Rãfi' also was one of the attending companions (*Mawla*) of God's messenger ﷺ, upon whom be peace. He accepted Islam and embraced God's religion along with al-'Abbãs, but both of them concealed their faith during their stay in Mecca.

At one time, the polytheist Meccans and the Muslims relationship was governed by a temporary agreement of suspension of hostility for one year, known as the Truce of H̲udaibiyya. Among the articles of the agreement, it was covenanted that Muslims who desired to renege on their faith and return to Mecca were free to do so. On the other hand, the treaty stipulated that should a Meccan seek to become a Muslim and take refuge in Madina, to join the believers, he was to be extradited and returned to the Meccans. Such was the demand of the Meccans, who, even soon after that covenant broke their fragile truce, and hence, events deteriorated rapidly and led into the Muslims taking back Mecca in 630 C.E., eight years after their *Hijra* migration to Madina.

During the period of the truce of H̲udaibiyya, Aslam lived in Mecca, and he was commissioned by the heathen and polytheist Quraishis of Mecca to deliver a letter to God's messenger ﷺ, upon whom be peace. As soon as Aslam arrived to Madina, he declared his acceptance of Islam, and he sought permission to remain in Madina along with the early émigrés. However, because of the truce of H̲udaibiyya, God's messenger ﷺ, upon whom be peace, ordered him to return to Mecca, saying: "We can neither control the cold weather, nor do we take our covenants lightly."

Hence, Aslam returned to Mecca, and shortly after that incident, God's message reined throughout the Arabian peninsula. The Muslims took back Mecca, and Aslam moved to the blessed city of Madina and became a close companion of God's messenger ﷺ, upon whom be peace. God's messenger ﷺ foretold Aslam that poverty was going to become one of his major trials, and he also forbade him to stash any excess money he earns, and he informed him about the punishment reserved in the hereafter for one who hoards money and stash it for later.

Among the many narrators of prophetic traditions and sayings, Aslam Abu Rãfi' is often quoted in many collections of prophetic sayings, including in S̲ah̲ih̲ Bukhãri and S̲ah̲ih̲ Muslim, among others.

**418-** Kathïr bin Zaid narrated that Aslam Abu Rãfi' said: "I was with God's messenger ﷺ, upon whom peace, and he took me to visit al-Baqï' Cemetery (in Madina). When we reached one of the graves, God's messenger ﷺ, grumbled in extreme displeasure with something while turning his head to the other side, and thrice he said, 'Phew, phew, phew!' as though he disapproved something." Rãfi' thought that it concerned him, and he exclaimed: "O messenger of Allah, surely you are more dear to me than my own father and mother, please tell me what is it that disappointed you?" God's messenger ﷺ, upon whom peace, replied: "I once employed the man in this grave pit to go to the tribe of so and so to collect alms, and he cheated us in remitting a cloak. As I passed by his grave today, I was shown the man wearing that same cloak which is turned into a blazing fire inside his grave."

**419-** Sãlim Mawla Abu Rãfi' narrated that God's messenger ﷺ, upon whom be peace, once said to Aslam Abu Rãfi': "O Abu

Rãfi', what would you say should you one day become extremely poor?" Abu Rãfi' replied: "Would it not be better for me then to start by giving away what I have?" God's messenger ﷺ answered him: "That will be good! Tell me, how much money have you saved?" Abu Rãfi' replied: "Forty thousands, and, I am offering it right now for Allah' pleasure." God's messenger ﷺ said: "No! Don't do that. Give away some of it, save some, and satisfy the satisfy the needs of your own children with the balance." Abu Rãfi' then asked: "O messenger of Allah, do our children have rights upon us?" God's messenger ﷺ replied: "Yes, indeed! The right of the child upon his father, is that the father must teach him the Book of Allah."

**420-** 'Uthmãn bin Abdu- Rahmãn narrated in reference to the children's rights upon their parents, also quoting God's messenger ﷺ, upon whom be peace, to have said: "To teach him the Book of Allah, and to train them in the art of archery, and swimming,"

**421-** Yazïd, another narrator of the above prophetic tradition added that God's messenger ﷺ, upon whom be peace, also said: "And to bequeath him his birthright."[1]

**422-** 'Uthmãn bin 'Abdu-Rahmãn narrated, re Abu Salïm that when God's messenger ﷺ, upon whom be peace, told Abu Rãfi' about his fate, Abu Rãfi' asked: "O messenger of Allah, when is it that I will become poor?" God's messenger ﷺ replied: "After I leave this world."

Abu Sãlim added: "After God's messenger ﷺ passed, I saw Abu Rãfi' sitting in on a sidewalk, begging, 'Who wishes to give charity to and old blind man? Who wishes to give charity to a man who was foretold by God's messenger ﷺ, upon whom be peace, that he will be tried with poverty after him? Is there any one who wishes to distribute money in charity today? Indeed, Allah has the upper hand, the charitable person has the middle hand, and the recipient has the lower hand. Indeed, whoever begs for money he does not need, it will become a distinguished mark of shame by which he will be branded and known on the Day of Resurrection.

---

[1] i.e., to teach his children knowledge about Allah and the Religion of Islam.

Surely it is not permissible to give charity to a rich person, or to a healthy strong man."[1]

Abu Sãlim said: "A man once gave him four dirhams in charity, and Abu Rãfi' returned one of them back. The man became upset and said to him, 'O servant of Allah, do not reject my charity or deny me the right of this duty!' Abu Rãfi' replied, 'I am not rejecting your charity, but God's messenger ﷺ, upon whom be peace, had ordered me not to save anything over and above my immediate needs.' "

Abu Sãlim further added: "Later on in his life, I witnessed Abu Rãfi' regain his stature in the world, he became rich again, and he further begot ten children. I also heard him say about himself, 'I wish Abu Rãfi' had died poor.' "

## 30- Salmãn Al-Fãrisi

All praises are due to Allah, the Lord and Creator of the universe, and the best peace and blessings be upon His blessed messenger Muhammad ﷺ, upon whom be peace.

Salmãn al-Fãrisi, is the forerunner and the champion of the believers of Persia. He was adamant and relentless in his pursuit of his exalted goal, and he abounded with profound knowledge and deep wisdom.

Abu 'Abdullãh, (that is his patronym), Salmãn al-Fãrisi sought and embraced Islam at the hand of God's messenger ﷺ, upon whom be peace, and he became a beacon of knowledge and wisdom, and he became a close companion of God's messenger ﷺ, upon whom be peace. Salmãn was a noble and a compassionate man, and he was foretold by God's messenger ﷺ, upon whom be peace, that paradise longed to meet him.

Because of his clarity, correct understanding, and his close relationship with God's messenger ﷺ, upon whom be peace, Salmãn bore patiently the hardships and material adversities of this world, and his superior knowledge and wisdom helped him make his uphill

[1] In reference to impermissibility of giving charity to a healthy person, this does not mean that one should not help his brother when in need, but rather it connotes, and depending on one's means, that such help may be considered as a gift or a loan.

battle with life easy and manageable, and his legacy will surely live forever.

The particular spiritual aspect we wish to elucidate in this record about Salmãn al-Fãrisi, God be pleased with him, deals with enduring one's challenges in this life with patience and perseverance, to overcome anxiety with lucid faith, and the benefit of giving things their proper worth.

**423-** Anas bin Mãlik, God be pleased with him, narrated that God's messenger ﷺ, upon whom be peace, once said: "The forerunners[1] are four: I am the forerunner of the Arabs, Suhayb is the forerunners of the Byzantines, Salmãn al-Fãrisi is the forerunner of the Persians, and Bilãl is the forerunner of the Abassinians."

## A Wedding In Kinda

**424-** Muzãhim reported that Salmãn once told the story of his marriage to a wealthy woman from Kinda, Persia. After the traditional wedding ceremony which took place at a relative's house, Salmãn's friends walked with him in a procession to the bride's house, and when they arrived at her door, Salmãn turned to his companions and said: "Now you may return to your homes, may Allah reward you for coming to bless this wedding." Hence, Salmãn did not invite them to enter his bride's house, nor did he introduce her to them as it were the so-called civilized popular customs of the culture of the time in Persia.

When Salmãn looked at the dwellings of his wealthy wife and found the house fully draped, he commented: "Are your walls damaged by humidity or something so that you had to cover them, or was the Ka'ba, the House of God Almighty, moved to Kinda?" Hence, Salmãn did not enter the house until all the decorative curtains were taken down except for the curtain covering the main entrance door. Finally, when he entered the house, he found it excessively furnished as well, and he asked: "To whom does this furniture and their fineries belong?" The family of the bride replied: "To you and to your wife!" Salmãn responded: "My bosom friend ﷺ, upon whom be peace, did not advise me thus. My bosom friend ﷺ advised me

---

[1] Arb. *Sãbiqün*; forerunners in responding to God's message

not to append more accessories and furnishings than a traveler would carry with him for a short journey."

Salmãn then saw several servants in the house, and he asked: "What are these female servants doing here?" The family of the bride replied: "They are here to serve you and your wife!" Salmãn pondered for a moment and said: "My bosom friend ﷺ, upon whom be peace, did not advise me thus. He advised me to only keep the woman I wed in my house. Should I become attracted to their silkiness and femininity, and should I victimize any of them, they would have brethen, and my sin will be equal to their." Salmãn looked again, and he saw other maidens attending to his wife, and he addressed them by saying: "Are you going to stay here all night? Wouldn't you be so kind to leave me alone with my wife?" They replied in the affirmative, and they withdrew and left the house. Salmãn followed them to the door, and he locked the main entrance, and closed the curtain behind it.

When he returned to his bride, Salmãn sat with her for a moment, and he gently anointed her forehead with his hand, prayed for God's blessings upon their union, and he said to her: "Would you be willing to do something if I ask you?" She replied: "I am sitting in the company of a sire who must be obeyed." Salmãn then said: "My bosom friend ﷺ, upon whom be peace, advised me that when I join with my family, we should first join together in praying to Almighty Allah, and to do what pleases Him." Following that conversation, Salmãn and his bride went to separate quarters in their house for prayer, and they prayed as much as God willed. When they concluded their prayers, they joined together in their matrimony, and Salmãn satisfied in her what a husband satisfies with his wife, and she satisfied in hi what a wife satisfies in her husband.

In the morning, some of his friends saw him, and they asked him: "How did you find your Persian wife?" Salmãn ignored their question, and turned to the other side. His friends insisted on asking the same question again, and Salmãn pretended not to hear it. On the third time, he retorted: "God Almighty created the curtains, the veils, and the doors to conceal what is behind them. Therefore, must one of you ask a question, it should relate to what he witnesses, and on the other hand, what is veiled to his knowledge, he should refrain from investigating it. I heard God's messenger ﷺ, upon whom be peace, say: 'Whoever talks about his wedding night to a friend, the bride and the groom will be like two donkeys mounting one another in the open.' "

**425-** Also in reference to the above account, and prior to Slamãn's wedding in Kinda, Ibn 'Abbãs, God be pleased with him, said: "One time, Salmãn returned from a journey, and Omar bin al-Khattãb came out to welcomed him, saying, 'I truly accept and recognize your trueness to your Lord, and I am proud of you as a servant of God Almighty.' In his reply, Salmãn said, 'If you think so, then give me a woman from your family in marriage.'"

Omar remained silent. Seeing that, Salmãn commented: "You accept me as a true servant of Allah, and yet you do not accept me to become your in-law?"

Salmãn went to his house, and in the morning a delegation from the family of Omar knocked at his door, and Salmãn said to them: "Is there something you need?" They replied: " Yes indeed." Salmãn asked: "First of all, what is it? And then, I do not know whether I have the means to satisfy what you want!" The people said, 'We have come to ask you to halt your intention of betrothal to Omar's family.' Salmãn replied: "I swear by God Almighty, it is not his political status or influence that I sought! When Omar welcomed me the way he did, I said to my self that he is indeed a righteous man, and perhaps Allah will bring out of my seed and his seed a blessed servant."

Ibn 'Abbãs, God be pleased with him, continued: "Hence, the question of betrothal to Omar's family was put aside, and later on Salmãn got married to a most beautiful and rich woman from Kinda, Persia..." *ibid.*

**426-** 'Abdul-Malik bin Juraij, narrated that Zãthãn al-Kindi said: "We once visited 'Ali, God bless his countenance, and the people felt happy in his company, and they found him in a comforting pleasant mood. Someone asked, 'O prince of the believers, tell us something about your close companions.' 'Ali replied, 'Which one of my companions do you want to know about?' They said, 'The companions of God's messenger ﷺ, upon whom be peace, of course!' 'Ali further inquired, 'All of the companions of God's messenger ﷺ, upon whom be peace, are my companions. Which one do you want me to talk about?' They replied, 'Tell us about those of whom you spoke most reverently, and affectionately, and who are most blessed, — tell us about Salmãn al-Fãrisi!' 'Ali, God bless his countenance, then said, 'Who else besides Salmãn do you expect to be a gnostic of the prophetic caliber of Luqmãn al-Hakïm? Salmãn is one of us, the family of *Ãl al-Bait,* the household of God's messenger ﷺ, and he is a blessed treasure of which we all benefit. He fathomed the primal knowledge and the ultimate one, and he read both the primal book and the last revelation. Surely, Salmãn is an inexhaustible ocean of knowledge.' "

**427-** 'Ammãr bin Zuraiq narrated, re Umu Ddardã', the wife of Abu Dardã', that Salmãn al-Fãrisi, God be pleased with him, once visited Abu Dardã'' house, and he found Umu Ddardã', his wife, looking unhappy, apathetic, and disinterested in her appearance. Salmãn asked her: "What is disturbing you, O Umu Ddardã'?' She replied: "Your brother Abu Dardã' has no more interest in women. He fasts his days, and prays all his nights!" Salmãn then turned to Abu Dardã' and gently said: "Surely your family has rights upon you. Surely you can pray, rest, and fast, and you may also break your fast as well!"

When the story reached God's messenger ﷺ, upon whom be peace, he commented: "Indeed, Salmãn is endowed with great knowledge."

**428-** In another narration of the above account, 'Aoun bnu Abi Juhaifa narrated that Salmãn al-Fãrisi, God be pleased with him, once visited Abu Dardã', and he found his wife Umu Ddardã' emotionally upset and neglectful of her appearance. Salmãn asked her: "What is upsetting you?" She replied: "It seems that your brother Abu Dardã' has lost interest in this world. He stands up all night in prayers, and he fasts his days!"

Later on, Salmãn invited Abu Dardã' to visit him, and he presented him with some food. Abu Dardã' replied: "I am fasting." Salmãn said: "I will not eat until you eat!" Abu Dardã' felt some pressure to share food with Salmãn, hence, he broke his fast and stayed overnight at Salmãn's house. In the middle of the night, Abu Dardã' walk up to pray, Salmãn was up, and he delayed him for a moment and said, 'O Abu Dardã', surely your Lord has rights upon you, your family has rights upon you, and your body has rights upon you! Give each one of them their due rights. Therefore, you may fast, break your fast, sleep, and have marital relations, etc.' "

"Before dawn, Salmãn said to Abu Dardã', 'Let us go now.' Hence, they refreshed their ablution, prayed two *rak'ãt* at the house, after which, they went to join the congregational prayer at the mosque. As soon as God's messenger ﷺ, upon whom be peace, finished leading the prayers, Abu Dardã' went to him and told him what Salmãn did. God's messenger ﷺ, reiterated, 'O Abu Dardã', surely your body has rights upon you ...' and he repeated everything, exactly as Salmãn said it."

**429-** 'Amru bnu Murra narrated, re Abi al-Bakhtari that a man from the tribe of Bani 'Abbãs travelled once with Salmãn al-Fãrisi, and when they reached the *Dajla*, Tigris River, they stopped to drink some water. Salmãn said to his companion: "Drink more!" The man replied: "My thirst is quenched." Salmãn instanced: "Do you see how much your drink of water has decreased this river?" The man replied with astonishment: "And what could a man's drink of water decrease of this giant river?" Salmãn replied: "Knowledge is like that! It is an ocean, and it does not diminish. Take from it what benefit you."

**430-** 'Ubaid bin Wãqid narrated that Salmãn al-Fãrisi once said to Huthaifa: "O brother of the Tribe of Bani 'Abs, knowledge is an ocean, and surely one's span of life in this world is too short to encompass all of it, and no one can ever encompass all of it. Get the share of knowledge which is most advantageous for your religious success, and forgo the balance. You do not have to suffer its greater hardships."

**431-** Al-Thawri narrated that Tãriq bin Shahãb once desired to learn about the nature of Salmãn al-Fãrisi's devotion, so he invited himself and stayed overnight at his house. Salmãn understood Tãriq's intention, and he opted to provide an easy to follow tradition that common people can comply with.

At Salmãn's house, T̲ãriq bin Shahãb stayed up most of the night only to find out that just shortly prior to the *fajr,* dawn prayers, Salmãn woke up, took his ablution, and he prayed two *rak'ãt sunna* prayer at home prior to attending the congregational prayers at the mosque. It seems that Salmãn's performance did not meet with T̲ãriq's expectations, and hence, he inquired about it. After the mourning prayers, Salmãn used this opportunity to address the question in public, wherein he said: "O people! You must be keen in your devotion, and you must observe the obligatory five daily prayers, for they are protection against evil, and they are penance for the expiation of one's own failures, as well as they wash away sins committed in-between the two prayers by one's limbs, with the exception of the major sins."

**432-** T̲ãriq bin Shahãb narrated that Salmãn said: "Once people offer their nightly *'Isha* prayers, they branch into three distinct ranks: (1) One person looses and he does not benefit from his prayers; (2) another person is blessed by his attentiveness to his devotion, and therefore, he is free of indebtedness; and, (3) a third person comes out of his prayers empty handed, he earns nothing, and owes nothing."

"As to the first person, he takes advantage of the darkness of the night and of people's sleep to indulge in evil doing, hence, he loses and does not benefit. The second person takes advantage of the darkness of the night and of people's sleep to stand up all night in prayers, hence, he benefits and he owes nothing, and finally, the third person, earns nothing and loses nothing, for as soon as he finishes his nightly prayers, he goes to sleep until dawn. O Brothers! Forthermore, try not to indulge in deep investigation of others' performances. Instead, take advantage of your own opportunities, persevere, and be steadfast."

**433-** Abu Buraida narrated that God's messenger ﷺ, upon whom be peace, said: "Gabriel, the Trustworthy Spirit (*ruh̲u'l Amin*), descended upon me, and he told me that Allah, the Most Exalted particularly loves four people from among my companions." People asked: "O messenger of Allah, who are they?" He replied: " Ali, Salmãn, Abu Tharr, and al-Miqdãd."

**434-** Anas bin Mãlik, God be pleased with him, narrated that he heard God's messenger ﷺ, upon whom be peace, say: "Paradise particularly yearns to meet four of my followers, 'Ali, al-Miqdãd, 'Ammãr, and Salmãn."

## Embracing Islam

**435-** Abu't-T̲ufail 'Ãmir bin Wã'ilah narrated that Salmãn al-Fãrisi, God be pleased with him, said: "I come from the Tribe of Jai, from of Isbahan, Persia, and the people of my town used to worship snow-white Caucasian horses.[1] In my heart, I knew that what they worshiped lacked substance and had no truth to their claim of its divinity. I often inquired about God Almighty, and one day, I was told by a wise man: "You will find the true religion you are seeking in the West of Persia."

One day, I left my homeland, and I traveled as far West as the city of Mosul, in Northern Iraq. Thereat, I inquired about the city's most renowned gnostic, and I was directed towards a hermitage, wherein lived a monk who worshiped the Almighty Allah, the Lord of the universe. When I arrived to his cell, I introduced myself, 'I am a man from the East, and I have come to seek what is good. If you agree, I wish to remain in your company, I will serve you here, and in return, I wish you to teach me some of the knowledge with which Allah has endowed you?' The monk accepted, and hence I remained in his company as long as Allah intended. My master shared with me his limited ration of grains, vinegar, and oil, and thus we lived. One day, my master fell in his last illness, and when I saw him dying, I sat near his head, and I cried. The monk said to me, 'Why are you crying?' I replied, 'I am now faraway from my family and roots, and before I found you, I had left my homeland in search of the truth, and indeed, Allah has blessed me to meet you and to stay in your company, this long. You treated me well, and you taught me some of what Allah, the most exalted, has taught you, and now that death has come to take you, I do not know what to do, or where to go!'

The dying monk replied: "Do not worry. I have a brother who

---

[1] Arb. *Balqã.*

lives in such and such place. Go to him, for he is on the right path, convey to him my best regards of peace, and tell him that I have entrusted you to his care."

Salmãn continued: "After his death, I traveled to the place he described, and there I found the monk he told me about, I said to him, 'Your brother so and so sends his best regards of peace to you.' He replied, 'Peace and blessings be upon him as well. Tell me his news?' I replied: 'He passed away.' I then narrated my story, and I told him that his brother had instructed me to accompany him. The monk accepted me, and I remained in his company as long as Allah, the most exalted, intended, and he shared with me his food rations as his brother did earlier. My new master also was advanced in age, and when he fell in his last illness, I came and sat near his bed, and I cried over him. He asked me, 'Why are you crying?' I replied, 'I left my homeland, and Allah granted me the good company of so and so who was extremely good to me, and he taught me some of what Allah taught him. On his death bed, he entrusted me to your care, and indeed, you took good care of me, and you taught me some of what Allah taught you. Now that death has come to take you, here again, I do not know where to turn or where to go!'

The dying monk replied: "Do not worry. I have a brother who lives on the way to Rome. Go to him, for he is surely on the right path, convey to him my best regards of peace, and tell him that I have ordered you to go to him, and that I have entrusted you to his care."

Salmãn continued: "After the death of the monk, I traveled to where he told me, and when I reached the man the second master told me about, I said to him, 'Your brother so and so sends his best regards of peace to you.' He replied, 'Peace and blessings be upon him as well. Tell me his news?' I replied: 'He passed away.' I then narrated my story, and I told him that his brother had instructed me to remain in his company. The man accepted to keep me in his company, he treated me well, and he taught me some of what Allah, the Lord of majesty and glory, taught him."

Salmãn continued: "The third monk was very old, and again, when he fell ill, I sat near his bed, and when he saw me crying near his bed, he asked me, 'Why are you crying?' I replied: "You know my story since I left my homeland, and then Almighty Allah blessed me with your good company. Now that death has come to take you, I still do not know where to turn or where to go!"

The monk replied: "Not anywhere! In these days, my dear brother, I am not acquainted with any living person who even follows the true religion of Jesus, the son of Mary, peace be upon him. However, to the best of my knowledge, in this era, there may have appeared, or yet to come, a messenger of God Almighty, in the land of the Tribe of Tihāma, in the southwestern coast of Arabia, and who would reveal God's message. After I die, stay here at my hut, and inquire from the traveling caravans that cross this land. Ask the Arab Hijazite merchants whether a prophet had appeared among them lately. If they answer you in the affirmative, then this is the one who is foretold by Jesus, peace be upon him. Among his signs, you will see the seal of prophethood in-between his shoulders, he accepts and eats from a gift, and he does not eat from charity."

Salmān continued: "After the man died, I stayed in his hermitage and whenever a caravan passed by, I inquired, 'What country do you come from?' Finally, one day, a caravan from Mecca came by me, and when they told me that they were from Hijāz, I asked, 'Has there appeared among you someone who claims to be a prophet?' They replied, 'Yes, indeed!' I said: 'Would someone among you accept me to be his slave for the price of carrying me on the back of his camel, and feeding me the needed chunk of bread until we reach Mecca, and when we arrive there, he can either sell me as a slave to someone to recuperate his money, or he may keep me for himself.' Someone in that group said, 'I will do that.' Hence, I became his salve, and he carried me behind him and fed me the little morsel of food I needed per day until we reached Mecca. Therein, the man used me to work for him in a date plantation field along with other slaves he owned."

"One day, I took a walk through the streets of Mecca, and by chance, I met a woman servant who had come originally from my homeland. I chatted with her, and I was extremely happy to speak again in my mother tongue. I was also happy to learn from her that her master and her entire household had secretly accepted God's message of Islam, and that they follow His messenger ﷺ. I asked the woman to tell me where to find God's messenger ﷺ, upon whom be peace, and she told me that he usually sits with his companions near the Black Stone at the Ka'ba, and that they gather there from the time you hear the cockcrowing of the Meccan cock, and they disperse after dawn and before the sunrise."

"That evening, I cut short my stay with my co-workers, claiming to have some stomach irregularity, in fear that they may discover my intent. I stayed up all night, and at the right time before dawn, I went to the Ka'ba, and I found God's messenger ﷺ, upon whom be peace, sitting by the black stone, and his companions were sitting in a semi-circle before him. I was coming towards them from behind, and as I neared the gathering, he knew my intention, and he allowed his cloak to slip down his shoulders. I looked astonishingly, and I saw the seal of prophethood in-between his shoulder blades.. I breathed a sigh of comfort, saying to myself, *Allahu Akbar* (surely Allah is the greatest), this is the first sign my teacher told me about."

"The following night, I did the same thing with my companions, so that they would not discover my plans or question of my intention, and in fear that they would report me to our master. I also kept some dates aside, and just at the right time I knew that God's messenger ﷺ, upon whom be peace, would be meeting with his companions, I went to the Ka'ba again, and when I reached them, I gently placed the dates before him. He asked me, 'What is that?' I replied, 'A charity!' God's messenger ﷺ, upon whom be peace, then said to his companions, 'Eat from it.' However, he did not touch them. I again breathed a sigh of comfort, saying to myself, *Allahu Akbar* (surely Allah is the greatest), this is the second sign my teacher told me about."

"On the third night, again I did the same with my co-workers, and before dawn, I brought some dates to the gathering at the time when God's messenger ﷺ, upon whom be peace, gathered with his companions by the Ka'ba. This time, when I placed the dates before him, and when he asked me, 'What is this?' I replied, 'A gift!' He immediately reached them, he ate some, and the people did the same. I immediately exclaimed, 'I bear witness that there is no god except Allah, and I bear witness that you are His messenger.'"

"After I sat there for a moment, God's messenger ﷺ, upon whom be peace, asked me to relate my story. When I told him what happened, he said to me, 'Go and buy back your freedom.' "

Salmān continued: "When I reached my companion-master, I said to him, 'I have come to buy back my freedom!' He replied, 'Yes indeed! I will give you back your freedom for the price of planting one hundred seedlings of date palm trees, and when I verify that they all took roots, and that they are free from disease, you also must bring me the weight of a date pit in gold, and only then you may go free.' "

Salmān said: "I went back to God's messenger ﷺ, upon whom be peace, and I related to him what the man said. He replied, 'Give him what he asks of you, and also bring me a bucket of water from the well you will use to irrigate the plants.' "

"I immediately went to the man, and I made the deal with him following the conditions he stipulated. With his permission, I then filled a bucket of water from the central well in the plantation field, and I took it back to God's messenger ﷺ, upon whom be peace, who in turn prayed over it. God's messenger ﷺ also asked the companions to collect and to give me the needed one hundred seedlings, and when they did, I went back, and I planted the seedlings."

Salmān continued: "I swear by God Almighty that not a single seedling failed us, and as soon as the man verified that, I went back to God's messenger ﷺ and told him the same. God's messenger ﷺ then called upon the companions to bring him a piece of gold of the weight we agreed upon with the man, and again, I immediately went back to the man and placed the piece of gold before him. When the man placed his specified measure on the other scale of the balance, my piece of gold seemed to weigh more, for nothing moved, and the man accepted the barter."

"I brought back to God's messenger ﷺ the date pit that determined the conclusion of the deal, and he looked at it and commented, 'I swear by Allah, that even if you had agreed with him to give him the weight of such and such measure of date pits, the piece you gave him would weigh more.' "

Salmãn continued: "From that day on, I went to God's messenger ﷺ, upon whom be peace, and I stayed in his company until the end."[1]

**436-** Yazīd bin Abi Habīb narrated, re Abi al-Tufail al-Bakri, that Salmãn al-Fãrisi told him: "I come from the city of Jai (in Asbahan, Persia). One day, the Almighty Allah inspired my heart to ponder the question, 'Who created the heavens and the earth?'"

"Hence, prompted by such concerns and inner quest, I sought an old man I knew, who spoke very little and who, out of self restraint, had kept a distance from the city people. When I reached him, I asked, 'What is the best of religions, (way of life)?' He replied, 'Why would you want to talk about this subject? Are you seeking a religion other than that of your fathers?' I cautiously answered: 'No, I am not, but I would like to know, 'Who created the heavens and the earth, and what is the best religion to follow?' The old man said to me, 'To my knowledge, only one monk follows the true religion today, and he lives in the city of Mosul, in Iraq.'"

"Hence, I traveled to Mosul, and I found the monk I was told to meet. Thereat, I stayed with him, and I worshiped what he worshiped. He was an old man, and he lived on little provisions. He fasted all his days, and he prayed all his nights. Approximately, three years later, at his deathbed, I asked him, 'You must advise me what to do now, and where to go?' The man replied, 'I know of no one in the East who believes and worships what I worship. Go West. Find a monk I once knew and who lives at the edge of the Arabian peninsula, and give him my regards of peace.'"

"After the monk died, I traveled to where he told me, and I found the man he described. I conveyed to him the greetings of his brother, and I told him of his death. Thereat, I remained in his company for another three years, and again, at his deathbed, I

---

[1] We must note here that it is commonly known that Salmãn al-Fãrisi's story took place in Medina, the City of God's messenger ﷺ, upon whom be peace, as supported by many prophetic traditions and accounts reported by the companions. The entire story can also be found in the book *Tãrikh Baghdad* (History of Baghdad). However, the above narration is reported hereinabove as I found it in the book of Imam al-Asfahãni, *Hilyat'ul Awliya*, and the reader will find in the next account 434, a variation of the same story as quoted and reported by different narrators, referring to a different gathering, and also as told by Salmãn al-Fãrisi, God be pleased with him.

requested him to guide me where to go after he dies. He replied, 'I am not acquainted with any one on this earth today who worships what I worship except for a very old monk who lives in the region of 'Amoriya, in Philistine, and I am not sure whether he is still alive!' "

"After the monk died, again I traveled to where I was told, and luckily, I found the man he described to me. Thereat, I stayed with him, and this time, the man was financially comfortable. Sometimes later, when he neared his death, I sought his advice, and I inquired from him, 'Where do you want me to go after you die?' He replied, 'I am not acquainted with any living person who worships what I worship. However, if you happen to live in a time, where a man from the descendants of the House of Abraham, upon whom be peace, will appear, — and I am not sure whether you will live to meet him or not! — I myself have had a strong desire to live to meet him, however, if you should meet him, then follow him, for that is the true way,and that is the religion of God Almighty. Among his signs, is that some of his people will label him a magician, an insane person, and a prognosticator. He accepts and eats from what is given to him as a gift, and he does not eat from charity; and you will also see the seal of prophethood in-between his shoulder blades.' "

Salmān continued: "I resided in my place for a while, and one day, a caravan of merchants from Madina crossed out path. I inquired from them, 'Who are you?' They replied, 'We are merchants. We make a living from trading. However, there appeared a man from the descendants of Abraham in Mecca, and he migrated to Madina, and the entire city is now under his control. As a result, his people from Mecca have declared war on him and on his followers, so we feared for our livelihood, and therefore, we decided to seek shelter and safety somewhere else.' "

"I asked, 'What are they saying about him?' The merchants replied, 'They say that he is a magician, a prognosticator, or maybe he is an insane person!' Hearing that, I said to myself, 'These are his signs.' I further inquired, 'Who is the leader of this caravan, would you please guide me to him?' When I came before the leader of the caravan, I requested him, 'Would you please take me to Madina?' He replied, 'What would you pay me?' I said, 'I have nothing to give you, but if you agree to carry me there, I will be indebted to you, and I will be your slave.' The man accepted the barter, and he carried me to Madina. Thereat, he placed me to work for him at a date plantation he owned, and I worked there very hard. I seldom had any food, and I mostly lived on water, just like cattle, until the bones of my back protruded, and I could see my pectoral bones. I did not know Arabic then, and not many people in that city spoke my Persian tongue."

"One day, an old woman of Persian origin came by the date plantation to get some water. When I spoke to her in my mother tongue, she understood me, and as we chatted a little, I asked her, 'Do you know that man that appeared lately, and would you please point him out to me?' She replied, 'He usually passes by here after the dawn prayers, or sometime in mid-morning.'"

Salmãn continued: "The next day, I kept some dates aside, and I waited for him. As he passed, I followed him to the mosque, and as he sat amidst his companions, I went there, and I presented him with the dates. God's messenger ﷺ, upon whom be peace, looked at them and then said to me, 'What is this? Is it a charity or a gift?' I understood what he meant, and I made a gesture pointing out that it is a charity. He immediately said, 'Give it to these people sitting here.' As I did, I said to myself, 'This is one of his signs.' The next morning, I brought another measure of dates and placed them before him. God's messenger ﷺ, upon whom be peace, again inquired, 'What is this?' I hastened to say, 'A gift!' He ﷺ then ate one, and he called his companions to share them with him. He then saw me stealthily attempting to look over his shoulders. He recognized my intention, and he allowed his cloak to slowly drop below his shoulders, and when I saw what I saw, I became bewildered, and I jumped out of my place, I kissed him all over, and I held tight to him. God's messenger ﷺ, upon whom be peace, then asked me, 'What do you want?' And after I told him my story, he said, 'You sold yourself to these people and chose the condition of slavery in order to come here, and now, you must go back to them, and buy back your freedom.' " *ibid.*, (*See Account 433*)

**437-** Sulaimãn al-Taymi narrated that Salmãn al-Fãrisi, God be pleased with him, said: "I served a dozen of masters, one after another, before I met God's messenger ﷺ, upon whom be peace."

**438-** Sa'ïd bin al-Musayyib, God be pleased with him narrated that Salmãn God be pleased with him, said: "God's messenger ﷺ, upon whom be peace, entrusted us with a promise which none of us fulfilled. He said, 'Suffice yourselves in this world with as little provisions as a traveler carries on a short journey,' and we all failed to follow his admonition."

**439-** In another narration of the above account, al-A'amash reported that Sa'ad once visited Salmãn during his last illness, and he said to him: "Be happy O Abu 'Abdullãh! When God's messenger ﷺ, upon whom be peace, passed away, he was most pleased with you." Salmãn replied: "How is that O Sa'ad? I heard God's messenger ﷺ, upon whom be peace, say, 'Suffice yourselves with as little provisions[1] in this world, and as much as a traveler may carry with him on a short journey.' "

**440-** Again in another narration of the above account, al-A'amash narrated that Sa'ad bin Abi Waqqãss visited Salmãn during his last illness when Salmãn cried. Sa'ad inquired: "Why would you cry when you will soon reunite with your beloved companions, you will see and drink from the *Hawdh*, the pond of eternal satisfaction of God's messenger ﷺ, upon whom be peace, and when you know that God's messenger ﷺ, upon whom be peace, passed away, he was pleased with you!"

Salmãn replied: "I am not crying in fear of death, nor am I in any way attached to this world, but I happen to remember the words of God's messenger ﷺ, upon whom be peace, saying, 'Suffice yourselves in this world with as little provisions as a traveler carries with him on a short journey,' and here I am, and when I just look around me now, and I saw all these luxury pillows surrounding me, this made me cry!"

Sa'ad bin Abi Waqqãss, God be pleased with him, commented: "I immediately looked around, and I saw nothing but a timeworn washing basin next to his bed!"

Sa'ad then asked Salmãn: "Advise us O Abu 'Abdullãh. We want to make a covenant with you, and which we promise not to break after you pass." Salmãn replied: "Remember your Lord when

[1] Arb. *bulgha*, i.e., leather slippers.

you endeavor something, remember Him when you judge something, and remember Him when you raise your hand to pledge something."

**441-** Mawriq al-'Ujali narrated that after Salmãn's death, they searched his house, and they found no more than a day's provision for a single person, a saddle blanket, a couple of cooking utensils, and no more than twenty dirhams."

**442-** 'Abdullãh, son of Imam Ahmad bin Hanbal, God be pleased with him, narrated that al-Hassan, God be pleased with him said: "Salmãn was once commissioned to govern over about thirty thousand men, and he was given a salary of five thousand dirhams, most of which he distributed in charity. Once he had spent his wage, he never solicited more. His light infrequent meal sometimes did not exceed more than a handful of dates or grains, and he lived a simple modest life. Salmãn had a single oversized timeworn cloak which he rolled up and held by hand to ease his movement, and when he delivered a sermon, half of it was hung over his shoulders, and he stood over the other half."

**443-** 'Abdul A'alã bin Abi al-Masãwir narrated that al-Hãrith bin 'Umaira said: "I once went to the marketplace in the city and I met some friends with whom I chatted a little. Somewhere within the range of my view, I noticed a man wearing an old worn garment, and he was sitting in front of his house, busy wielding a red leather belt. When he perceived that I noticed him, he looked at me, nodded his head, and he made a gesture with his hand, and he shouted, 'O servant of Allah, wait in your place for me!' I immediately stood up and I asked my friends, 'Who is that man?' They replied, 'This is Salmãn!' Meanwhile, the man went inside his house, and he came out shortly after that wearing a clean white robe, and he cheerfully hastened towards me, shook hands with me, and he then said to me, 'How are you doing?' I was in shock, and I said to him, 'O servant of Allah, who are you? We have never met before this day, nor do we know each other! What do you want?' Salmãn replied, 'But of course! I swear by Him Who holds the destiny of my life that as soon as I saw you, my soul recognized your soul. Are you not al-Hãrith bin 'Umaira?' I said in amazement, expecting him to explain himself, 'Indeed I am!' He continued, 'I heard God's messenger ﷺ, upon whom be peace, say, 'Souls are loyal soldiers.

Among them, those who recognize the sovereignty of Allah will know one another and live in harmony; while those that negate the sovereignty of Allah, will disagree and be indifferent towards one another.' "

**444-** Müsa al-Jahni narrated that 'Atiyya bin 'Ãmer said: "Salmãn al-Fãrisi, God be pleased with him, was once invited to a meal at a companions's house, and as a gesture of pleasure in hospitality and love for his guest, the host insisted earnestly on Salmãn to eat more, Salmãn pulled out, excused himself, and said, 'Enough for me! That is enough food for me. God's messenger ﷺ, upon whom be peace, once said to me, 'People who eat their fill in this world, will be the most hungry in the hereafter. O Salmãn, this world is a confinement for the believer, and it is a paradise for the disbeliever.' "

**445-** 'Abdullãh, son of Imam Ahmad bin Hanbal, God be pleased with him, narrated that Salmãn al-Fãrisi, God be pleased with him, used to regularly shave his head, and when someone asked him about it, he replied, 'God's messenger ﷺ, upon whom be peace, said, 'True life is that of the hereafter.' "[1]

**446-** Habib bin al-Shah¨d narrated that 'Abdullãh bin Buraida said: "Salmãn used to earn his livelihood by working with his hands, and when he earned some money, he used to buy meat, or fish, and invite the deprived ones to share in his meal."

**447-** Abu Ghaffãr narrated that Salmãn al-Fãrisi, God be pleased with him, said: "I like to earn my livelihood from my own sweat, and I like to work with my own hands."

**448-** Sulaimãn al-Teemi narrated that Salmãn al-Fãrisi, God be pleased with him, said: "If only people know how much help Allah grants the weak, they would never take pleasure in showing off the excess Allah endowed them with."

**449-** 'Abdullãh bin Siwãr narrated that Salmãn al-Fãrisi, God be pleased with him, once had the intention to betroth a woman from the Tribe of Bani Laith, and he took Abu Ddardã' with him to ask for her hand in marriage on his behalf. When they arrived

[1] i.e., The true comfort and delight of living is surely that of the eternal life in the abode of the hereafter.

to that family's house, Salmãn waited outside, and Abu Ddardã' sought permission and entered to speak to her father. Abu Ddardã' spoke highly of his friend Salmãn al-Fãrisi, his illustrious qualities, his early acceptance of Islam and his lofty companionship of God's messenger ﷺ, upon whom be peace. Abu Ddardã' then informed the family of Salmãn's intention. The girl's father replied: "We will not give our daughter in marriage to Salmãn, but should it be your wish, we will be honored to give her hand to you in marriage!" Abu Ddardã' felt favored and honored to accept the offer, and sometimes later, and under the circumstances of the moment, he only came out of the house hours later being married the girl.

When Abu Ddardã' came out of the house, he said to Salmãn: "Something else happened here today, and I am ashamed to tell you about it!" Salmãn asked: "What is it, and why where you there so long?" When Abu Ddardã' told him the story, Salmãn congratulated him and remarked: "I am the one who should be ashamed of himself before you my brother, and for seeking to betroth a woman Allah has destined her to be your wife!"

**450-** Imam Ahmad bin Hanbal, God be pleased with him, narrated that a man once visited Salmãn al-Fãrisi, God be pleased with him, and saw him engaged in kneading a dough for backing his daily bread. The man was surprised, and he commented: "What are you doing! Do you regularly do that yourself?" Salmãn replied: "I heave sent my helper in an errand, and I hate to impose two jobs on him in the same day." The man then said: "I bring you the greetings of so and so." Salmãn asked: "When did you arrive to this town?" The man replied: "It's been some time since I arrived to this town!" Salmãn then commented: "To convey someone's greeting is a trust, and should one fail to deliver it at the time he reaches his destination, he will be asked about it on the Day of Judgment."

**451-** Muhammad bin 'Abdullãh al-Hadhrami narrated that al-Ash'ath Ibn Qays and Jurair bin 'Abdullãh al-Bajãli once stayed in Madina, but they had never met Salmãn al-Fãrisi, God be pleased with him. One day, they arrived from a journey to Syria, and they asked to see Salmãn, and after greeting him, one of them inquired: "Are you Salmãn al-Fãrisi?" He replied in the affirmative. The man then asked: "Are you the bosom companion of God's messenger ﷺ, upon whom be peace?" Salmān replied: "I do not know what do you mean by that!" The two men became suspicious, and they said to one another: "May be he is not the man we are looking for?"

Hearing that, Salmān said: "Indeed, I am the man you are looking for, and I have seen God's messenger ﷺ, upon whom be peace, and I sat with him. However, his true companions should be the ones who will ultimately enter paradise with him on the Day of Judgment. Now, tell me what do you want?" They replied: "We were sent by one of your brethren who lives in Syria, and who had asked us to visit you." Salmān asked: "Who is it?" They replied: "Abu Ddardā' " Salmān smiled as he asked the two men: "Then where is the gift he sent me with you?" The two men looked surprised by the question, and they replied: "He did not trust us with anything to bring you!" Salmān continued insisting and pressuring the two men: "Fear Allah, and deliver the trust. No one has ever visited me, coming from his side, but carrying a gift from my brother for me."

The two men became agitated, as they replied: "Do not accuse us of such allegation. If you do not trust us, here is our merchandise, keep it in your custody until you receive news from him." Salmān said: "I have nothing to do with your merchandise. Just give me the gift my brother has entrusted you to bring me!" The men replied: "We swear by God Almighty that he did not send you any gift with us. He just said that 'There is a man who lives in your city, and whenever God's messenger ﷺ, upon whom be peace, sat with him, he did not wish that anyone else join them. Therefore, should you meet him, please convey to him my regards of peace.' Salmān then said: "And peace upon him as well. This is it! What better gift do you want me to expect you to carry from my beloved brother? And is there a gift better than the regards of peace — a bounteous and a blessed salutation from Allah, the Lord of majesty and glory?"

**452-** Al-A'amash narrated that 'Abdullāh bin Hanzala said: "We once joined a campaign lead by Salmān al-Fārisi, God be pleased with him. One evening, we were sitting listening to a recital from *Suratu Maryam,*[1] and someone in the audience became extremely

[1] *Qur'an; Mary, Chapter XIX.*

upset, and to the point that he insulted her and her son! We immediately jumped at him and hit him without mercy in defense of God's messenger Jesus and his mother, upon both of whom be peace. The injured man went to Salmãn, the commander of the army then, and he reported us to him. Immediately, Salmãn came to see us, and he said firmly, 'Why did you people beat this man?' We replied, 'We were reading *Suratu Maryam*, and he unjustly insulted her and her son!' Salmãn said: 'And why do have to challenge people's feelings? Have you not heard Allah, the Lord of Majesty and Glory's say, ‹ Do not insult those who call upon lords besides Allah, thus causing them to insult Allah in ignorance, and without knowledge (of what they are saying) › (*Qur'an 6:108*). Salmãn then turned to the people who had gathered around him by then, and he addressed them, saying, 'O Arabs! Did you not at one time uphold the most evil – so called – religious practices humanity has ever known? And did you not at one time live below most standards humanity has ever known? And is it not true, that later on, Allah has blessed you with the religion of Islam, and He honored you with His generous gifts? How dare are you now to raise the might of Allah against other people, an authority He alone disposes of? I swear by Almighty Allah, that either you stop such unwarranted provocations, or expect Allah, the Lord of Majesty and Glory, to strip you off His gifts and bounties and hand them over to other nations.' "

A. bin Hanzala continued: "Salmãn then taught us the correct Islamic stance towards other faiths, and he said, 'Join your two nightly prayers (*Maghrib and 'Isha*) by regularly reading the Qur'an in-between them. By doing so, a man renders his reckoning easy on the Day of Judgment, and by occupying himself in reading the Qur'an during such times, he can spare himself any nonsense associated with social gatherings that usually take place at the early part of the evening, for indeed, inequities in the beginning of the night can only beget havoc by the end of it.' "

**453-** Imam Ahmad bin Hanbal, God be pleased with him, narrated that Huthaifa once said to Salmãn al-Fãrisi, God be pleased with both of them: "O Abu 'Abdullãh, let me build a house for you?" Salmãn looked at Huthaifa and showed a degree of despise towards his suggestion. Huthaifa realized what happened and he further explained himself, saying: "Slow down. Let me explain myself. I meant to build you a house, wherein, your head will lay at one end, and your feet at the other, and when you wish to raise your head, it will hit the ceiling." Salmān, having understood it to mean a grave, he replied: "You seem to have read my mind!"

**454-** 'Abdullāh bin Muhammad bin Ja'far narrated that Salmān once said to Jurair: "O Jurair! Do you know what is darkness on the Day of Resurrection?" Jurair replied: "Nay, I do not know!" Salmān said: "On the Day of Resurrection, darkness represents the deeds which people unjustly incur against one another in this world." Salmān then took a tiny straw, he closed his fist on it, and said: "You cannot even find a straw like this in the garden of paradise!" Jurair shook and said: "O Abu 'Abdullāh! Then what about the palm trees among others described in the prophetic traditions?" Salmān replied: "The trees of paradise are created of different substance. Their roots and trunks are created of pearls and gold, and their fruits blossom at the top."

**455-** Imam Ahmad bin Hanbal, God be pleased with him, narrated that Salmān al-Fārisi, God be pleased with him, said: "On the Day of Judgment, the most sinful people among the Muslims, are those who cater to confabulations and sinful casual conversations in this world."

**456-** Al-Thawri narrated that Salmān al-Fārisi, God be pleased with him, said: "I sometimes count the leftover bones in a pot, in fear that I may falsely suspect my servant of stealing."

**457-** Al-A'amash narrated that a man from the Tribe of Ashja' said: "The people of Madā'in, Iraq, once heard that Salmān al-Fārisi, God be pleased with him, was praying at the central mosque of their city. Within a short time, nearly one thousand man came out to meet Salmān and to greet him. Every one felt a special honor in being there, and every one took great pleasure in welcoming him, and to sit in his company, and they aspired to hear him talk. Salmān was touched by their overwhelming welcome, and he kept on humbly thanking them, and asking them to sit down! When every one finally sat down, and the atmosphere was favorable, Salmān stood up, and he opened the Qur'an, and started reading to them from *Surat Yusuf.*[1] Slowly, slowly, the crowd started to break up, and they thinned down to about one hundred man. When Salmãn suddenly looked up and noticed what happened, he became upset, and he addressed the remaining people, saying, 'Have you come here to listen to flowery and ornate personal opinions or what? And now, when I read to you from the glorious Book of Allah, the most exalted, you leave?'"

**458-** In another narration of the above account, al-Thawri quoted Salmãn al-Fãrisi, God be pleased with him, to have also said at that occasion: "Have you gathered here to hear a personal ornate speech or what? Do you only sit down if you are entertained with a verse from this chapter, mixed with a verse from that chapter, or else you leave...?"

**459-** Imam al-Bakhtari narrated that a man once said to Salmãn al-Fãrisi, God be pleased with him: "It is a wonder how great and kind hosts are people today! By God, whenever I visit one of them, he makes me feel as though I am staying with my own father's son." Salmãn replied: "O my brother's son. This is most natural. It is the remarkable achievement and the legacy of faith and Islam. Don't you see, when you first load an animal with merchandise, it wants to move forward at once! At the beginning of its journey, it embarks with speed and assiduity, and when it finds out that there is still a considerable distance to be covered, it slows down!"

**460-** 'Atã bin al-Sã'ib narrated that Salmãn al-Fãrisi, God be pleased with him, said: "There are two sides to every human being, inner and outer. When one corrects his inner disposition, Allah will make his outer being look more beautiful, hence, when the people see that, they like him, and when one tarnishes his inner being with sins, Allah will make his outer being look contemptible."

## The Idol Worshipers & The Fly

**461-** Tãriq bin Shahãb narrated that Salmãn al-Fãrisi, God be pleased with him, delivered a sermon, wherein he said: "Once upon a time, two men travelled together and had a unique experience with a fly. When they died, one of them entered hell-fire because

[1] *Qur'an; Joseph, Chapter XII.*

of it, and the second entered paradise because of it as well." The people inquired: "What happened to them?" Salmãn replied: "In times past, two men once traveled together. On their way, their journey led them to a pathway, whereat, they met with a group of people who worshiped a deity they made. The idol worshipers had placed their deity at a junction of the road, and they imposed on every passerby to make an offering to their deity. When the two men arrived at that junction, the idol worshippers said to them, 'You must make an offering to our deity!' One of the men replied, 'I have nothing to offer!' They said, 'You can sacrifice anything, even a fly will do!' The man consented, and he immediatelylooked around, and he caught a fly and sacrificed it before their deity, and the idol worshippers were extremely pleased with him, and hence, later on, when the man died, he entered hell-fire because of his own doing. When the idol worshipers required the same thing from his companion, he replied, 'I do not offer anything before anyone except Almighty Allah.' The idol worshippers argued with him with great anger, and they killed finally him, and thus, when he died, he entered paradise because of his true faith."

**462-** Jurair narrated that Salmãn al-Fãrisi, God be pleased with him, once said: "Even should a man spend all his nights freeing slaves from bondage, yet, one who spends his nights in reciting the Qur'an and celebrating Allah's praises (*zikr*) is in a higher station."

**463-** Sulaimãn al-Teemi narrated a similar saying by Salmãn al-Fãrisi, God be pleased with him, who said: "Even should a man spend his entire night fighting the enemies of God Almighty, yet one who spends his night in reciting the Qur'an and celebrating Allah's beautiful attributes (*zikr*) receives a greater reward."

**464-** Laith narrated that Salmãn al-Fãrisi, God be pleased with him, said: "Should Allah, the most exalted, require one of His creation to suffer the consequences of his sins, or should Allah decree the adverse outcome and destruction of one of His creation because of his evil actions, He first deprives him of modesty and correctness, so that whosoever sees him, he finds his appearance contemptible and depressing, and once he becomes contemptible, mercy will be taken out of his heart, and once he becomes merciless, his heart turns callous and ruthless. Once he becomes ruthless, he will be stripped off trustworthiness; therefore, whenever you see him, he will look unworthy of trust and a traitor in everyone's eyes. At this point, his face will lose the radiant beauty of Islam, and he then becomes damned, abominable, and accursed."

**465-** Salam bin 'Aṯiyya al-Asadi narrated that Salmãn al-Fãrisi, God be pleased with him, once visited a dying man, and he prayed: "O Angel of death, be compassionate and kind towards him!" The dying man turned to Salmãn and said: "The angel of death have just asked me to tell you that he is most compassionate and kind towards every believer."

**466-** Abu Is<u>h</u>ãq narrated that Aows bin <u>D</u>ham'aj said: "We asked Salmãn al-Fãrisi, God be pleased with him, to teach us something new about supererogatory religious devotion, and he replied, 'Greet everyone with the regards of peace, share your food with others, and pray at night when people are asleep.' "[1]

**467-** Sulaimãn al-Teemi narrated that Salmãn al-Fãrisi, God be pleased with him, said: "Should a Muslim stand alone in a vast desert at a great distance from his home, and when it is time for prayers, should he take his *wu<u>d</u>hu'* (ritual ablution), or substitute that with a ritual *tayammum,* and then, when he calls out to prayers and then establishes the prayers (*iqãma*), he will be leading myriads of angels in prayers, no sight can behold the horizon where they end!"

**468-** Sulaimãn al-Teemi narrated that Salmãn al-Fãrisi, God be pleased with him, said: "If a man spends his entire night freeing slaves from bondage, and another man spends his night reading the Qur'an, and invoking the remembrance of Allah's (*zikr*), the second man would be in a higher state."

**469-** Sulaimãn al-Teemi narrated that Salmãn al-Fãrisi, God be pleased with him, said: "If a man spends his entire night fighting the evil spirits, and another man spends his night remembering *zikr* Allah, and reading the Qur'an, the second man would realize a superior status."

---

[1] *i.e., Greeting everyone with the regards of peace will spread unity; inviting people to share one's food will promote mutual love, affection, and satisfaction; and, praying at night when people are asleep will promote one's own spiritual excellence, and brings him closer to his Lord.*

**470-** Imam Ahmad bin Hanbal, God be pleased with him, narrated that Abu Ddardã' wrote a letter to Salmãn al-Fãrisi, God be pleased with both of them, inviting him to visit Jerusalem: "Come to the blessed holy land!" In his reply, Salmãn wrote back to Abu Ddardã': "Surely a land does not make one holy, but good deeds are what render the human being holy."

Salmãn also wrote in his letter: "I am told that you have become a physician. If in fact you are able to cure people's illnesses, then enjoy the blessings. Otherwise, if you merely self-profess such degree of medical knowledge and dexterity, then beware that should you accidentally kill someone with your diagnosis or with your prescribed medication, you will enter hell-fire for murdering another human being."

**471-** Al-A'amash narrated that Salmãn al-Fãrisi, God be pleased with him, once said: "The parable of the heart and of the human body is like that of a blind man who lives with a disabled companion. The disabled companion (i.e., the heart) once said to the blind man (i.e., the body), 'I see a fruit tree nearby, but I cannot reach it on my own, carry me there, and I will guide you to it.' The blind man did what he was told, and when they reached the tree, they both ate from it and enjoyed its fruits."

**472-** Al-Mughïra bnu 'Abdu-Rahmãn narrated that Salmãn al-Fãrisi once met 'Abdullãh bin Salãm, God be pleased with both of them, and in the course of their conversation, Salmãn said: "Should you die before me, then, God willing, come and tell me about your findings, and should I die before you, and God willing, I will come and let you know about what happens."

Salmãn died first, and 'Abdullãh bin Salãm saw him in a dream and he asked him: "O Abu 'Abdullãh, how are you doing?" Salmãn replied: "I am well." 'Abdullãh bin Salãm then asked: "What deeds in this world receive the best of rewards in the hereafter?" Salmãn replied: "I find *tawakkul 'ala Allah* (reliance and unswerving dependence upon Allah, the most exalted), for all of one's needs receive the most phenomenal reward."

**473-** Sulaimãn al-Teemi narrated that Salmãn al-Fãrisi, God be pleased with him, was once talking about the story of the wife of Pharaoh, Ãsiya, God be pleased with her, who died in the dungeon of Pharaoh's palace of torture at the hand of her husband and his men, because of her faith in Allah and her acceptance of the truth of the messengership of her adopted son, God's prophet Moses, upon whom be peace. Salmãn al-Fãrisi said: "During her torture, 'Ãsia suffered excruciating pain at the hands of her prosecutors, and sometimes the the angels would cover her with their wings, and this protected her from feeling pain, and she would be able to see her dwellings in paradise, and towards which she kept on aspiring."[1]

**474-** Sulaimãn al-Teemi narrated that Salmãn al-Fãrisi, God be pleased with him, said: "Nemrod starved out two lions, and then released them to devour God's bosom friend, Abraham, upon whom be peace, but when the lions reached him, and by God's leave, they stood before him with reverence, and they both lovingly licked him all over and then prostrated themselves at his feet."

**475-** Abi al-Bakhtari narrated that Salmãn al-Fãrisi, God be pleased with him, had a female servant from Persian descent, and he once spoke to her in her Persian tongue, and said: "Prostrate yourself even once before Allah!" She replied with disdain: "I do not prostrate to any one!" Someone asked Salmãn: "O Abu 'Abdullãh, what would she benefit from a single prostration?" Salmãn replied: "Each link is an important part of a chain, and perhaps should this woman accept to offer a single prostration before God Almighty, then this may lead her to regularly engage in offering the five times prayers. In fact, one who has a share in the blessings of Islam is not equal to someone who has naught of it."

**476-** Al-A'amash narrated that Salmãn al-Fãrisi, God be pleased with him, once visited a friend from Kinda, Persia, who was ill. In the course of their conversation, Salmãn said to his friend: "When Almighty Allah tries His faithful servant with adversities and then cures him, the servant's sufferings become atonement for his sins,

---

[1] In another narration of the above tradition, it is reported that during her torture, suddenly, Ãsia looked up and smiled, and whatever physical torture descended upon her, it felt painless, and that boggled the minds of her torturers, who immediately stopped and called their master to witness, but when Pharaoh arrived, Ãsiya, God be pleased with her, had passed.

and his reckoning on the Day of Judgment will consist of censure. On the other hand, when Allah, blessed be His Name, tries a brazen insolent person with adversities, and then cures him, the latter becomes like a pack animal who is hobbled by his owner and later on he was unloaded, yet the burro does not understand why did his owner disencumber him, nor does it realize why was he hobbled to begin with."

**477-** Safwān bnu 'Amru narrated that Salmān al-Fārisi, God be pleased with him, once said: "The parable of a believer in this world is like that of a patient under the direct supervision of his physician. The physician knows the patient's illness and cure. Should the patient desire a variety of food that otherwise would hamper his recovery, the physician will say to him, 'Do not touch this food, if you do, it will kill you.' Hence, the physician will keep on advising his convalescing patient, and he will enjoin on him a strict diet until he is completely recovered. Like that, a believer may desire many comforts in this world, some of which, Allah, blessed is His holy Name, has availed as worldly favors bestowed upon other than His particular cherished servant. Therefore, Allah, the most exalted, may deprive His true servant from many desirable comforts in this world, and He may further prevent them from reaching him, and He will do so over and over, and until He takes back his soul, and only then will He let him enter the paradise of eternal bliss."

**478-** Imam Ahmad bin Hanbal, God be pleased with him, narrated that Salmān al-Fārisi, God be pleased with him, said: "Three things make me laugh, and three things make me cry. I laugh at someone who stretches his hopes in this world, being unmindful of death which is steadily seeking to end his life. I laugh at someone who is heedless and unaware that Allah is not unmindful of him. And finally, I laugh at someone who grins from ear to ear, unaware whether his loud laughter is pleasing to his Lord, or perhaps whether it is incurring His wrath. On the other hand, I cry for missing the fellowship of Muhammad ﷺ, upon whom be peace, and his companions. I cry when I think about a man experiencing the throes of death, and his grief and agony with his overwhelming newly unveiled encounter. And finally, I cry when I think about my having to stand up on the Day of Reckoning before Almighty Allah, blessed is His Name, not knowing whether I will be thrusted into hell-fire, or let to enter paradise!"

## His Death

**479-** Muhammad bin 'Abdullãh al-Hadrami narrated that Baqira, the wife of Salmãn al-Fãrisi, God be pleased with him, said: "When death approached Salmãn, he was staying in a room on the second floor of the house. His room had four doors, one facing each direction. Salmãn called me and said, 'O Baqira, today I am having special guests who are neither jin nor humans. Leave all the doors wide open, for I do not know through which of the doors will they enter.' "

The wife continued: "Salmãn then asked me to bring some powdered musk mix it in water, and to sprinkle it around his bed. When I did so, he said to me, 'You may go downstairs now and wait there, when you come up later, you will find me on my bed.'

Baqira further continued: "I did what he asked me to do, and sometime later, when I went to see him, I found him laying in his bed, his soul had departed, and he looked peaceful, just like someone resting."

## 31- Abu Ddardã

Also among our peers and sires of the believers, the blessed companion of God's messenger ﷺ, upon whom be peace, there lived great thinker and a gnostic, Abu Ddardã', God be pleased with him. His true understanding awakened in him constant remembrance of his Lord Whom he recognized correctly, and he cherished His gifts. Both in times of comfort as well as in times of adversities, Abu Ddardã', God be pleased with him, pondered incessantly upon the work of the Divine Lord. He nestled comfortably in his niche of continuous devotion, and he forsook any interest in materialism. He was most devoted to his spiritual life, and he was most eager to meet his Lord. Once he became free from worldly concerns and worries, the gate of true understanding became open before him. Here are few of the *ãthãr* (accounts) of this blessed companion of God's messenger ﷺ, upon whom be peace, and who was endowed with true knowledge and wisdom.

On this subject, it is said that the fruit of spiritual success lies within enduring intense yearning for one's beloved with quietude and serenity, and to submit willingly to the supreme power of the Lord Who draws nigh unto Himself whosoever He pleases, and to Whom, ultimately, everything will return.

**480-** Abu Zar'a al-Dimashqi narrated that after Abu Ddardã' died, 'Aoun bnu 'Abdillãh bnu 'Utba asked Umu Ddardã', the wife of Abu Ddardã', God be pleased with him: "What was the best form of devotion Abu Ddardã' offered?" She replied: "Contemplation upon the divine work, and deference for the divine admonition."

**481-** Qays bin 'Ammãr al-Duhni narrated that Abu Ddardã', God be pleased with him, once said: "To contemplate upon the work of Almighty Allah for one hour is greater than standing up in supererogatory prayers for an entire night."

**482-** Imam Ahmad Ibn Hanbal, God be pleased with him, narrated that someone asked Abu Ddardã' to advise him, he replied: "Remember Allah when you are comfortable, He will remember you when you are in difficulty, and when you set your eyes upon something in the world, think about how it will end!"

**483-** Sufyãn al-Thawri narrated that Abu Ddardã', God be pleased with him, once passed by two oxen in the work field. One of them was working, and the other was stretching out. As soon as they saw him, the one working stopped and looked, and the second ox stood up. Abu Ddardã', God be pleased with him, commented: "Surely there is a lesson one must learn from this incident!"

**484-** Al-'Alã bin al-Musayyib narrated that Abu Ddardã', God be pleased with him, once said: "I was a merchant (in Mecca) when God's messenger ﷺ, upon whom be peace, proclaimed the divine message of Islam. At that time I wanted to combine business and devotion, but it did not work out that way. Finally, I renounced the business, and I eagerly sought true comfort in religious devotion. I swear by Him in Whose presence my soul stands, I would not even wish to own a shop adjacent to the main gate of the mosque, whereat, I will never miss a congregational *fajr* prayer at dawn, and even if it were to bring me a net forty dinars every day, and which I would spend freely in their entirety in charity."

Someone asked: "What is wrong with that?" Abu Ddardã' replied: "I fear the rigorousness of our accountability before Almighty Allah on the Day of Reckoning."

**485-** In another narration of the above account, al-A'amash narrated that Abu Ddardã', God be pleased with him, said: "I was a merchant before Muhammad ﷺ, upon whom be peace, was sent as the messenger of God Almighty. When he proclaimed the message of Islam, I kept my business alongside a common degree of spiritual devotion. I did so painstakingly and with great toil for sometime, but it did not work for me, nor did it bring me any spiritual satisfaction. Soon after that, I gave up trading, and I devoted my life entirely to worship."

**486-** Imam Ahmad Ibn H̲anbal, God be pleased with him, narrated that Abu Ddardã', God be pleased with him, said: "It would not be my greatest pleasure to open a vending shop at the threshold of the mosque, and even if it were to bring me three hundred dinars of net business per day, or even if it would help me, by being their, not to miss a single congregational prayer at the mosque. I am not saying that Allah, the Lord of majesty and glory, did not make trading permissible or that He did not forbid usury, I am only desiring to be among those, ﴾ Men who are not distracted from remembering Allah by traffic or by selling merchandise, and who establish their prayers regularly, who pay their due alms, and who fear a Day (of Reckoning), when the hearts and the visions are caught by uncertainty and apprehension (as to the final outcome of their judgment.) ﴿" (*Qur'an 24:37*)

**487-** 'Abdullãh, son of Imam Ahmad Ibn H̲anbal, God be pleased with him, said: "I read before my father a narration wherein 'Aouf bnu Mãlik said, 'I once saw a vision in my sleep, wherein I was walking with people I could not identify, and there was a tent with a dome made of animal skin, and the place was surrounded with green pasture, and herds of sheep were grazing; some were resting, and others were chewing cud, and scattering the fields with their dung. I asked, 'Whose tent is this?' I was told that it belonged to 'Abdu-Rah̲mãn bnu 'Aouf, who incidentally was a very successful merchant and an extremely rich man. We waited until he came out from under his tent, and I said to him, 'O 'Aouf! This is the only material comfort that we have earned because of our faith and pursuit of the Qur'anic admonition. Yet, if you only look behind that trail, you would be able to behold what your sight has never laid eyes upon, you would hear (i.e., learn) what your ears could never have perceived otherwise, and you would find something your heart could have never thought of, — all of which, Allah, the Lord of the universe, and the most exalted has prepared to reward Abu Ddardã'; and all of that gratifying reward is because, during his entire life, Abu Ddardã' unfailingly resisted and rejected any comfort in the world, and every time worldly attractions paraded themselves before him, he repelled them."

**488-** Imam Ahmad Ibn H̲anbal, God be pleased with him, narrated that Abu Ddardã', God be pleased with him, said: "Whosoever does not recognize Allah's infinite bounty except in his food and drink, has little or no rewarding deeds, and his real sufferings are near; and whosoever is not rich beyond the need of this material world, he has neither understood the reality behind it, nor will he ever be comfortable in it."

**489-** Abu Muhammad bin H̲ayyãn narrated that Abu Ddardã', God be pleased with him, said: "How infinite is God's bounty even in a still plant."

**490-** 'Amru bnu 'Abdu-Wãh̲id narrated that Abu Ddardã', God be pleased with him, said: "You will be safe as long as you love the best amongst you, and as long as you acknowledge just and constructive criticism when they befit you, for whosoever recognizes what is just and true is like the one that does them."

**491-** Abu H̲ãmed bin Jabla narrated that al-Qãsim bin Muhammad said: "Abu Ddardã', God be pleased with him, was one of Allah's servants whose virtues are stated in the Qur'an, and he was ‹ Endowed with knowledge › (*Qur'an 28:80*).

**492-** Ja'far bin Barqãn narrated that Abu Ddardã', God be pleased with him, said: "What an awful end awaits someone who does not know, and had it been Allah's will, He would have taught him; and the end that awaits a learned person who does not act upon what he knows is seven times more awful!"

**493-** Imam Ahmad Ibn Hanbal, God be pleased with him, narrated that Abu Ddardã', God be pleased with him, once said: "You will not become fully learned (Arb. *faqïh*) until you realize that the Qur'an contains varying levels of depths. Furthermore, you will not become fully learned until you stand on the side of Allah, blessed is His name, and despise the class of evildoers for the sake of your love for Him, and after you do that, you should go back to yourself and despise its own failures more than you despise others."

**494-** Qutaiba bin Sa'ïd narrated that Abu Ddardã', God be pleased with him, said: "One of the signs of man's true understanding (*fiqh*), is his compassion towards himself by adopting a simple life."

**495-** Imam Ahmad Ibn Hanbal, God be pleased with him, narrated that Abu Ddardã', God be pleased with him, once said: "The sign of man's true understanding (*fiqh*) also involves his personal conduct, where he goes, from where he comes, whom he sits with, and his perseverance in oft-soliciting to sit in the company of the learned ones."

**496-** Imam Ahmad Ibn Hanbal, God be pleased with him, narrated that Abu Ddardã', God be pleased with him, said: "It is indeed a blessing when the so-called smart people oft-sleep through their nights and do not observe supererogatory fasting during the day, for how can they find fault in the devotion of those whom they label as stupid people who stay up long nights in prayers and read the Qur'an, who incessantly celebrate Allah's praises (*zikr*), and who observe voluntary fasting? Surely the value of an atom's worth of a good deed of pious person, besides the surety of his faith, is greater and more beneficial than mountains of devotion by self-deceived, moralizing, canting, and presumptuous people."

**497-** Bishr bnu Müsa narrated that Abu Ddardã', God be pleased with him, said: "Do not ask people to do more than what they are required to do, or to exert more what they are capable of doing, and do not judge people when only their Lord holds such authority. O son of Adam, just take care of yourself. For one who pries into the affairs of others will be afflicted with the disease of an extended and oft-recurring periods of depression, and he will not be able to overcome irritation, frustration, and infuriation."

**498-** Abu Bakr bin Abi Shaiba narrated that Abu Ddardã', God be pleased with him, said: "Worship Allah as though you can see Him. Regard yourselves as though you have joined the dead, and understand that having a little that suffices you in this world is better than having a lot that distracts you from your true objective. You must realize that *birr* (trueness) in one's deeds is a virtue, and virtues appreciate in value and they do not depreciate. You must also remember, that not even the slightest remote sin is ever forgotten."

**499-** Khãlid Ibn Dinar narrated that Abu Ddardã', God be pleased with him, said: "Blessings are not measured by the size of your wealth or by the number of your children, rather they are measured by the maturity of your forbearance, the breadth of your knowledge, and in vying with other devotees in worshipping God Almighty. At that stage, when you do good, be grateful and praise the Almighty Allah for guiding you, and when you fail, ask Allah, the Lord of majesty and glory, to forgive you, and implore Him to help you out of it."

**500-** Sa'ïd bin Abi Ayoub narrated that Abu Ddardã', God be pleased with him, said: "Had it not been for three blessed favors, I would not have liked to remain in this world." Someone asked: "What are they?" He replied: "1) To prostrate my face before my Creator and Lord in submission and adoration, and to do so throughout the rotations of the day and the night, and to know this to be the preface of my life in this world and its introduction to the hereafter; 2) to maintain the struggle of keeping up the control over my desires and thirst for the forsaken habits; and, 3) to sit in the company of exalted people who chose their words in the same way one picks up the better fruit on a plate."

Abu Ddardã', God be pleased with him, then said: "The epitome of piety is when the servant shows reverence to Allah, blessed is His Name, and when the servant fears the consequences of wrongdoing. That is when one shields himself with piety against any breach of the divine law, and when he upholds justice, even if it concerns an atom's worth in the balance of right and wrong. Therefore, a believer must pursue such thin edge of the balance of righteousness to the degree of giving meticulous attention to every detail, and even if it leads him to the point of withholding from taking in much of what is lawful in fear of becoming victim to unforeseen ramifications. Allah, blessed is His Name, has surely identified such ramifications for His creation when He defined the law, saying: ❮ Whosoever does an atom's worth of good will harvest its reward, and whosoever does an atom's worth of evil will reap its consequences ❯ (*Qur'an 99:7*). Therefore, do not overlook the ramification of committing the slightest wrongdoing, and do not belittle the importance of doing of good deeds which may sometimes seems insignificant."

**501-** Sãlem bin Abi al-Ja'ad narrated that Abu Ddardã', God be pleased with him, said: "Why do I find your scholars departing from this world, and yet your ignorant ones refuse to learn? Surely the one who teaches what is good and beneficial and the one who learns them receive equal reward; and besides these two categories, humanity is at loss."

**502-** Ya<u>h</u>ya bin Is<u>h</u>ãq narrated that Abu Ddardã', God be pleased with him, said: "There are three categories of people in this world: 1) A learned; 2) a student, and 3) a useless dreg."

**503-** Al-<u>D</u>ha<u>hh</u>ãk narrated that upon noticing some dislike on the part of the residents of Damascus, Syria, to hearing the admonitions of Abu Ddardã', God be pleased with him; he gave a sermon, wherein he said: "O honorable people of Damascus! You are indeed our brethren in the religion of Islam, you are our neighbors, and you are our helpers against our common enemy. Tell me what is preventing you from showing kindness to my presence amidst you? I have not come here to solicit your support. Surely my livelihood depends on someone other than you. Why do I find your learned ones departing steadily from this world, and your ignorant ones refusing to learn? I find you eager to grab what you are already guaranteed to receive from God Almighty, while you have forsaken what you are commanded to do! Let me remind you of a story of an earlier nation who had worked and built a city of strong foundations, they amassed excessive wealth, and they stretched their hopes beyond their means. One day, their strong edifices turned upside-down on them and became their graves, their ambitions deceived them, and their hands became barren of what they collected. I advise you to acquire the required knowledge and to teach it to others, for the scholar and the student receive equal reward, and there is no benefit in anyone besides these two categories."

**504-** Imam Ahmad Ibn Hanbal, God be pleased with him, narrated that Abu Ddardã', God be pleased with him, said: "You hear me asking you to do something which I myself may sometimes fail to practice, and yet, I still hope that Almighty Allah will reward me for suggesting what is good and beneficial."

**505-** Dhumra bin Habib narrated that Abu Ddardã', God be pleased with him, said: "One does not become truly pious unless he becomes learned, and one does not enjoy the beauty and benefits of his knowledge unless he practices what he knows."

**506-** Bishr bnu Müsa narrated that Abu Ddardã', God be pleased with him, used to say: "When I contemplate the Day of Judgment, I immediately begin to fear to be asked the question, 'You were endowed with knowledge, so tell Us, what have done with it'?"

**507-** In another narration of the above account, Imam Ahmad Ibn Hanbal, God be pleased with him, reported that Abu Ddardã', God be pleased with him, said: "The most serious question I terrified to be asked on the Day of Reckoning, is, 'O 'Uwaymir![1] Where you a learned person or an ignorant one in the world?' — Being ignorant in the world, one knows the consequences, — and should I reply, 'I indeed have acquired knowledge,' then there will not be a single revealed verse in the Qur'an commanding the believers to do good, or a verse forbidding them to indulge in what is prohibited that I will not be required to meet the consequences of failing to fulfilling them. Therefore, I seek refuge in Allah, blessed be His Name, against acquiring a knowledge from which one does not benefit, I seek refuge in Him against having a craving or a greed in this life that is insatiable, and I seek refuge in Him from a prayer which He disregards."

**508-** In another narration of the above account, Qutaiba bin Sa'ïd reported that Abu Ddardã', God be pleased with him, said: "The most I fear on the Day of Reckoning, is to be called forth before

[1] 'Uwaymir: i.e., one who lived a short life in the world.

the entire creation, and should it be said to me, 'O 'Uwaymir! Did you learn the truth in the world?' And when I reply, 'Yes indeed, I learned the truth!' And the, the next question will be, 'How did you perform?' "

## A Letter To Salmãn al-Fãrisi

**509-** Al-H̲assan bin Sufyãn narrated that Abu Ddardã' once sent a letter to Salmãn al-Fãrisi, God be pleased with both of them, wherein he wrote: "My dear brother, take advantage of your health and independence today, before a day comes, wherein people will suffer a most horrifying calamity as a divine justice, and which they will have no power to eschew. My dear brother, ask a believer who is suffering from a calamity to pray for you, and take advantage of his prayers, for his supplications will surely be answered favorably. My dear brother, make the mosque your house, for I have heard God's messenger ﷺ, upon whom be peace, say that, 'Allah's mosques are the house of every pious person.' Indeed, Almighty Allah, the Lord of majesty and glory, has guaranteed such people who regard His mosques as their house to strengthen them with a spirit of His own, to give them comfort and peace, to make their passage over the bridge of judgment (*s̲irãt̲*) easy, and to receive them at the end of their crossing, having won the cheer blessings of their Lord. My dear brother, have compassion towards orphans. Bring them nigh unto you, and feed them from your own food. A man once complained before God's messenger ﷺ, upon whom be peace, about the roughness of his heart. God's messenger ﷺ, upon whom be peace, then said to him, 'Would you like your heart to soften?' The man replied, 'Indeed I do!' God's messenger ﷺ, upon whom be peace, said, 'Then befriend the orphans, be compassionate towards them, bring them nigh unto you, comfort them, feed them from your own food, and your heart will then soften, and you will be able to win success in your life.' "

Abu Ddardã' continued: "O my dear brother, do not amass more money than what you are capable of thanking Almighty Allah for. I have heard God's messenger ﷺ, upon whom be peace, say, 'On the Day of Judgment (*Youm al-H̲isãb*), and on the bridge of judgment (*s̲irãt̲*) , a man will walk ahead of the money which he paid its dues, and every time he staggers or hesitates, his money will say to him, 'Go forward, for you have paid your dues! On the other hand, a man who did not obey Allah's commands concerning his monies, he will be impelled to walk the awful crossing of the bridge of judgment, and he will be forced to carry his money on his back. In his stress, every time the weight of his money causes him to stagger, and as he stumbles and falls, time after time, his money will impel him and rebuke him, saying, 'O man! What an awful destiny is awaiting you! Why didn't you use me according to Allah's commands?' As the crossing becomes harder and harder to bear, and as the man keeps on hearing the rebuke of his money, his depression heightens, his legs tremble, and his steps keep on failing to obey him until he breaks down, and he bursts out crying, pleading for his own annihilation, but to no avail.' "

"My dear brother, it came to my knowledge that you have acquired a servant, and I have heard God's messenger ﷺ, upon whom be peace, say, 'The *'abd* (servant) remains the recipient of Allah's favors, and Allah remains his Provider and Helper, as long as he does not become a beneficiary of others' servitude. Once he does, then he also becomes subject to accountability.' O my dear brother, I was once financially comfortable, and when my wife, Ummu Ddardã' saw that, she asked me to hire a servant to help her in her daily chores, but when I reflected upon the reckoning associated with such comfort, I disapproved, and I discounted the idea. And now, my dear brother, who do we have to guarantee us, when we reach the Day of Judgment, that you and me can be unconcerned of the just, accurate, and scrupulous divine reckoning? My dear brother, do not burst with pride because of your fellowship with God's messenger ﷺ, upon whom be peace, a unique blessing you and me have once enjoyed, for indeed, we have lived an short span of life after him, and only Allah knows what actually befell us since he left."

**510-** Imam Ahmad Ibn H̲anbal, God be pleased with him, narrated that the caliph, Yazi'd bin Mu'ãwiya once asked Abu Ddardã' for the hand of his daughter in marriage, but Abu Ddardã' declined the offer. Later on, someone who frequented the court of Yazi'd privately remarked to Abu Ddardã': "May Allah help you correct your attitude; nevertheless, since you do not wish to accept him to become you in-law, then would you give me permission to betroth your daughter?" Abu Ddardã' became upset, and he scalded the man, saying: "Get out of here. You do not need to incur my fury!" The man temperately reiterated his offer, saying: "May Allah help you have a better attitude, give me permission to marry your daughter." Hearing that, Abu Ddardã', God be pleased with him, thought about it for a moment, and he consented, saying: "You have my permission." Hence, with the daughter's consent, and after the wedding, the event became the talk of the town, and the people kept on talking about 'Yazïd, the son of Mu'ãwiya, who asked to betroth the daughter of Abu Ddardã', and that he was rejected, and then when a common poor Muslim tested his chances, Abu Ddardã' accepted him.' When the hearsay reached Abu Ddardã', God be pleased with him, he defended himself, saying: "I thought about it, and a thought flashed in my mind, what will happen to her faith should my daughter al-Ddardã' wake up one morning to see maidens at her head and feet, and should she look around her and see the glitters and fineries of palaces and spacious homes! I then I said to myself, how far my daughter will then be from the religious norms and environment she grew up to know? Hence, this thought helped me to make my decision."

**511-** 'Abdullãh bin Muhammad al-Makhzoumi narrated that Dãwoud bin Mihrãn said: "I was a young boy when I stopped by al-Fudhayl bin 'Iyãdh, and I paid my respects to him, saying, 'Peace be on you,' but he did not reply. Al-Fudhayl's eyes were wide open, and I thought that he was looking straight at me, but yet I waited long enough before he suddenly look down, and he addressed me, 'For how long have you been standing here my son?' I replied, 'For some time!' Al-Fudhayl then said, 'Excuse me my son, you and me are occupied in entirely two different thoughts!' "

**512-** Abu 'Aouf 'Abdu-Rahmãn bin Marzouq narrated that Abu Ddardã', God be pleased with him, once said to him: "One must be aware not to be caught oblivious of being reprobated by the hearts of the believers." Abu Ddardã' then asked Sãlem bin Abi al-Ja'ad: "Do you understand what this means?" Sãlem replied: "No I do not understand that, explain it to me!" Abu Ddardã' said: "It indicates that the servant is indulging privately in immoral actions that incur Allah's displeasure. The Almighty Lord of majesty and glory, blessed be His Name, will then cast such reprobation towards that person in the hearts of His pious servants. They in turn will reflect such stance towards the sinner, and most likely, he will not recognize what is causing them to loath him and to treat him with despise!"

**513-** Ahmad bin Ishãq narrated that Abu Ddardã', God be pleased with him, once prayed: "O Allah, I seek refuge in Your divine protection from the hearts of the scholars should they ever curse me!" Hassãn bin 'Atiyya heard Abu Ddardã's prayer, and he asked him: "How do the hearts of scholars curse you?" Abu Ddardã' replied: "They do so if they despise me."

**514-** Qutaiba bin Sa'ïd narrated that Abu Ddardã', God be pleased with him, once said: "It is better to hearken to the censure and criticism of your brother than to loose him. Otherwise, who else can assume such unfeigned and integral relationship but him? Hearken to your brother and soften your attitude towards him in order to protect your unique human bond with him. Beware not to follow the insinuations of someone who is jealous of your brother, otherwise, you could become a jealous person just like him! Tomorrow when the angel of death comes to collect your soul, you will surely realize how awesome is your loss, when you are laid in your grave, and when you become prisoner to your loneliness, or should your brother die before you do, then why would you cry for your separation, when you realize how wrong was it to rupture your relationship with him when he was still alive?"

**515-**Imam Ahmad Ibn Hanbal, God be pleased with him, narrated that Abu Ddardã', God be pleased with him, once said: "If only you knew what you will certainly see upon your death, you would never again eat a single bite out of a craving appetite, and you would never again drink an extra sip of water for the pleasure of an unquenchable and insatiable thirst. Hence, you will remain outdoor in perpetuity, bewildered and awaiting the unexpected, and you will never again seek comfort in a shelter or seek a shade. You will wander aimlessly and climb the hilltops of every mountain, you will look up towards the heavens and beseech your Lord for mercy, and you will beat on your chest and cry endlessly, and you will wish that your were a little vegetable — a plant which is protected to grow, and then plucked to be eaten by a hungry person passing along."

**516-** K͟hãlid bin Ma'dãn narrated that Abu Ddardã', God be pleased with him, said: "The epitome of faith is to endure patiently the judgment of the Just Lord, to willingly accept one's fate as the inheritance of one's own doing, to have sincerity in one's dependence and reliance upon his Lord, and to wholly accept and surrender (*Islam*) to the Lord of majesty and glory, the Creator, Originator, Sustainer and Controller of every life form."

**517-** 'Abdu-Ra͟hmãn bin Muhammad al-Mu͟hãribi narrated that Abu Ddardã', God be pleased with him, once sent a letter to one of his brethren, and after greeting him with the peace of Allah, blessed be His Name, he wrote: "My dear brother, remember that there is nothing which is in your possession today that did not belong to someone else before you, and which will not soon become the trust of someone else after you. The only benefit you can partake of what is under your you control today, is the way you use it to allow your soul to reap its benefits tomorrow! Therefore, give preference to charitable deeds over and above beefing up the size of the inheritance of any one of your righteous children, and whom you do not know how will he use it! Otherwise, you will pass from this world to stand before someone Who will not excuse your failure, meanwhile, you would have worked hard in this world to bequeath one who will be grateful to someone other than you. The wealth you worked hard to amass in this world will eventually culminate in one of two possibilities: 1) It will either fall into the hands of someone who will use it in obedience to Allah's commands, and whose deeds will benefit him, while you would have worked hard and deprived yourself of the benefits of such deeds; or, 2) it will fall into the hands of someone who disobeys Almighty Allah, blessed be His Name, and who will use it in an evil way, whereby you will share in his punishment and sufferings for what you have bequeathed him to nurture his weaknesses. I swear by Almighty Allah, blessed be His Name, that neither of the above-described two categories of people is more worthy than yourself to receive Allah's mercy, and none of them merits more than you what you have worked hard and sweated to bequeath them to pacify their life and to assuage their comfort in this world after you depart from it. The best you can do for them is to pray for their sake. Ask for Allah's mercy for those who died, and as for those who will remain the dwellers of this world after you die, trust that Almighty Allah, blessed be His Name, has guaranteed their sustenance, as well as that of everyone else, and for as long as they dwell herein. I bid you peace."

**518-** Imam Ahmad Ibn H̲anbal, God be pleased with him, narrated that when the bangs of death descended upon Abu Ddardã', God be pleased with him, he shook and sweated profusely while fumbling in a low voice: "Is there anyone who wishes to prepare for a day like the one I am having today? Is there anyone who wishes to prepare for an hour like the one I am now experiencing? Is there anyone who wishes to prepare himself for his final lay down helplessly as I am today?" Abu Ddardã', God be pleased with him, then read from the divine revelation addressing the hypocrites: ❮ We will surely cause their hearts and eyes utter confusion, just as it happened to them at first when they heard the message, and deemed it untrue ❯ (*Qur'an 6:110*).

**519-** Imam Ahmad Ibn H̲anbal, God be pleased with him, narrated that Abu Ddardã', God be pleased with him, used to say: "Woe unto him, and what an agony is awaiting one who cares only about amassing money in this world! Woe unto him who opens his mouth agape and drools at hearing the sound of money, who looks aghast, just like an idiot when he thinks about it, who stares at what people have, and who does not see what he has; and if he could, he would pursue such an obsession by day and night. Woe unto him! What an austere reckoning and a grievous punishment are awaiting him!"

**520-** Ismã'ïl bin 'Iyãsh narrated that whenever Abu Ddardã', God be pleased with him, passed a funeral, he used to say: "Go ahead, we will surely follow you. Go back to your Lord, and God willing we will tomorrow follow you. This is the strongest admonition the human being will ever bear witness to. Surely this is a soul shaking moment, a heedless and an oblivious person will most likely overlook. People will depart from this world, one after the other, and yet, the latter ones will remain unprepared, and he will stick to his hot temper and his lack of patience and endurance."

**521-** Mu'ãwiya bin Qurra narrated that Abu Ddardã', God be pleased with him, said: "I love three things which most people hate, 1) poverty; 2) illness; and 3) death."

**522-** In another narration of the above quote, Shu'uba narrated that Abu Ddardã', God be pleased with him, said: "1) I love death because of my yearning to meet my Lord; 2) I love poverty because it forces me to stand humble before my Lord; and 3) I love illness because it embodies penance and atonement that expiate my sins before I meet my Lord."

**523-** Sa'ïd bin Abi Hilãl narrated that Abu Ddardã', God be pleased with him, said: "O citizens of Damascus! Aren't you ashamed of yourselves? You hoard more than what you can eat, you build dwellings you do not inhabit, and you stretch your hopes beyond your reach! Aren't you ashamed of yourselves? Before your time, there lived nations that were more conscious of what they harvested, they designed plans and pondered seriously what they aspired for, and they built their cities with great anticipation for a lasting future, and yet, what they gathered turned into ruins, what the hoped for and anticipated deceived them, and their dwellings were turned upside-down to become their graves! Think about the ancient nation of Sodom, they filled in-between Eden and Oman with wealth and children, and now look at what happened to them? Is there anyone among you here today, who is in his right mind, and who would buy from me the entire inheritance of the people of Sodom for two dirhams (i.e., two pennies)?"

**524-** Safwãn bnu 'Amr narrated that Abu Ddardã', God be pleased with him, said: "O wealthy people! Use your money today as you are commanded by Almighty Allah, blessed be His Name, to cool down the intense heat of hell-fire tomorrow, and before you and us become equally penniless in our graves. Today, both of us are looking at our monies, but with opposing concerns."

Abu Ddardã', God be pleased with him, further said: "I fear for you to develop a covert desire and to become fascinated with a divine favor regarding your worldly achievements that will distract you from what should be your ultimate goal. This too will happen on the day when food will be aplenty, and when you fill your stomachs to satiety, but yet, you will hunger for true knowledge."

"surely, the best amongst you is one who says to his friend, 'Let us make the intention, and together, observe a fast for one day before we die! On the other hand, the worst and most evil amongst you, is one who says to his friend, 'Let us enjoy ourselves and take advantage of today, let us eat and drink to satiety, and have fun before we die."

**525-** Safwãn bnu 'Amr narrated that Abu Ddardã', God be pleased with him, once passed by a gathering of people who were building a house, and he commented: "You work hard to build this world of yours, and Allah, blessed be His Name, has mandated that it will ultimately turn to ruins! Allah's decree will surely prevail."

**526-** Muhammad bin Hayyãn narrated that when Abu Ddardã', God be pleased with him, would see an abandoned ruin, he used to stop by it and address it, saying: "O ruin which took place before the last destruction! Tell me, what happen to your dwellers?"

**527-** Mu'ãwiya bin Qurra narrated that when Abu Ddardã', God be pleased with him, fell ill, some companions visited him, and they inquired from him: "O Abu Ddardã', what is ailing you, and of what are you complaining?" He replied: "My sins!" They asked again: "Is there anything you wish for?" Abu Ddardã' replied: "Paradise!" They further asked him: "Should we call a physician to see you?" He replied: "He is the One Who confined me to my bed."

**528-** Muhammad bin Bishr narrated that Abu Ddardã', God be pleased with him, said: "One who always inspects what he has will eventually discover something missing, and one who does not build up his patience to help him meet calamities will become their victim. Consider this, if you praise the people, they will praise you, but if you mind your own business and turn away from the people, they will criticize you." Someone asked: "What would you advise me?" Abu Ddardã', God be pleased with him, replied: "Constantly praise the One Who will surely bring you to account on a Day when your true poverty is exposed."

**529-** Ismã'il bin Is<u>h</u>ãq al-Sarrãj narrated that some people asked Abu Ddardã', God be pleased with him, to pray to Almighty Allah, blessed be His Name, on their behalf. Abu Ddardã' replied: "I do not know how to swim, and I am afraid of drowning."

**530-** Shaibãn bin Faroukh narrated that Abu Ddardã', God be pleased with him, used to say: "Three things I fear for your sake: 1) The slip of the tongue of a scholar; 2) an argument with a hypocrite about the Qur'an, although the Qur'an is true in its entirety, and it carries a most resplendent light to guide the seekers, just like that of a lighthouse; and finally, 3) I wish to state here that one who is not spiritually rich beyond the need of this world has no world."

**531-** Al-Aouza'i narrated that a poor man once heard Abu Ddardã', God be pleased with him, pray: "Lord, I seek refuge in You from the shattering of the heart." The man went to him and asked: "What is the shattering of the heart?" Abu Ddardã' replied: "It is somehow similar to someone who gives me a large some of money in coins scattered between several distant valleys."

**532-** 'Abdu-Ra<u>h</u>mãn bin al-Mahdi narrated that Abu Ddardã', God be pleased with him, said: "Those whose tongues are soothed with continuous hymns, (Arb. *zikr Allah*), glorifying and celebrating Allah's praises, blessed be His Name, they will enter paradise smiling."

**533-** Imam Ahmad Ibn <u>H</u>anbal, God be pleased with him, narrated that someone told Abu Ddardã', God be pleased with him, that Abu Sa'ad bin Munbih bought and freed one hundred slaves from bondage in a single night. Abu Ddardã' commented: "To pay for the freedom of one hundred slaves from the earnings of a single man is indeed a lot of money, but if you want, I will tell you about a single deed which is greater than that; — that is to be consistent in one's faith day and night, and to soothe one's tongue with continuous hymns, glorifying and celebrating Allah's praises, blessed be His Name."

**534-** Ja'far bin <u>H</u>amdãn narrated that Abu Ddardã', God be pleased with him, said: "To glorify the name of Allah, blessed be His Name, one hundred times is dearer to my heart than to give one hundred Dinar in charity."

**535-** Kathir bin Murra al-H̲ad̲hrami narrated that Abu Ddardã', God be pleased with him, once said to his companions: "Would you like me to tell you which of your deeds pleases your sovereign Lord most and raises you in station, — a deed which is better than mounting an expedition against your enemy, killing them, and being killed by them, and a deed which is better than regularly giving money in charity?" The people asked: "O Abu Ddardã', tell us what kind of deed is that?" He replied: "Always celebrate the *zikr* (remembrance of Allah), glorify and praise His divine attributes, blessed be His Name, and continuously attest to the supremacy of Allah's divine sovereignty and control over the entire creation, by solemnizing and continuously celebrating *Allahu Akbar* (surely Allah is the greatest off all)."

**536-** Abu Bakr Ibn Mãlik narrated that Abu Ddardã', God be pleased with him, said: "There is not an organ in the body of a believer which is dearer to Allah than the tongue, and because of it, Allah permits the believer to enter paradise. On the other hand, there is not an organ in the body of a disbeliever which is more abominated by Allah than the tongue, and because of it, Allah casts the disbeliever into hell-fire."

**537-** Ibrãhim al-Teemi narrated that Abu Ddardã', God be pleased with him, said: "One who oft-remembers death will have a little or nothing to rejoice about, and he will have less envy and jealousy towards others."

**538-** 'Abdu-Rah̲mãn bin Yazid narrated that Abu Ddardã', God be pleased with him, once prayed: "Lord, let me die in the company of the true ones, and do not let me live in the company of the evil ones."

**539-** Muhammad Ibn Ish̲ãq narrated that Abu Ddardã', God be pleased with him, once prayed: "Lord, let me not be tried with an evil deed, so that I may not be called an evil man."

**540-** Abu Bakr bin Abi Shaiba narrated that Abu Ddardã', God be pleased with him, said: "Whenever I retire at night knowing that some people have not accused me of to blaspheme, or crafted a fallacy against me, I also recognize that Allah, blessed be His Name, has indeed favored me with His subtle kindness and protected me for that day."

**541-** Imam Ahmad Ibn H̲anbal, God be pleased with him, narrated that Abu Ddardã', God be pleased with him, said: "Whenever I retire at night, knowing that people have not committed a blaspheme or crafted a fallacy against me, and whenever I wake up in the morning safe from people's evil fallacies against me, I generally have a most healthy day, both physically and spiritually."

**542-** Muhammad bin Fud̲hayl narrated that Abu Ddardã', God be pleased with him, said in one of his speeches: "O ye people! Why do I find you most anxious and athirst to seek what you are guaranteed to receive while neglectful of what you were entrusted to perform? I certainly know your evil ones better than a veterinarian or a blacksmith knows his horses. Such are those who drag their feet and come late to prayers, who disinterestedly hearken to the Qur'anic revelation, and who do not let go of their attachment to their property of slaves, although they understand well that Islam has come to guarantee their freedom. Such are the morally corrupt people."

**543-** Al-Faraj bin Fad̲hãla narrated that Abu Ddardã', God be pleased with him, said: "Beware of the divine justice in response to the call of the oppressed ones and the orphans, for their prayers are answered right away, and the effects of the divine retribution take place at night when people are asleep."

**544-** Imam Ahmad Ibn H̲anbal, God be pleased with him, narrated, that Abu Ddardã', God be pleased with him, said: "I dreadfully and extremely hate to commit an injustice against someone who only calls upon Allah's justice and help against me."

**545-** Muhammad bin Ish̲ãq narrated that Abu Ddardã', God be pleased with him, once saw Kurayb bin Abraha riding a horse while one of his servants walked steadily behind him. Abu Ddardã', God be pleased with him, then commented, 'The distance separating Allah, the Lord of glory and majesty, blessed be His Name, and His servant keeps on widening as long as the latter requires someone to walk behind him in obeisance like a peon in bondage."

**546-** Imam Ahmad Ibn H̲anbal, God be pleased with him, narrated that whenever Abu Ddardã', God be pleased with him, heard the voices of people reciting the Qur'an in the middle of the night, he used to say: "The mourners over their own souls insist on holding tight to the rope of Allah regardless of what may come upon them on the Day of Resurrection. They persevere in cooling the yearnings of their hearts with the *zikr* (remembrance) of Allah, and by solemnly and regularly rehearsing His revelation."

**547-** Abu Bakr bin Abi Shaiba narrated that Abu Ddardã', God be pleased with him, said: "Seek and anticipate Allah's bounty all your life. Expose yourselves at all times to the amplitude of Allah's presents, for Allah, blessed be His Name, has designated auspicious presents filled with His divine mercy, and He, in His infinite mercy and compassion, allots such blessings to whosoever He pleases among His obedient servants, and whenever He pleases. Furthermore, beseech Allah, the Lord of Majesty and glory, to veil your imperfections and weaknesses, and ask Him to alleviate your sorrow and anxiety."

**548-** Sa'ïd bin Wahab narrated that a man once came to Abu Ddardã' and said: "Teach me something I can practice and through which Almighty Allah, blessed be His Name, will bless me!" Abu Ddardã', God be pleased with him, faithfully replied: "I will teach you two, three, four, or even five things, whosoever acts upon them and observes their rights, Allah, the Lord of majesty and glory, will exalt his reward and raise his station to be among the most illustrious believers:

1) Eat only what is permissible and healthy; 2) do not accept any money save that which is blessed and lawful; 3) do not let into your house anything except that which is beneficial and pleasing to Allah; 4) pray to Allah, blessed be His Name, to provide for your earnings, one day at a time; 5) when you wake up in the morning, count yourself among the dead, for then you are one step closer to joining them; 6) entrust your guardianship to the sovereign Hand of Almighty Allah, for He is the best of protectors; 7) should someone insult you, offend you, or aim to fight you, then walk away from him, and do not avenge yourself, let Almighty Allah exonerate and defend you; 8) when you do something wrong, repent sincerely, and immediately pray for Allah's forgiveness; and finally, 9) when you do something right, thank Allah, most exalted is His Name, for His guidance and countless favors."

**549-** Bakr bin Sawãda narrated that Khãlid bin Hudayr al-Aslami visited Abu Ddardã', God be pleased with him, during his last illness, and he found him in pain and sweating profusely. The room was empty, and there he found Abu Ddardã' laid on the floor on a thin piece of hide, and he wore an old piece of lambskin, and next to him, there also laid an old basket made of animal hide. Khãlid said to Abu Ddardã', God be pleased with him: "If you wish, I will be happy to fit your bed with a more comfortable woolen pad such as those provided to us by the Prince of the Believers." Abu Ddardã' replied: "We surely do need that, for we do have a home, we will soon get there, and indeed, we toil awfully hard in this world to reach it safely."

**550-** Abu Shu'aib al-Harrani narrated that some friends of Abu Ddardã', God be pleased with him, came to visit him, and he welcomed them with adequate hospitality. Their visit carried through the middle of the night, and they did not feel like returning to their homes that night, so they slept in his house. Some slept on a piece of hide or on a lambskin, and others slept on the bare floor with their clothes on. In the morning, Abu Ddardã', God be pleased with him, apologized for his narrow means, saying: "We have a home, and what we collect here determines what we will have when we get there, and towards it we are unfailingly faring."

**551-** Sulaimãn bin Ahmad narrated that Abu Ddardã', God be pleased with him, was in Syria, and he addressed his audience, saying: "O people of Damascus! Are you deriving satisfaction in this world from merely filling your stomachs with wheat bread year after year while the Name of Allah, the most exalted, is never mentioned in your leagues? Why do I find your scholars trickling down in number, and those who lack knowledge among you are not seeking to learn? Should the intelligent ones among you use their brains, then God willing, they can expand their knowledge, and should your ignorant ones solicit the true knowledge, they will surely find it readily available and easy to reach! You must pay the dues for what you receive from Allah, the Lord of majesty and glory. I swear by Him, in Whose presence my soul stands, that no nation has ever perished except when the people pursued their own fancies, praised their own devotion, and took pride in their personal achievements."

**552-** Abu Bakr bin Abi Dãwoud narrated that Abu Ddardã', God be pleased with him, once saw a man walking in the marketplace holding the hand of his child, whom he adorned and dressed up beautifully, and the man seemed to take great pride in his son. Abu Ddardã' then made an audible comment, saying: "Adorn them as you please, and this will surely help boost their ego and self deception!"

**553-** Al-Aouza'i narrated that a man came to Abu Ddardã' and complained about his older brother who did him an injustice. When Abu Ddardã', God be pleased with him, heard and verified the account, he said to the man: "Do not worry, surely Allah, the Lord of majesty and glory, will exonerate you, and He will grant you victory over your brother."

Later that year, the brother's wife gave birth to a son, and the man visited the caliph Mu'ãwiya who handed him a present of one hundred Dinars. Shortly after that, the younger brother visited Abu Ddardã' who in the course of the conversation said: "You see, it happened just as I told you! Indeed Allah has exonerated you, and He granted you victory over your brother. I heard that your brother has begotten a son, and that Mu'ãwiya awarded him a gift of one hundred Dinars!"[1]

**554-** Abu Muhammad bin Hayyãn narrated that Abu Ddardã', God be pleased with him, said: "On the Day of Resurrection, the most evil of people in Allah's sight, is a scholar people could not benefit from his knowledge in the world."

**555-** Abu Bakr bin Mãlik narrated that Abu Ddardã', God be pleased with him, said: "What an awful punishment awaits someone who lies, who disobey the commands of his Lord, and who breaks the divinely witnessed covenant. Hence, regardless of what devotion he observes, neither his speech nor his offerings will ever be regarded as true."

**556-** 'Abdu-Rahmãn bin Yazïd bin Jãbir narrated that Abu Ddardã', God be pleased with him, said: "O ye People! Your appetite,

[1] Cf. #302

lust, and passion for the pleasures of this world seem to grow increasingly afresh, just like those of a youth, when even your collarbones are bent together of old age, except for ‹ Those whom Allah has tested their hearts, and qualified their piety to be true› (*Qur'an 49:3*), and alas, how rare are such true people today!"

**557-** Imam Ahmad Ibn Hanbal, God be pleased with him, narrated that Abu Ddardã', God be pleased with him, said: "O son of Adam! You have the power to affect the outcome of three things and to turn them to your advantage. 1) Never complain about your difficulties; 2) do not tell others about your pain and sufferings; and 3) do not praise yourself with your own tongue."

**558-** Ahmad bin Yahya al-Halwãni narrated that Whenever Abu Ddardã' wrote a letter to Salmãn al-Fãrisi, he often reminded him of the miracle of the serving plate. We talked earlier about this awesome miracle, when Abu Ddardã' and Salmãn al-Fãrisi were eating together from a plate, and when suddenly, the plate and the food together started to praise Allah, the Lord of majesty and glory, blessed be His Name, and in an audible human voice.

**559-** Al-A'amash narrated that Salmãn al-Fãrisi was once visiting with Abu Ddardã', God be pleased with both of them. Abu Ddardã' went to light a fire under the cooking pot, when suddenly he heard a sound coming from inside the pot. Abu Ddardã' hearkened closely, and to his amazement, he heard a soft human voice resembling that of a young child, emanating from inside the pot, and praising Allah, blessed be His Name. Abu Ddardã' was further startled with reverence as the pot rose on its own, floated in the air, and gently whirled a complete turn on its own axis before it returned to its first position over the fireplace. Miraculously, not a single drop of food spilled out of it, and the sound then evanesced! Abu Ddardã' shook in exhilaration as he shouted: "O Salmãn, O Salmãn! Come here, come here and behold this wonder! Hurry on, come and see what neither you nor your father have ever dreamt to see, come now!" From inside the room, Salmãn replied: "Alas! If only you had kept your quiet, you would have further heard the resonance of some of the most magnificent and glorious signs of Allah, blessed be His Name."

**560-** 'Abdullãh bin Sa'ïd, son of Rabï'a al-Dimashqi, narrated that one evening, late at night, Abu Ddardã', God be pleased with him, sought the mosque to pray, and as he entered the mosque, he passed by a man in prostration who was praying: "O Lord, I am afraid, and I am seeking shelter in the safety of Your custodianship. Lord, shield me from Your punishment. I am a poor beggar beseeching You to endow me with a favor of Yours. I am not a sinner who is justifying his wrongdoing, nor do I have the means to protect myself against Your punishment, but here I come before You as a repenting sinner. O Lord, accept my repentance."

Abu Ddardã', God be pleased with him, loved this supplications, so he memorized them, and he taught them to his companions in the morning.

**561-** Al-Faraj bin Fadhãla narrated that Umu Ddardã' once prayed to God Almighty, saying: "O Lord, Abu Ddardã' betrothed me in this world, and I am asking You to make me his wife in paradise." Abu Ddardã', God be pleased with him, heard her prayer, and he commented: "If you wish to become my wife in paradise, and if I am your first husband, then do not marry any one after me."

Al-Faraj bin Fadhãla continued: "Umu Ddardã' was extremely beautiful, and she was a most dignified looking woman. When Abu Ddardã', God be pleased with him, died, the caliph Mu'ãwiya asked for her hand in marriage, but she declined his offer, and said, 'Let Allah be my witness, I will not marry another man until, God willing, I rejoin Abu Ddardã' in paradise.' "

**562-** Sulaimãn bin Ahmad narrated that Abu Ddardã', God be pleased with him, once passed by a crowd gathering around a man who committed a wrongdoing, and they were chastising and rebuking him. Seeing that, Abu Ddardã' said to them: "You see! Suppose that you discover that your brother had fallen into a deep well, would you not try to help him and pull him out of his predicament?" The people replied: "Indeed, we would!" Abu Ddardã' then added: "Therefore, do not insult your brother because of his shortcoming. Instead, praise Allah, blessed be His Name, Who has guarded you against committing such a sin, and Who protected you against walking into the same predicament." The people said: "Do you not hate him for what he did?" Abu Ddardã' replied: "In truth, what I abhor is his act, and once he repents and refrains from committing it again, he will always be my brother." Abu Ddardã', God be pleased with him, then said: "O man! Pray to Allah, blessed be His Name in a good day when you are prosperous. Praise His holy Name and beseech Him to grant you guidance, protection, and strength when you are at ease, perhaps He will answer your prayers on an arduous day, when you meet with trials and difficulties."

Abu Ddardã', God be pleased with him, was a gnostic, a sage, and a wise man, and he possessed exceptional control of balance and reasoning. He was a most skilled physician of the hearts. He spoke extensively, and his speeches abounded with wisdom and subtleties. His wisdom and knowledge were medicine for the sick at heart, and warmth for the hearts of the equitable and the pondering ascetics. When Abu Ddardã' spoke, his words penetrated the hearts of his listeners, and when he invoked a verse from the divine revelation and celebrated and praised Allah, the Lord of majesty and glory, blessed be His Name, the hearts of his listeners were filled with coherence, and they bonded instantly with his prayers. Abu Ddardã' was free from ostentatiousness or pride, and he forsook any so-called desirable features of this world. Through his extensive knowledge, dedicated skills, and unrivaled devotion, he recognized and sought the rewarding stations of the hereafter, and he was an expert collector of *Hilyatul Awliyã*, the fineries reserved for the most exalted believers in the hereafter.

**563-** Yazïd bin Mu'ãwiya said: "Abu Ddardã', God be pleased with him, was a great scholar and a wise man, and he was an expert physician who knew how to heal the sick, both physically and spiritually."

**564-** Abu Hãmed bin Jabla narrated that someone asked Abu Ddardã', God be pleased with him: "Why have you not poeticized? Surely, there is not a single man from Madina who did not expressed himself in poetry." Abu Ddardã' replied: "I did. Listen to this poem I once said:

*Man desires to have everything he wishes for in this world,*
*Yet Allah will sanction only what He decrees.*

*Man cries out, 'My benefits, my money,'*
*although the best interest he should muster*
*is piety towards his Lord.*

**565-** Abu 'Amru bnu Hamdãn narrated, re Abu Ddardã', that God's messenger ﷺ, upon whom be peace, said: "If you clearly recognize the absolute sovereignty of Allah, He will forgive you your sins."

**566-** Marwãn bin Muhammad al-Tatari elucidated in reference to the above prophetic tradition, saying: "Clearly recognize the sovereignty of Allah, means to submit in Islam to Him."

**567-** Al-A'amash narrated, re Abu Ddardã', God be pleased with him, that God's messenger ﷺ, upon whom be peace, said: "Whoever dies believing in Allah and associating none of His creation with Him will enter paradise."

In fact, when sometimes someone probed Abu Ddardã' regarding the above tradition, saying: "Is this true even if one had committed a major sin such as adultery or thievery?" Abu Ddardã' would reply: "Yes, even if he had committed adultery or thievery, and that is in spite of what Abu Ddardã' may think!"

**568-** 'Abdullãh bin Ja'far narrated, re Abu Ddardã', God be pleased with him, that God's messenger ﷺ, upon whom be peace, said: "Everyday, when the sun rises in the mourning, there will be tow angels standing by its sides, and they will call out, 'O people, come to the Lord of majesty and glory, come to your Master. Surely, to satisfy yourselves with what is less yet sufficient is better than to become distracted with excess.' "

God's messenger ﷺ, upon whom be peace, then added: "All life forms will hear this cry, except for the humans and the jinn."

**569-** Al-'Ã'ithu-Billãh Abu Idris narrated, re Abu Ddardã', God be pleased with him, that God's messenger ﷺ, upon whom be peace, prayed: "My Lord, grant me to love You, to love those who love You, and guide me to do what will earn me Your love. O Lord, grant me to love You more than myself and my family, and more than my thirst for a drink of cold water on a day of scorching heat."

**570-** Umu Ddardã' narrated, re her husband, Abu Ddardã', God be pleased with him, that God's messenger ﷺ, upon whom be peace, said: "Free yourselves from the worries of the world as much as you can, for whosoever treats his worries in this world as his most serious concern, Allah, blessed be His Name, will minimize his real loss in his eyes, and He will cause his fear of poverty to broaden and to be constant. On the other hand, whosoever regards the hereafter as his major concern, Allah, blessed be His Name, will group his immediate needs together to become manageable, He will fill his heart with richness, and broaden his satisfaction and contentment. In fact, whenever a servant turns his hearts wholly towards his Lord, then Allah, blessed be His Name, will cause the hearts of His believing servants to flow towards him with love, kindness and mercy, while abundant divine blessings will flow towards him to serve his immediate needs more expeditiously."

**571-** Sulaimãn bin Ahmad narrated, re Abu Ddardã', God be pleased with him, that God's messenger ﷺ, upon whom be peace, said: "Allah, the most exalted, blessed be His Name, said, 'O Jesus, after you, I am establishing a nation which people will be grateful and thankful to Me when they receive what they like, and they will submit to My decree and exercise patience when afflicted by what they do not like. However, they will lack forbearance, and they will be unlettered." Jesus, peace be upon whim, inquired: "My Lord, how can they have all of that, yet they would lack forbearance and knowledge?" Almighty Allah, blessed be His Name, said: "I will ensure that they will have forbearance and knowledge of My own, and which they will receive directly from Me as they need them and pray for them."

## 32- Mu'ãṯh bin Jabal

The next of our peers is Mu'ãṯh bin Jabal, patronymed Abu 'Abdu-Raẖmãn, God be pleased with him. Mu'ãṯh was most industrious and diligent, he gave careful attention to details, and his performances were characterized by his adherence to the highest level of excellence. His deeds were free from affectation or inequity, and he was a brave master and a leading scholar who was also versed in the knowledge of the Qur'an and that of the *ẖadïth* (prophetic traditions). Mu'ãṯh's words expressed the highest level of sagaciousness and insight, and he was a most generous host.

Mu'ãth bin Jabal, God be pleased with him, memorized the entire Qur'an by heart, and he regularly read it avidly with percipience, pensiveness, and pondering. His true and pure love for Almighty Allah, the Lord of majesty and glory, blessed be His Name, and for His blessed messenger ﷺ, upon whom be peace, was forthright and ever-intensifying.

Mu'ãth, God be pleased with him, enjoyed a most forbearing and a cheerful character. He sat regularly with God's messenger ﷺ, upon whom be peace, and he was a meritorious and a most trustworthy companion. Mu'ãth, God be pleased with him, also was most loyal, faithful, and unfailing to his duties by the divine guidance and protection, and his trustworthiness and excellence of character added to his success and assurance in his pursuit of the divine acceptance, and they earned him strength and victory over his trials and asperities.

On this subject, it is said that spiritual success also means clarity, balance, and constancy in exercising kindness. Such success also requires one to cultivate the pure essence of faith in the sacred meadows of one's inner being.

**572-** 'Abdullãh bin Ja'far narrated that God's messenger ﷺ, upon whom be peace, said: "Among my entire *Umma* (of followers), Mu'ãth bin Jabal is the most knowledgeable person regarding *halãl* and *harãm*."[1]

**573-** Abu Hãmed bin Jabla narrated that Omar bin al-Khattãb, God be pleased with him, said: "Should I decide to appoint Mu'ãth bin Jabal to govern the affairs of the Muslims after me, and should my Lord ask me on the Day of Judgment, 'What made you do it?' I will say that I heard Thy prophet ﷺ, upon whom be peace, say that, 'On the Day of Judgment, when the scholars and gnostics come before their Lord, Mu'ãth will lead them, and he will stand at a distance of a stone's throw ahead of them.' "

**574-** 'Abdullãh bnu 'Amru, God be pleased with him, narrated that God's messenger ﷺ, upon whom be peace, said: "Learn the Qur'an at the hands of four people, 'Abdullãh bnu 'Amru, Mu'ãth bin Jabal, Ubiyyu bnu Ka'ab, and Sãlem Mawla Abu Huthaifa."

---

i.e., knowledge about the Lawful and the unlawful.

**575-** Abu Is<u>h</u>ãq bin <u>H</u>amza narrated that Anas bin Mãlik, God be pleased with him, said: "During the time of God's messenger ﷺ, upon whom be peace, the Qur'an was compiled at the hands of four people, Ubiyyu bnu Ka'ab, Mu'ã<u>th</u> bin Jabal, Zaid bnu <u>Th</u>ãbit, and Abu Yazïd." Someone asked: "Who is Abu Yazïd?" He replied: "One of my paternal uncles."

**576-** Muhammad bin Is<u>h</u>ãq narrated that Ibn Mas'oud, God be pleased with him, said: "Mu'ã<u>th</u> bin Jabal, God be pleased with him, was indeed an excellent model (*umma*) for the believers, he was devoutly obedient to his Lord (*qãnit*), and he a sincere believer (*birr*)."

Someone replied to Ibn Mas'oud's comment: "But God Almighty said that ❮ Abraham was indeed a model, he was devoutly obedient to his Lord, and true in faith ❯ (*Qur'an 16:120*)." Ibn Mas'oud replied: "Do you know what *umma* and *qãnit* mean?" The man replied: "Allah knows best!" Ibn Mas'oud expounded: "*Umma* means one who recognizes what is beneficial (Arb. *<u>k</u>hair*), and *qãnit* means one who is obedient to Allah and to His messenger ﷺ, upon whom be peace."

**577-** In another narration of the above tradition, reported by Firãs bin Ya<u>h</u>ya, son of Mas'oud, God be pleased with him, said: "We used to liken the character of Mu'ã<u>th</u> to that of God's prophet Abraham, upon whom be peace."

**578-** Abu Bakr bin <u>K</u>halãd narrated that Abi Muslim al-<u>K</u>hawlãni said: "I once entered the central mosque of the city of Homs, Syria, and there I found some thirty elderly men from among the blessed companions of God's messenger ﷺ, upon whom be peace. A man of younger age with bright eyes and long dark eyelashes also sat quietly near them, and whenever the elders needed a reference or an explanation, they went to him, and they addressed him with great love and reverence. I asked someone who sat next to me: "Who is this man?" He replied: "This is Mu'ã<u>th</u> bin Jabal, God be pleased with him." Instantly, I felt a sudden intense love and admiration for him, and I stayed near their circle, and listened attentively to their discussion until they dispersed."

**579-** Is<u>h</u>ãq bin Ibrãhïm al-<u>H</u>an<u>z</u>ali narrated that Yazid bin Abi Ba<u>h</u>riyya said: "I once entered the central mosque of the city of <u>H</u>oms,

Syria, and I saw people gathered around a young man who looked most dignified, sagacious, and versed. When he spoke, his words were full of light and wisdom, and they came out like radiant gemstones. I asked, 'Who is this man?' Someone replied, 'This is Mu'ãt̲h bin Jabal.' "

**580-** Ahmad bin Muhammad bin Sanãn narrated that Shahru bnu H̲awshab said: "Whenever the companions of God's messenger ﷺ, upon whom be peace, gathered, and when Mu'ãt̲h bin Jabal was sitting with them, they all looked towards him with great love and respect, and he had a dignified look that inspired solemn reverence."

**581-** Imam Ahmad bin H̲anbal, God be pleased with him, narrated that Ka'ab bin Mãlik said: "Mu'ãt̲h bin Jabal was a very handsome-looking man, and he was among the best of his clan. He was most generous, and he gave people whatever they asked him. One day, Mu'ãt̲h had to borrow some money, and he had no means to repay it. Later on, when his debtors pressured him to make payment, he went to God's messenger ﷺ, upon whom be peace, and asked him to speak to his debtors on his behalf, so that they may give him some time. However, when God's messenger ﷺ spoke on his behalf, the debtors insisted on receiving their money all at once. Hence, God's messenger ﷺ called Mu'ãth, God be pleased with him, and when he saw their attitude, he immediately divided all his belongings between them, and he walked out owning nothing and owing nothing. Hence, Mu'ãth became the first Muslim whose property was confiscated to pay for his debts. On that year, Mu'ãth sought permission to perform the pilgrimage to God's House in Mecca, and God's messenger ﷺ, upon whom be peace, wanted to comfort his heart, so he also appointed him to head a mission in Yemen. Mu'ãth fulfilled his duty, but he only returned to Madina after God's messenger ﷺ, upon whom be peace, had passed, and the *k̲hilãfa* (vice regency) was borne by Abu Bakr, God be pleased with him."

**582-** Al-A'amash narrated that after God's messenger ﷺ, upon whom be peace, passed, the vice regency was borne by Abu Bakr, God be pleased with him, and in turn, Abu Bakr appointed Omar bin al-K̲hatt̲ãb to head the pilgrimage season to Mecca for that year. Also in that same year, it happen that Mu'ãth bin Jabal, God be pleased with him, was returning from Yemen after leading his mission, and he too performed a pilgrimage that year. In Mecca, Omar met Mu'ãth who had brought with him a number of servants from Yemen, and he said to Omar: "Those were presented as a gift to stay in my company, and the remaining servants were sent to Madina to Abu Bakr to serve." When Omar heard that, he commented: "May be it is better that you should talk to Abu Bakr about that!"

In Mecca, the next mourning, Mu'ãth passed by Omar and said to him: "O Ibn al-Khattãb! I saw you in a dream last night. I saw you holding me firmly from my waist belt and dragging me down into hell-fire. Therefore, I have no solution but to obey what you dictated regarding the servants."

Upon completing their pilgrimage, when Mu'ãth returned to Madina, he took the servants to Abu Bakr and said to him: "These were offered to me to remain in my service, and the others were offered as a gift to you." Abu Bakr replied: "All right, and we hereby decree to release your gift to your care."

Later on that day, Mu'ãth went to the mosque, and when he finished his prayers, he noticed that his servants were praying behind him. Mu'ãth asked them: "Who were you praying to?" They replied: "To Almighty Allah, the Lord of majesty and glory, blessed be His Name." Mu'ãth immediately said to them: "Then you belong to Allah. You may go now, you are free men." Thus, he released them from their obligations.

**583-** Idris al-Khawlãni narrated that Mu'ãth Bin Jabal, God be pleased with him, said in one of his sermons: "Coming your way are awful trials were money will be aplenty, and the Qur'an will be read by the believer as well by the hypocrite, the young and the old, the strong and the weak, and people from all nations will read the Qur'an. A man rehearsing the Qur'an in public will be astounded and bewildered as he says to himself, 'How is it that I happen to be reading the divinely revealed Qur'an, and people seem to neither heed, nor would they comply with its admonitions?' "

Mu'ãth further continued: "O people! Beware, beware of innovations, for innovations lead to straying from the right path.

I also warn you about the potential aberration of a scholar, or the possible blunder of a teacher, for it is possible that a wise man's own Satan utters a misleading statement through him, while it is also possible that a hypocrite speaks a word of truth. Therefore, accept only the truth, for truth is a radiant light."

Someone asked: "How are we to know whether a wise man is right or wrong?" Mu'ãth replied: "A wise man may utter a word in error, and you will feel uncomfortable with it. You will say to yourselves, 'What is this?' Therefore, do not feel awkward about questioning it, and perhaps he will retract his expression on his own when he recognizes what you already know, and he may change his opinion. Knowledge and faith are indeed an effulgent light, and their clarity and distinctiveness will remain radiant thus until the Day of Resurrection. Therefore, whosoever seeks true knowledge and faith with sincerity and perseverance, he will surely find them."

**584-** Ibn Shahãb narrated, that Yazïd bin 'Umaira, a close companion of Mu'ãth bin Jabal, God be pleased with him, said: "Whenever Mu'ãth joined a *zikr* and Qur'an reading session, he always began with the invocation, 'Allah is a just Lord, blessed be His Name. Whoever is in doubt about that will surely meet with perils.' "

Abu Yazïd bin 'Umaira continued: "One day, during a discourse, Mu'ãth, God be pleased with him, said, 'Coming your way are awful trials were money will be aplenty, and the Qur'an will be opened for reference by the believers as well by the hypocrites and the disbelievers, and it will be read by men and women, young and old, strong and weak, and by a free man as well as by a slave. A preacher rehearsing the Qur'an in public will say to himself, 'How is it that I happen to be reading the divinely revealed Qur'an, and people seem not to be interested, nor would they follow its admonitions! Perhaps they will only follow what I say if I invent a new book for them.' "

Mu'ãth further continued: 'Beware of innovations, for innovations lead to erring. I also warn you about the potential aberration of the scholars, or the possible blunder of the teachers, for it is possible that even a wise man's own satan utters a misleading statement through him, as well as it is possible that a hypocrite speaks a word of truth. Therefore, accept only the truth, for truth is radiant."

Someone asked: "How are we to know whether a wise man is right or wrong in what he says?" Mu'āth replied: "A wise man may utter a word lightly, and you feel uncomfortable with it and question it in your heart. Do not feel awkward, nor impel yourselves to agree without questioning such statement should your heart not agree with what the wise man may have said, for perhaps, and should his words be unquestionably wrong, he will retract his expression when he hears the truth from you, and therefore he will correct his own statement, for indeed, truth is a radiant light, and it is assertive of itself."

**585-** 'Abdullāh, son of Imam Ahmad bin Hanbal, God be pleased with him, narrated that a man asked Mu'āth bin Jabal, God be pleased with him: "Teach me something." Mu'āth replied: "Would you obey me?" The man humbly replied: "I am most eager to obey you." Mu'āth then instructed the man: "Fast and pray regularly, earn your livelihood in a lawful way, and do not err in that regard. Strive not to die except in Islam, and beware not to become liable before the divine justice regarding the grievance of someone with whom you have dealt unjustly."

**586-** Sulaimān bin Ahmad narrated that when Mu'āth bin Jabal, God be pleased with him, stood up to pray in the middle of the night, he used to pray: "Lord, the eyes are asleep, the stars have ebbed out, and You remain the ever living watchful Controller over all. Lord, my soliciting Your paradise is indeed slow, and my flight from hell-fire is tenuous. Lord, grant me the gift of a hidden guidance which You will demonstrate as an award out of Your generosity on the Day of Resurrection, for surely You do not fail Your promise."

**587-** Mu'āwiya bin Qurra narrated that Mu'āth bin Jabal, God be pleased with him, once said to his son: "My dear son, when you stand up in prayers, do so as a departing person bidding farewell to this world, and do not assume that you will have another chance to thus pray again. My dear son, understand that a believer dies ranking in-between two deeds, one he offers for his present day, wherein he will immediately garner its blessings, and the second deed he offers towards the Day of Resurrection, and that is when he will reap its ultimate benefits."

**588-** Imam Muhammad Ibn Seerïn narrated that a man once came with some friends to visit Mu'ãth bin Jabal, God be pleased with him, and the man asked for his advice. Mu'ãth replied: "I advise you to observe two things, if you do, they will surely protect you. First of all, you must know that you cannot circumvent receiving your share in this world, and the second advice is that you are in dire need of your personal share of the divine blessings in the hereafter. Therefore, give preference to offering deeds that will benefit you in the hereafter over struggling to garner what is already destined to come to you in this world anyhow. Keep on doing so until you string your deeds together for the benefit of the hereafter like you string your prayer beads to carry them with you wherever you go in this world."

**589-** Al-Fudhayl bin 'Iyãdh narrated that a man came to see Mu'ãth bin Jabal, God be pleased with him, during his illness, and he wept in his presence. Mu'ãth asked the man: "Why are you crying?" The man replied: "Let Allah be my witness, I am not crying because of a blood relationship or propinquity between you and me, nor am I crying for the loss of a business between us in this world, however, I used to come and listen to your sermons, and I have learned from you what I am afraid may soon cease." Mu'ãth, God be pleased with him, replied: "Then do not cry my brother, for whoever seeks the path of knowledge and faith, Allah, blessed be His Name, will grant him his wish, and He will endow him with both of them as He did with Abraham, upon whom be peace. In truth, during his time, his people sought neither knowledge nor did they recognize faith, and yet, Allah, blessed be His Name, chose to endow Abraham with both of them."

**590-** Imam Ahmad bin Hanbal, God be pleased with him, narrated that Mu'ãth bin Jabal, God be pleased with him, said: "Nothing better than *zikr Allah* (the remembrance of Allah), that is constantly glorify and celebrate Allah's praises, the Lord of majesty and glory, blessed be His Name, can save the son of Adam from punishment for his sins." Someone asked Mu'ãth: "Is *zikr Allah* greater than carrying one's sword and fighting in the cause of Allah in three campaigns?" Mu'ãth replied: "Even that is not equal to *zikr Allah*, and unless one fights incessantly until he earns his martyrdom."

**591-** In another narration of the above quoted account, Jurair bin 'Uthmãn reported that Mu'ãth bin Jabal, God be pleased with him, replied to the man, saying: "Not even *Jihãd* (warring), and unless one fights incessantly until he earns his martyrdom, for Allah, the most exalted, blessed be His Name, says: ❮ Surely celebrating Allah's praises (*zikr Allah*) is greater. ❯ (*Qur'an 29:45*)."

**592-** Sa'ïd bin al-Musayyib narrated that Mu'ãth bin Jabal, God be pleased with him said: "According to my understanding, — to celebrate God's praises (*zikr Allah*) from dawn till nightfall is more rewarding than mounting a horse from dawn to nightfall in *jihãd*, warring to defend the cause of Allah."

**593-** Abu Ahmad al-Ghitrifi narrated that Ya'qoub bin Zaid said: "I once entered the central mosque of Homs, Syria, where I heard Mu'ãth bin Jabal, God be pleased with him, say, 'Whoever likes to meet Allah, blessed be His Name, feeling safe, and being free from anxiety, then let him regularly attend to his five daily prayers at the mosque, and that is where they are called for. This is the blessed *sunna* (tradition) of the perfectly guided believers, and this is what your prophet ﷺ, upon whom be peace, has instituted for you. Let no one say, 'I have a prayer niche in my house, and I only pray there, for should you do so, you would have departed from the *sunna* traditions of your prophet, and should you depart from the *sunna* traditions of your prophet ﷺ, upon whom be peace, you would surely stray from the path.'"

**594-** Abu Hãmed bin Jabla narrated that al-Aswad bin Hilãl said: "We were walking with Mu'ãth, God be pleased with him, when he suddenly turned to us and said, 'Let us sit here for an hour and reconfirm our faith.' "

**595-** Imam Ahmad bin Hanbal, God be pleased with him, narrated that Mu'ãth bin Jabal, God be pleased with him, said: "Whenever you sit with people and find that some of them have lost their focus, or perhaps they become distracted, or should they engage in secular conversations, or even doze a little, then stand up immediately and turn to Allah in prayers (*salãt*), for such is an auspicious hour for solicitation, and it is an hour where one's personal supplications to Almighty Allah are subject to His favorable answer."

**596-** Al-Walid bin Muslim, who also narrated the above account, added: "We mentioned Mu'ãth's saying to 'Abdu-Rahmãn bin Yazid bin Jãbir, who replied, 'Indeed, what Mu'ãth said is true. I heard Abu Talha Hakim bin Dinar describing one of the signs of one's prayers being answered favorably, he said, 'When you see people indulging in heedlessness, then stand up and turn to your Lord in prayers, for such is an auspicious hour for one's personal solicitations.' "

**597-** Abu Muhammad bin Hayyãn narrated that when Mu'ãth bin Jabal, God be pleased with him, came to their land, their *mashãyikh* (elders and leading scholars) came to welcome him, and to honor his visit, they suggested: "Should you order us, we will happily carry those rocks and gather the needed lumber to build up a mosque for you here!" Mu'ãth replied: "Nay, not for me, but for the pleasure of Allah, blessed be His Name! I fear to be ordered to carry it on my back on the Day of Resurrection."

**598-** Abu 'Amru bnu Hamdãn narrated that 'Amru bnu Maimoun al-'Aoudi of Yemen, said: "Mu'ãth bin Jabal, God be pleased with him, once stood up and gave a sermon, wherein he said, 'O tribe of 'Aoud, surely I am the emissary of God's messenger ﷺ, upon whom be peace, to you, and he has indeed delivered the divine message. You must understand that at the appointed Hour, the creation will ultimately reach the presence of Allah, blessed be His Name, and from there, people will either be destined to enter the heavenly paradise, or to dwell in hell-fire. You also must understand that the hereafter is a permanent abode, not a transient one, and people will dwell there eternally in permanent immortal bodies.' "

**599-** 'Abdullãh bin Muhammad, son of Ja'far, narrated that Mu'ãth bin Jabal, God be pleased with him, said: "Learn whatever knowledge you wish to acquire, and Allah will not reward you unless you act upon what you have learned."

**600-** Imam Ahmad bin Hanbal, God be pleased with him, narrated that Mu'ãth bin Jabal, God be pleased with him, said to

Rajã' bin Haiwa: "Your earlier trials consisted of harsh adversities (*dharrã'*), and you had limited resources towards which you exercised extreme patience and endurance, however, your future trials will consist of comfort and prosperity (*sarrã'*). Furthermore, the most I fear for you are the trials of women, and the time will come, when women will adorn their forearms with bracelets of gold and silver decorated with alike matching bangles, and that will become the fashion, and then, they will be dressed up with damask linen and silk from Syria, and they will tie up their heads with embellished headbands and ligatures from Yemen, and then women will become a burden for the rich and a worry for the poor."

**601-** Imam Ahmad bin Hanbal, God be pleased with him, narrated that Mu'ãth bin Jabal, God be pleased with him, once said: "There are three types of actions, whosoever engages in any of them will earn himself the divine abomination, and those are; 1) To laugh without astoundment; 2) to sleep without exhaustion from staying up late in devotion; and, 3) to eat or nibble on food without hunger."

**602-** Mãlik al-Dariny narrated that Omar bin al-Khattãb, God be pleased with him, once placed four hundred dinars in a bag, and he said to his attendant: "Give this to Abu 'Ubaida al-Jarrãh; wait their for an hour or so, and find out what will he do with them!"

The attendant went to Abu 'Ubaida and said to him: "This is a gift from the Commander and Prince of the believers. Use it as you see fit." Abu 'Ubaida graciously accepted the gift, and he replied: "May Allah unite him with whom he loves, and show mercy towards him." Abu 'Ubaida then addressed a women serving his family, saying: "Take these seven dinars and give them to so and so, and give these five dinars to so and so, then these five dinars to so and so..." and thus he did with the balance of the money until nothing remained in his possession.

When the attendant returned to Omar and narrated what he witnessed, Omar, God be pleased with him, handed him another bag of four hundred dinars, and said: "Take these to Mu'ãth bin Jabal, tarry there for an hour or so, and find out what will he do with them!"

The attendant went to Mu'ãth at once and said to him: "The commander and prince of the believers has sent you this gift, and he asked that you use it for some of your personal needs." Mu'ãth graciously accepted the gift, and he replied: "May Allah show mercy towards him and unite him with whom he loves." Mu'ãth then called a female servant and said to her: "Take this money to the house of so and so..." As Mu'ãth was dividing the gift, his wife looked and realized what was happening, and she said to her husband: "By God, listen, we too are poor, and therefore, you better leave something for our own needs as well!" Mu'ãth looked inside the bag, and there were two Dinar coins left in the bottom of the sack, so he rolled them down to her.

When Omar's attendant returned and narrated what he witnessed, Omar smiled and commented: "Surely these two men are brethren from the same household."

## A Letter to Omar bin Al-Khattãb

**603-** Marwãn bin Mu'ãwiya narrated that Muhammad bin Souqa said: "I visited Na'ïm bin Abi Hind, who brought me a letter from Abu 'Ubaida al-Jarrãh and Mu'ãth bin Jabal to Omar bin al-Khattãb, which read as follows:

'Peace be upon you. After all, we know that you are a responsible individual, and that you are well aware of your true interest. Now that you have been elected to guard the interests of this nation, you will also have to serve the interests of the red and the black, the noble and the lowly, the avowed enemy and the truthful friend, all of whom will sit before you, and each one of them will receive his share of justice. O Omar, therefore, consider carefully your position in the eyes of Allah, before Whom you yourself will stand on the Day of Judgment for reckoning. We warn you of such a day when people's faces will convey tormenting worries, their hearts will dehydrate, their rationalization of their actions will be in vain, and when they will all submit to the clear proof of the supreme omnipotent King Who will defeat their false alibis. On that day, all the creation will have no choice but to submit to His judgment, that's when they will all hope and be in dire need of His mercy, and they will all fear His punishment.'

'We have all been taught by God's messenger ﷺ, upon whom be peace, and he has told us that near the end of times, this *umma* (nation) will be exceptionally divided, and people will express brotherly love outwardly, although they will conceal strong jealousy and enmity inwardly.'

'Finally, we pray, and we seek refuge in the protection of Almighty Allah that these words of ours will not be perceived by you other than with the same sincerity our hearts were inclined to expressed them, for we have wrote this letter only to advise you. Peace be upon you.'

Upon reading their letter, Omar, God be pleased with him, wrote back:

'From Omar bin al-Khattāb, to Abu 'Ubaida and Mu'āth, peace be upon you both. 'In reply to your subject letter, your message have reached me, wherein, you noted your awareness that I am a well concerned person, and that I am well aware of my true interests, and since I have been elected to guard the interests of this nation, and to serve the interests of its red and black, the noble and the lowly, the avowed enemy and the truthful friend, who will all come and sit before me, and each one of them will receive his share of justice, and you further outlined, 'O Omar, consider carefully your position in the eyes of Almighty Allah before Whom you yourself will stand on the Day of Judgment for reckoning. I therefore testify that indeed, Omar has no will or power on his own, and except for what Allah, the Lord of majesty and glory, wills, and I testify that Allah alone has the absolute power of managing the affairs of His creation.'

'You also wrote in your letter, and you apprised me regarding what earlier nations have been warned against, and in fact, in the past, people had to experienced their judgment first in this world, and where the briefness of the night and day had expedited people's encounter with their destiny, reduced the new to old, and hastened the arrival of what was considered to be distant. Subsequently, earlier nations knew their just reward in advance, and they realized their ultimate destination, which can either be heaven or hell.'

'You also wrote in your letter, and warned me regarding the

end of times, when this *umma* (nation) will be most divided, and when people will express brotherly love outwardly, while concealing extremely enmity inwardly. In this respect, I say that you are not such brethren, nor is this such an era, and which is yet to come! At such times, both the propensity of desires and the burden of solemn concerns will shatter people's hearts. In fact, at such a times, people may also cooperate, but they will mostly concentrate their focus on enhancing and embellishing their own worldly status.'

'You also wrote in your letter seeking refuge in Almighty Allah that your words will not be perceived by me other than with the same sincerity your hearts were inclined to expressed them, and that you have wrote your letter only to advise me.'

'In repose to that, may I add that I indeed believe that you are most truthful and sincere in your efforts. Please do not stop writing to me, for I cannot afford to be spared of your advice. Peace be upon both of you.' "

## The Need for Acquiring True Knowledge

**604-** Muhammad bin Ibrāhīm, son of Yahya, narrated that Mu'āth bin Jabal, God be pleased with him, said in one of his sermons: "Acquire knowledge for the pleasure of Allah, blessed be His Name, for learning thus engenders piety, reverence for one's Lord, and fear of wrongdoing. Seeking knowledge for God's pleasure is an act of worship, studying it is a celebration of God's glory (*zikr*), and searching for it is a most rewarding struggle (*jihād*), teaching it to someone who realizes that he needs to acquire it is charity (*sadaqa*), and applying it in one's own home strengthens family unity and kinship. Knowledge indeed helps the believer to discern between the lawful (*halāl*) and the forbidden (*harām*), and it is the guiding light for the seekers on the path of Allah, and the future dwellers of the heavenly paradise."

Mu'āth further said: "Knowledge is a comforting friend in times of loneliness, it is the best companion during travels, and it is the inner friend who speaks to you in your privacy. Knowledge is the discerning proof of what is right and what is wrong, and it is the positive force that will help you surmount the trials of comfort, as well as those of hardships. Knowledge is your most powerful sword against your enemy, and finally, it is your most dignifying raiment in the company of your close companions."

"Through knowledge, Allah, blessed be His Name, raises some people in rank, and He makes them leaders in righteousness and models in morality. The vestige of their faith is avidly sought, their deeds are emulated perceptively, and people will seek and sanction their opinions solicitously and unequivocally. The heavenly angles seek their company and anoint them with their wings, every fresh or withered life they pass by implore Almighty Allah to forgive them their sins, even the fish in the oceans, the beasts of the lands, and every bird of prey and migratory bird pray and solicit the mercy of Almighty Allah on their behalf. This is because knowledge revives the dead hearts and drives them out of darkness into light, and because knowledge is the light of the inner eyes that cures one's blindness and restores his inner sight."

"With knowledge, one attains the stations of the chosen ones, and with it, one earns good esteem and blessings in this world as well as in the eternal life to come thereafter. In fact, to ponder upon knowledge equals fasting, and to study it equals standing up all night long in supererogatory prayers. With knowledge, families unite in love and compassion, and with it, they recognize right from wrong, and finally, knowledge is the leader and the guiding light of the masters, while rewarding deeds can only follow that."

**605-** Imam Ahmad bin Hanbal, God be pleased with him, narrated that when Mu'ãth bin Jabal, God be pleased with him, was in his deathbed, he said to his companions: "Go and look out, is it dawn yet?" At once, someone went to the door and came back to report: "Not yet!" Mu'ãth immediately turned to another person and said to him: "You go and find out, is it dawn yet?" The next companion went to the door and came back with the same answer: "It is not the morning yet!" Mu'ãth waited a little and then he became annoyed as he kept on inquiring about the morning, and finally, as the time drew closer to daylight, and to appease his anxiety, someone looked out and then he returned to report: "Yes, it is the morning!"

Mu'āth, God be pleased with him, then prayed: "I seek refuge in Allah, blessed be His Name, to protect me from a night that delivers its visitant to hell-fire by the morning. Welcome to death, and welcome to the long awaited caller and the harbinger of the Beloved; — Indeed, you are a pleasant relief who arrives at a moment of painful anguish and vacuity. O Allah! I lived a lifelong of reverence and fear of You, and today, I am beseeching You for mercy. Beloved Lord, You know that I was never fond of this world, nor did I ever hoped for a long life herein to watch the rivers flow, or to plant trees. You know well that my greatest endeavors were bent around willingly thirsting and fasting from ephemeral pleasures, striving arduous hours of long nights worshipping You and celebrating Your praises, and competing on my knees with the scholars and sages wherever and whenever people gathered to celebrate Your praises and to glorify Your Name."

**606-** Imam Ahmad bin Hanbal, God be pleased with him, narrated that a plague once befell Syria, and people became bewildered by the contagious and destructive disease. Several rumors spread around, and some people attributed the disease to a major flood that may have taken place in a distant land. When Mu'āth heard people's hearsay, he stood up at the mosque and delivered a sermon, wherein, after praising Almighty Allah, blessed be His Name, and after paying tribute to His messenger ﷺ and invoking the divine blessings (*salawāt*) upon him, Mu'āth said: "It has come to my attention that you are bewildered by your adversities, and I also heard how you are interpreting it in accordance with your personal whims, and therefore, I am afraid that perhaps you are seized by oblivion. Nevertheless, you must realize that this is a munificent mercy from your Lord, blessed be His Name. This is the answer of the prayers of your prophet ﷺ, upon whom be peace, and after all, this is the answer to the collective prayers of all the righteous believers before you. In truth, this is the lightest of adversities a believer may have to face to expiate his sins. What your peers feared most was to leave the door of one's house in the morning, not aware whether he is a believer or a hypocrite, and they also feared to experience a day, when people are governed by a generation of mutant dissenting youths who will someday subordinate them, impose their immature and dangerous will upon them, and dictate their affairs."

**607-** Al-Hãrith bin 'Umaira said: "Mu'ãth, Abu 'Ubaida, Sharhabīl bin Hasana, and Abu Mãlik al-Ash'ari, all four were struck by the plague on the same day. When Mu'ãth fell ill, he commented, 'This is the mercy of your Lord, blessed be His Name, this is indeed the answer of the prayers of your prophet ﷺ, upon whom be peace, and this is how the souls of many of the righteous believers before you were taken back to their Lord.' Mu'ãth then prayed, 'Lord, grant the family of Mu'ãth the largest share of this mercy.' "

Al-Hãrith bin 'Umaira continued: "Mu'ãth's eldest son, 'Abdu-Rahmãn, by whose name Mu'ãth was patronymed, and who was more dear to him than the entire world, was struck by the plague that same evening. When Mu'ãth returned home from his evening congregational prayers at the mosque, he discovered that, and he asked him, 'O 'Abdu-Rahmãn, how are you feeling?' 'Abdu-Rahmãn replied with a Qur'anic verse: 'O my father, ﴾ This truth comes from your Lord, have no doubt therein ﴿ (*Qur'an 3:60*).' Mu'ãth also quoted from the Qur'an in his reply, saying, ﴾ God willing, you will find me patient (with His decree) ﴿ (*Qur'an 37:102*).' "

'Abdu-Rahmãn died that same night, and Mu'ãth buried him in the morning. Shortly after that, Mu'ãth himself fell ill with the same plague, and his share of physical suffering with his mortal throes were most severe and forbidding, and no one has ever suffered thus before him. After each stroke, and every time Mu'ãth regained his consciousness, he struggled to open the side of his eye, and with extreme difficulty he prayed: "My Lord, crush me with Your mightiest blow. I swear by Your mighty firm Hand, that You know how much my heart loves You."

**608-** 'Abdullãh bin Muhammad bin Ja'far narrated, re Mu'ãth bin Jabal, God be pleased with him, that God's messenger ﷺ, upon whom be peace, said to him: "O Mu'ãth, go and prepare your camel then come back to me, for I am sending you to Yemen."

Mu'ãth continued: "At once, I went home and I prepared my camel then returned and stood by the gate of the mosque, awaiting permission from God's messenger ﷺ, upon whom be peace. When he came out, he took me by the hand, and we walked together for a while, and he then said: "O Mu'ãth, I am asking you and I am advising you to be pious with Allah, and to fear wrongdoing. Be truthful when you speak, fulfill what you promise, deliver what you are entrusted with, and shun treason. I advise you to have compassion towards the orphan, to guard and protect your neighbor, to swallow your anger, to be humble, to lower your wing to the believers, to maintain constancy with your faith, to learn and understand the Qur'an, to love the hereafter, to worry about the Day of Reckoning, to curtail your hope, and to do your best no matter what you do. I forbid you to insult any Muslim, to belie a truthful person, or to believe a liar, and I enjoin upon you to disobey a just *Imam* (i.e., guide and a leader). O Mu'ãth, always remember Allah, blessed be His Name. Remember Him with each breath, and keep His remembrance as you cross each and every rock and tree. Repent immediately each time you commit a wrongdoing. Repent privately for each wrongdoing you commit in private, and repent in public for each wrongdoing you commit in public."

**609-** The above tradition was also reported by 'Abdullãh bin Omar, God be pleased with both of them, who said: "When God's messenger ﷺ, upon whom be peace, intended to send Mu'ãth to Yemen, he too a short walk with him, and he advised him, 'O Mu'ãth, I advise as a compassionate brother would advise his precious brother. I advise you to be steadfast with your piety and reverence for Almighty Allah, blessed be His Name.' "

Upon reporting most of the above narrated tradition, 'Abdullãh bin Omar, God be pleased with him, also quoted God's messenger ﷺ, upon whom be peace, to have told Mu'ãth: "I advise you to visit the sick, to hasten to fulfill the needs of the widowed women and the weak, to often sit in the company of the poor and the meek. I advise you to always be just even if justice stands between you and your personal interests, always tell the truth, and fear no one's censure when it comes to Allah's rights."

**610-** Bishr bin Müsa narrated that Mu'ãth bin Jabal, God be pleased with him, said: "God's messenger ﷺ, upon whom be peace, once took me by the hand, and he said to me, 'O Mu'ãth, I swear that I love you in Allah.' Mu'ãth replied, 'O blessed messenger of

Allah, surely you are more dear to me than my own father and my own mother, I swear by Allah that I love you too.' God's messenger ﷺ, upon whom be peace, then added, 'O Mu'āth, I advise you not to fail to recite the following supplication, after each *Ṣalāt* (prayer), say, 'O God, help me to have constancy in remembering You, to always thank You, and help me to Lord duly worship You.' "

**611-** Anas bin Mālik narrated that Mu'āth bin Jabal, God be pleased with him, came one mourning to see God's messenger ﷺ, upon whom be peace, who asked him: "How did you wake up this mourning?" Mu'āth replied: "I woke up a believer in Allah, exalted be His Name." God's messenger ﷺ, upon whom be peace, said: "Every statement must be substantiated, and every claim must be supported by the truth, hence, what is the proof of your claim?" Mu'āth replied: "O prophet of Allah, blessed be His Name, I never woke up in a mourning thinking that I will live to see the evening, and I never come upon an evening thinking that I will be there to witness another mourning. O prophet of Allah, blessed be His Name, I never walked a single step thinking that the second foot will follow it. Deep in my heart, it a vivid perception, and it is as though I am seeing all nations kneeling before their Lord in the Final Hour, all are brought in as promised, for their deeds to be judged by the Book of the divine criterion. I sometimes also see them standing up, and each nation is headed by its prophet, with them, the people bring the statues and carry the idols they carved and worshiped besides Allah. It is as though I am witnessing the punishment of the dwellers of hell-fire and the reward of the dwellers of the heavenly paradise!" God's messenger ﷺ, upon whom be peace, then said: "Now that you have such realization, thence, it is imperative for you to act upon it and to be steadfast."

**612-** Al-Qāsim bin Mukhaimara narrated that Mu'āth bin Jabal, God be pleased with him, once returned from Yemen to Madina on a mission, and one evening, God's messenger ﷺ, upon whom be peace, inquired from him: "In what state did you leave the people?" Mu'āth replied: "I left them having no anxieties except those of cattle!"[1] God's messenger ﷺ, upon whom be peace, commented: "Then what would you say when you will come upon

[1] i.e., merely worried about their livelihood.

a time when people will correctly recognize and know what these people do not understand, and yet, they will nurture no concerns other than those of cattle!"

**613-** Mãlik bin Yakhmãr narrated that Mu'ãth bin Jabal, God be pleased with him, said: "I turned to God's messenger ﷺ, upon whom be peace, while circumambulating the Ka'ba, and I asked him, 'O messenger of Allah, show us what is most evil in people!' He replied, 'Ask only about what is good, and do not ask about evil.' God's messenger ﷺ, upon whom be peace, then said: "The most evil of people are the evildoers among the learned ones."

**614-** 'Abdu-Rahmãn bin Ghanam narrated that he was with Mu'ãth bin Jabal, God be pleased with him, when his son died, and when he received a letter saying:

"In the Name of Allah, the Merciful, the most Compassionate. Peace be upon you. To you I thank Allah besides Whom there is no god. As to the purpose of this letter: I pray to Allah, blessed be His Name, to expound your reward, to inspire you patience, and to endow us and you with increasing gratitude. Indeed, our souls, families, properties, and children are comforting endowments He graciously bestows upon us, and they are His exposed trust. He grants such comforts for a term, and He then takes them back at the appointed time. Allah, blessed be His Name, also ordained us to show gratitude to Him when He gives us, and to exercise patience when He tries us."

"Your son was indeed Allah's comforting endowments, and His exposed trust. He allowed you to appreciate him and to enjoy such a praiseworthy gift. Then He took him back from you for a prodigious reward. Indeed, should you bare your trial with patience and gratitude, then the divine blessings, mercy, and guidance are your prize. Be warned you not to have two opposing complexions, which together denote defect in character: 1) One is gratitude when Allah gives, and 2) discontent when He calls back for His trust. Otherwise, your reward will be forfeited, and you will immensely regret your losses. When you reflect upon your trial, you will find that it does not measure up to your reward, and therefore, you will be able to receive what Allah promised. Allow the scope of your sorrow to transcend what befell you, for what passed is past, and peace be upon you."[1]

**615-** 'Amru bnu Murra narrated that when God's messenger ﷺ, upon whom be peace, sent Mu'ãth bin Jabal, God be pleased with him, to Yemen, he said to him: "When you are true to your *Deen* (i.e., faith and religious commitment), then a mere little effort will be sufficient to satisfy your needs."

## 33- Sa'ĩd Bin 'Ãmer

The next of our peers and beacons of true theism is Sa'ĩd Bin 'Ãmer, God be pleased with him. Sa'ĩd understood the essence of true Islam, and he readily forsook any allegiance to the delusory attraction and destructive fascination of this mind mesmerizing world. He looked down at the seekers of this world and loathed their strife, while he sought the natural higher inclinations of the earlier companions with steadfastness, commitment, and loyalty to his covenant. Although Sa'ĩd Bin 'Ãmer, God be pleased with him, was appointed during the time of the caliphate of Omar bin al-Khattãb, God be pleased with him, to a governing position in Syria, and he proved to be a true servant of Almighty Allah, blessed be His Name, and he served the dependants of God Almighty as a true ascetic with piety, sincerity, and devotion, as well as he delivered his trust with clarity and impeccable justice.

It is said that the path of spirituality calls for bearing one's difficulties with patience, and without giving much regard to personal expectations.

**616-** On this subject, Hassãn bin 'Atiyya narrated that when the commander of the believers, Omar bin al-Khattãb, God be pleased with him, removed Mu'ãwiya from his post as the governor of Syria (*Shãm*), he assigned Sa'ĩd Bin 'Ãmer, God be pleased with him, to that position. Sa'ĩd Bin 'Ãmer immediately left Madina with his wife, and he travelled north to serve.

---

[1] It must be noted here that although the above letter is sometimes attributed to God's messenger ﷺ, upon whom be peace, and should it be so, then it is probable that it was addressed to someone else, and on an earlier date, since the son of Mu'ãth died after the passing of God's messenger ﷺ, upon whom be peace. It is also possible that a copy of the above letter was sent to Mu'ãth by one of the companions to comfort him when his son passed.

Sometimes later, Omar heard that Sa'ïd Bin 'Ãmer was experiencing difficulties with his basic needs, and therefore, Omar sent him one thousand Dinars. When the money was delivered, Sa'ïd Bin 'Ãmer brought it home to his wife, and said to her, 'Omar sent us this gift. See what do you wish to do with it.' The wife delighted as she replied: "Why don't you buy ourselves some direly needed food along with other supplies for now, and then save the balance for later!" Sa'ïd Bin 'Ãmer pondered for a moment, and said: "Let me suggest a better way to use this gift. Let us invest this money and put it to work for us. — Let us give it to a merchant to trade with it, he will guarantee the capital investment, and we will earn our daily bread from its return." The wife consented, and Sa'ïd went out and bought some food and provisions for his house, and he also bought two camels and two servants to attend to them, and then, he decided to distribute everything to the poor and the needy in that town, but did not confide his real intention to his wife.

Shortly thereafter, the wife said to Sa'ïd: "We have used up such and such supplied, and I wish that you would go to that man and ask him to give us some of the profits so we may buy extra needed supplies." Sa'ïd heard what his wife said but he did not answer her, nor did he do anything about it. A couple of days later, the wife inquired anew, but Sa'ïd had no reply. Consequently, the wife said something harsh that hurt the feelings of her husband and made him spend most of his days at the mosque and return to his house late every night.

One evening, a friend of Sa'ïd Bin 'Ãmer, God be pleased with him, came home with him and said to the wife: "What can you do! Surely you have hurt your husband's deep feelings, while he can do nothing about his investment, for he has distributed the entire amount in charity!" The wife was surprised when she heard the story, she was shocked, and she cried in pain, and then she kept to herself for some days thereafter.

Few days later, Sa'ïd Bin 'Ãmer came home and he found his wife depressed. Sa'ïd turned to her and said: "Take it easy! I once had some true companions, they all have died a short while ago, and today, I would prefer to be in their company rather than to have the entire treasures of this world at my disposal or even to live eternally herein. Let me tell you, to my perception, should one of the *houri* (nymphs) of the heavenly paradise now glance upon the earth, the effulgent light of her face will shine evenly for the inhabitants of the entire planet all at once, and such glance will surely render pale the glow of the sun and the radiance of a full moon. In my view, surely the purity of her veil is a more superior wear than the entire world and all its treasures, and in truth, you are more precious to my heart than to let you be engrossed in such mundane accessories, or to allow them to deceive you."

When the wife heard what her husband said, and when she understood Sa'ïd's pious intention, she excused him and accepted his explanation.

**617-** Khãlid bin Ma'dãn narrated that the commander of the believers, Omar bin al-Khattãb, God be pleased with him, appointed Sa'ïd Bin 'Ãmer Ibn Juthaim al-Jamhi, God be pleased with him, to the post of governor of Homs, Syria. One day Omar himself came to visit Homs, and he privately asked its citizens, 'How do you find your employee?' The people complained to Omar about their governor Sa'ïd Bin 'Ãmer — incidentally, the people of Homs were labeled *'the citizens of little Küfa,'* because, like the citizens of the city of Küfa, Iraq, the people of Homs invariably complained about their administrators; — and here again, they were critical about their governor as they said, 'We basically have four complaints about him!'

Omar, God be pleased with him, was surprised, and he asked, 'What are they?' The people replied, 'He only comes out of his house in the mid-morning to attend to our needs.' Omar became upset, and he said, 'This is a serious allegation, what else?' They said, 'He never answers any calls at night.' Omar commented, 'This is another serious allegation as well. What else?' They continued, 'He has reserved one day in each month for himself, where he does not come out at all.' Omar said, 'Surely this is another serious one, and what else?' They said, 'From time to time, he gets extremely sick, and he remains at home.'

Omar, God be pleased with him, immediately called for Sa'ïd Bin 'Ãmer to meet the people face to face and answer their allegations, and he prayed, 'My Lord, do not disappoint me with my opinion of Sa'ïd Bin 'Ãmer today.'

When sa'ïd sat in their midst, Omar, God be pleased with him, turned to the people and said, 'Tell me again, what charges do you have against your *wãli* (governor)?' The people said, 'He only comes out of his house in the mid-morning to attend to our needs.' Sa'ïd Bin 'Ãmer, God be pleased with him, answered, 'Allah is my witness, I was hoping that I did not have to answer to this one. After all, my wife has no helpers, and for this reason, I kneed my dough every mourning, and I wait for it to rise before I take my ablution and come out to attend to their needs,'

Omar further asked the people, 'Voice your next complaint?' The people replied, 'He never answers any calls at night.' Omar turned to Sa'ïd Bin 'Ãmer, God be pleased with both of them, and inquired, 'What do you have to say about that?' Sa'ïd replied, 'I also hoped that I did not have to speak regarding this matter, however, since this subject has come up thus, then I feel that I must explain that in fact, I have allotted the day to serve the needs of the people, and as to the night, I have kept it to my personal devotion and worship of Almighty Allah, blessed be His Name.'

Omar then turned to the people and he asked, 'What other complaints do you hold against him?' The people replied, 'He has reserved one day a month when he does not come out until late in the day.' Omar turned to Sa'ïd and inquired, 'What do you have to say about that?' Sa'ïd replied, 'O Commander and Prince of the believers, I have no one to wash my clothes, nor do I have a second set of clothing. Once a month, I wash my cloth, I wait until they dry out, and then, I smooth them by hand before I come out of my house to attend to the needs of the people.'

Omar further asked the people, 'What other complaints do you have about him?' The people replied, 'From time to time, he gets extremely sick, and he stays in his bed for a while, as though if he was sick!' Omar again turned to Sa'ïd Bin 'Ãmer, God be pleased with both of them, and asked him, 'What do you say about that?' Sa'ïd pondered stared for a moment, and then he replied, 'O Commander and Prince of the believers, before embracing Islam,

I lived in Mecca, and I watched when Khubaib al-Anṣāri was murdered and his body mutilated at the hands the polytheist Quraishis who had tortured him for a long time, and then, they pierced him with their spears repeatedly, and furthermore, they carried him on a stick; — and there I stood during his last agonizing moments. The disbelievers asked Khubaib, 'At this junction, wouldn't it be better for you to renounce your faith and to spare your life; and wouldn't you rather see Muhammad in your place instead?' Khubaib, God be pleased with him, replied, 'Let Allah be my witness that I would rather not be resting in comfort in the midst of my family and children tonight, knowing that even a small thorn has hurt God's messenger, Muhammad ﷺ, upon whom be peace.' Khubaib then called out with a piercing voice, 'O Muhammad!' Immediately, the Quraishis became extremely furious, and in their rage, they executed him at once, and then, they mutilated his body with great fury.'

Sa'ïd Bin 'Ãmer continued: "Whenever I remember the scene of that soul terrorizing sinister dark day, being a polytheist and an atheist then, and having no faith in Almighty Allah, whenever I recall how I failed to support him under such circumstances, I become extremely tormented and agitated thinking that Allah, the Lord of majesty and glory, blessed be His Name, will never forgive me for such a sin, and hence I become sickened and seized by depression and distraught, as if I am entrapped by the throes of death.'

Omar then commented: "All praises be to Allah, blessed be His Name, Who did not let my keenness fail me when I appointed him to serve."

Later on, when he returned to Madina, Omar, God be pleased with him, sent one thousand Dinars to Sa'ïd Bin 'Ãmer, God be pleased with him, with the message: "Use them for your personal needs."

When the wife of Sa'ïd Bin 'Ãmer, God be pleased with him, saw the gift, she said: "All praises be to Allah, blessed be His Name Who provided us with these means to make your duty lighter." Sa'ïd then turned to his wife and said: "Would you like to know about a better way to use this money? Let us invest it in a business that will insure a satisfactory return when we need it most!" The wife replied favorably: "Indeed."

Immediately, Sa'ïd Bin 'Ãmer, God be pleased with him, called someone he trusted in the family, and he divided the money in several pouches, and said to him: "Go and give this bag to the widow of so and so, and this bag to the orphan and such and such family, and this back to that neighbor who is confined to his bed ..." Sa'ïd Bin 'Ãmer did thus until only a single coin of money remained, which he passed to his wife, and said: "Spend this for your immediate needs." Sa'ïd then went back to his work.

As Sa'ïd was leaving the house, the wife asked him: "Why don't you hire a servant to help us? What can this little money do?" Sa'ïd Bin 'Ãmer, God be pleased with him, replied: "Do not worry. Your true return will come at a time when you need it most!"

**618-** 'Abdu Rahmnan bin Sãbit al-Jamhi narrated that Omar bin al-Khattãb, God be pleased with him, once called a man from the tribe of Bani Jamh, named Sa'ïd Bin 'Ãmer, son of Juthaim al-Jamhi, and he said to him: "I am appointing you to serve in such and such land." Sa'ïd replied: "O commander of the believers, please do not let my focus be distracted by such a rank!" Omar became upset, and he said: "I swear by Allah, that I will not let you get away with it, or let you be free of responsibility. You have elected me to this position, and you have laid this monumental responsibility upon my shoulders, and then you wish to leave the burden on me alone to carry! Nay."

Omar then said to Sa'ïd: "We will pay you for your services as well as we will give you the necessary funds for any extra needs you may have." Consenting to his fate, Sa'ïd replied: "Surely Allah has made the remuneration of the post sufficient, and I do not wish to receive any extra supplement thereto."

Sa'ïd complied with the orders, and he went to serve his function. Every time he received his salary, Sa'ïd would go out and buy his family their immediately needed provisions, and he then would distribute the balance in charity. Whenever his wife inquired from him, 'Where is the balance of your salary?' Sa'ïd replied, 'I loaned it to someone.'

One day, his relatives came to visit him, and they said to him: "Surely your family has rights upon you, and your in-laws also have rights upon you, and accordingly, you must satisfy their needs as well!" Sa'ïd Bin 'Ãmer, God be pleased with him, replied: "I am neither excluding my family from any considerations, nor am I giving preference to others over them, and I will not waste my life soliciting anyone's pleasure; — the cost of which is extremely high, and which means that I would have to circumvent my personal aspiration to join the *houri* of the heavenly paradise in the life after. Let me tell you that should one of such most beautiful and chaste *houris* glance upon the earth, the effulgent light of her face will shine evenly for the inhabitants of the entire planet. Moreover, you must understand that I do not wish to miss the first cluster of believers, for I have heard God's messenger ﷺ, upon whom be peace, say, 'When Allah, the Lord of majesty and glory, blessed be His Name, will gather the people for judgment, the poor ones among the believers will flock in a solemn procession and head towards the heavenly paradise, advancing in balanced formations, just like flocks of pigeons in flight. Shortly before arriving there, the angels will stop them, and they instruct them, 'You must first stop by the station of reckoning and await the final judgment!' The believers that were poor in the world will reply, 'What judgment is there for us? We have nothing to report, nor did you ever give us anything to be reckoned for.' At once, Almighty Allah will assert, 'My servants spoke the truth,' and immediately the gates of the heavenly paradise will open to them, and they will enter it without questioning, seventy years before its dwellers are admitted to their permanent abode.'

## 34- 'Umair Bnu Sa'ad al-Ansãri

Here is another unique companion of God's messenger ﷺ, upon whom be peace. His name is 'Umair bnu Sa'ad, God be pleased with him. He was true to his covenant, loyal to his promise, trustworthy, quick thinking, and appreciative of learning. His charisma embodied the needed spiritual soundness and strength to achieve decisive control over his surrounding circumstances. His persona portrayed his unique fabric, and he was a pious theist who became the crown of governors, as well as he was Allah's witnessing proof amidst His creation.

Here is another account of an incident that portrays the unique character of this pious ascetic and blessed companion of God's messenger ﷺ, upon whom be peace:

**619-** Sulaimān bin Ahmad narrated that the Commander of the Believers, Omar bin al-Khattāb, God be pleased with him, once appointed 'Umair bnu Sa'ad al-Ansāri, as administrator of the city of Homs, Syria. Thereat, 'Umair bnu Sa'ad stayed one full year without reporting to the caliph in Madina, and no news came from that direction for such a long time.

In a manner intended to teach a lesson on the importance of communication, coordination, and formal reporting between the distant regions and the central state, Omar, God be pleased with him, appeared suspicious, and to create a precedent in managing the affairs of the people, he said to his log keeper: "I think that 'Umair has betrayed us. Write to him the following message, 'Upon receiving my letter, return to Madina immediately, and bring back with you all the dues and alms taxes you have collected up to date from the Muslims (of Homs).' "

When 'Umair bnu Sa'ad, God be pleased with him, received the letter, and on the spot, he immediately gathered his meager belongings, which consisted of a haversack, a small cooking pot, and few personal tools which he wrapped in a piece of cloth. 'Umair then prepared some food for the journey, and he roped his goat and left Homs on foot, dragging the goat behind him, and he walked until he entered the city of Madina weeks later.

When he arrived to Madina, 'Umair had lost weight, his face was pale and dirty, his hair long, and he was covered from head to toe with the dust of the journey. Upon entering the city of Madina, 'Umair bnu Sa'ad, God be pleased with him, and even prior to going to the mosque, he headed immediately towards Omar's house. When he entered, 'Umair greeted him reverently: "Peace be upon you, O Commander of the Believers, may Allah's mercy and blessing descend upon you."

When Omar looked up and saw 'Umair's condition, he looked

at him with obvious shock and said: "What happened to you?" 'Umair replied: "What wrong do you see happened to me! Do you not see me standing up with a healthy body, my blood renewed and pure from the journey, and here I am in your presence, having walked all this distance, dragging the world[1] by its horn behind me?"

Omar then asked him: "What are you carrying with you?" 'Umair replied: "I am carrying my haversack, wherein I placed my food, a pot which I sometimes use to cook my food and to wash my head and clothes, besides a special pouch for my personal tools I use for my ritual ablution and for drinking, and furthermore, I brought my goat, which I sometimes leaned on, and at other times, it was useful to counter or to scare an enemy. Let Allah be my witness that the whole world is of no importance after that."

Omar asked: "Did you come back walking on foot?" 'Umair replied: "I did." Omar further asked: "Was there no one to donate an animal for you to ride on for this arduous long journey?" 'Umair replied: "They neither offered me anything, nor did I ask any one for anything." Omar then commented: "Most inauspicious are such Muslims you have left behind you." 'Umair replied: "O Omar, you must fear Allah! You know well that Allah forbade you to backbite others. Let me clarify here that when I last saw them, they were engaged in a *dhuha,* mid-mourning supererogatory prayers, and to this I bear witness."

Omar further asked: "How much alms tax have you collected? And would you report to me about the state of affairs you were sent to conduct?" 'Umair replied: "O Commander and Prince of the Believers, please enunciate your question clearly! What do you mean?" Omar exclaimed: "Glory be to Allah the All-Knowing Lord!" 'Umair then said: "I was afraid to tell you the news should they depress you. However, I must report to you since you have sent me to that town to govern. As soon as I reached there, I called upon the righteous and most trustworthy citizens, and I appointed them to collect the due alms. Each time they brought me the money, I placed it where it belongs, and that is to serve the town's immediate interest, and to improve people's lives. Should there have been any money over and above that, surely I would have brought it back to you."

Omar exclaimed: "Then you have brought us nothing?" 'Umair replied in the affirmative: "Nothing!" Omar pondered for a moment, and he then turned to his immediate circle and said: "Renew for 'Umair his contract of employment." Hearing that, 'Umair became upset and he said: "That's something different! I expressly refuse to work for you or for anyone after you from this day on. O Omar, I thought that you will be on my side! Is this humiliation you brought me in public the best of what you can offer as a reward for my services? Surely the worst of my days are those which I had to share the responsibility of this government with you."

'Umair immediately asked Omar for permission to leave, and he walked back on foot to his house which was situated at a distance of several miles from Madina.

Omar wanted to pursue his intention, and as soon as 'Umair left, Omar turned to his companions and said: "I have the feeling that he betrayed us!" Omar then gave someone called al-Hārith one hundred Dinars and said to him: "Follow 'Umair to his house, and pretend to wish to stay there as his guest. If you find something unusual, come back and tell us about it. However, if you find him in dire need, then give him this one hundred Dinars."

When al-Hārith arrived near 'Umair's house at the outskirts of Madina, he found him sitting near the wall outside his house boiling some water and washing his shirt. Al-Hārith paid his regards to 'Umair who replied: "Come down, be our guest, may Allah's mercy descend upon you." Hence, al-Hārith dismounted his mule, and he sat near 'Umair, God be pleased with him.

'Umair asked al-Hārith: "Where do you come from?"

- "From Madina." Al-Hārith replied.

'Umair inquired: "How did you leave the commander of the believers when you left the city?"

- "He was well when I left him." Al-Hārith replied.

'Umair further inquired: "How are the Muslims doing in the city?"

Again, al-Hārith replied: "They are all fine."

'Umair asked: "Does the commander of the believers execute the divine laws?"

Al-Hãrith replied: "Indeed he does. He lately caused the death of one of his own sons, when he required him to pay for a major sin the son had committed."

'Umair then prayed: "O Allah, help Omar, for I only know him to have intense love for You."

'Umair had a single batch of barley bread his wife prepared, and al-Hãrith stayed as his guest for three days and nights. 'Umair offered his guest a single meal every day, while he and his wife slept hungry for the next three nights. After the three days passed, 'Umair and his wife were exhausted, and 'Umair said to his guest: "You have made us hungry. If it agrees with you to take leave and return to your home, then please do so."

Immediately al-Hãrith pulled out one hundred Dinars from his pouch and said: "The commander of the believers have sent you this gift to use for your basic needs."

'Umair became extremely upset as he exclaimed: "No, I have no need for it. Take it back to him!"

The wife suggested with a humble low voice: "Take it, and if you need it, then use it, otherwise, place it where it should be."

Hearing his wife, 'Umair immediately regained his calm as he replied to his wife: "Allah is my witness, that I do not even have a pouch to keep it!"

The wife immediately tore a piece from the bottom of her robe and handed it to him. 'Umair, God be pleased with him, wrapped the one hundred Dinars inside the cloth, and he went along with his guest to a nearby village where he distributed the money between the orphans among the children of the martyrs as well as other poor residents. All the way through, al-Hãrith also had hoped to receive some of it, but 'Umair ignored his intuition. When they returned home, 'Umair said to al-Hãrith: "Go back now, and convey my regards of peace to the commander of the believers."

Thus, al-Hãrith returned to Omar, God be pleased with him, who asked him: "What did you find out?" Al-Hãrith replied: "O commander of the believers, I witnessed austere conditions." Omar precipitated rigorously: "What did he do with the money you gave to him?" Al-Hãrith became apprehensive as he replied: "I have no idea!"

Omar immediately wrote a message to 'Umair, saying: "Come here at once upon reading this notice, and before you put down this message."

Shortly after that, 'Umair arrived, and Omar, God be pleased with him, asked him: "What did you do with the money?" 'Umair replied: "I did with it whatever I did. Why do you have to ask?" Feeling remorse, Omar appealed with tears in his eyes: "I implore you earnestly to tell me about what did you do with the money!" 'Umair replied: "I offered it in charity for my personal benefit in the hereafter." Omar commented: "Indeed, Allah has shown you the way to receiving His mercy."

Immediately, Omar ordered that a parcel containing a generous measure of food to be prepared and two new garments be given to 'Umair. When they were brought in, 'Umair said: "As for the food, I truly have no need for it, for I have left two measure of wheat barley, and until they are consumed, I am confident that Allah, blessed be His Name, will provide the needed provisions for what will come next. However, as for the two garments, I will take them, for I have left my wife with a torn robe, and she can use them."

'Umair then graciously took the two garments, and he left immediately after this conversation with Omar, and returned to his house.

'Umair died few days after that event, may Allah's eternal mercy descend upon him died having fulfilled his duties to the Allah, and content in His mercy. When Omar heard the news, he felt for him and prayed for Allah's mercy to encompass him. That day, Omar walked along with few of his companions to the *Baqï'* cemetery to visit 'Umair's grave. On their way, Omar, God be pleased with him, said: "Let each one of you make a wish." Someone said: "O commander of the believers, I wish that I had the needed money to free such and such number of slaves from bondage for Allah's pleasure." Another man said: "O commander of the believers, I wish that I had large sums of money to spend in charity for Allah's pleasure." A third person said: "I wish that I had the physical strength to stand by the well of Zamzam, and to draw out the needed water to quench the thirst of all the pilgrims who visit Allah's House." Omar, God be pleased with him, then prayed: "I wish that I had another man such as 'Umair bnu Sa'ad to help me serve the needs of the Muslims."

**620-** Abu Talha al-Khawlãni said: "I once visited the house of 'Umair bnu Sa'ad in Palestine. He had a unique personality, and he was frequently labeled *'a fabric of his own.'* Thereat, I found him sitting on a bench in his yard, and nearby there was an artificial shallow pond made of stones which collected some drinking water for the livestock he managed.

'Umair bnu Sa'ad, God be pleased with him, turned to a servant who was standing by, and he said to him: "Young man. Take the horses inside." When the servant did what he was told, 'Umair looked towards the horses and he discovered that a female horse was missing. 'Umair asked: "What happened to the other horse?" The servant replied: "She is mangy, and she carries a festering wound dripping blood." 'Umair asked: "Bring her in!" The servant replied: "I am afraid that her mange could affect the other horses!" 'Umair reiterated: "Bring her in, for I once heard God's messenger ﷺ, upon whom be peace, say: "A disease does not spread on its own, a bad omen does come except when invited, and only the heedless will wander aimlessly."

'Umair pointing out to emphasize the divine control of God Almighty, blessed be His Name, continued: "Don't you see the camels in the desert, how unexpectedly, and without contact with previously diseased animals, sometimes they too develop festers or mange in varying parts of their body! Tell me, who introduced the first virus?"

## 35- Ubai Bnu Ka'ab

Also among our peers and blessed sires, the foremost among all Muslims and the highly esteemed companions of God's messenger ﷺ, upon whom be peace, there is Ubai Bnu Ka'ab, God be pleased with him. He was regularly sought by the believers to explain profound spiritual questions, to expound upon uncommon issues, and he was blessed to arrive at uncommon, yet most convincing interpretations. Ubai transcended yearning and its agony, and he rose to an exalted spiritual state above common norms.

**621-** 'Abdullāh bin Rabāh narrated, re Ubai Bnu Ka'ab, God be pleased with him, that God's messenger ﷺ, upon whom be peace, once asked him: "O Abal-Munthir, which verse from the revealed Book of Almighty Allah you consider most magnificent?" Ubai replied: "The verse of the Divine Throne, and he recited: ﴾ Allah, there is no god except Him, the ever Living, the sovereign controller. He is not subject to slumber nor sleep. To Him belongs everything the heavens and the earth hold. Who is there to intercede before Him except as He permits. He knows what awaits the people and what will come thereafter. They encompass naught of His knowledge except as He wills. His Throne encompasses the heavens and the earth, and it does not weary Him to preserve them, for He is the Most Exalted, the Magnificent ﴿ (*Qur'an 2:255*). God's messenger ﷺ, upon whom be peace, then stroke Ubai's chest and said: "O Abal-Munthir, most blessed is your knowledge."

**622-** Anas bin Mālik, God be pleased with him, narrated that God's messenger ﷺ, upon whom be peace, once said to Ubai Bnu Ka'ab, God be pleased with him: "Allah, the Lord of majesty and glory, blessed be His Name, has commanded me to rehearse the revelation to you." Ubai became extremely emotional, he was struck with awe and reverence of his Lord, and he inquired: "O messenger of Allah, did Allah, the Most Exalted, mention me to you by name?" God's messenger ﷺ, upon whom be peace, replied: "Yes indeed, Allah mentioned you to me by name;" and immediately Ubai burst into tears.

**623-** In another narration of the above account, Ja'far bin Muhammad bin 'Amr narrated, re Ubai Bnu Ka'ab, God be pleased with him, that God's messenger ﷺ, upon whom be peace, said to him: "I was commanded to rehearse the Qur'an before you." Ubai replied: "I ask you in the Name of my Lord and your Lord of majesty and glory, did He mention me by name?" God's messenger ﷺ, upon whom be peace, answered: "Yes indeed, He mentioned you by your name." God's messenger ﷺ then recited: ﴾ Say: It is (only) by the grace of Allah and His mercy. Let them enjoy such a divine favor, for indeed He is better than all what they cater to › (*Qur'an 10:58*).

**624-** Also in another narration, Mu'ãth bin Ubai Bnu Ka'ab narrated, re his father, that God's messenger ﷺ, upon whom be peace, said to him: "I am commanded to rehearse the Qur'an before you." Ubai replied: "O messenger of Allah! You are the one who guided my faith, I embraced Islam at your hand, and it is from you that I learn!" When God's messenger ﷺ, upon whom be peace, reiterated his statement, 'Ubaid asked: "O messenger of Allah! Was I mentioned by name?" God's messenger ﷺ replied: "Yes indeed, you were mentioned in the upper realms by name and lineage." Upon hearing that, Ubai Bnu Ka'ab, God be pleased with him, said: "Then read O messenger of Allah."

**625-** Al-Rabi' bin Anas, God be pleased with him, narrated that Abul 'Ãliya said: "When Ubai heard what God's messenger ﷺ, upon whom be peace, had to say, he burst out crying, and I do not know whether he was moved by love or fear."

**626-** Ja'far bin Muhammad narrated that Ubai Bnu Ka'ab, God be pleased with him, said: "I went to God's messenger ﷺ, upon whom be peace, and he placed the palm of his hand on my chest, and he prayed, 'I call upon Allah's protection to shield you against doubt and refutation.'

Ubai Bnu Ka'ab, God be pleased with him, commented: "Immediately, my eyes became filled with tears, and it was as though I was witnessing the distinct presence of my Lord."

**627-** Qays Bnu 'Ubãd narrated: "I once traveled to Madina to meet the companions of God's messenger ﷺ, upon whom be peace, and I longed mostly to meet Ubai Bnu Ka'ab, God be pleased with him. As soon as I arrived to Madina, I went to the mosque and I sat in the front raw near the *miḫrãb* (prayer niche). When Ubai Bnu Ka'ab came out, he lead the congregational prayers, and when he finished, he sat down and spoke. Surely, I have never seen before people who were so eager to hear someone, with their heads poked out and listening attentively. During his speech, Ubai Bnu Ka'ab, God be pleased with him, said, '... I swear by the Lord of the Ka'ba that the loyalists who make their covenant with the leaders of the world, and who pay their allegiance to its princes, have called for their own demise!' — Ubai repeated this statement thrice, and then he added, — 'In fact, they have called for their own destruction as well as that of others. I am not sorry for them, I am only sorry for the innocent Muslims they deceive and steer to their destruction as well.' "

**628-** Qays Bnu 'Ubād narrated: "I prayed in the mosque of God's messenger ﷺ, upon whom be peace, in Madina, and I was in the front raw, when suddenly a man came towards me, and he pulled me to the side and then stood up in my place to pray two *rak'āt*. I looked at him, and I recognized him to be Ubai Bnu Ka'ab, God be pleased with him. As soon as he concluded his prayers with the regards of peace, Ubai looked straight at me and said, 'Young man, Allah is not iniquitous, do not misconstrue the divine wisdom. This is the promise, God's messenger ﷺ, upon whom be peace, entrusted us to keep up.' Ubai then turned towards the *Qibla*, the communal direction of prayers, and said, 'I swear by the Lord of the Ka'ba that the loyalists who make their covenant with the leaders of the world, and who pay their allegiance to its princes, have called for their own demise!' — Ubai, God be pleased with him, repeated this statement thrice, and he added, — 'I am not sorry for them, nay, let Allah be my witness, I am not sorry for them, but rather I feel sorry for the innocent Muslims they lead astray.' "

**629-** Muhammad bin Ahmad bin al-Hassan narrated that in one of his sermons, Ubai Bnu Ka'ab, God be pleased with him, said: "O ye people! Follow the leading path (*sabīl*) and the prophetic traditions (*sunna*), for the fire of hell does not touch a servant of Allah who is committed to the leading path, and whose eyes overflow with tears whenever he remembers the Merciful Lord. Surely a servant of Allah who follows the leading path and the prophetic traditions of *zikr*, regularly remembering the merciful Lord, his sins will fall off his shoulders whenever he develops goose flesh, and whenever he is seized by reverence and awe for Almighty Allah, the Lord of majesty and glory, just as the dried leaves of a withered tree fall off when the wind swings by them. To be steadfast with moderation on a leading path, and to follow the prophetic traditions of *zikr*, oft-remembering the merciful Lord, is better than toiling to achieve a personal interpretation which may lead one to stray from the direction of God's path and that of the prophetic traditions. Therefore, consider your deeds and endeavors carefully, and whether you pursue steadfastness in moderation, or exert extraneous efforts in religious interpretations (*ijtihād*), always make sure that they follow the exalted pathway of God's prophets and their blessed traditions."

**630-** Al-Rabi' bin Anas narrated that a man said to Ubai Bnu Ka'ab, God be pleased with him: "Advise me!" Ubai Bnu Ka'ab replied: "Let the Qur'an, the Book of Allah be your guide (*Imam*). Accept it as your supreme judge and arbitrator, for indeed the glorious Book of Allah, the most exalted, is the everlasting inheritance His messenger ﷺ, upon whom be peace, has left for you. Regularly reading its divine words will bring it to intercede on your behalf on the Day of Judgment, and its admonitions must never be disobeyed. In fact, God's Book is an infallible witness, it is flawless, and its clarity and lucidity are irreproachable. It talks about your generation, and the history of nations that preceded you. In it, you will find the needed justice to interpret and resolve your conflicts. It reconfirms the earlier prophecies about your time, and those relating to the generations that will come after you, and up to the Day of Judgment."

**631-** Imam Ahmad bin H̲anbal, God be pleased with him, narrated that Ubai Bnu Ka'ab, God be pleased with him, interpreted the Qur'anic verse, ❮ Say: He it is that has the power to send calamities upon you from above you and from beneath you, to try you with confusion and dissension among yourselves, and to let some of you taste sufferings at the hands of each others. - See how We explain the signs, so perhaps they may understand¤ (*Qur'an 6:65*), and Ubai said: "These are four major trials, all of which are awesome calamities, and all of them will unfailingly take place. Two of them started to take place about twenty five years after the passing of God's messenger ﷺ, upon whom be peace. They are the calamity of confusion and dissension, and the calamity of torment and sufferings at the hands of each others. The other two calamities will unfailingly take place, and these represent major earthquakes and death by stoning."

**632-** Abu Muhammad Hāmed bin Hayyān narrated that Ubai Bnu Ka'ab, God be pleased with him, said: "There is nothing in this world which God's servant renounces for the pleasure of Allah, the Lord of majesty and glory, blessed be His Name, and for which the Almighty Lord will not compensate him and reward him with what is better, and He will provided him with such replacement from sources he does not anticipate. On the other hand, whenever God's servant disesteems, or contemptuously accepts something he regards as trivial, when he should not, Allah, the Lord of majesty and glory, blessed be His Name, will inflict him with what is more harmful in areas he cannot foresee."

**633-** Muhammad bin Ishāq narrated that Ubai Bnu Ka'ab, God be pleased with him, said: "When we were with God's messenger ﷺ, upon whom be peace, we stood up united as one front, and with one aspiration, and only after he passed that we began to look different."

**634-** 'Atiy Bnu Dhumra narrated that Ubai bnu Ka'ab, God be pleased with him, said: "When we were with God's messenger ﷺ, upon whom be peace, we stood up united as one front, and with one aspiration. Only after he departed that we dispersed right and left."

**635-** 'Abdullāh bin Ja'far narrated that Ubai bnu Ka'ab, God be pleased with him, said: "The food of the human being gives us a good parable to better understand the potentiality of this world, even if people garnish it and add salt to it."

**636-** also in reference to the above account, attributing the origin of the above saying to a prophetic tradition, re Sufyān al-Thawri, re Ubai bnu Ka'ab, God be pleased with him, that God's messenger ﷺ, upon whom be peace, said: "Human's food illustrates what this world is worth. Consider what the human being excretes, — although he may add salt to his food and garnish it, and yet, he knows well what it will eventually become."

**637-** Abu Muhammad bin Hayyān narrated that a man came to Ubai bnu Ka'ab, God be pleased with him, and said: "O Abul' Munthir, there is a verse in Allah's Book which causes me extreme uneasiness!" Ubai inquired: "Which verse is that?" The man read ‹ Whoever commits an evil act will have to pay for it › (*Qur'a*

*4:123*)." Ubai, God be pleased with him, replied: "In essence, this verse is a blessing in disguise, and it describes a believing servant in Allah, blessed be His Name, for in this world, when a believing servant bears his adversities with patience, his exercise will cleanse him and render him sinless when he meets his Lord."

**638-** Sa'ïd bin Qatãda narrated that Ubai bnu Ka'ab, God be pleased with him, said: "In paradise, Adam, peace be upon him, was a tall man, his chest was covered with furry-like long and thick hair, and from a distance, he looked like a towering hollow palm tree. When he committed his sin, his lost his hair, and feeling ashamed of himself, he ran aimlessly across paradise, seeking a place to hide out but to no avail. While he was running, a branch of a tree stubbornly clung to his head. Adam tried to free himself from it, but to no avail, and he said to it, 'Let go of me!' The tree replied, 'I will not do that.' At that moment, his Lord called him, 'O Adam, are you running away from Me?' Adam, peace be upon him, humbly replied, 'I feel ashamed of myself before You my Lord!' "

**639-** Ahmad bin Ja'far bin Ma'bad narrated that Ubai bnu Ka'ab, God be pleased with him, said: "A believer is recognized by four characteristics, 1) He is patient during trials; 2) he is grateful when he receives a gift; 3) he is truthful when he speaks; and, 4) he is equitable when he sits to judge. Hence, a true believer revolves between five dimensions of radiant lights. Such are the lights described by Allah, blessed be His Name, in His saying, ❬ Light upon light ❭ (*Qur'an 24:35*), 1) His words are full of light; 2) his knowledge is full of light; 3) the avenues he embarks upon are radiant with light; 4) the gates from where he emerges are radiant with light; and finally, 5) on the Day of Resurrection, his destination is towards the most sublime heavenly light."

"As to the atheist, he revolves around five spheres of darkness, 1) His speech is full of darkness; 2) his deeds are made of darkness; 3) his goals drive him from one avenue of darkness into another; 4) the gates from where he emerges are mazes of darkness; and 5) on the Day of Resurrection, his fate will carry him to the abysmal abode of darkness."

**640-** 'Abdullãh bin al-H̲ãrith, son of Nawfal, narrated: "I was once in a crowded fruit market, standing under the canopy of a palm tree, and next to me stood Ubai bnu Ka'ab, God be pleased with him. Ubai said, 'Do you not see how people are branching out in different directions, each one of them soliciting the better comfort of this world?' I replied, 'Indeed, I do!' Ubai bnu Ka'ab, God be pleased with him, said, 'I once heard God's messenger ﷺ, upon whom be peace, say, 'Approaching is an horrific advent, the Euphrates river will recede to unveil a mountain of gold that is hidden beneath it. As soon as people from all over the world hear about it, they will hurry with impetuousness towards it. The inhabitants of the land will say, 'If we let the nations take away what belongs to us, we will have nothing left for our own needs.' Hence, a war will escalate, and nations will fight and kill one another, and only one out of a hundred people will escape the onslaught.'"

**641-** Sulaimãn bin Ahmad narrated that Ubai bnu Ka'ab, God be pleased with him, once asked God's messenger ﷺ, upon whom be peace: "O messenger of Allah, what is the reward of suffering a fever?" God's messenger ﷺ, upon whom be peace, replied: "A fever carries forth countless blessing upon its sufferer, and he is rewarded for every step he takes with hardship, and for every drop of sweat he perspires." Ubai then prayed: "My Lord, I ask You to bestow upon me the blessing of a fever that does not impede me from striving on Your path, a fever that does not stop me from making a pilgrimage to You House, or from praying at the mosque of Your prophet ﷺ, upon whom be peace."

Muhammad Ibn Mu'ãth commented on the above narration, saying: "Since that prayer, Ubai bnu Ka'ab, God be pleased with him, suffered a fever each night for the balance of his life."

**642-** Abu 'Amru bnu H̲amdãn narrated, re Ubai bnu Ka'ab, God be pleased with him, that God's messenger ﷺ, upon whom be peace, said: "Announce to this nation the tidings of a high rank which is reserved exclusively for them, the advantage of divine help and ultimate victory, and the blessing of a divine investiture. Nevertheless, whosoever takes advantage of the deeds of the hereafter to benefit from them in this world, will have no share to partake of in the hereafter."

**643-** Sulaimãn bin Ahmad narrated, re al-Tufail bnu Ka'ab, that his father, Ubai bnu Ka'ab, God be pleased with him, said: "God's messenger ﷺ, upon whom be peace, used to say every night, 'O ye people! The great day of upheaval, the day of ﴾ the great quickening (of the souls) has arrived, and coming thereafter is the day of the greater commotion, ﴿ (upon resurrection) (*Qur'an 79:6*). Indeed, death has come whole, and the doomsday is coming soon after it.' God's messenger ﷺ, upon whom be peace, used to repeat this call thrice as soon as the first quarter of the night fell."

**644-** Abu 'Amru bnu Hamdãn narrated, re Ubai bnu Ka'ab, God be pleased with him, that God's messenger ﷺ, upon whom be peace, said to him: "Would you like me to teach you few words Gabriel, peace be upon him, has taught me?" Ubai replied: "O messenger of Allah, indeed, I would like so very much." God's messenger ﷺ, said: "Pray regularly, 'O My Lord forgive me all my faults, my intentional ones, my joshing wittiness, and my sober earnestness. O My Lord, do not deprive me of the benefits and blessings embodied in what You bestow upon me, and do not try me with what You deny me.' "

## 36- Abu Müsa al-Ash'ari

Here is another revered sire and a peer, a model and a teacher who practiced what he taught. His name is Abu Müsa al-Ash'ari, the sincere companion and the treasured companion of God's messenger ﷺ, upon whom be peace. He exercised self restraint, and he riveted his aspirations to respond with constancy to his spiritual longing. Abu Müsa al-Ash'ari, God be pleased with him, was a savant in religious jurisprudence, a wise man, and an equitable judge. Abu Müsa was often seen sitting alone contemplating and meditating in the valleys of the enamored seekers in love with the spiritual reality. Hence, Abu Müsa was filled with gratitude, and he was always focusing upon the minutely marvelous and majestic display of the unfathomable divine work. He was often heard reciting the Qur'an in the middle of the night with a most superbly expressive and rich melodic voice, engrossed in his prayers and savoring the meaning of the Qur'anic revelation, word by word, and verse by verse, contemplating their admonitions. Abu Müsa, God be pleased

with him, often fasted during the scorching heat of the days, and he exhausted his long nights in prayers.

On this subject, it is said that spiritual attainment is the feasting of the enthusiastic and mystified heart in the lush fields of the everlasting divine protection and comfort.

**645-** Imam Ahmad Ibn Hanbal, God be pleased with him, narrated that God's messenger ﷺ, upon whom be peace, sent Mu'ãth Ibn Jabal and Abu Müsa al-Ash'ari, God be pleased with both of them, to Yemen, and he asked them to teach the Qur'an to its people.

**646-** Qurra bin Khãlid narrated that Abu Rajã' al-'Atãridi said: "Abu Müsa al-Ash'ari, God be pleased with him, used to move between our Qur'an studying circles in al-Basra mosque, in Iraq, and he used to sit with us and instruct us. I can still remember him sitting with us, wearing his white cloak, and teaching me the Qur'an. It is from him that I have learned and memorized the first revelation, ❮ Read in the Name of your Lord Who created (everything). He is the One Who creates humankind from a coagulated blood. Read and proclaim His glory, for your Lord is the most bounteous (Teacher). He teaches by the writings of the (primordial) Pen, and He teaches the human being (by revealing) a knowledge, he (otherwise) does not know ❯ (*Qur'an 96:1-5*).

Abu Rajã' al-'Atãridi further continued: "This chapter was the first revelation that descended upon God's messenger Muhammad ﷺ, upon whom be peace."

**647-** Sulaimãn bin Ahmad narrated that when Abu Müsa al-Ash'ari, God be pleased with him, arrived to Yemen, he said in his opening sermon: "The commander of the believers, Omar bin al-Khattãb, God be pleased with him, sent me to teach you the Book of your Lord, blessed be His Name, the Lord of majesty and glory. He also commissioned me to teach you the blessed traditions (*sunan*) of your prophet ﷺ, upon whom be peace, and to cleanse and purify your conventions."

**648-** Muhammad bin Ja'far bin al-Haytham narrated that Abu Müsa al-Ash'ari, God be pleased with him, once called the Qur'an readers to a meeting, and he asked that only those who have memorized the entire Qur'an by heart should come to see him. Some three hundred of them came to hear his admonition and he said to them: "You are responsible for rehearsing the divine revelation to the people of this city. Do not let your hearts harden as time pass by, and as did the hearts of the People of the Book before you."

"We have heard a prophetic admonition which is similar in length and might to the warning revealed in *Süra Barã'a,*[1] where God's messenger ﷺ also said, 'If the son of Adam had two valleys filled with gold, he will strive to own a third one to increase his possessions, although, nothing will eventually fill the hollowness of the son of Adam but dirt (when he lies in his grave).' "

"In another revelation, we called *musabbiḫãt* (hymns of glorification), the beginning of which is kept as the first verse of *Süra Al-Ṣaff,*[2] and where Almighty Allah says, ❮ O ye who (claim to) have faith, why do you say things which you do not act upon?❯ (*Qur'an 61:2*), a testimony which you will carry upon your shoulders, and which is inscribed in your records, and for which you will be accountable on the Day of Judgment."

**649-** Also in reference to the above account, Abu Kinãna, who also was present during the abovementioned meeting, narrated that Abu Müsa al-Ash'ari, God be pleased with him, after praising the divine revelation and glorifying the magnificence of the holy Qur'an, he added, that for merely knowing the truth of its revelation, "this Qur'an can either be your blessed reward, or it can become your unwieldy burden on the Day of Reckoning. Follow the Qur'an, and do not let the Qur'an follow you! For whosoever follows the Qur'an, it will lead him to the heavenly gardens of paradise, and whosoever is followed by the Qur'an, it will chase him and impel him until it shoves him into the abyss of hell-fire."

**650-** 'Abdullãh bin Buraida narrated that God's messenger ﷺ, upon whom be peace, once heard Abu Müsa al-Ash'ari, God be pleased with him, recite the Qur'an, and he said: "Surely this man is given one of the most beautiful melodious voices and a spirit as those emitted by the flutes of the family of God's prophet David, peace be upon him."

---

[1] *Süra Barã'a,* Repentance, Qur'an, Chapter 9
[2] *Süra Al-Ṣaff,* The Ranks, Qur'an Chapter 61:1

When Buraida reported what he heard from God's messenger ﷺ, upon who be peace, to Abu Müsa al-Ash'ari, God be pleased with him, Abu Müsa said to him: "Now that you have told me what God's messenger ﷺ, upon who be peace, have said, surely you have become my true and sincere friend."

**651-** Imam Ahmad bin Hanbal, God be pleased with him, narrated, re Abu Müsa al-Ash'ari, God be pleased with him, that God's messenger ﷺ, upon whom be peace, was once walking along with the mother of the believers, 'Aisha, God be pleased with her, and as they passed by his house, they heard him reciting the Qur'an. God's messenger ﷺ and 'Aisha stopped by the wall of his house and they listened for a while before they continued on their way home.

The next morning, Abu Müsa came to see God's messenger ﷺ, upon who be peace, who said to him: "O Abu Müsa, I was walking last night with 'Aisha, and when we reached your house, we heard you rehearsing the Qur'an, so we stopped and listened for a while to your recital." Abu Müsa replied: "O blessed prophet of Allah, I wish I knew you were there, for I would have enhanced my voice, and improved my rendition."

**652-** Thãbit al-Banãni narrated, re Anas bnu Mãlik, God be pleased with him, that God's messenger ﷺ, upon whom be peace, said: "Surely Abu Müsa is endowed with a beautiful melodious voice and a spirit such as those that once emanated from the flutes of the family of God's prophet David, peace be upon him."

**653-** Muhammad bin Omar bin Salam narrated that Omar bin al-Khattãb used to say to Abu Müsa al-Ash'ari, God be pleased with both of them: "Remind us of our Lord, all glory and majesty are His, and blessed be His Name," and Abu Müsa would immediately read from the Qur'an.

**654-** Sulaimãn al-Teemi narrated that Abi 'Uthmãn al-Nahdi, said: "Abu Müsa al-Ash'ari, God be pleased with him, once led us in the dawn *fajr* prayer, and I have never heard a voice of such beautiful resonance and melodiousness, neither from a resonant cymbal, nor from the plucking of a sonorous lute."

**655-** Imam Ahmad bin Hanbal, God be pleased with him, narrated that Masrouq said: "We were traveling with Abu Müsa al-Ash'ari, God be pleased with him, and the night led us to take rest in a cultivated farm. That night, Abu Müsa stood up to pray, and he recited the Qur'an with a most melodious voice and eloquent diction, and he read long chapters from the Qur'an. When he stood up in *qunüt,*[1] Abu Müsa prayed, 'My Lord, indeed Thou art the Peace, and peace comes from Thee. Thou art the Believer, and Thou loveth the believer; Thou art the Controlling Guardian, and Thou loveth one who controls his stimuli and guards his covenant; and indeed Thou art the Truthful, and Thou loveth the truthful."

**656-** Imam Ahmad bin Hanbal, God be pleased with him, narrated that Anas bnu Mãlik, God be pleased with him, said: "We once traveled with Abu Müsa al-Ash'ari, God be pleased with him, and during our journey, he heard people discussing the path with a great lucidity and intellectual input, using the most eloquent and stylistic expressions. Abu Müsa looked towards me and said in dismay, 'What happen to me O Anas? Why do people's talking in such manner depresses me? Let's go somewhere else and remember our Lord, for the sharp tongues of these (intellectuals) can even gnaw apart food that is hard to chew on.' "

As we moved on, Abu Müsa added: "O Anas! Do you know what obstructs people from seeking the hereafter and hinders their perseverance and pursuit of its promise?" Anas replied: "I guess wantonness and satan will do that!" Abu Müsa replied: "Nay, I swear by Allah, it is not that, but it is their attachment to the ephemeral pleasures of this world that attracts them to such a degree, making the permanent comfort of the hereafter seem distant in their minds; and yet, even if they were to behold its physical form and examine its trueness, they will still be adamant in their pursuit of the pleasures of this world, and they will not waiver or relinquish their attachment to it, nor will they turn back to the straight path."

**657-** Imam Ahmad Ibn Hanbal, God be pleased with him, narrated that Abu Müsa al-Ash'ari, God be pleased with him, once learned that some people were so poor and had no clothes to wear

[1] *Qunüt:* A pre-concluding segment of one's prayers, where one submissively implores and praises his Lord, blessed be His Name.

in public, and that's what prevents them from attending the Friday congregational prayers. Upon hearing that, Abu Müsa immediately threw his cloak over his shoulders, and he went out to the mosque to lead the congregational prayers and to speak on this subject."

**658-** Bishr bin Müsa narrated that his father Abu Müsa al-Ash'ari, God be pleased with him, once said to him: "O my dear son: during the time of God's messenger ﷺ, upon whom be peace, — (during the Meccan period) if only you could see us then. We were so poor, and we had no change of clothes that when it rained on us, we smelled like sheep."

**659-** Abu 'Amru bnu Hamdān narrated, re Abu Müsa al-Ash'ari, God be pleased with him, that God's messenger ﷺ, upon whom be peace, once said: "Seventy of God's prophets walked barefooted by the rock in Jerusalem, near the lower plains, having nothing to wear but a mere worn out cloak, with which, each one of them wrapped himself to guard his modesty."

**660-** Abi Burda narrated that Abu Müsa al-Ash'ari, God be pleased with him, said to him: "We once embarked on a campaign by sea. One evening, the sails were raised, and the wind was favorably, hauling our ship with the right pace. In the middle of that night, we heard a deep loud voice calling from above, 'O people of this ship! Come out and let me tell you something.' — The loud voice of the imperceptible being thus called us seven times. _ I Immediately left my bed and went to the deck, and I looked up and said, 'Who are you, and where do you come from?' The voice replied, 'Would you like me to tell you about a decree, Allah, the Lord of majesty and glory, exalted be His Name, has taken upon Himself?' I said, 'Indeed, tell us!' The voice said, 'It is decreed that whosoever thirsts himself on a hot day for the sake of Allah, He, the most exalted, has taken it upon Himself to quench his thirst on the Day of Resurrection.' "

Abi Burda continued: "From that day on, Abu Müsa al-Ash'ari, God be pleased with him, used to fast during the hottest days of the summer, when one's skin could nearly burn under the scorching heat of the sun ."

**661-** Imam Ahmad Ibn Hanbal, God be pleased with him, narrated that Abu Müsa al-Ash'ari, God be pleased with him, said: "I take my bath in a dark room, and yet, I do not stand up unless I put on my robe, because I shy to stand up naked before my Lord."

**662-** Abu Muhammad bin Hayyãn narrated that Abu Müsa al-Ash'ari, God be pleased with him, said: "A true believer should expect this world to offer him nothing but sorrowful and tiresome labor, besides luring and haunting trials."

**663-** Abu Dãwoud narrated that Abu Müsa al-Ash'ari, God be pleased with him, once said: "What destroyed earlier nations and lead to their annihilation was nothing but their love for the Dinar and dirham, and it will unfailingly do the same to you."

**664-** Ghunaim bin Qays narrated that Abu Müsa al-Ash'ari, God be pleased with him, said: "The heart is the seat of emotions and temperaments, and thus it is called *qalb* in Arabic, because of its constant motion and change of temperament. In fact, the parable of the heart is like that of a drifting feather in a desert, the lightest breeze moves it around.

**665-** Imam Ahmad Ibn Hanbal, God be pleased with him, narrated that Abu Müsa al-Ash'ari, God be pleased with him, once delivered a sermon at a mosque in Basra, Iraq, where he said: "O ye people! Cry as much as you can, and if you could not find such deep emotions in your hearts, then feign your crying in the hope of receiving the divine mercy, for the dwellers of hell-fire will cry endlessly, and until there will be no more tears in their eyes, and after that, they will have nothing but tears of blood in sorrow, and which will run profusely like huge rivers where even ships can float because of what they have brought upon themselves."

**666-** 'Utba bin Ghazwãn al-Raqãshi narrated that Abu Müsa al-Ash'ari, God be pleased with him, saw his eyeball protruded, and he asked him: "What happened to your eye?" 'Utba replied: "I once glanced at a group of men, and I noticed a beautiful maiden serving them. My eyes were fixed on her for a moment before suddenly my eyeball projected as you see." Abu Müsa said: "Ask your Lord for forgiveness, for surely you have been needlessly unjust towards your own eye. In protecting the chastity of your eyes, you should know that you are not liable for an inadvertent passing first glance, but then, you are accountable for the next glance."

**667-** Al-A'amash narrated that Abu Müsa al-Ash'ari, God be pleased with him, said: "On the Day of Resurrection, the sun will be positioned vertically over people's heads, and their deeds will either shade them or expose them to its intense heat."

**668-** Abi Burda narrated that Abu Müsa al-Ash'ari, God be pleased with him, said: "On the Day of Judgment, the believing servant will be brought before his Lord for his individual reckoning, and Allah, the most exalted, blessed be His Name, will veil His servant with His own presence, away from the sight of the creation, so that they cannot see him. For every good deed, Almighty Allah sees in the records of His servant, He says, 'I accept,' and immediately the servant will prostrate himself in gratitude before his Lord, and for every wrongdoing, God Almighty sees in the records of His servant, He says, 'I forgive.' and again, the servant will prostrate himself in gratitude before his Lord. When the personal reckoning of the believing servant is finally brought to conclusion, and when the creation see him anew, they will say, 'Blessed be this servant, for surely he has never committed a single wrongdoing.' "

**669-** 'Abdullāh bin Muhammad narrated that Abu Müsa al-Ash'ari, God be pleased with him, said: "The soul of a believing servant comes out his body having a sweet scent that is more fragrant than musk. The angels in charge will escort it up, and when they meet the guardian angels of the lower firmament, the latter will inquire, 'Whose soul are you bringing with you?' They will reply, 'This is the soul of so and so,' and they will speak of him referring to the best of his deeds. The guardian angels of the lower firmament will rejoice, and they will say, 'May Allah receive you and the person you are bringing with you with His utmost favorable regards.' Immediately, the gates to the upper firmaments will open, the believer's countenance will immediately glow with light, and he will be brought before the divine Lord Whose presence is distinct and readily perceivable like the daylight."

"On the other hand, when the soul of the evildoer comes out of his body, it emits a mephitic smell which is more repugnant than a decaying corpse. The angels in charge will escort it up, and when they meet the guardian angels of the lower firmament, the latter will inquire, 'Whose soul are you bringing with you?' They will reply, 'This is the soul of so and so,' and they will speak of him referring to the most evil of his deeds. The guardian angels of the lower firmament will become disgusted, and they will say, 'Take him back, for Allah was never unjust to him.' "

Abu Müsa al-Ash'ari, God be pleased with him, then read: ‹They will not enter paradise until a camel fits through the eye of a needle › (*Qur'an 7:40*).

**670-** 'Amru bnu Khãlid narrated that when Abu Müsa al-Ash'ari, God be pleased with him, laid on his deathbed, he called his children to his side, and he said to them: "Go and dig a grave, and make it spacious and deep." When the children completed what their father asked them to do, they came back and reported to their father: "We dug a grave, and we made it large and deep as you asked." Abu Müsa, God be pleased with him, then said: "I swear by Allah, that it will soon come to one of two conclusions: 1) Either my grave will expand to form angles stretching up to forty yards wide, and then a doorway to paradise will open to reveal my house, family, stations, blessings, and honors Allah has reserved for me, and I will then know my way to my dwellings therein better than I know the road to my house in this world; and I will smell the fragrance of paradise and perceive the vivacity of that station up to the Day of Resurrection; or 2) should it be the opposite, — *and we too seek refuge in Allah's mercy from such culmination,* — then my grave will tighten down to be smaller than the bushing of a spearhead, and then a doorway to hell-fire will open to reveal my chains, shackles, and the like concatenations reserved for fellows who dwell in *gahannam* (hell-fire), and I will immediately know the way to my seat of punishment therein better than I know the road to my house today; and moreover, I will smell the baneful stench of its poisons, and experience the intensity and fieriness of its blazes up to the Day of Resurrection."

**671-** Abi Burda narrated that when Abu Müsa al-Ash'ari, God be pleased with him, was dying, he called his children to his bedside, and he said to them: "My dear children! Remember the story of 'The Man With A Loaf of Bread.' Listen carefully to his story: Once upon a time, there lived a man in a hermitage who for seventy years had dedicated his entire existence to worshipping Almighty Allah, and he only left his cell one day a week to acquire his basic needs. One day, while in the market, satan made an attractive woman seduce him, and the man was lured to stay with her for seven days and nights. On the seventh day, the veil of darkness that shrouded his clarity was lifted, and the man left the woman's house repenting to God Almighty. With every step the man took, he prayed and prostrated himself to Allah, ashamed of himself, fearful of the consequences of his sin, and he kept on imploring for forgiveness. By nightfall, his steps led him to a shop, near which sat twelve paupers."

"In that town, there lived a monk who daily sent these twelve paupers a loaf of bread each. That night, his servant carried the twelve loaves of bread and brought them for distribution, and in the dark, the servant distributed a loaf of bread for each indigent, and when he reached the extra man who sat in their midst, not counting their number, the servant thought him to be one of indigents, and he handed him a loaf of bread. As he was leaving, the one pauper who did not receive his share for that night, shouted, 'Why have you not given me my usual loaf of bread? You have never done that before!' The servant who had not realized what happened became upset, and he replied, 'Do you think that I have kept anything away from you, or do you think that I kept it for myself?' Ask around you, did I give any one sitting here two loaves of bread instead of one?' They replied, 'No!' The servant then said, 'You are probably accusing me of keeping it for myself! I swear by Allah, that I will not give you anything for tonight.' Immediately, the repenting man made what happen known, and he handed his loaf of bread over to the person who did not get his share for that night."

"By sunrise, the repenting man was found dead in the street near that shop. When the angels came and weighed his deeds, the seventy years of worship he offered did not measure up to the weight of his sin during the last seven nights of his life, but when the angels weighed the sin of the last seven nights and his last peace offering of the single loaf of bread he gave to that pauper, his charity weighed heavier, and thus he was saved from eternal damnation."

Abu Müsa al-Ash'ari, God be pleased with him, then added: "My dear children, always remember this story of 'The Man With A Loaf Of Bread'."

**672-** Qutaiba bin Sa'ïd narrated that Abu Müsa al-Ash'ari, God be pleased with him, once visited the church of John the Baptist, in the city of Homs, Syria, and when he heard the call to prayers from a distant mosque, he turned towards the direction of the Ka'ba in Mecca, and he offered his regular prayer. When he left, Abu Müsa thanked Allah, the most exalted, blessed be His Name, and he then turned to the people who accompanied him, and said, 'O ye people, you are living in a time where one who offers his deeds solely for the sake of Allah, the most exalted, will be awarded one reward, and there will come a time, when one who offers his deeds solely for the sake of Allah, the most exalted, blessed be His Name, will be awarded double his reward.'

## 37- Shaddãd bin Aows

Among our peers, the blessed companions of God's messenger ﷺ, upon whom be peace, there also lived Shaddãd bin Aows al-Anşãri, patronymed Abu Ya'lã, God be pleased with him. He always weighed his words carefully, and he spoke with flawless clarity and superb vision and perspicacity. Shaddãd bin Aows was vigilant, wary, pious, godly, and reserved. He cried often because of his love for Almighty Allah and in fear of His displeasure, and he mostly tied up his tongue, and was humble and reserved.

**673-** Al-Faraj bin Fadhãla narrated that every night when Shaddãd bin Aows, God be pleased with him, went to bed, he mostly stayed up restless nights pondering the hereafter, and he prayed: "My Lord! Thinking about the fire of hell makes me sleepless." Shaddãd would then leave his bed and stand up in prayers until dawn.

**674-** Abu Muhammad bin Hayyãn narrated that Shaddãd bin Aows, God be pleased with him, said: "O people! I am afraid that as long as you are in this world, you have only seen the antecedent of good and evil. The real good in its entirety is in paradise, and the real evil in its entirety is in hell-fire. In fact, what one experiences in this world is a preview evincing what is to come. In fact, in the world, both the truthful pious and the insolent profligate eat on its table, yet, the hereafter is a genuine truthful promise which is governed by a mighty King. O people! Everything has offspring, therefore, strive to be the children of the permanent abode of the hereafter, and not the children of this ephemeral world."

**675-** Abu Ddardā', God be pleased with him, once extolled Shaddād bin Aows, God be pleased with him, saying: "Some people are endowed with knowledge but are deprived of forbearance, while God Almighty has endowed Abu Ya'lā with both knowledge and forbearance."

**676-** Shaddād bin Aows, God be pleased with him, narrated that God's messenger ﷺ, upon whom be peace, said: "O people! This world is a display evincing what is to come, for in this world, both the truthful pious and the insolent profligate eat on its table. Surely the hereafter will come, and it is a genuine truthful promise which is governed by a supreme mighty King. In it, truth will permeate everything, and falsehood is nonexistent. O people! Be the children of the hereafter and not the children of this ephemeral world, for children follow their mother by nature."

**677-** Abu 'Amr bin Hamdān narrated that during that speech, Shaddād bin Aows, God be pleased with him, also quoted God's messenger ﷺ, upon whom be peace, to have said during the above-quoted speech: "O people! Do what is good, and be wary of Allah. You must also know that you will surely have to face your deeds in the hereafter, and that you will unfailingly meet your Lord. Therefore, ﴾ Whosoever does an atom's weight of good will reap its benefit, and whosoever does an atom's weight of evil will have to face its consequences ﴿ (*Qur'an 99:7*)."

**678-** Abu Muhammad bin Hayyān narrated that Abu Ddardā, God be pleased with him, said: "Every nation has an expert theologian (*faqih*), and the expert theologian of this nation is Shaddād bin Aows."

**679-** Thābit al-Banāni narrated that Shaddād bin Aows once said to a companions: "Bring us this food to ail with!" The companion was surprised as he replied: "Since I met you, I have never heard you utter such a slang!" Shaddãd replied: "Indeed, since the passing of God's messenger ﷺ, upon whom be peace, I am not aware to have had a slip of a tongue which was not misconstrued, or perhaps sometimes misunderstood, although I try my best to weigh my words, and to tie up my tongue. I swear by Allah, that you will never hear another slip of a tongue from me again!"

**680-** Also in reference to the above account, Abu 'Amru bnu Hamdãn narrated that Shaddãd bin Aows, God be pleased with him, once said to some of his companions: "Get us this food to play with." Subsequently, and for few days, some people used that slang jestingly during their own conversations.

It was well known in the community that Shaddãd bin Aows does not speak in vein, or talk jestingly, and someone commented: "Listen to what Abu Ya'lã has come up with!"

When Shaddãd heard what the people were saying, he called them up and said: "O my brothers' children, listen to me. I have never had a slip of a tongue since I took my covenant with God's messenger ﷺ, upon whom be peace, and I have often tried my best to weigh my words and to tie up my tongue. Come and let me teach you something better than what you heard, but promise me not to use the expression you perceived earlier, and instead use what is better. Pray, 'Our Lord, we ask You to strengthen our endeavors, endow us firmness against temptations, and grant us with an unwavering determination, certitude, and wisdom. Endow us with thankfulness for Your bounty and blessings, and teach us how to worship You best. Our Lord, grant us a healthy heart and a truthful tongue. Grant us the benefit of what You know is best, and protect us against what You know to be evil.' "

**681-** Also in reference to the above account, Imam al-Awza'i narrated that Shaddãd bin Aows, God be pleased with him, once visited some friends, and when he got hungry, he said: "Bring us some food to toy with." Someone said: "O Abu Ya'lã, what did you say?" Somehow, it seemed that a group of people took offense to the expression. When Shaddãd realized that, he immediately said:

"Since I became Muslim, whenever I spoke a word, I first selected it, and chewed on it for a while, and only when it felt right, I spoke it, except for the expression you have just heard. Please do not quote me, and instead you may quote the following account. I once heard God's messenger ﷺ, upon whom be peace, say, 'When you see people hoarding gold and silver, then remember these words, and pray, 'My Lord, I ask You to grant me strength against temptations and firmness in my faith, and strengthen me with resoluteness and determination to seek forthrightness. My Lord, I ask You to forgive me all my sins, surely there is nothing is hidden from You, and indeed You are the All-Knowing Lord.' "

**682-** In his narration of the above account, Abu Ash'ath al-San'ãni quoted Shaddãd, that God's messenger ﷺ, upon whom be peace, said to him: "O Shaddãd, when you see people hoarding gold and silver, then invoke this prayer, 'My Lord, grant me strength against temptations, firmness in my faith, and strengthen me with resoluteness, determination, and forthrightness. Lord, guide me to do deeds that yield Your mercy upon me, and inspire me intentions which further Your compassion upon me, to forgive me my sins. Lord, embody me with gratitude for Your favors, and teach me how to worship You rightly. Grant me a heart filled with piety, and endow me a truthful and a chaste tongue."[1]

**683-** Abu Bakr bin Khallãd narrated, re Shaddãd bin Aows, God be pleased with him, that God's messenger ﷺ, upon whom be peace, said: "A good person is one who casts no blame upon any ones except himself, and he labors hard for the benefit of his own life after death, while a weak person is one who follows his carnality and hastens to satisfy his mind and desire, and yet, he anticipates his Lord to confer upon him the best of divine favors in the hereafter."

**684-** Abu 'Amru bnu Hamdãn narrated that when Shaddãd bin Aows, God be pleased with him, was on his deathbed, he said to his companions: "The most I fear for you are hypocrisy and concealed wantonness."

[1] The added quote to the above prophetic prayer is attributed to the narration of al-Shu'aithi.

**685-** 'Atã' bin 'Ajlãn narrated that Shaddãd bin Aows, God be pleased with him, once passed by 'Ubãda bin Nasiy, and together, they went to Shaddãd's house. A moment after they sat down in his house, Shaddãd burst into tears, and his crying caused 'Ubãda to cry as well. When Shaddãd recovered, he inquired from 'Ubãda: "Why are you crying?" The latter replied: "I saw you cry, and that affected me!" Shaddãd said: "I cried because I remembered something God's messenger ﷺ, upon whom be peace, had said, 'The most I fear for my *umma* (of followers) is polytheism and concealed wantonness.' "

Shaddãd then said to God's messenger ﷺ, upon whom be peace: "As to one of the two, there is no way to escape it!" God's messenger ﷺ, upon whom be peace, further expounded: "They will not worship a sun nor a moon, nor will they set up idols for worship, but they will offer deeds for other than the pleasure of Allah, the Lord of majesty and glory."

'Ubãda and Abu Ddardã' immediately exclaimed: "Lord forgive all of us. O Shaddãd, didn't God's messenger ﷺ, upon whom be peace, tell us that 'satan has lost all hope to ever be worshiped in the Arabian peninsula.' Now, as to the concealed desires, that one everyone knows about, and that is desire for women and wealth, then what is this *shirk* (polytheism) you are warning us about O Shaddãd?" He replied: "Do you see, if a man worships

**686-** In his account of the above prophetic tradition, Sulaimãn bin Ahmad also narrated that Shaddãd bin Aows, God be pleased with him, quoted God's messenger ﷺ, upon whom be peace, to have said: "The most I fear for my *umma* (of followers) is if they should ascribe an associate to Almighty Allah, and to be overtaken by concealed desires. As to such hidden desire, this is when a man wakes up fasting in the morning, and then, when he sees something that excites him, he asks for it and breaks his fast. As to the polytheists, these are people who do not worship stones nor idols, and yet they do what they do for show."

**687-** Laith bnu Saleem narrated, re Shaddãd bin Aows, God be pleased with him, that God's messenger ﷺ, upon whom be peace, also commented on the abovementioned type of polytheism, saying:

"Allah, the most exalted, says, 'I am the best to justly divide the shares with someone who associates a partner with Me. Therefore, whosoever associates someone with Me, I will let his body, deeds, effects, and aspirations become the possession of the one he associates with Me, to do with them whatever he wants, for I do not need him!' "

**688-** Shaddãd bin Aows, God be pleased with him, narrated that God's messenger ﷺ, upon whom be peace, said: "Surely repentance washes away a sin committed in ignorance; good deeds abrogate bad deeds, and when a believing servant remembers his Lord in comfort, Allah, exalted be His Name, will help him during his trials. This is because Allah, the most exalted, says, 'I never grant My servant two safe havens, and I do not make him suffer two kinds of fear. Should My servant feel at ease with Me in the world, he will surely be struck with fear and dreadfulness on the day I gather My creation for judgment, and should he fear Me and revere Me in the world, I will grant him safety and peace on the Day I assemble My true servants in paradise, wherein, his sense of safety will embrace him forever, and I will not cause him to suffer the horrific punishment that will effect those I will hurl to their eternal demise.'"

## 38- Huthaifa Bnul Yammãn

Among our peers and sires, there is also the blessed companion of God's messenger ﷺ, upon whom be peace, Huthaifa Bnul Yammãn, God be pleased with him. His experiences involved grim visitations, and the suffering of awesome trials and perturbations that affect the heart in the process of its transformation and development. He observed the sickness of vice and deception of the heart, and his inquiries focused on the nature of evil, which he shielded himself against, and furthermore, he pursued what is good and rewarding, which virtues he solicited avidly.

During his trials of poverty and scarcity, Huthaifa, God be pleased with him, controlled his stance with stillness and contentment, he attributed his condition to the supreme judgment of the divine wisdom, he sought the avenues of repentance and regret to deepen the soundness of his spiritual conformity, and he patched up the fissures of his days with devotion and gratitude to his Lord. Such are some of the distinct attributes of a true spiritual seeker.

Huthaifa Bnul Yammãn, God be pleased with him — patronymed Abu 'Abdullãh — spent his life contemplating upon the magnificent work of the Merciful Lord, and he consented to His decree without questioning its wisdom. Huthaifa never objected to God's will, and he willingly accepted his fate in this world, and even when his trials involved the vicissitude of extreme poverty and privation.

**689-** Ahmad bin 'Abdu-Rahmãn al-Saqti narrated that Huthaifa Bnul Yammãn was visiting Omar bin al-Khattãb, God be pleased with both of them. During that visit, Omar asked his guests: "Who amongst you have heard the prophetic statement of God's messenger ﷺ, upon whom be peace, referring to the trials of deception, or deceptive attraction (*fitan*), that will befall people, and which trials will descend one after another just like the heaving waves of a heavy storm in the high seas?" Huthaifa thought that Omar intended him for the answer, and he said: "I heard it." Omar exclaimed: "Indeed your heart is truly dedicated to Allah, tell us what you heard !"

Huthaifa, God be pleased with him, then paraphrased the prophetic tradition, saying: "These trial will affect the hearts of all people without exception. Whosoever refutes them, the trials will etch a white spot in his heart, and whosoever absorbs them and is deceived by them, the trials will etch a black spot in his heart. Thus, people's hearts will be of two kinds: 1) A kind that is clear and spotless, and which nothing can affect as long as the heavens and the earth remain; and, 2) the second heart is one which is dark and opaque and it looks like a crooked corncob, and it will tilt one's balance and lead him to his eternal demise on the Day of Judgment." — Huthaifa then tilted the palm of his right hand to the left, and he further commented: "Such a twisted heart will not acknowledge what is right, it will not deny what is wrong, and it will only accept what it already absorbed of rapacity and wantonness in this world as normal."

Huthaifa, then turned to Omar, God be pleased with both of them, and said: "The time of such trials to begin is only held up by a closed door under the unremitting blows of destiny is almost shattering into pieces."

Omar inquired: "You mean breaking open?" Huthaifa replied: "Nay, I mean shattered into small pieces!"

Omar then said: "Perhaps if it becomes open, someone can close it again!"

Huthaifa replied: "Nay, it is certain that such a door will shatter into pieces." Huthaifa further expounded: "This door represents a man who kills the true prophetic traditions, disallows teaching them, and denies their authenticity."

**690-** 'Abdullãh bnu Ja'far narrated that Huthaifa Bnul Yammãn, God be pleased with him, said: "God's messenger ﷺ, upon whom be peace, informed us about two major events, one of which I have witnessed, and the second I am still awaiting. He told us that the divine trust (*amãna*) descended upon alert, but cautious hearts of men, nevertheless, it helped them to learn something about the Qur'anic revelation, and it helped them to learn something from the prophetic traditions (*sunna*) as well."

Huthaifa continued: "God's messenger ﷺ, upon whom be peace, then informed us about the time when the divine trust (*amãna*) will be recalled. He said, 'A man will go to rest, and while sleeping, a black spot will etch in his heart, and its stain will stand out as an irremovable black smudge, — just as if you were to strike out a piece of smoldering coal with your shoe, and how its ashes will leave an irremovable stain that will overshadow the rest of the shoe. Similarly, the etched black smudge of such heart will eclipse the balance of the heart, and when people wake up in the morning, they will not have a single trustworthy man among them. Furthermore, there will come a time when people will no longer be evaluated by their piety or faith, and when they praise someone, they say, 'What a fun and a nice man to be with! What an intelligent man!' Although of faith, his heart will not possess the weight of a single grain of wheat.' "

**691-** Abi Bakr bin Khalãd narrated that Nasr bin 'Ãsim al-Lïthi, said: "I came to the city of Küfa, Iraq, and when I entered the mosque, people were sitting in a circle, listening in awe to a prominent speaker who seemed to have captured everyone's attention. I asked someone, 'Who is this man?' He replied, 'Huthaifa Bnul Yammãn.' I immediately sat down, and I heard him say, 'People used to ask God's messenger ﷺ, upon whom be peace, about what is good (*khair*), and I always asked him about what is evil (*sharr*), and therefore, I understood that goodness was still on earth then. I once inquired, 'O messenger of Allah, will there be any evil after this kind of good?' I asked this question three times, and every time, God's messenger ﷺ, upon whom be peace, replied, 'O Huthaifa, learn God's book, and follow its admonitions.' God's messenger ﷺ further added, 'However, there will also come an awesome trial of deceptive attractions (*fitna*).'"[1]

Huthaifa Bnul Yammãn, God be pleased with him, asked: "O messenger of Allah, what does the stagnant black cloud represent?" God's messenger ﷺ, upon whom be peace, replied: "It is a time when the hearts of some nations will no longer be able to return to what they were! At such an era, an awesome blind, deaf, innovative, misleading and deceptive trial will take place, — a loud cry from hell-fire. — At such a time, should you tie yourself up to the trunk of a tree, or stay put by it, that will be better for you than to follow any of such men."

**692-** Abu Idris al-Khawlãni narrated that he heard Huthaifa Bnul Yammãn, God be pleased with him, say: "People used to ask God's messenger ﷺ, upon whom be peace, about what is good, and I always asked him about what is evil, in fear that it may befall me. I once said, 'O messenger of Allah, we lived a pagan life in ignorance, and that was evil (*sharr*), and then Allah, blessed be His Name, sent us this blessing (*khair*); will there be any evil after this?' God's messenger ﷺ, upon whom be peace, replied, 'Yes there will be evil after this, and it will come in the form of a stagnant black cloud of smoke.' I asked, 'And what is that cloud?' He replied, 'People who will pursue other than my traditions (*sunna*), and they will instruct others by other than my guidance. Some you will recognize, and others you don't.' I asked, 'What evil could there be after that?' God's messenger ﷺ, upon whom be peace, replied, 'The rise of the harbingers of hell-fire, whosoever answers their call, they will seize him and thrust him in hell.' I asked, 'O messenger of Allah, what

[1]Abu Dãwoud reported this prophetic quote as 'A stagnant black cloud'.

would you command me to do should I witness such a time?' God's messenger ﷺ, upon whom be peace, replied, 'Remain close to the Muslim community and to their Imam.' I hasten to inquire, 'And what if the Muslims were divided, or what if they did not have a community or an Imam?' God's messenger ﷺ, upon whom be peace, replied, 'Then forsake all such groups, and do so solely for Allah's pleasure, and then, it will be better for you to seek refuge and pray near a stump of a distant tree. Remain there until death comes and finds you in such a state.' "

**693-** Bishr bin Müsa narrated that H̲uthaifa Bnul Yammãn, God be pleased with him, said: "The trial of deceptive attractions (*fitna*) will be paraded before all the hearts, and whoever acquiesces in and yields to it, the trial will etch a black mark in his heart, and whichever heart refutes it, the trial will etch a white mark therein. Should one of you desire to know whether he is affected by such trials of deceptive attractions (*fitan*) or not, then let him look within himself to find out, if his hearts is accepting what is unlawful (*harãm*) to be decent, or if his heart finds what is lawfully just and permissible (*halãl*) as offensive and unacceptable, then in fact, he is struck by the *fitna*."

**694-** Abu Muhammad bin H̲ayyãn narrated that H̲uthaifa Bnul Yammãn, God be pleased with him, said: "When a servant commits a sin, it will etch a black mark in his heart. Such a mark will grow until it takes over his entire heart and makes him look like a frowning ashen sheep."

**695-** Al-A'amash narrated that H̲uthaifa Bnul Yammãn, God be pleased with him, said: "I swear by Allah Whom there is no god but He, that when the trials (*fitan*) befall the nations, a man wakes up in the morning having his sight, and he goes to sleep at night having lost it."

**696-** In another reference to the above accounts, Zaid bin Wahab narrated that H̲uthaifa Bnul Yammãn, God be pleased with him, said: "At first, the trials of deceptive attractions (*fitan*) will come in the form of a fog , or a light cloud overshadow your lives, and have little or no effect on your faith. Then, the second wave of trials will come to cast you with hot brimstones, causing major shaking of your lives and faith, and the third wave of such trials will come as an opaque cloud that will blind the majority of people."

**697-** Al-Fadhl bin Müsa narrated that Huthaifa Bnul Yammãn, God be pleased with him, said: "There will come three awesome trials of deceptive attractions (*fitan*), and the fourth will drive people straight to the hands of the imposter.[1] The first trial will come as a light cloud that will cause major droughts, the next trial will cast people with hot brimstones, and the third trial will cause major shaking of people's lives and faith, just like the heaving waves of a giant life threatening storm in the high seas, and finally, the forth trial will drive people straight to the hand of the imposter."

**698-** 'Ammãra bin 'Abdullãh narrated that Huthaifa Bnul Yammãn, God be pleased with him, said: "Beware of the trials of deceptive attractions (*fitan*). Do not become their victim, and when you see them, do not stare at them. I swear by Allah, blessed be His Name, that should anyone stare at them, and even if it were out of curiosity, they will destroy him, just as a torrential rain washes away the newly gathered harvest. When such trials arrive, they will create confusion as to whether they are the prophesied chain of events or not! Having doubt, the ignorant person will say, 'Surely this resembles the prophesied cataclysm.' However, when people see the ramifications and massive destruction caused by their violent upheaval, they will recognize them as the prophesied trials of deceptive attractions (*fitan*). O people, when you see such trials arriving, gather at your homes, guard your faith, break down your swords, and wish for death to seize you in-between the intervals of their successive destructive waves."

**699-** In another narration also dealing with the above trials, Zaid bin Wahab narrated that Huthaifa Bnul Yammãn, God be pleased with him, said: "Surely the waves of the trials of deceptive attractions (*fitan*) have interim periods of calm, and they have swift and unexpected destructive strikes. Should one die during the interim periods of their calm, he would surely be lucky."

**700-** Jurair narrated that Huthaifa Bnul Yammãn, God be pleased with him, said: "There will come a time when only those

[1] i.e., the Deceiver; Arb. Dajjãl, or the pseudo Massiah.

who pray the prayer of a drowning person will escape from destruction."

**701-** Abu 'Amru Bnu Hamdān narrated that Abu Mas'oud once asked Huthaifa Bnul Yammān, God be pleased with both of them, he said: "I know that the trials of deceptive attractions (*fitan*) have started, would you tell me anything else you heard in their regard?" Huthaifa replied: "Haven't you witnessed and verified the evidence yet? — The Book of Allah, the Lord of majesty and glory, blessed be His Name!"

**702-** Al-A'amash narrated that Huthaifa Bnul Yammān, God be pleased with him, said: "Not even the drunkenness caused by excessive drinking of wine can inebriate or obfuscate the minds of men more than the trials of deceptive attractions (*fitan*) will do!"

**703-** Imam Ahmad Ibn Hanbal, God be pleased with him, narrated that Huthaifa Bnul Yammān, God be pleased with him, said: "The trials of deceptive attractions (*fitna*) are put in charge of destroying three kinds of people: 1) The learned hot-headed and arrogant person who whenever he raises a challenge, the sword of destiny will strike at it and destroy it obdurately; 2) the leader (*Imam*) who calls upon such destruction to come; and, 3) the self-proclaimed sire. The first two kinds of people, the massive destruction will humiliate them, demean them, throw them to the ground, and mar their faces with mire; and as to the self-proclaimed sire, the *fitna* will scatter his possessions to waste, one blow after another, and until he will have nothing left."

**704-** Abu't Tufail narrated that Huthaifa Bnul Yammān, God be pleased with him, said: "O ye people! Why don't you inquire from me about this religion? Surely people used to take their questions to God's messenger ﷺ, upon whom be peace. They used to ask him about what is good and beneficial (*khair*), and I used to ask him about what is evil and harmful (*sharr*). Why don't you ask me about who is a living dead?"

As the people hearkened, Huthaifa Bnul Yammān, God be pleased with him, expounded: "Allah, the most exalted, blessed be His Name, have sent His messenger Muhammad ﷺ, upon whom be peace, to call humanity to come out of heedlessness and to receive the divine guidance. God's messenger ﷺ also asked them to forsake atheism, to know Allah their only Lord, and to have faith in Him. The lucky ones accepted his invitation, while others failed. By doing so, one who is a living dead comes back to life by recognizing the truth (*haqq*), and by rebutting falsehood (*bãtil*), and one who thinks that he is alive becomes a living dead by upholding falsehood."

Huthaifa continued: "The era of prophethood then ended, and it was followed by a caliphate system of Islamic polity that asserted and observed the jurisprudence established by God's messenger ﷺ, upon whom be peace, and after that, there will come an era of authoritarian monarchism."

"Some people will ward off falsehood with their hearts, actions, and words, and hence, they will have embraced the whole truth. Others may reject falsehood with their hearts and words, although they will do nothing about it, and hence, they will have abandoned a cardinal branch of what is true and just. A third group of people will rebut falsehood with their heart only, but they will keep quiet and do nothing about it, and such group of people will have abandoned two constitutive branches of what is true and just. Finally, a forth group of people will not even refute falsehood with neither their hearts nor their tongues, and this is what is known as a living dead."

**705-** Al-A'amash narrated that Huthaifa Bnul Yammãn, God be pleased with him, said: "Let Allah be my witness, that I know one thousand authentic prophetic sayings relating to the commands of Allah, the most exalted, and to the admonitions of His messenger ﷺ, upon whom be peace, and when you hear them, you will surely love me, follow me, and believe me. I also know another one thousand authentic prophetic sayings, and when you hear them, you will hate me, avoid me, and accuse me of lying."

**706-** In another narration of the above account, reported by 'Amru Bnu Murra that Huthaifa Bnul Yammãn, God be pleased with him, said: "I can tell you one thousand authentic prophetic sayings, and when you hear them, you will believe me, follow me, and support me; and I can also tell you another one thousand authentic prophetic sayings, but when you hear them, you will accuse me of lying, and you will avoid me, and insult me, although, Allah is my supreme witness that they are all true, and that they are truly the words of Allah, blessed be His Name, and those of His messenger ﷺ, upon whom be peace."

**707-** Jandab bnu 'Abdillāh, son of Sufyān, narrated that Huthaifa Bnul Yammān, God be pleased with him, said: "I have knowledge concerning an Imam who will dwell in the heavenly paradise, while his followers dwell in hell-fire." Jandab bnu 'Abdillāh asked: "Wouldn't that be a general statement referring to some of what you, the companions of God's messenger ﷺ, upon whom be peace, are constantly warning us about?" Huthaifa replied: "And what do you know about the facts and deeds of such a person that earned him such a blessed abode?"

**708-** Sa'īd bin Wahab narrated that Huthaifa Bnul Yammān, God be pleased with him, said: "It is as though I can perceive a rider who will soon descend upon you, and who will say to you, *'This land is ours, and this money is ours,'* and he will deprive the widows and the poor people from the wealth which Allah, out of His divine generosity, has conferred upon their forefathers."

**709-** 'Amru Bnu Murra narrated that Huthaifa Bnul Yammān, God be pleased with him, said: "There are four kinds of hearts: 1) A veiled heart, and that is the heart of an atheist; 2) a shielded heart, and that is the heart of a hypocrite; 3) a naked heart holding a glowing lamp, and that is the heart of a believer; and, 4) a heart filled with both hypocrisy and faith. The section of faith therein is like that of a tree which is watered with fresh spring water, and the section of hypocrisy is like that of a festering boil filled with puss and infected blood. Whichever of the two abounds and overruns the other at one time or another, the heart will reflect it."

**710-** Ahmad bin Ja'far, son of Hamdān al-Basri, narrated that Huthaifa Bnul Yammān, God be pleased with him, said: "I once complained to God's messenger ﷺ, upon whom be peace, about suffering from logorrhea,[1] and he replied, 'Why don't you regularly ask for God's forgiveness! I personally ask Allah, the Lord of majesty

---

[1] Logorrhea: Boils effecting the tongue; Arb. *Tharab al-Lissān,* it could also mean *glossorrhea,* i.e., excessive use of words.

and glory, blessed be His Name, for forgiveness one hundred times a day."

**711**- Abu 'Amru bnu Hamdãn narrated that Huthaifa Bnul Yammãn, God be pleased with him, said: "The best of my days are when I enter my house and find my family hungry and grousing around some dearth."

**712**- Abu Muhammad bin Hayyãn narrated that Huthaifa Bnul Yammãn, God be pleased with him, said: "I am most pleased when my family complains about poverty, for Allah, the most exalted, blessed be His Name, surely protects the believing servant from the syndromes of this world just as a concerned family prevents its sick member from eating certain foods that maybe harmful to his illness."

**713**- Attributing the abovementioned account regarding preventive medicine to God's messenger ﷺ, upon whom be peace, Sulaimãn bin Ahmad narrated that Huthaifa Bnul Yammãn, God be pleased with him, used to say: "There isn't a day where I am more gratified than when I enter my home and find my family hungry, and particularly when they censure me, saying, 'You do nothing for our sake, whether it is little or more!' This is because I heard God's messenger ﷺ, upon whom be peace, say, 'Allah, the most exalted, blessed be His Name, is more protective of the believing servant from the illnesses of this world than his own family when they place their sick person on a restricted diet. On the other hand, Allah, the most exalted, blessed be His Name, is more assuring to His believing servant to meet with salutary afflictions in this world than a father wishing the best benefits and success (*khair*) for his own born."

**714**- 'Abdullãh bin Muhammad bin Ja'far narrated that Huthaifa Bnul Yammãn once said to Sa'ad, son of Mu'ãth bin Jabal, God be pleased with both of them: "What do you think will happen to us should we become wealthy in this world?" Sa'ad replied: "I do not think that our generation will see such a day!" Later on, Huthaifa Bnul Yammãn, God be pleased with him, commented on Sa'ad's reply: "He was accorded what he anticipated, and I was given according to my expectation."

**715-** Imam Muhammad Ibn Seerīn narrated that when Huthaifa Bnul Yammān, God be pleased with him, first came to Madā'in, he arrived riding on a donkey, and he had little or no provisions. In fact, Huthaifa held a loaf of bread in one hand, and some distilled water in a carafe made of leather in the other hand, and he was eating while riding on his donkey."

**716-** Sulaimān bin Ahmad narrated that Huthaifa Bnul Yammān, God be pleased with him, said: "Beware not to find yourselves standing by the gate of deceptive attractions (*fitan*)!" Someone inquired: "O Abu 'Abdullāh, what is the gate of deceptive attractions?" Huthaifa replied: "That is the threshold of government officials, and that is when one of you seeks a government official, and in the process of hoping to earn some meager gains, he lies to him, soliciting the attention of his rank and authority, and pretending to be telling the truth. This is the threshold of deceptive attractions."

**717-** Imam Ahmad Ibn Hanbal, God be pleased with him, narrated, re Zaid bin Wahab, that a man came to Huthaifa Bnul Yammān, God be pleased with him, and said: "Ask Allah on my behalf to forgive me my sins!" Huthaifa replied: "I will not ask Allah to forgive you your sins." Huthaifa then turned to his companions and said: "Should I solicit Allah's forgiveness for this man's sins, he will then say on the Day of Reckoning, 'Huthaifa had interceded before Allah, the most exalted, to forgive me my sins!' And then, he may be told, 'Would you like Allah to place you where Huthaifa is placed?' "

Huthaifa then prayed: "O Allah, my Lord, I beseech Your divine generosity to grant this man to dwell where Huthaifa will dwell in Your mercy."

**718-** Rab'i bnu Khirāsh narrated that he heard Huthaifa Bnul Yammān, God be pleased with him, say at his deathbed: "O my Lord help me. One day I thought that when my death comes, my assurance will not be shaken. But today my Lord, my mind is moved by mixed specters,[1] unknown to me, and I do not know what final repercussions will they have on me!"

---

1 Specter: A visible appearance of something not present, associated with the time of death.

**719-** Mũsa bin 'Abdullãh bin Yazĩd narrated that Huthaifa Bnul Yammãn, God be pleased with him, once said: "At times, I wish I had someone to handle my business and to take care of my family, and then, I would have closed my doors, and stayed indoor until the day when I meet Allah, the Lord of majesty and glory."

**720-** 'Abdullãh, son of Imam Ahmad Ibn Hanbal, God be pleased with him, narrated that Huthaifa Bnul Yammãn, God be pleased with him, once said: "One of the best conditions in which Allah loves to see his servant, is when He sees his face covered with dust."[1]

**721-** Abu Muhammad bin Hayyãn narrated that Huthaifa Bnul Yammãn, God be pleased with him, once said: "The most I fear for this nation of believers (*umma*), is that they give preference to what they see over what they know, and to step into heedlessness without realizing it."

**722-** Al-A'amash narrated that Huthaifa Bnul Yammãn, God be pleased with him, used to say: "The best among you are not those who renounce the comfort of the world for the sake of that of the hereafter, nor those who relinquish the comfort of the hereafter for the sake of that of this world, rather the best among you are those who take a share of comfort from each one of them."

**723-** 'Abdullãh bin Ja'far narrated, re Huthaifa Bnul Yammãn, God be pleased with him, that God's messenger ﷺ, upon whom be peace, said: "On the Day of Judgment, people will be gathered in one plane, and not a single soul will utter a word. The first to be called is Muhammad ﷺ, upon whom be peace. He will reply, 'Here I am to serve Thy command, and I am surely bound by Thy favors, my Lord. Indeed, all what is good is Thy endowment, and evil has no rise nor appurtenance in Thine presence. Lord, surely there is no refuge nor escape from Thee but to Thee. Blessed and most exalted Thou art, Lord of the most blessed House."

"This is the meaning of the verse: ‹ Soon will your Lord raise you to a station of praise and glory. › (*Qur'an 17:79*)

**724-** Abu Muhammad bin Hayyãn narrated that someone asked

---

[1] *i.e., resulting from long prostrations and hard work.*

Huthaifa Bnul Yammãn, God be pleased with him: "Did the Children of Israel altogether depart from their religion in one day?" Huthaifa replied: "No, but whenever they were commanded to do something they abstained and whenever they were barred from doing something, they sought it. They did so invariably until they were striped off their religion, just as when a man takes the shirt off his shoulders."

**725-** 'Abdullãh bin Saydãn narrated that Huthaifa Bnul Yammãn, God be pleased with him, said: "Allah's wrath will surely descend upon those among you who do not exercise what we were ordered to practice. I swear by Allah, blessed be His Name, that either you engage in enjoining what is good and beneficial, and advise against what is wrong and evil, or you will be struck with internal wars, whereby, your evil ones will rise over your better ones, and they will kill them one after the other, and until there will not remain among you a single good person who enjoins what is good or forbid what is evil., At such an austere time when you pray to Allah, the Lord of majesty and glory, for help, and He will not answer your prayers, out of despise and repudiation for your contemptible attitudes."

**726-** Imam Ahmad Ibn Hanbal, God be pleased with him, narrated that Abi-r-Raqqãd said: "I was a young boy when my employer started taking me to the mosque, and he ordered me to sit down and to listen to the admonitions of Huthaifa Bnul Yammãn, God be pleased with him. On that day, I heard Huthaifa say, 'During the time of God's messenger ﷺ, upon whom be peace, a man may have said a word that turned him into a hypocrite, and even today, I can still hear such an expression from one of you, in the way he poses a question, and then he repeats it in various forms, and up to four times in one setting. Here me ye, it is either you obey God's command, to enjoin what is good, to forbid what is evil, and to spread the good news, or you will have to meet with the wrath of Allah, blessed be His Name, where you will be wiped out altogether with a horrid punishment, or He may order your evil ones to rise and to have the upper hand over you, and at such terrifying times, even the prayers of your better ones, asking for His help will not be accepted.' "

**727-** 'Abdul Malik bin Maisara narrated that al-Nazzãl bin Sabra said: "We were at the house of Huthaifa, when 'Uthmãn came and asked him, 'O Abu 'Abdullãh, what is this forewarning I heard that you have admonished the people with. Did you truly say that?' Huthaifa Bnul Yammãn, God be pleased with him, replied, 'No, I did not!' 'Uthmãn then said, 'I knew that you are their most truthful, and their most true to his Lord.'

Later on, when 'Uthmãn left, al-Nazzãl bin Sabra turned to Huthaifa and said, 'O Abu 'Abdullãh, did we not hear you say what you said?' Huthaifa replied, 'Yes, indeed you heard it right.' "

Nazzãl bin Sabra then said to his visiting companions: "Indeed, he did say it, and yet, in order to avoid alarming those who may disapprove such knowledge, he withheld having said it. Perhaps he wanted to mix his deeds between the common and the uncommon, and maybe he thought that should he propound what he knew then, it would brook opposition and panic among some people, and by doing so, he feared to lose his stand of servitude and trueness to his Lord."

**728-** 'Amru bnu Murra narrated that Huthaifa Bnul Yammãn, God be pleased with him, said: "In due time, you will live an era, wherein, the best among you will refrain from enjoining what is good or forbidding what is evil."[1]

**729-** Habı̃b Bnu Abi Thãbit narrated that Huthaifa Bnul Yammãn, God be pleased with him, said: "You may mix with both, the believers and the atheists, however, do not bring up the subject of religion in your conversations with the unbelievers."

**730-** Muhammad bin Ishãq narrated that Huthaifa Bnul Yammãn, God be pleased with him, said: "The era of religious hypocrisy (*nifãq*) has gone away for now, and therefore, there is no more religious hypocrisy today. What you see for now is the spread of atheism (*kufur*) after faith (*imãn*)."

**731-** 'Abdullãh bnu Ja'far narrated that Huthaifa Bnul Yammãn, God be pleased with him, said: "The hypocrites are more evil today than they were at the time of God's messenger ﷺ, upon whom be

[1] Perhaps this account denotes a time of monumental spread of corruption and evil that cannot be reversed until Doomsday. Allah knows best.

peace, for then, they used to hide their stance, and now, they are audaciously egregious about it."

**732-** Al-A'amash narrated that H̲uthaifa Bnul Yammān, God be pleased with him, once asked a man: "Would you like to kill the most immoral and profligate person in this world?" The man replied: "Indeed!" H̲uthaifa said: "If you do, then you will be even more iniquitous than him!"

**733-** 'Amru Bnu Marzouq narrated that H̲uthaifa Bnul Yammān, God be pleased with him, said: "I swear by Allah the most exalted that whenever a man distances himself from the Muslim community for even a span of one's hand, he would have forsaken Islam in its entirety."

**734-** Al-A'amash narrated that H̲uthaifa Bnul Yammān, God be pleased with him, said: "O readers of the Qur'an, O teachers of the Qur'an! Adhere to the path (*t̲arïq*), and if you do, you will attain a much higher success, but if you don't, and instead you wander right or left, you would have embarked on the furthest and most erring course."

**735-** Abi Salāma narrated that H̲uthaifa Bnul Yammān, God be pleased with him, said: "There will come a time when you will be governed by princes who will not be worth the weight of single flake of a grain of barley on the Day of Judgment, in the sight of Allah, blessed be His Name."

**736-** 'Abdullāh, son of Imam Ahmad Ibn H̲anbal, God be pleased with him, narrated that Ubai 'Abdu-Rah̲mān al-Salmi said: "I was in Madā'in, and one day I went with my father to the Friday congregational prayers. The central mosque was about one parasang[1] from our home, and at that time, H̲uthaifa Bnul Yammān, God be pleased with him, was the deputy (*wāli*) of the caliph in Madā'in.

When H̲uthaifa rose on the pulpit to give the Friday sermon, he commenced by praising Allah, blessed be His Name, and by glorifying His attributes, and later on, in the course of his *k̲hutba* (sermon), he said, 'Surely, the final hour has drawn near, and the moon has cleaven by God's leave. Surely this world has evinced

[1] Arb. *farsak̲h*, about three and one half miles distance.

the final signs of its conclusion. Indeed, today is the field of sowing the seeds of success, and tomorrow is the fast coming day for harvesting the reward of the forerunners.' "

Ubai then added: "I asked my father, 'What does he mean by the forerunners (Arb. *sãbiqün*)?' He replied, 'The ones who will win the heavenly paradise.' "

**737-** Abu 'Amru bnu Hamdãn narrated that Huthaifa Bnul Yammãn, God be pleased with him, once delivered the Friday sermon in the central mosque of Madã'in, where he said: "O People! Look into the source of revenues your workers collect. Find out if they are lawful, then bring them in, otherwise, disallow them, for I have heard God's messenger ﷺ, upon whom be peace, say, 'It is not possible for a flesh that grows on ill-gotten gains to enter the heavenly paradise.' "

**738-** Imam Ahmad Ibn Hanbal, God be pleased with him, narrated that Huthaifa Bnul Yammãn, God be pleased with him, said: "The sin of the one who sells wine is equal to the sin of the one who drinks it, and the sin of the one who sells pork is equal to the sin of the one who eats it. Therefore, inquire as to where from do your workers collect your revenues, for it is not possible for a flesh that grows on ill-gotten gains to enter the heavenly paradise."

**739-** Al-A'amash narrated that Huthaifa Bnul Yammãn, God be pleased with him, said: "To fear and revere Allah, the Lord of majesty and glory, is the least of knowledge, but the least an untruthful person can do upon telling a lie, is to ask for Allah's forgiveness, even though he may return to lying."

**740-** 'Akrama bin 'Ammãr narrated that 'Abdul 'Aziz, a nephew of Huthaifa Bnul Yammãn, God be pleased with him, said: "I personally heard it from Huthaifa, about forty five years ago, when he said, 'Absence of fear and reverence for Allah, the Lord of majesty and glory, will be the first loss in your religious observances, and foregoing the prescribed regular prayers (*salãt*) will subsequently be the final loss in your religious observances.'"

**741-** Al-A'amash narrated that Abu Yahya asked Huthaifa Bnul Yammãn, God be pleased with him: "Who is a hypocrite?" Huthaifa replied: "A hypocrite is one who can describe what is Islam, although he does not practice it!"

**742-** Ziyãd Mawla Ibn 'Abbãs, narrated that Huthaifa Bnul Yammãn, God be pleased with him, said when he was on his deathbed: "I would not speak had I not known that today is my last day in this world and my inaugural day in the hereafter. My Lord, You know that I preferred poverty over richness, meekness over honor, and death over life in this world. Indeed, a beloved has arrived on a day when the heart has much longing for him. So horrific is the loss of those who bring nothing but regret to this sure encounter."

Ziyãd added: "Huthaifa Bnul Yammãn, God be pleased with him, died on that same day."

**743-** 'Abdu-Rahmãn bin al-'Abbãs narrated that when Huthaifa Bnul Yammãn, God be pleased with him, was near his death, he said: "A beloved has arrived on a day when the heart has great deal of longing for him. Perdition is surely the share of those who bring nothing but regret for this sure encounter." Huthaifa then added: "I praise Allah, the most exalted, blessed be His Name, Who, by taking me back unto Him today, is sparing me the sure coming encounter with the calamitous trials of deception (*fitan*) that will soon befall the entire world. I am most grateful to Him for taking me back without having to meet its leaders and thugs."

**744-** Khãlid bin al-Rabi' al-'Absi said: "We came to see Huthaifa in Madã'in the day he died, and it was dark when we arrived. Near his death, and when he became heavy, Huthaifa asked: "What time is it?" We replied: "It is late at night." Huthaifa said: "I seek refuge in Allah, blessed be His Name, from a morning that leads to hell-fire." Huthaifa then turned to the people and asked: "Did you bring a shroud with you?" They replied: "We did." He then said: "Be not exorbitant in what you shroud me with. Should your departing friend be of any worth in the sight of his Lord, then Allah, blessed be His Name, will replace his shroud with what is better. Otherwise, should one be shrouded in what exceeds the indispensable, he will be stripped of it shortly after he dies."

**745-** Also in another narration of the above account, Abu Hãmed bin Jabla narrated: "Huthaifa was leaning on Abi Mas'oud's shoulder when he saw someone bringing a new shroud. He said: "Why would you shroud your friend in this new fabric? Surely should your friend be of any worth, then Allah, the most exalted, blessed be His Name, will replace it with what is better. Otherwise, should he be unfitting to wear such excess, his shroud will writhe him contortedly between the two walls of his grave, and it will throw him perpetually from one side of his grave to the other, from the time he is buried, and until the Day of Resurrection."

**746-** Sulaimãn bin Ahmad narrated that Silla bin Zafar said: "Huthaifa, God be pleased with him, sent me along with Abu Mas'oud to purchase a shroud for his burial. Hence, we went out and we bought him a complete vestment of the finest quality of cotton available, a fabric commonly used for turbans, and we paid three hundred dirhams for it. When we returned to his house, Huthaifa asked, 'Show me what you bought!' And when he saw it, he said, 'This is not a shroud for a man like me! It will be sufficient for me if you would use two white bed sheets, and without a shirt for a shroud, for it will not be long before they will be replaced with either a better raiment or a meaner one.'

Immediately, Silla bin Zafar and Abu Mas'oud returned to the market, and they bought him what he asked for."

**747-** Silla bin Zafar narrated that Huthaifa, God be pleased with him, said: "Learn how to exercise patience, for your turn of trials has drawn near. However, no matter how much difficulties you meet, they cannot measure to the awesome adversities we experienced at the dawn of Islam alongside God's messenger ﷺ, upon whom be peace."

**748-** 'Abdullãh bin Muhammad narrated that Huthaifa, God be pleased with him, said: "There is reckoning in the grave and another reckoning on the Day of Resurrection, and whosoever is brought before Almighty Allah for the questioning of the Day of Judgment will suffer."

## 39- 'Abdullãh Bnu 'Amru Bnul 'Ãss

Here is another example of a pious believer who observed high-minded morality, he fasted most of the days of his life, stood up in supererogatory prayers most of the nights, and he read the glorious Qur'an with utmost reverence for Allah, blessed is His Name, Who revealed it; this is the humble and beloved companion of God's messenger ﷺ, upon whom be peace, this is 'Abdullãh Bnu 'Amru Bnul 'Ãss, God be pleased with him. He spoke the truth, shunned falsehood, occupied himself in his work seriously, and he forsook vain talk. 'Abdullãh Bnu 'Amru Bnul 'Ãss was a generous host, he fed the poor, he was first to initiate the greeting when he met someone, and his speech was filled with utmost sagacity, sweetness, and sapience.

It is said that spirituality also involves embracing the character of the righteous, and to honor the genuineness of one's commitments.

**749-** On this subject, Sa'ïd Bnul Musayyib narrated that 'Abdullãh Bnu 'Amru Bnul 'Ãss, once said: "Someone brought it to the attention of God's messenger ﷺ, upon whom be peace, that I had made a vow to fast for the rest of my days, and to pray all my nights as long as I lived in this world. One day, when God's messenger ﷺ saw me, he said to me, 'Did you vow to fast for the rest your days, and to pray all the nights as long as you live?' I replied, "Indeed, and I beg for your permission, for surely you are more dear to me than my own father and mother!' God's messenger ﷺ, upon whom be peace, then said, 'There may come a time when perhaps it will be too hard for you to bear up this commitment.'

**750-** Also in reference to the subject of upholding one's commitment, Muhammad bnu 'Amru bnu 'Alqama narrated that 'Abdullãh bnu 'Amr Bnul 'Ãss, God be pleased with him, said: "One day, God's messenger ﷺ, upon whom be peace, came to my house, and he said to me, 'O 'Abdullãh bnu 'Amr, it came to my attention that you have imposed upon yourself to observe a perpetual night vigil in prayers, and to fast for the remainder of your days. Surely such a commitment is a self-imposed devotion which is uncalled for.' I replied, 'But I can do it, O messenger of Allah, and I find no hardship in doing so!' God's messenger ﷺ, upon whom be peace, then said, 'It will be deemed sufficient if you would only fast three days per week.' "

'Abdullãh bnu 'Amr continued: "I became more obdurate and

inflexible in my obstinacy, but on the other hand, God's messenger ﷺ, upon whom be peace, also became more firm in his instruction, and when I added, 'O messenger of Allah, I truly find the needed strength in me to do so!' He then said: 'O 'Abdullãh, your eyes have rights upon you, your guests have rights upon you, and also your wife has rights upon you.' "

**751-** Qutaiba bin Sa'ïd narrated that Abi Salma once asked 'Abdullãh bnu 'Amr Bnul 'Ãss, God be pleased with him: "Tell me about the day when God's messenger ﷺ, upon whom be peace, came to see you, and what he said to you regarding your extraordinary fasting commitment and outstanding inordinate prayers!" 'Abdullãh bnu 'Amr Bnul 'Ãss replied: "He came in and said, 'O 'Abdullãh bnu 'Amr, is what I heard true? Did you imposed upon yourself the observance of a perpetual night vigil in prayers, and to fast for the balance of your days in this life?' I replied, 'Indeed, I do that O messenger of Allah.' God's messenger ﷺ then said, 'It is sufficient to fast three days per month, and the reward of that will be equal to the benefit of fasting all year around.' "

'Abdullãh bnu 'Amr continued: "I became argumentative and more obdurate and inflexible in my obstinacy, and God's messenger ﷺ, upon whom be peace, further became more firm in his instruction, and when I said, 'O messenger of Allah, I truly find strength to do so!' He then said: 'The most balanced fasting in the sight of Allah is the fasting of David, upon whom be peace.' "

'Abdullãh bnu 'Amr further continued: "And now that I have reached old age, my body became frail, and I recognize that indeed I did tax my family and interests by being stubborn. I wish I had accepted the dispensation of my vow as suggested by God's messenger ﷺ, upon whom be peace, and that was to fast three days per month only."

**752-** Abi Salma bnu 'Abdu-Rahmãn also paraphrased the above account, re 'Abdullãh bnu 'Amr Bnul 'Ãss, God be pleased with him, who quoted God's messenger ﷺ, upon whom be peace, to have said: "Why wouldn't you then fast the fasting of David, upon whom be peace! He fasted one day, and he broke his fast the next day." 'Abdullãh bnu 'Amr again argued: "O messenger of Allah, I surely find strength in me to do more than that!" God's messenger ﷺ, upon whom be peace, then said: "Perhaps should you live a long life, your body will become weaker, and such a lifetime commitment may become a burden on you, think about it!"

**753-** Sulaimãn bin Ahmad narrated that 'Abdullãh bnu 'Amr Bnul 'Ãss, God be pleased with him, said: "When I memorized the entire Qur'an by heart, I read all of it in one night, and when God's messenger ﷺ, upon whom be peace, heard that, he said to me, 'As time goes, I am afraid that such avid reading of the Qur'an today may become tedious, and it could cause you to feel weariness towards it.' God's messenger ﷺ further suggested, 'Read it once in the course of each month.' "

'Abdullãh bnu 'Amr replied: "O messenger of Allah, allow me to enjoy my strength and youth as long as I have them!" God's messenger ﷺ replied: "Then read it once in the course of each twenty days," but 'Abdullãh bnu 'Amr further argued: "O messenger of Allah, please allow me to enjoy my strength and youth!" However, God's messenger ﷺ, upon whom be peace, disapproved.

**754-** 'Abdu-Rahmãn bin Rãfi' narrated that when 'Abdullãh bnu 'Amr Bnul 'Ãss, God be pleased with him, became old, and reading the entire Qur'an once a day became ponderous, demanding, and wearisome, he said: "When I memorized the entire Qur'an by heart, I went to God's messenger ﷺ, upon whom be peace, and said, 'O messenger of Allah, I have memorized the entire Qur'an by heart. Please enjoin upon me the requirement of reading it regularly.' God's messenger ﷺ, upon whom be peace, replied, 'Read it in the course of one month, (i.e., one *juzu'* per day).' I said, 'I do feel stronger than that!' God's messenger ﷺ then said, 'Read it twice in the course of each month,' but again I said, 'I surely feel stronger than that!' God's messenger ﷺ again said, 'Then read it in the course of six days period.' I answered, 'But I feel stronger than that!' He again said, 'Then read it in the course of three days period,' and again I argued, 'I certainly feel stronger than that!' "

God's messenger ﷺ, upon whom be peace, disliked this type of debating, and he said: "Then rise and go to your reading.

**755-** Imam Ahmad bin Hanbal, God be pleased with him,

Narrated that 'Abdullāh bnu 'Amr Bnul 'Āss, God be pleased with him, said: "My father chose a wife for me from a noble family from the Tribe of Quraish. When my wife entered my house, I avoided necking with her, and because of the spiritual comfort I deemed myself in need of, and which I felt attainable only through constant devotion, fasting, and prayers, I thus remained withdrawn."

"One day, my father, 'Amr Bnul 'Āss, came to visit his daughter in-law, and he asked her, 'How do you find your husband?' My wife replied, 'Surely he is the best of men. He never seeks our bosom nor does he ever near our bed.' My father became extremely upset, and he affronted me, and he was rough with his words, as he said to me, 'I gave you a wife whom I have chosen for you from one of the most noble families of Quraish, and surely you have delimited her spirit, and restricted her rights, and you did this and that ...' "

"My father then went to God's messenger ﷺ, upon whom be peace, and he reported me to him. Later on, God's messenger ﷺ called for me, and when I arrived, he asked me, 'Do you regularly fast during the day?' I replied in the affirmative. He further asked, 'Do you invariably stand up in prayers at night?' I replied, 'I do.' God's messenger ﷺ, upon whom be peace, then said, 'But I also fast, and I also break my fast, and I pray at night as well, and yet, I also take rest, and I also have intimate moments with my wife, therefore, whosoever feels disinclined to my *sunna* (traditions), he is not one of my followers.' "

"God's messenger ﷺ, upon whom be peace, then turned to me and said, "Read the Qur'an in the course of one month.' I replied, 'I find my self stronger than that!' He then said, 'Then read it in the course of ten days at a time.' I replied, 'But I do find my self stronger than that!' God's messenger ﷺ suggested, 'Then read it in the course of three days!' – And thus, he kept on reasoning with me, until he said, 'You may fast one day, and then break your fast the next day, for that is the best criterion of fasting, and such was the fasting tradition of my brother David, peace be upon him.' "

**756-** Husayn commented in reference to the above prophetic tradition, saying: "Every worshiper will undergo a temporary passion, and at times, such ardor may become excessive. However, sometimes, it can last for as long as one year, or otherwise, if it goes beyond that, it becomes innovation. Therefore, one whose inclinations and fervor last for up to, and no longer than one year, then he is surely well guided. Otherwise, if they last longer than that, then they could lead him to his demise."

**757-** Mujãhid also spoke apropos of the this subject, he said: "When 'Abdullãh bnu 'Amr Bnul 'Ãss, God be pleased with both of them, became old, his body became frail, and his strength debilitated, and he was only able to fast few days at a time, and then he would break his fast for few days as well. 'Abdullãh continued to maintain his regular reading taskwork (*hizb*) of the entire Qur'an, although, he took his time in doing so. Sometimes he would read it in the course of three days, or even in the course of seven days, and he was less stringent regarding maintaining a rigorous standard of his performance. 'Abdullãh bnu 'Amr Bnul 'Ãss, God be pleased with him and with his father, also used to say, 'To have accepted the dispensation of my vow as suggested by God's messenger ﷺ, upon whom be peace, would have been more dear to my heart today than my persistence regarding my personal feelings then. I wish I did not have to disagree with him concerning this matter, and by finally complying with his suggestion at this age, I hope that I will not have dissented on anything else.'"

**758-** Imam Ahmad bin Hanbal, God be pleased with him, narrated that Wãhib bin 'Abdullãh, son of 'Abdullãh bnu 'Amr, said: "I saw myself in a dream licking my fingers, and it was as though one finger was coated with ghee, and the other was coated with honey. In the morning, I related my dream to God's messenger ﷺ, upon whom be peace, who interpreted my dream, saying, 'You will study the two books, the Torah and the Qur'an.'

Imam Ahmad bin Hanbal, God be pleased with him, added that 'later on in his life, Wãhib bin 'Abdullãh grew up to be most learned and insightful in both revelations.'

**759-** 'Abdu-Rahmãn al-Hubali narrated that 'Abdullãh bnu 'Amr Bnul 'Ãss, God be pleased with him, said: "To do a good deed today is twice more pleasing to me than it was when we lived with God's messenger ﷺ, upon whom be peace. That is because, when we were with God's messenger ﷺ, upon whom be peace, we focused solely on the hereafter, and we gave no regards to this world, and lately, the balance of deceptive attractions in this world have tilted people's focus adversely and affected many of us."

**760-** Abu Bakr Ibn Khallãd narrated, re 'Abdullãh bnu 'Amr Bnul 'Ãss, God be pleased with him, that a man once asked God's messenger ﷺ, upon whom be peace: "What is considered as best of deeds in the way of Islam (submission to Allah)?" God's messenger ﷺ, upon whom be peace, replied: "To share your food, and to salute those you know and those you do not know with the greeting of peace, (*As-Salãmu 'Alaikum*)."

**761-** 'Atã bin al-Sã'ib narrated, re 'Abdullãh bnu 'Amr Bnul 'Ãss, God be pleased with him, that God's messenger ﷺ, upon whom be peace, said: "Worship the merciful Lord, give the regards of peace, and feed the hungry, and thus you will be let into paradise."

**762-** 'Amru Bnu Shu'aib narrated that his grandfather 'Abdullãh bnu 'Amr Bnul 'Ãss, God be pleased with him, said: "I once sat in a gathering with God's messenger ﷺ, upon whom be peace, and on that day, I felt a bliss I never felt before in my life, and I never delighted or felt a similar gratification since that day."

**763-** Abu 'Amru bnu Hamdãn narrated that 'Amru bnu Shu'aib said: "I went with 'Abdullãh bnu 'Amr to God's House, and as soon as we reached behind the Ka'ba, I said to him, 'Wouldn't you seek refuge in Almighty Allah from hell-fire?' 'Abdullãh bnu 'Amr immediately prayed, 'I seek refuge in Allah, the Lord of the Ka'ba against hell-fire.' 'Abdullãh then went to the Cornerstone (*hajar*), and after holding it for a moment, he stood in-between that corner and the gate of the Ka'ba, whereat, he placed his chest and face and spread his arms open against that wall for a short while in utter submission. Later on, he said to me, 'I once saw God's messenger ﷺ, upon whom be peace, do that.' "

**764-** Bishr bnu Müsa narrated that Hussain bnu Shafiy said: "We were once sitting with 'Abdullãh bnu 'Amr Bnul 'Ãss, God be pleased with him, discussing our religion when Tubai' arrived, and seeing him, , 'Abdullãh bnu 'Amr immediately exclaimed, 'Here comes the best of experts on this subject in the land today.' 'Abdullãh bnu 'Amr then asked Tubai', 'Tell us about the three greatest blessings a human being can have, and the three most evil things he must avoid!' Tubai' replied, 'Indeed. The three greatest blessings are: 1) A truthful tongue; 2) a God-fearing heart; and, 3) a pious wife; and the three most evil things to acquire are, 1) A lying tongue; 2) a dissolute heart; and, 3) a wicked wife.' 'Abdullāh bnu 'Amr then turned to his guests and said, 'Didn't I tell you that!'"

**765-** Ubai 'Abdu-Rahmān al-Hubali narrated that 'Abdullāh bnu 'Amr Bnul 'Āss, God be pleased with him, once said: "To be one of the last ten poor believers to enter paradise on the Day of Judgment is more pleasing to me than to be one of the last ten rich believers then, for the blessed majority on that day is the assembly of the poorest in this world, except for a rich person who freely gives away charity right and left." (*Also narrated by al-Laith*)

**766-** Al-Laith bnu Sa'ad narrated that 'Abdullāh bnu 'Amr Bnul 'Āss, God be pleased with him, said: "Paradise is forbidden to any lewd and shameless person."

**767-** Muhammad bin Ahmad bin al-Hassan narrated that 'Abdullāh bnu 'Amr Bnul 'Āss, God be pleased with him, said: "Whosoever offers a Muslim a drink of water, Allah, blessed be His Name, will distance him as far from hell-fire as a great stride of a leaping racing horse."

**768-** Sulaimān bin al-Mughīra narrated that 'Abdullāh bnu 'Amr Bnul 'Āss, God be pleased with him, said: "There was a time when people used to say, 'Walk away from what you can do nothing about, remain silent regarding what is not of your concern, and conserve your words the same way you keep away your savings.'"

**769-** Bishr bin Mūsa narrated that 'Abdullāh bnu 'Amr Bnul 'Āss, God be pleased with him, said: "It was revealed through the *Nāmous*, (the Holy Spirit) which came upon God's prophet Moses, upon whom be peace, that Allah, the most Exalted, abominates three types of people among His creation: 1) One that sows discord among brethren; 2) one who is swift in drumming up mischief; and 3) one who hunts for someone living in peace, and finds a way to cause him trouble and distress."

[1] Arb. *farsakh*, about three and one half miles distance.

**770-** Khãlid bin Yazïd narrated that 'Abdullãh bnu 'Amr Bnul 'Ãss, God be pleased with him, said: "It is written in the Torah that engaging in a business can develop profligacy and immorality, and that the schemer will fall into the pit which he digs for his brother."

**771-** Qutaiba bin Sa'ïd narrated that 'Abdullãh bnu 'Amr Bnul 'Ãss, God be pleased with him, said: "Iblis, the first accursed Satan, is presently shackled at the deepest layer of the earth, whenever he makes a moves, it fuels evil and sows dissension between two people or more."

**772-** Imam Ahmad bin Hanbal, God be pleased with him, narrated that 'Abdullãh bnu 'Amr Bnul 'Ãss, God be pleased with him, said: "If you only knew what I know, you would laugh little and cry a lot. Moreover, if you had really understood the truth, you would cry so loud continually until your vocal cords break down, and you would prostrate yourselves for a long lasting prostration, until your spinal column bends and then stiffens into one piece."

**773-** Imam Ahmad bin Hanbal, God be pleased with him, narrated that Ja'far bin Abi 'Omrãn said: "We learned that 'Abdullãh bnu 'Amr Bnul 'Ãss, God be pleased with him, once noticed himself hearing the hissing sound of fire in his house, and contemplating upon it, he exclaimed, 'Ooh, Ooh!' 'Abdullãh then heard a voice saying, 'O son of 'Amr, this is not it!'

Commenting on his experience, 'Abdullãh bnu 'Amr Bnul 'Ãss, God be pleased with him, said, 'I swear by Him Who controls the destiny of my soul, that this earthly little fire was beseeching its Lord for mercy, in fear of ever returning to *gehennam,* the grand fire of hell!'"

**774-** Abu 'Amru bnu Hamdãn narrated, re 'Abdullãh bnu 'Amr Bnul 'Ãss, God be pleased with him, that a man once came to him to solicit an endowment, and he said: "Aren't we considered party to the poor Meccan immigrants?"

'Abdullãh bnu 'Amr replied: "Do you have a wife with whom you confide?" "I do!" The man replied.

'Abdullãh bnu 'Amr further asked the man: "Do you have a house where you can retire at night?" "I do!" The man answered.

'Abdullãh bnu 'Amr then commented: "Then you are not

considered a party of the poor Meccan *muhãjireen* (immigrants). However, if you want, we will give you something, or if you want, we will mention your needs to the governor in charge!"

The man then said: "Do nothing! God willing, we will endure with patience, and we will ask for nothing!"

**775-** Imam Ahmad bin Hanbal, God be pleased with him, narrated that 'Abdullãh bnu 'Amr Bnul 'Ãss, God be pleased with him, once spoke to a gathering of believers, where he said: "You will be gathered on the Day of Reckoning, and a call will come, 'Where are the poor and the meek of this *Umma* (nation of followers of God's messenger ﷺ, upon whom be peace)?' When they all come forth, they will be asked, 'What do you bring with you?' They will reply, 'Our Lord, we were subjected to all kinds of miseries and trials in the world, and by Thy grace, we endured that with patience. Thou already know all of that, and Thou have put others in charge of managing wealth and authority!' Then it will be said to them, 'You spoke the truth.' "

"Hence, they will be let into the heavenly paradise, and that is a long time before the rest of those who are also destined to enter it,[1] while the exact, critical and demanding accountability, remains the lot of those who occupied a seat of command and presided over others and who had money in this world."

**776-** Khãlid bin Sa'dãn narrated that 'Abdullãh bnu 'Amr Bnul 'Ãss, God be pleased with him, said: "Paradise is enwrapped, and it is suspended by the horns of the sun. Once a year, paradise is spread open, and the souls of the believers wing freely inside it, carried by starling-like green birds. They know one another, and together, they enjoy the fruits of paradise."

**777-** Imam Ahmad bin Hanbal, God be pleased with him, narrated that 'Abdullãh used to often close his doors for an extended period of time, and he used to with great chagrin in private until eventually his sight was affected by his grief and sorrow. As a result of his excessive crying, 'Abdullãh developed serious inflammation of the eyes, and consequently, the mother of Ya'lã Ibn 'Atã' used to make a special mixture of kohl for 'Abdullãh bnu 'Amr Bnul 'Ãss to treat his eyes.

[1] i.e., Five hundred years.

Ya'lã Ibn 'Atã' said: "My mother used to regularly make him a special ointment mixed which she with Kohl to treat his eyes."

**778-** 'Amru Bnu Nãfi' narrated that 'Abdullãh bnu 'Amr Bnul 'Ãss, God be pleased with him, once passed by a man resting after the *fajr* dawn prayers, and he woke him up, saying: "Didn't you know that Allah looks upon His creation at this hour, and that out of His mercy, He lets into paradise three types of people who otherwise would be destined to enter hell-fire!" (*Also narrated by al-Muqri'*)

**779-** Ya'qoub bin 'Ãsim narrated that 'Abdullãh bnu 'Amr Bnul 'Ãss, God be pleased with him, once said: "Whoever is asked to give something in charity in the Name of Allah, and if he obliges, will be rewarded seventy fold."

**780-** Abu Hãmed bin Jabla narrated that Sulaimãn bin Rabi'a once went on a pilgrimage from Basra, Iraq, to Mecca in a caravan of Qur'ãn readers and the caravan was led by Mu'ãwiya. In their company also traveled al-Muntasir bin al-Hãrith. When they completed their pilgrimage, they all decided not to return to Basra until they had met one of the companions (*sahãba*) of God's messenger ﷺ, upon whom be peace, and hear an authentic prophetic admonition. Hence, they inquired everywhere, and finally someone told them that 'Abdullãh bnu 'Amr Bnul 'Ãss, God be pleased with him, had a house somewhere near the edge of the city of Mecca.

When the pilgrims arrived at that locality, they noticed a large convoy of three hundred camels, consisting of one hundred camels saddled and ready for a journey, and the other two hundred were loaded with goods. They inquired: "Who do these camels belong to?"

"They belong to 'Abdullãh bnu 'Amr Bnul 'Ãss." The Meccan residents accompanying them replied. The pilgrims commented: "We were told that he lived a most modest life!" The Meccans replied: "This is true, but 'Abdullãh keeps one hundred camels to help his local brothers of the region when they need them most, and the other two hundred camels, he maintains at all times to supply the needs of his visitors from distant lands, and to serve his local guests."

The pilgrims received that comment with great astonishment. Seeing that, the Meccans further said: "Do not be astonished, for 'Abdullāh bnu 'Amr Bnul 'Āss is indeed a very rich man, but he deems that his guests have the foremost rights upon him, including the right to be supplied with the needed provision upon traveling back to their homeland."

The pilgrims immediately asked: "Point him to us!" The Meccans replied: "His is not at home right now, but you may find him praying at the sacred mosque."

Sulaimān bin Rabī'a continued: "Hence, we went back to the Ka'ba, and we found him sitting in prayers near the edge of the mosque. He was a short man, his sight was partially dimmed by cataract, he wore a turban and a simple mantle over his robe, and he had his sandals tied-up to his left shoulder."

## 40- 'Abdullāh Bin Omar Bin al-Khattāb

Among our peers there also lived a remarkable pious man, and a most blessed companions of God's messenger ﷺ, upon whom be peace. He led a humble and a pious life, and he was disinterested in leadership, as well as he was indifferent to earthly ranks. His name is 'Abdullāh, the son of Omar bin al-Khattāb, God be pleased with both of them.

'Abdullāh bnu Omar was a steadfast, persevering, and a sincere seeker of the nearness of his Lord. He demanded from himself the highest level of devotion, and he observed the most exalted virtues one would expect from the witnesses of God's revelation, the blessed companions of God's messenger ﷺ, upon whom be peace. 'Abdullāh bnu Omar, God be pleased with him, was a beacon of piety, and he lived a devout religious life, wholly engaged in worshipping God Almighty, blessed be His Name.

'Abdullāh bnu Omar stayed up long nights in devotion, praying, celebrating the praises of God Almighty, reading the Qur'an, and contemplating its miracle. He sought and emulated the most exalted character of faith and truth witnessed by humanity, the sublime model of God's messenger ﷺ, upon whom be peace. He hearkened to him wholeheartedly, and he received with great sincerity every word of his admonitions and guidance, as well as he earned the blessings they carried with them.

'Abdullāh bnu Omar, God be pleased with him, was often seen worshipping at mosques, and he mostly resided in their vicinage. When he needed a short rest, he often laid on an uneven gravely grounds, unconcerned with his personal comfort. He considered himself a stranger in this world, and he correctly perceived the hindmost advent of the hereafter as very near. He always solicited and prayed for God's forgiveness, and he incessantly invoked His *zikr* (remembrance).

It is said that spiritual attainment is also dependent on one's fear of falling in the trap of presumption, arrogance, and haughtiness, and it is the fruit of one's sincere solicitation of the true and exalted seat of nearness to his Lord.

**781-** On this subject, Muhammad bin Is<u>h</u>āq narrated that Nāfi' once saw 'Abdullāh bin Omar enter the mosque to pray, and in his prostration, Nāfi' heard 'Abdullāh pray: "Lord, You know well that nothing except my fear of You that prevents me from vying with the people of Quraish in striving to win stature and wealth in this world."

**782-** Abu <u>H</u>ārith bin Jabla narrated that when people came to 'Abdullāh bnu Omar to offer him the *<u>k</u>hilāfa* (vice regency) of the Muslim caliphate after the murder of his father, Omar bin al-<u>K</u>hat<u>t</u>āb, God be pleased with him, 'Abdullāh bnu Omar replied: "I swear by Allah that this is not what I hoped for. However, if you happen to call me to prayers, I will come, if you call me to harvest success, I will join you, but if you are divided, I will disagree with you, and yet, when you become united again, I will support you wholeheartedly and never leave you as long as you are united in Allah."

**783-** Al-A'amash narrated that 'Abdullāh bin Mas'oud said: "The best young man in the whole Tribe of Quraish who has faithfully guarded his dignity, integrity, and chastity, and who was able to protect himself against the deceptive attractions (*fitan*) of this world, is 'Abdullāh bnu Omar."

**784-** Imam Ahmad bin <u>H</u>anbal, God be pleased with him, narrated that Jābir, God be pleased with him, said: "I have not met anyone who was not affected by the deceptive attractions of this world except for 'Abdullāh bnu Omar, since the passing of God's messenger ﷺ, upon whom be peace."

**785-** Nafi', the attending companion of 'Abdullāh bnu Omar, said: "Whenever 'Abdullāh bnu Omar found himself attached to something he owned, he immediately gave it away in charity for the pleasure of Allah, the Lord of Majesty and glory, blessed be His Name."

**786-** Muhammad bin Ishāq narrated that Nafi' said: "The bondsmen of 'Abdullāh bnu Omar knew of his soft spot. One day, some of them took permission for a spiritual retreat in the mosque, and when 'Abdullāh bnu Omar saw them inclined to their devotion, he immediately released them from bondage. Some friends of 'Abdullāh bnu Omar witnessed that event and they turned to him and said, 'O Abu 'Abdu-Rahmān, they are pretending to be so religiously devoted only to take advantage of your good heart!' 'Abdullāh bnu Omar replied quietly, 'Whosoever assumes a spiritual character under the cover of Allah to trick us, we will lower our wings for the sake of Allah, and we will pretend to be fooled by his presumption.' "

**787-** Qutaiba bin Sa'īd narrated that Nafi' said: "One evening, we went along with 'Abdullāh bnu Omar, riding on our horses, and he rode one of his most cherished highbred possessions which he had bought for a large some of money. As we went on riding, and as soon as 'Abdullāh bnu Omar felt some vainness about the distinction and worth of his noble bred horse, he drove it to the side of the road, dismounted it, and said to me, 'Take off its bridle and saddle, place a blanket over its back, and keep this horse in the stable for now.' "

**788-** Abu'l 'Abbās al-Thaqfi narrated that Nafi' said: "On another occasion, 'Abdullāh bnu Omar, God be pleased with him, was riding his camel, and when he felt some attachment to his possession, he immediately become upset with himself, as he muttered , 'Phew, phew!' 'Abdullāh then made his camel kneel down, he dismounted it, and he said to me, 'O Nafi', put down its saddle!' I immediately understood that he felt a misgiving regarding something! I dismounted the saddle, and I said to him, 'I beg you to sell it and to buy something else instead!' But he immediately offered the camel in charity.' In fact, this was the nature of 'Abdullãh bnu Omar, God be pleased with him, whenever he liked something he owned, he offered it in charity for Allah's pleasure."

**789-** Ahmad bin Muhammad bin Sanãn narrated that 'Abdullãh bnu Omar, God be pleased with him, once let go of a woman servant called Ramĩtha, and before she left, he said to her: "O Ramĩtha, I heard the words of Allah, the Lord of majesty and glory, in His book, addressing the believers: ‹ By no means will you receive the benefit of trueness to your Lord, unless you spend freely out of what you love most. › *(Qur'an 3:92).*

'Abdullãh then said to her: "Let Allah be my witness, that I surely feel most comfortable about having you as a member of my household, and you have certainly become dear to me in this world, I therefore release you for the pleasure of Allah. You may go now, you are a free woman."

**790-** Imam Ahmad bin Hanbal, God be pleased with him, narrated, re Nãfi' that whenever 'Abdullãh bnu Omar felt attached to something he owned, he gave some of it away in charity for God's pleasure. Sometimes, he would distribute about thirty thousand dirhams during a single setting. Ibn 'Ãmer came to 'Abdullãh bnu Omar at two occasions and offered him thirty thousand dirhams to engage Nãfi' in his service, but 'Abdullãh refused the barter. On the second occasion, and after Ibn 'Ãmer had left, 'Abdullãh turned to his attending companion (*Mawla*) Nãfi' and said: "O Nãfi', I am afraid that the generous money Ibn 'Ãmer is offering me to acquire you may occupy my thoughts and distract my focus, and that could lead me astray, therefore you may go now, you are a free man."

**791-** Imam Ahmad bin Hanbal, God be pleased with him, narrated, re Nãfi' that 'Abdullãh bnu Omar, God be pleased with him, would subsist on food other than meat for a long stretch of time. In general, he only ate meat regularly during his travels, or during the fasting month of Ramadan. Otherwise, perhaps he would go for an entire month without eating a single bite of meat.

**792-** Abu Hãmed bin Jabla narrated that Nãfi' said: "By the time 'Abdullãh bnu Omar, God be pleased with him, died, he had bought the freedom of over one thousand slaves."

**793-** Imam Ahmad bin Hanbal, God be pleased with him, narrated, re Nãfi' that 'Abdullãh bnu Omar, God be pleased with him, once bartered a land he owned for two hundred camels. He then placed one hundred of them to serve God's path at once, and he made it conditional upon their new owners not to sell any of them should they have to do so, until they had passed the distant valley of *Wãdi al-Qurã* in the North.

**794-** Nãfi' narrated that Mu'ãwiya once sent one hundred thousand dirhams to 'Abdullãh bnu Omar, God be pleased with him, who in turn distributed the entire amount in charity before the end of that year.

**795-** Ismã'ïl bin Ishãq al-Qãdhi narrated that Ayoub bin Wã'il al-Rãsi said: "One day I visited the city of Madina, and a neighbor of 'Abdullãh bnu Omar told me that a man came a day earlier and delivered to 'Abdullãh bnu Omar four thousand dirhamsas a gift from the caliph Mu'ãwiya, four thousand dirhams as a gift from someone else, and another two thousand dirhams as a gift from a third person, plus a new shawl. The next day, 'Abdullãh bnu Omar was seen in the market trying to buy some fodder for his horse for one dirham on credit."

The neighbor continued: "I recognized the person who delivered the four thousand dirhams from the caliph, so I hastened to his detachment before they would leave the city, and when I saw the man, I said to him, 'I wish to ask you something personal, and I would like you to tell me the truth! Aren't you the man who came yesterday and delivered to 'Abdullãh bnu Omar four thousand dirhams from Mu'ãwiya, four thousand dirhams from someone else, and another two thousand dirhams from a third person, plus a new shawl?' The man replied, 'Indeed, I did.' "

The neighbor remarked: "I saw him today trying to buy some feed for his horse for one dirham on credit!" The man said: "In fact, 'Abdullãh bnu Omar did not even go to sleep before he had distributed the entire endowment he received. As for the shawl, I later learned that he had send it to a needy person in town as soon as he left."

The neighbor then returned to the market and exclaimed: "O merchants, wake-up! What are you wasting your time doing competing with one another in this world while 'Abdullãh bnu Omar lives amidst you! Last night he received a gift of over ten thousand dirhams, and this morning you found him trying to buy a little forage for his horse for one dirhams on credit! Wake-up, O merchants wake-up!"

**796-** Imam Ahmad bin Hanbal, God be pleased with him, narrated that Nãfi' said: "One time, 'Abdullãh bnu Omar fell sick, and I bought him a cluster of grapes[1] for one dirham. As soon as I placed the grapes before him, a beggar knocked at the door, and 'Abdullãh said to me, 'Take these grapes and give them to that man.' I said, 'First taste some of them!' He replied, 'No, give all of them to him.' So I did, but I also went out after the beggar, I bought the grapes back from him for one dirham, and I brought them back to 'Abdullãh. The beggar who took the one dirham went away for few moments, but shortly after that, he returned to the door and asked for something in charity. Again 'Abdullãh bnu Omar said to me, 'Give these grapes to the man at the door,' and again I said, 'Eat some at least, taste them!' He insisted, 'No. Give all of them to that man,' and I did as he told me. Like that, for the third time — or perhaps for the fourth time — I handed the grapes to the same beggar, and I further went after him and bought them back for one dirham, and every time, he took the money, he went away for a moment before he returned to the door and asked for something in charity. After the third or the fourth time, I became upset, and I went after the beggar and I said to him, 'Aren't you ashamed of your actions?' Finally, I bought the cluster of grapes from him for another dirham, and he agreed to leave, and at last, I brought the grapes to 'Abdullãh bnu Omar who ate some."

**797-** Ibn al-Mubãrak narrated, re the above account that Nãfi' said: "Had 'Abdullãh bnu Omar known my story with the beggar, he would have never tasted the grapes."

**798-** Qutaiba bin Sa'ïd narrated that 'Abdullãh bnu Omar, God be pleased with him, once traveled with his family to the town of al-Juhfa, and one day, he said to his wife Safiyya bint Abi 'Ubaid: "I would like to eat some fish today!" Immediately someone went

[1] A scarce fruit in the Arabian desert then.

out to buy some fish, but he couldn't find more than a single fish in the marketplace, and which he eventually bought. Safiyya prepared the fish for her husband, and as soon as 'Abdullāh bnu Omar sat with his family to eat, a beggar came to his door and asked for some charity. 'Abdullāh bnu Omar immediately said: "Give this fish to the man at the door." The wife did so, but then she turned to her husband and said: "You know how much trouble we went through to get this fish and to prepare it for you, and then you simply give it away in charity! We could have given the man some money instead!"

**799-** In another narration of the above account, Muhammad bin Hayyān narrated that 'Abdullāh bnu Omar once desired to eat some fish, and as soon as the meal was brought to him, a beggar knocked at the door, and when 'Abdullāh knew that, he immediately said: "Give this fish to the needy man." His wife said: "Why don't we give him some money instead! It will be of more use to him, and then you can satisfy your desire for the fish!" 'Abdullāh bnu Omar, God be pleased with him, replied: "I care little for my desire."

**800-** Qutaiba bin Sa'īd narrated that someone once reproved the wife of 'Abdullāh bnu Omar, saying: "How is it that you fail to take good care of this old man?" She replied: "What can I do, every time we cook for him, he invites someone to share in his meal, and he himself barely eats anything!"

Qutaiba bin Sa'īd continued: "That same day, Safiyya bint Abi 'Ubaid went out to a group of needy people who usually posted along his path to the mosque, she fed them, and said to them, 'Please sit somewhere else today, and should 'Abdullāh invite you for a meal, make an excuse and do not come.' That evening, when 'Abdullāh bnu Omar, God be pleased with him, came home after the *'Isha* evening prayers, and when his wife, brought him his dinner, he said to her: "Call our neighbor so and so to partake some of our food!" Safiyya also had sent that family some food, and she also had requested them not to come should he invite them to dinner. After waiting for a while, and when no one answered his invitation, 'Abdullāh turned to his family and said: "It is you who wanted me not to have dinner this evening," and he retired to his bed that night without eating."

**801-** Muhammad bin Qays narrated that 'Abdullãh bnu Omar, God be pleased with him, would not eat unless some poor people shared his meal with him, and this caused him to lose weight and rendered his health poor. When he grew older, and when his wife would prepare some dates for him, she would also bring him a drink of water to help his digestion.

**802-** Hamza, the son of 'Abdullãh bnu Omar, God be pleased with him, narrated that even when his father had extra food at home, he never fully appeased his hunger, and particularly when it was imperative that he finds someone to partake in his meal.

One day, Ibn Muti' visited 'Abdullãh bnu Omar during an illness, and he remarked that he had lost weight. Ibn Muti' turned to Safiyya and said: "Why don't you take better care of this old man! Make him some nutritious food, perhaps he may regain his health?" She replied: "We do that regularly my brother, but whenever we bring him his meal, he does not let anyone of his family, or his neighbors, or even his present guests but calls them to partake in his meal. Why don't you talk to him about his eating habits?"

Ibn Muti' then turned to 'Abdullãh and said: "O Abu 'Abdu-Rahmãn! Why don't you take better care of your health and help yourself regain some weight!" 'Abdullãh replied: "My dear brother, I have lived some eighty years now, and I do not remember whether I ever ate my full, or maybe I did so once, I am not sure! Do you now want me to change my eating habits at this age, and when I have no more than a donkey's last leg in this world!"

**803-** Imam Ahmad bin Hanbal, God be pleased with him, narrated that Omar bin Hamza bin 'Abdullãh, said: "I was once sitting with my father when a man walked by us, and my father asked him, 'Tell me, what did you say to 'Abdullãh bnu Omar, when I saw you two, and I saw you talking to him at Jaraf?' The man replied, 'I said, 'O Abu 'Abdu-Rahmãn, your bite has become softer, you have reach old age, and your guests do not recognize your rights and personal needs, nor do they understand your honors and status. If only you would order your family to take better care of you, and to prepare you some special food to strengthen your body!' He replied, 'Alas, alas! Let Allah be my witness that I have not had my fill even once for the past twelve years, or perhaps thirteen or fourteen years, and now, at this junction of my life, what do you expect me to do, when what I have left in this world could not last beyond the fatal brief thirst of a donkey!' "

**804-** Nãfi' narrated that 'Abdullãh bnu Omar, God be pleased with him, said: "The truth is that I have never once ate my fill since I became Muslim."

**805-** 'Abdullãh, son of Imam Ahmad bin Hanbal, God be pleased with him, narrated that Abu Bakr bnu Hafs said: " 'Abdullãh bnu Omar, God be pleased with him, never sat to eat a meal unless an orphan had a share in it."

**806-** Imam Ahmad bin Hanbal, God be pleased with him, narrated that whenever 'Abdullãh bnu Omar, God be pleased with him, took his lunch or dinner, he also invited the orphans of his neighborhood to partake in his meal. One day, when he sat to eat, 'Abdullãh asked his family to invite a neighboring orphan, but the boy was not home. 'Abdullãh then commenced eating his lunch with his family, and when they he had just finished eating, and as soon as he reached out to take his daily sweet drink, the young orphan arrived, 'Abdullãh looked at him, and smiled, and handing him his cup to drink from, he said: "Drink this, I do not think that you have missed much."

**807-** Sãlim bin 'Ãsim narrated that 'Abdullãh bnu Omar, God be pleased with him, never turned away a beggar unsatisfied, and that he sometimes ate with a leper from the same plate, and at times the leper's hand may have been plasmatic.

**808-** 'Abdullãh bin al-Mughïra narrated that 'Ubaidullãh bin 'Adiy, an early servant of 'Abdullãh bnu Omar, once arrived to Madina from Iraq, and he went to pay his respect to him. During his visit, 'Ubaidullãh said: "I brought you a gift." "What is it?" 'Abdullãh asked. 'Ubaidullãh replied: "A special mix of crushed nuts called *Jawãrish*." "What is *Jawãrish*[1]?" 'Abdullãh inquired. 'Ubaidullãh replied: "It is a special mix of nuts and grains, and they are very good for digestion!"

'Abdullãh bnu Omar then said: "I have not filled my stomach to surfeit for some forty years, therefore, what do you want me to do with a digestive?"

**809-** In his narration of the above account, Imam Muhammad Ibn Seerïn, reported that a man said to 'Abdullãh bnu Omar, God be pleased with him: "Would you like me to prepare some *Jawãrish* for you?"

'Abdullãh bnu Omar inquired: "What is *Jawãrish,* and what do you do with them? The man replied: "It's a special mix of nuts and grains, and they are used to cure constipation."

'Abdullãh bnu Omar then said: "I have not had a full stomach for the past four months, and believe me, it is not because I do not have the means to buy food, but rather I was accustomed to the company of people who alternated their eating habits, — one meal they ate their fill, and the next meal they stayed hungry."

**810-** Imam Ahmad bin Hanbal, God be pleased with him, narrated that someone once brought 'Abdullãh bnu Omar fruits of a caper tree (Arb. *kabar*). 'Abdullãh bnu Omar asked: "What is it?" The man replied: "This fruit is a very nutritional fruit, and it helps to soften the digestive system!"

'Abdullãh commented: "As for my eating habits, perhaps an entire month goes by before I fill my stomach once, or maybe twice!"

**811-** Qutaiba bin Sa'ïd narrated that Maimoun bin Mihrãn said: "A throng of people who followed Najda al-Harouri once passed by a camel herd belonging to 'Abdullãh bnu Omar, God be pleased with him, and they unjustly decided to seize the herd and to drive it away with them. The shepherd escaped, and he ran back to 'Abdullãh bnu Omar, crying loud:

"O Abu 'Abdu-Rahmãn! Look out for your camels!' " 'Abdullãh bnu Omar inquired eagerly: "What happened to them?"

"A band of Najda al-Harouri came by and drove them away!" The shepherd replied 'Abdullãh asked: "How is it that they have taken the camel herd and let you go?" The shepherd replied, 'At first they captured me as well, but then I was able to escape."

'Abdullãh asked: "What made you decide to run away from them and to come back to me?" The shepherd replied: "Because you are more dear to me than them." 'Abdullãh then said: "Would you swear to Allah Whom there is no god be He that I am more

[1] Arb. *Jarash;* pl. *Jawãrish.*

dear to you than them?" "I do." The shepherd replied.

'Abdullāh then said: "As far as I am concerned, neither you nor these camels belong to me. Go, you are a free man."

A short while later, someone came to 'Abdullāh bnu Omar, God be pleased with him, and said: "Would you like to see your she-camel so and so?" The man named her, and then added: "It is being sold right now in the marketplace!"

'Abdullāh replied: "Lead me to my coat;" but when he stood up and placed his coat over his shoulders, he pondered for a moment and then sat down again before he serenely said to the man: "I thought about that she-camel and as to its whereabouts, but then I decided not to look for it."

**812-** Maimoun bin Mihrān narrated that 'Abdullāh bnu Omar, God be pleased with him, once signed a contract with one of his servants to release him from his duties upon payment of a specified some of money in easy installments. When the first installment was due, the servant brought the money, and 'Abdullāh bnu Omar asked him: "Where from did you get this money?" The servant replied: "Some of it I earned by working overtime, and the balance was a charity I begged for."

'Abdullāh became agitated and he said: "Do you want me to feed my family and children of people's filth and of what they cast away to cleanse their own earnings and actions? Go, I release you of your obligations for the sake of Allah's pleasure. You may take away what you brought here and leave, you are free man."

**813-** Maimoun bin Mihrān narrated that one of the sons of 'Abdullāh bnu Omar, God be pleased with him, once asked his father for a new *izār*[1] explaining that his *izār* was worn out, and it also had a couple of holes in it, and that he shied to wear it any more in public. 'Abdullāh replied: "You can cut off the part that is worn out, mend it and wear it again!" Somehow, it appeared that the young boy disliked his father's suggestion, and when 'Abdullāh saw discontent on the face of his son, he said to him: "My son, beware of Allah, and fear him. Do not become like people who use Allah's favors to merely satisfy their hunger and to display them over their shoulders!"

**814-** Abu Hãmed bin Jabla narrated that Maimoun bin Mihrãn said: "I visited the house of 'Abdullãh bnu Omar, God be pleased with him, and I noticed that the value of its combined contents did not equal the price of my shawl."

**815-** 'Abdullãh, son of Imam Ahmad bin Hanbal, God be pleased with him, narrated that 'Abdullãh bnu Omar, God be pleased with him, once stayed in the town of al-Juhfa, and the people flocked in crowds to visit with him. When a rich man called Ibn 'Ãmer bin Kuraiza saw that, he asked his servant to take what he baked for that day to 'Abdullãh bnu Omar' house. Hence, the servant brought the first tray of food, and 'Abdullãh bnu Omar asked him to put it down before his guests. Shortly after that, the servant returned with a second tray of food, and he wanted to take back the first tray before placing the second one in its place, but 'Abdullãh asked him: "What do you want?" The servant replied: "I want to take the first tray back!" 'Abdullãh said: "Leave it where it is, and place the contents of the second tray on top of the first tray." The servant reluctantly did what he was told, and every time he brought a new tray, 'Abdullãh bnu Omar asked him to replenish the main tray.

When the servant finally fulfilled his duty and returned to Ibn 'Ãmer bin Kuraiza, and having not recognized the identity of the man he had to serve, he said: "Surely this man is one of the rudest bedouin Arabs I have ever met!" Ibn 'Ãmer bin Kuraiza immediately responded: "Watch out what you say; — this is your true master, he is 'Abdullãh, the son of Omar bin al-Khattãb, God be pleased with both of them!"

**816-** Also in reference to the above account, Imam Ahmad bin Hanbal, God be pleased with him, narrated that Abu Ja'far al-Qãri said: "My master, 'Ãmer bin Kuraiza, asked me to accompany 'Abdullãh bnu Omar, God be pleased with him, during his stay in al-Juhfa and to serve his needs. During his travels, in every place 'Abdullãh bnu Omar stopped to drink some water or to pray, he asked me to invite the people of that locality to a share his food. Whenever the elders among his children came to eat, they would take a couple of bites and leave immediately after that to allow the guests to eat."

---

[1]*Izãr*: A surround, a long cotton wrapper, traditionally worn by Middle Eastern men.

"One day, 'Abdullãh bnu Omar invited his neighbors from al-Juhfa to share his meal. During their meal, a poor black boy who had no shirt to cover his back arrived. When 'Abdullãh bnu Omar saw him, he invited him to eat. The young boy replied, 'I would like to do so, but it looks too crowded here, I cannot even find a place for me to sit down!' 'Abdullãh bnu Omar then moved to one side, and the young boy sat to eat in a very tight spot, practically leaning on 'Abdullãh's ribs."

**817-** 'Abdullãh, son of Imam Ahmad bin Hanbal, God be pleased with him, narrated that Qur'a said: "I once saw 'Abdullãh bnu Omar, God be pleased with him, wearing a coarse garment, and I said to him, 'O Abu 'Abdu-Rahmãn, I see you wearing a coarse garment, and I have brought you a robe of Persian soft fabric made in Kharasãn to wear instead.' 'Abdullãh replied, 'Show it to me.' When he saw it and felt it, 'Abdullãh inquired, 'Is it made of silk?' I replied, 'Not at all, this is pure cotton.' 'Abdullãh looked at it again and said, 'I will be afraid to wear it. I will be afraid that should I wear it, I may develop a feeling of haughtiness and pride, and Allah does not like the haughty person or the proud.'"

**818-** Muhammad bin 'Abdullãh al-Hadhrami narrated that someone asked 'Abdullãh bnu Omar, God be pleased with him: "What kind of clothing are commendable to wear?" 'Abdullãh replied: "Wear something which the common narrow-minded impudent does not find fault in it, and which a wise and a forbearing person does not censure you for wearing it!" The man further asked: "Of what worth should such garment be?" 'Abdullãh replied: "Something you can buy for in-between five and twenty dirhams."

**819-** Sulaimãn Bin Ahmad narrated that 'Abdullãh bnu Omar, God be pleased with him, said: "I was a young man and single, and during the time of God's messenger ﷺ, upon whom be peace, I mostly slept at the mosque. At that time, it was common when someone saw a dream to narrate it to God's messenger ﷺ, upon whom be peace, to hear his interpretation. Witnessing such daily events, I too wished to see a dream to report it to God's messenger ﷺ, upon whom be peace, and to hear his interpretation. Soon after that, one night, in my sleep, I saw as though two angels came and took me on a journey to see hell-fire. When we reached there, I saw it enclosed, just like a deep well, having a huge caldrons similar in shape to those used to draw water from a well. In hell, I also saw some people I knew, and I immediately started praying, '*I seek refuge in Allah from the fire of hell, I seek refuge in Allah from the fire of hell.*' A third angel came by and said to me, 'You do not have to worry!' In the morning, I told my dream to my sister Hafsa, (the wife of God's messenger ﷺ), and she in turn narrated my dream to him. God's messenger ﷺ, upon whom be peace, commented to her, 'Surely 'Abdullãh is a good man. I only wish that he offers supererogatory *nafl* prayers during some parts of the night.' "

Hafsa reported to her brother what God's messenger ﷺ, upon whom be peace, said, and from that day on, and throughout the balance of his life, 'Abdullãh used to sleep but a little of the night.

**820-** Nãfi' narrated that when 'Abdullãh bnu Omar, God be pleased with him, missed his evening *'isha* prayers in congregation, he would stand up all night in prayers until the dawn *fajr* congregational prayers."

**821-** Nãfi' narrated that 'Abdullãh bnu Omar, God be pleased with him, used to stand up all-night in *tahajjud* prayers. Two thirds through the night, intending to fast the following day, 'Abdullãh would ask his companion-attendant: "O Nãfi', is it time for the predawn *suhür* meal?" Nãfi' replied: "Not yet!" 'Abdullãh bnu Omar then would resume his prayers, standing up, reading long chapter of the Qur'an, until sometimes later, and then he would ask again: "O Nãfi', is it time for the predawn *suhür* meal yet?" And only when Nãfi' replied in the affirmative that 'Abdullãh bnu Omar, God be pleased with him, would sit down, ask for Allah's forgiveness, and invoke special supplications until the dawn *fajr* prayers, where he would join the congregation at the mosque.

**822-** 'Abdullãh, son of Imam Ahmad bin Hanbal, God be pleased with him, narrated that whenever 'Abdullãh bnu Omar, God be pleased with him, visited Mecca, he used to stay at the house of Abu Ghãlib, and he was known to stand up all-night in *tahajjud* prayers. One night, shortly before the dawn *fajr* prayers, he woke up his host, and said to him: "O Abu Ghãlib! Wouldn't you like to wake up and read one third of the Qur'an before dawn?" Abu Ghãlib, while still in his bed, half asleep, looked out and replied: "How can I finish reading one third of the Qur'an when it is almost dawn?" 'Abdullāh bnu Omar, God be pleased with him, then said: "Don't you know that the reward of reading *surat-ul Ikhlās*[1] one time equals the benefit of reading one third of the Qur'an!"

**823-** 'Abdullāh, son of Imam Ahmad bin Hanbal, God be pleased with him, narrated that 'Abdullāh bnu Omar, God be pleased with him, used to stand up regularly between the noon *zuhur* prayer and the mid-afternoon *'asr* prayer in supererogatory prayers.

**824-** Ibrāhīm Ibn Maisara narrated that Tāwous, said: "I have not seen devotion and sedulousness during prayers such as those of 'Abdullāh bnu Omar, God be pleased with him. In fact, I have never ever seen anyone who is wholly absorbed with his entire body and heart when he turns towards the Ka'ba during prayers such as he does."

**825-** Mu'ar bin Sa'īd narrated that Abi Burda once prayed next to 'Abdullāh bnu Omar, God be pleased with him, and he heard him pray during his prostration: "My Lord, be Thou the One I love most, and the One I fear most. My Lord, I swear by Thy bounty, guidance, and countless favors upon me, that I shall never become a helper to the *kuffār* who deny Thy revelation. My Lord, since the day I embraced Thy revelation and accepted Islam by Thine guidance, I have always hoped that my prayers and devotion will qualify as *kaffāra* (absolution) for my sins."

**826-** Sulaimān bin Ahmad narrated that 'Abdullāh bnu Omar, God be pleased with him, prayed at dawn, every morning: "My Lord, grant me to receive the greatest share of benefits and blessings Thou distribute among Thy servants for this morning. My Lord, make me a light by which Thou guides the people, a mercy that Thou showers upon them, and a wholesome nourishment which Thou extends for them. My Lord, rescind any harm destined for them for this day, lift any calamity which Thou have justly brought down upon them, and dispel any misleading deception which they may have attracted towards themselves."

**827-** Ahmad bin Ja'far bin Hamdān narrated that 'Abdullāh

[1] Qur'an, Chapter 112, Sincerity.

bnu Omar, God be pleased with him, stood up in prayers, and he recited the verse: ‹ What a woeful destiny is awaiting those who defraud others, — those who, when they buy, they demand full measure, and when they sell they cheat and short weigh their merchandise. Do they not think that they will not be resurrected for judgment? This will surely take place on an awesome Day, the day when all humanity will stand up before the Lord of all creation (for reckoning). › (*Qur'an 83-1-6*). When 'Abdullãh bnu Omar, God be pleased with him, read this verse, he burst out crying until he fell on the floor from exhaustion. He then completed his prayers sitting down, and he did not read the rest of the chapter."

**828-** Imam Ahmad bin Hanbal, God be pleased with him, narrated that Nãfi' said: "Whenever 'Abdullãh bnu Omar, God be pleased with him, read the last three verses of *Surat-ul Baqara*, beginning with the divine utterance, ‹ Whether you unveil what you think or conceal it, Allah will question you about it, ›(*Qur'an 2:284-286*), 'Abdullãh bnu Omar would burst out crying, and when he completed his reading, he would say, 'Surely this is an awesome, a ponderous, and a scrupulous reckoning.' "

**829-** Imam Ahmad bin Hanbal, God be pleased with him, narrated re Nãfi', that whenever 'Abdullãh bnu Omar, God be pleased with him, read a verse wherein hell-fire is mentioned, he used to stop, and pray to Allah, the most exalted, beseeching Him to shield him from it."

**830-** Ahmad bin Sanãn narrated that Yusuf bin Mãhik, once saw 'Abdullãh bnu Omar, God be pleased with him, giving a talk, and his eyes were overflowing with tears.

**831-** 'Abdullãh bin Muhammad narrated that Nãfi' said: "Whenever 'Abdullãh bnu Omar, God be pleased with him, read the verse, ‹ Is it not time for those who believe (in God) to let their hearts submit in reverence and awe, and to accept His message when they hear His admonition? › (*Qur'an 57:16*), and by the end of the verse, 'Abdullãh bnu Omar would be overcome by crying."

**832-** Al-Hassan narrated that 'Abdullãh bnu Omar, God be pleased with him, said in one of his sermons: "Let whosoever wishes to follow a *sunna* (convention) emulate the traditions of those who passed. Those are the companions of God's messenger ﷺ, upon whom be peace, for they are the best of what this family of believers (*umma*) have ever produced. They possessed the most true hearts, and the deepest of knowledge and understanding, and they were the least assumptuous. Allah, the most exalted, chose them for the fellowship of His prophet ﷺ, upon whom be peace, and to transmit His religion. Hence, imbibe their characters and follow closely their conventions,[1] for they are the companions of God's messenger ﷺ, upon whom be peace. They truly walked on the straight path, and I swear to this truth by Allah, the Lord of the Ka'ba."

During that sermon, 'Abdullāh also said: "O son of Adam, be in this world with your body only, but depart from it with your heart and concerns. Surely you are answerable for your actions on the Day of Grand Standing. Therefore, do what you can today for the benefit of what you will reap tomorrow upon death, and God willing, by doing so, you would have qualified yourself to receive the best of rewards."

**833-** 'Abdullāh bin Muhammad narrated that 'Abdullāh bnu Omar, God be pleased with him, said: "One does not become a truly knowledgeable *'ālim* except: 1) If he is not met with the jealousy of those higher in rank; 2) if he is not belittled by those who are less knowledgeable than he; and 3) as long as he does not take advantage of his knowledge for monetary gain."

**834-** Sālem bin Abi'l Ja'ad narrated that 'Abdullāh bnu Omar, God be pleased with him, said: "A man does not attain the station of true faith (*īmān*) unless he regards others as incapable of understanding the reasons behind his immoderate religious exertions."

**835-** Yusuf bin Ya'qoub al-Nujairami narrated that 'Abdullāh bnu Omar, God be pleased with him, once said: "Sometimes, it is even better to vaunt about one's good deeds rather than to speak boastfully about one's evildoing."

**836-** Abu Muhammad bin H̲ayyān narrated that 'Abdullāh bnu Omar, God be pleased with him, once said: "Any comfort a servant solicits and achieves in this world will demote his standing before

[1] Arb. *T̲arīqa*, sing.; *T̲arā'iq*, pl.

Allah, the Lord of majesty and glory, in the hereafter, and that's even if the servant is generous in sharing the benefits of his success with others."

**837-** Muhammad bin Hayyãn narrated that someone said to 'Abdullãh bnu Omar, God be pleased with him: "O Abu 'Abdu-Rahmãn, Zaid bin Hãritha al-Ansãri has just died." 'Abdullãh replied: "May the mercy of Allah encompass him." The man continued: "O Abu 'Abdu-Rahmãn, he left one hundred thousand Dirhams behind him!" 'Abdullãh bnu Omar replied: "Yet they did not leave him."

**838-** 'Abdullãh bin Muhammad bin Ja'far narrated that 'Abdullãh bnu Omar, God be pleased with him, was at the mosque when he heard a man shouting: "Where are those who have renounced the world and who are truly desirous of the hereafter?" 'Abdullãh bnu Omar immediately went to the man , and he took him by the hand, and he led him to the site of the graves of God's prophet ﷺ, upon whom be peace, and its adjacent two graves of his blessed companions, Abu Bakr and Omar, God be pleased with them; 'Abdullãh pointed to them and said: "Are you asking about these people?"

**839-** Sulaimãn bin Habïb narrated that he heard 'Abdullãh bnu Omar, God be pleased with him, say: "I swear by Allah, that even if I unintentionally place my finger in a glass of wine, I would not wish for that finger to follow me!"

**840-** Yusuf bin Mihrãn narrated that 'Abdullãh bnu Omar, God be pleased with him, said: "I would rather drink boiling water from hell, or even to burn in hell-fire, and to remain therein as long as one may remain, rather than to drink a single sip of wine!"

**841-** Qays bin Sa'ad narrated that someone asked 'Abdullãh bnu Omar, God be pleased with him, to give an opinion regarding a Muslim man who was forced under exceptionally adverse circumstances to drink wine and to eat the flesh of swine, 'Abdullãh bnu Omar replied: "It will be good for him if he refrains from further doing so until he dies, or otherwise, should he continue to eat the flesh of swine and to drink wine, then in fact, this disease lies in him."

**842-** Nãfi' narrated that 'Abdullãh bnu Omar, God be pleased with him, said: "The best thing a man must cleanse is his tongue."

**843-** Al-Zahri narrated that 'Abdullãh bnu Omar, God be pleased with him, never cursed any of his servants except for one whom he released from his service immediately after that incident.

Al-Zahri expounded: " 'Abdullãh bnu Omar was once extremely upset with the manners of one of his servants, and he wanted to curse him. As soon as 'Abdullãh began to utter the word 'Cur...', he held his tongue, and he swallowed the balance of the word, then said: "I do not like to utter this word!"

**844-** Sulaimãn bin Ahmad narrated that someone once addressed 'Abdullãh bnu Omar, God be pleased with him, saying: "O the best of men, — or perhaps he said, 'O son of the best of men!' — When 'Abdullãh bnu Omar heard that praise, he replied: "I am not the best of men, nor am I the son of the best of men. I am only a simple *'abd*, (a dependent creation) of Allah, the most exalted, just an *'abd* amidst the infinite multitudes of His creations. I place my hope in Him as well as I fear Him." 'Abdullãh then added: "O people! I swear that a time will come when you will keep on glorifying, praising, and flattering a man until you bring about his demise."

**845-** Abu Bakr bin Khallãd narrated, re Nãfi', that during his pilgrimage to Mecca, 'Abdullãh bnu Omar, God be pleased with him, used to invoke the same *talbiya* (proclamation of compliance) as those recalled by God's messenger ﷺ, upon whom be peace, and 'Abdullãh also prayed:

*Here I come my divine Lord, here I come.*
*Here I am at Your service my Lord, here I come.*
*In compliance with Your command, here I come.*
*Responding to Your call, here I come.*
*Indeed, most fortunate am I to receive Your command,*
*here I come!*
*Here I come my divine Lord, here I come.*
*Surely all the favors and blessings are in Your Hand,*
*Here I come.*
*Here I come my divine Lord, importunately thirsting and soliciting*

*Your divine acceptance, here I come.*
*Surely all the good deeds we do are Your favors,*
*and all are rewarded solely by You my divine Lord,*
*here I come.*

**846-** Hafs bin 'Amr al-Hawdhi narrated that Nãfi' heard 'Abdullãh bnu Omar, God be pleased with him, pray at the Hill of Safa, during a pilgrimage to Mecca: "My divine Lord, protect me by helping me to correctly comply with Your religion (of Islam). Guide me to obey Your commands and to comply with the guidance of Your messenger ﷺ, upon whom be peace. Lord, protect me against infringing upon the limitations sat by You. Lord, fill my heart with love for You, and gather me among those who love Your angels, Your messengers, and Your righteous servants. My divine Lord, write me among those You love, and whom Your angels, Your messengers, and Your righteous ones love. My divine Lord, help me to do my deeds with ease. Help me to avoid the avenues of difficulties, forgive me my sins in this world, do not require them from me thereafter, Lord, and gather me among the blessed pattern of the pious ones in the hereafter. Lord! You said, 'Call upon Me, and I will answer your prayers.' Lord, surely You do not fail Your promise. O Allah, indeed, You are the One Who guided me to Islam. I beseech You not to divest me of Your gift. Do not deprive me of it, nor take it away from me. Keep me thus until You take my soul back to You in a state of perfect Islam, submitting to You."

Nãfi' added: "This was only a short passage of an extensive prayer, 'Abdullãh bnu Omar, God be pleased with him, prayed at the hills of *Safa* and *Marwa,* and he repeated them again at the Valley of 'Arafãt, and later on, he invoked the same prayers near the Sacred Monument at Jamarãt, and then during his final circumambulation of the Ka'ba."

**847-** Bishr bin Müsa narrated that whenever 'Abdullãh bnu Omar, God be pleased with him, arrived to Madina, and prior to entering his house, he would first visit the grave of God's messenger ﷺ, upon whom be peace, and facing it, he would greet him, and invoke Allah's *salawãt* (blessings) upon him. 'Abdullãh then would move few steps to the right, facing the grave of Abu Bakr, God be pleased with him, invoke Allah's blessings upon him, and pray for him. Finally, 'Abdullāh would move a couple of steps further to the right, and he would be stand facing the grave of his father, Omar bin al-Khattāb, God be pleased with him, he would invoke Allah's blessings upon him, pray for him, and then burst out crying: "O my beloved father! O my father! O my dear father!"

**848-** 'Urwa bin al-Zubair narrated: "We were pilgrims in Mecca, and while circumambulating the Ka'ba, I turned to 'Abdullāh bnu Omar, God be pleased with him, and I asked him for the hand of his daughter Sawda' in marriage, but he did not acknowledge. I said to myself that had he accepted my offer, he would have replied, and I vowed not to open the subject with him again. After completing our pilgrimage, it happened that 'Abdullāh had to return to Madina before I did. Few days later, when I arrived to Madina, I first visited the mosque of God's messenger ﷺ, upon whom be peace, and after paying the due respect to his resting place, I went to join the circle were 'Abdullāh bnu Omar was sitting with some companions. I paid my respect to him, and he welcomed me cheerfully, and he asked me, 'When did you arrive?' I replied, 'Just now.' He then said to me, 'It happened that you asked me for the hand of Sawda, daughter of 'Abdullāh, during our *tawāf* (circumambulating the Ka'ba), and at that station, we were occupied in apperceiving and appreciating the presence of Allah, the Lord of majesty and glory, before our own eyes. Surely you also may have had other opportunities to express your interest in this marriage, and at other than such a sacred station. However, when you did, I remained silent, and I told my self that this was Allah's decree. Now that we have completed our pilgrimage, tell me, what do you think about your earlier proposal?' I rejoiced and I replied enthusiastically, 'I am most keen, and certainly I am more solicitous than ever to succeed at winning the honor of this betrothal.' 'Abdullāh bnu Omar, God be pleased with him, then called his two sons Salem and 'Abdullāh as witnesses, and after she consented, he gave me the hand of his daughter Sawda in marriage."

**849-** Sulaimān bin Ahmad narrated that Mus'ab, 'Urwa, and 'Abdullāh, children of al-Zubair, and 'Abdullāh bnu Omar, God be pleased with him, were sitting together near the Black Stone at the

Ka'ba in Mecca, when one of them suggested that each one makes a wish. 'Abdullãh bin al-Zubair said: "I wish to become a caliph." 'Urwa bin al-Zubair said: "I wish to become a scholar, and that people acquire knowledge from me." Mus'ab bin al-Zubair said: "I wish to govern Iraq, and to marry 'Aisha, the daughter of Talha, and Sakïna, the daughter of al-Hussain." Finally, as to 'Abdullãh bnu Omar, God be pleased with him, he said: "I wish for Allah's forgiveness."

Abi al-Zinãd, who also reported the above account, commented: "The first three had their wishes fulfilled, and we pray that Allah has fulfilled the wish of 'Abdullãh bnu Omar."

**850-** 'Abdullãh bin Ja'far narrated that during the caliphate of Ibn al-Zubair and at the time of violent political turmoil with his adversaries the Kharijites (dissenters), some people came to 'Abdullãh bnu Omar, God be pleased with him, and said: "How can you accept to pray alongside such people as well as pray together with their opponents, when they both are murdering one another?" 'Abdullãh bnu Omar replied: "As to me, whosoever proclaims, 'Come to pray,' I will answer his call, and whosoever announces the divine invitation, 'Come to reap success,' I will answer his call as well, but whosoever calls for the murder of another Muslim brother and to unjustly seize his property, I will say 'No' to that!'

**851-** Bishr bin Müsa narrated that 'Abdullãh bnu Omar, God be pleased with him, said: "Our parable during this ordeal of dissension is like that of the story of a people who traveled on a road they knew. Suddenly, an opaque cloud descended upon them and befogged their vision. Some strayed to the right, and others to the left, and thus, both of them lost their way, while we camped in our place until Allah, blessed be His Name, caused the cloud to dissipate. Only then, and when we were able to see the road, we recognized what happened, and we continued on our journey. These two groups are the children of Quraish, and they are murdering one another to win leadership and control of this world. As for me, I have no interest in what they are fighting for, and I will not even barter my two worn out old sandals for the sake of what they are hoping to win."

**852-** Müsa bin 'Uqba narrated that Nãfi' said: "In my mind, and following common perceptions, if I was to look at 'Abdullāh bnu Omar, God be pleased with him, and examine his unrelenting and faithful pursuit of the footsteps and traditions of God's messenger ﷺ, upon whom be peace, I would say that this man is crazy!"

**853-** 'Abdullāh bin Numair narrated that 'Āsim al-Ahwal said: "Sometimes, when one looks at 'Abdullāh bnu Omar, God be pleased with him, one would think that he is different from the common people, and that's because of his unrelenting and faithful pursuit of tracing the footsteps and exact traditions of God's messenger ﷺ, upon whom be peace."

**854-** Abu Bakr bin Abi Shaiba narrated, re Nãfi', that on his way to Mecca, sometimes 'Abdullāh bnu Omar, God be pleased with him, would lean forward on his camel, throws his arms around its neck, and attempts to steer it, saying: "Perchance your hoofs would step into the footprint of the hoofs of his camel."[1]

**855-** Zaid bin Aslam narrated that his father Aslam said: "No she-camel who is bewildered by the loss of her newly weaned babe in a vast desert would search the traces of her lost babe's footprints better than 'Abdullāh bnu Omar's constant pursuit of the legend of his father, Omar bin al-Khattāb, may God be pleased with both of them, in the way they both embraced and emulated the traditions of God's messenger ﷺ, upon whom be peace."

**856-** Abu Bakr bin Khallād narrated that when Ishāq bin 'Abdullāh visited 'Abdullāh bnu Omar, God be pleased with him, Ishāq would sometimes accompany him to the marketplace. Walking through it's streets, 'Abdullāh would unfailingly greet everyone; — a locksmith, a merchant, or an indigent, — no matter who he passed by, and in fact, he would never let any Muslim pass by without greeting him before 'Abdullāh would return to his house, having bought nothing.

Ishāq asked him: "Why do you even take me with you to the marketplace? You never stop to ask about a merchandise or a price! You do not bargain with anyone, nor do you sit with anyone, and sometimes, I say to myself, perhaps he would stop here by these people and chat with them, but you don't do that neither!"

[1] i.e., the footsteps of the camel of God's messenger ﷺ, upon whom be peace.

'Abdullãh bnu Omar, God be pleased with him, replied, teasing his companion: "O paunchy! — In truth, we go to the market for the sake of spreading *salãm* (peace), by greeting everyone. Therefore, you too should pay your regards to everyone you pass-by!"

**857-** Mãlik bin Anas narrated that 'Ubaidullãh, son of 'Abdullãh bin 'Utba said: "*Ikhlãs*, (sincerity) was easily recognizable in Omar bin al-Khattãb and in his son 'Abdullãh bnu Omar, may God be pleased with both of them, and anyone could clearly recognize their *birr* (trueness to their Lord) in the way they way they spoke, and in their actions."

**858-** Muhammad bin Ishãq narrated that 'Abdullãh bnu Omar, God be pleased with him, once said to Mujãhid: "O Abu'l Ghãzi! For how long did God's prophet Noah remain amidst his people?" Mujãhid replied: "Some nine hundred and fifty years!" 'Abdullãh then commented: "Since then, people's life span have decreased gradually, their bodies have become smaller, and their aspirations have grown narrower."

**859-** Qatãda narrated that someone asked 'Abdullãh bnu Omar, God be pleased with him, about the companions of God's messenger ﷺ, upon whom be peace, and whether they ever laughed? 'Abdullãh replied: "Of course they laughed, but their faith was mightier than mountains."

**860-** Adam bin 'Ali narrated that 'Abdullãh bnu Omar, God be pleased with him, said: "On the Day of Judgment, a group of people will be called the 'Deficient Ones'.' Someone asked: "What does the 'deficient ones' means?" 'Abdullãh replied: "Such are the ones whose ablutions and prayers are inadequate through lack of concentration and hastiness."

**861-** Al-A'amash narrated that while on a journey, Nãfi' and 'Abdullãh bnu Omar, God be pleased with him, once stayed for few days as guests at someone's house, and after three nights of being guests, 'Abdullãh said: "O Nãfi', from today on, you may spend of our own money for our needs."

**862-** Qatãda narrated that someone asked 'Abdullãh bnu Omar, God be pleased with him, about the testimony of *Lã ilãha il Allah* (Surely there is no god except Allah), saying, 'Can any deed be ever harmful after testifying to it, just as in its antithesis, where one's deeds are of no worth when denying it?' 'Abdullãh replied, 'Brother, live your life as decreed by Allah, but avoid self adulation.'

**863-** Ma'abad al-Jahni once asked 'Abdullãh bnu Omar, God be pleased with him: "What do you say about a man who never misses an opportunity to embark on a good deed except that he may have some doubt about Allah, the Lord of majesty and glory?" 'Abdullãh bnu Omar replied: "He is doomed no doubt." Ma'abad further asked: "Then what about a man who never misses an opportunity to engage in mischief, except that he bears the testimony, *Lã ilãha il Allah, Muhammadur-Rasul Allah* (I testify that there is no God except Allah, and that Muhammad is the messenger of Allah), and the man has never had the slightest doubt about it?" 'Abdullãh bnu Omar replied: "O Ma'abad, live your life as destined by Allah, and spare yourself the reckoning for self adulation."

**864-** Imam Ahmad bin Hanbal, God be pleased with him, narrated that Mujãhid said: "I was walking with 'Abdullãh bnu Omar, God be pleased with him, and we passed by a ruin. 'Abdullãh said to me, 'Say, O ruin, tell me, what did your people do?' I turned to the ruin and said, 'O ruin, tell me, what did your people do?' A moment of silence passed, then 'Abdullãh bnu Omar said, 'They have gone, and these are the effects which they have left behind them!' "

**865-** Imam Ahmad bin Hanbal, God be pleased with him, narrated that 'Abdullãh bnu Omar, God be pleased with him, passed by a group of people who stood around a man from Iraq, and who was struck by an epileptic seizure. 'Abdullãh asked: "What happened to him?" The people replied: "Whenever he hears the Qur'an, he is seized with such fit!" 'Abdullãh commented: "We too fear Allah when we hear the Qur'an as well, but we do not have fits!"

**866-** Mujãhid narrated, re 'Abdullãh bnu Omar, God be pleased with him, that God's messenger ﷺ, upon whom be peace, said to him: "Love for the sake of Allah, abominate for the sake of Allah, support others solely for the sake of Allah, and vie for the sake of Allah, for otherwise, you will never receive the *wilãya* (guardianship) of Allah, and no man will ever enjoy the taste of *Imãn* (faith) otherwise, and that's even if he prays and fasts extensively."

**867-** Mujãhid narrated that 'Abdullãh bnu Omar said: "Today, loyalty (*muwãlat*) to people is centered exclusively around selfish worldly interests, and such politically motivated endorsements bring its people nothing but havoc."

'Abdullãh bnu Omar also said: "God's messenger ﷺ, upon whom be peace, once said to me, 'O son of Omar, when you wake up in the morning, do not think about the evening, and when you come upon the evening, do not think of the next morning. Take advantage of your health today to balance your deeds when you fall ill, and take advantage of your life in this world by offering good deeds to benefit you when you die, for O 'Abdullãh son of Omar, you never know what will your name be tomorrow.' "

'Abdullãh continued: "God's messenger ﷺ, upon whom be peace, then took hold of my shoulder, and he added, 'O 'Abdullãh son of Omar, be in this world like a stranger, or a traveler, and consider yourself among the dwellers of the graveyards.' "

**868-** Mujãhid narrated, re 'Abdullãh bnu Omar, God be pleased with him, that a young man stood up and asked God's messenger ﷺ, upon whom be peace: "O messenger of Allah, who is the most diligent among the believers?" He replied: "The one that remembers death most, and who is best prepared for it, such are the most diligent ones."

**869-** Abu Bakr bin Khallãd narrated, re 'Abdullãh bnu Omar, God be pleased with him, that God's messenger ﷺ, upon whom be peace, said: "Some people are extremely cognizant, and they have correctly understood the commands of Allah, the most exalted, although, they may look ugly, and they maybe lowly and despised in the eyes of others today, but yet, they will be saved tomorrow. Others may speak with eloquence and have a charming tongue, people like their look, and yet, they will be doomed tomorrow, on the Day of Resurrection."

**870-** 'Abdullãh bnu Ja'far narrated, re 'Abdullãh bnu Omar, God be pleased with him, that when God's messenger ﷺ, upon whom be peace, completed the building of the mosque in Madina, he dedicated one of the doors exclusively for women, and he said: "Let no man walk through this door."

Nãfi' added: "Since that day, I have never seen 'Abdullãh bnu Omar ever walk through or step out from that door."

**871-** Al-Qãdhi Abu Ahmad narrated that 'Abdullãh bnu Omar, God be pleased with him, said: "Here comes a time upon us, when no one has right over his money more than his own Muslim brother. In fact, it became so to fulfill a prophetic saying which I have heard from the lips of God's messenger ﷺ, upon whom be peace. He said, 'When people become stingy about their Dinar and dirham, when they buy and sell using monetary specimen (Arb. *'aina*), when they follow the cowtail, and when they forsake their struggle on God's path, Allah will inflict them with humiliation, and He will not rescind it, until they review their practices, understand the reason behind their failures, and correct the way they perform their religious obligations.'"

**872-** Sa'ïd bin al-Musayyib said: "On the day 'Abdullãh bnu Omar, God be pleased with him, died, there was not a single person I wished to have had his deeds when I meet my Lord except him."

**873-** Abu Hãmed bin Jabla narrated that al-Siddy said: "I met 'Abdullãh bnu 'Amru, Aba Sa'ïd, and Abu Huraira, among others, and all of them have recognized that no one has departed from this world being in a state akin to that of God's messenger ﷺ, upon whom be peace, except for 'Abdullãh bnu Omar, God be pleased with him."

**874-** 'Abdullãh, son of Imam Ahmad bin Hanbal, God be pleased with him, narrated that sometimes after the passing of 'Abdullãh bnu Omar, God be pleased with him, 'Aisha, the mother of the believers, God be pleased with her, said: "Lately, I have not seen anyone who resembles the blessed companions of God's messenger ﷺ, upon whom be peace, better than 'Abdullãh bnu Omar, who was also buried enshrouded in an old *izãr*."

## 41- Ibn 'Abbãs ('Abdullãh bin al-'Abbãs)

In attempting to further learn about the spirituality of the blessed companions of God's messenger ﷺ, upon whom be peace, and in this section, God willing, we will also explore through authentic referenced accounts, some aspects of the true spiritual commitment of the blessed and noble companion 'Abdullãh bin al-'Abbãs, also known as Ibn 'Abbãs, God be pleased with him. We will also endeavor to view other areas of his blessed character, attempt to benefit from his spiritual model, and try to learn from his understanding, and from few of his explanations and commentaries, among other referenced testimonies of his companions.

It is narrated in the prophetic traditions that God's messenger ﷺ, upon whom be peace, once saw his nephew Ibn al-'Abbãs as a young boy, and he made an exceptional prayer on his behalf. Hence, Ibn 'Abbãs was destined to memorize the holy Qur'an by heart with great ease, and he became gifted with quick understanding, as well as he became an inspiring teacher since his early youth. Even the elders among the early companions learned from his explanations, and they hearkened with great interest to his Qur'anic interpretations, as well as they accepted them with utmost respect.

Ibn 'Abbãs was a most discerning listener, and a sagacious speaker since his young age. He also was perspicacious and most sensitive to his surroundings, and his explanations were most clear and to the point. He was endowed with luminous wisdom and understanding, for he was taught at the hand of the best of teachers, the inspired deliverer of the final revelation of God Almighty, and the seal of His prophets, God's messenger Muhammad ﷺ, upon whom be peace.

In fact, Ibn 'Abbãs will always be perceived by all Muslims as the radiant moonlight of all the learned ones, the pillar of the accomplished scholars, and the source of the impeccable and unparalleled fountainhead of Qur'anic interpretations. Ibn 'Abbãs is regarded as the ever unfolding ocean of knowledge, and to this date, the most insightful interpretations of the Qur'an and of the prophetic quotes came via Ibn 'Abbãs, God be pleased with him. In fact, his interpretations, commentaries, and his in-depth explanations (*ta'wīl*) of the inner meanings of Qur'anic verses and prophetic sayings remain a cardinal reference for the most acquainted Muslim scholars, and indeed, Ibn 'Abbãs, God be pleased with him, is the most cherished endowment of all Muslims, and he will always remain one of the most revered gnostics for Muslims all over the world.

Ibn 'Abbãs always dressed in white, he was a generous host as well as he was most respectful to his guests, and he was extremely charitable. He acknowledged and strove to nurture the blessings which Almighty Allah has bestowed upon him, as well as he struggled continuously to free himself from attachment to any ephemeral interests and what maybe fancied by the majority of people as material pleasure.

**875-** Al-Zahri narrated, re Ibn 'Abbãs, God be pleased with him, that God's messenger ﷺ, upon whom be peace, once saw him as a young child, and he said to him: "Young boy, let me teach you few words and Allah, the most exalted, will bless you if you would live up to them: 1) Constantly maintain your awareness of Allah, and you will find Him omnipresent; 2) Recognize Allah's blessings when you are in comfort, and He will sustain your needs whenever you face hardships; 3) if you were to ask for anything, then ask only of Allah; 4) if you needed a helper, seek only the help of Allah; 5) the divine pen of destiny has already dried, after it has written the divine decree confirming the divine primordial knowledge of what will happened.' 6) Hence, even if the entire creation assembles to give you something Allah did not write in your destiny, they cannot give it to you; 7) and even if they altogether unite their efforts to prevent you from receiving something Allah has written in your name, they cannot do that neither, 8) therefore, devote your deeds solely to Allah and offer them with contentment, full acceptance, and certitude. Understand, that 9) there are ample benefits if you can exercise patience towards what you dislike; 10) that victory comes with persevering in patience; 11) that the gateway to safety and comfort is wide opens during adversities; and finally, 12) realize that ample access to ease is most present during difficulties."

**876-** 'Amru bnu Dinar narrated that Ibn 'Abbãs, God be pleased with him, said: "I once stood behind God's prophet ﷺ, upon whom be peace, to pray during the later part of the night, and just before he entered the sacrament of *salãt*, he brought me forward, and he made me stand next to him. When we completed the prayers, and prior to leaving, I said to him, 'O messenger of Allah, is it permissible for any one besides you to stand at that station, when you are the messenger of Allah, and when that rank is God's exclusive gift to you?' God's messenger ﷺ, upon whom be peace, heard what I said, and he prayed to Allah, Blessed be His Name, to expand my knowledge and understanding."

**877-** 'Abdullãh bin Muhammad bin Ja'far narrated that Ibn 'Abbãs, God be pleased with him, said: "I was at the house of God's messenger ﷺ, upon whom be peace, when he, peace and blessings be upon him, went to a nearby pitcher in the house, where he took his ablution and then drank some water while standing up. When I saw that, I said to myself, 'By God, I would certainly like to do what God's messenger ﷺ, upon whom be peace, just did.' Hence, I went to that same pitcher, I took my ablution, and I drank some water while standing up, and then, I followed him and stood behind him to pray. When God's messenger ﷺ, upon whom be peace, saw me, he pointed out to me to come forward, and to stand next to him to the right, but I shied away, and insisted on standing up behind him. When he completed the prayers, he said to me, 'What prevented you from standing next to me in prayers?' I replied, 'O messenger of Allah, you are more revered and more exalted in my eyes, that I should ever dare to stand next to you in prayers.' God's messenger ﷺ, upon whom be peace, then prayed, 'O Allah, endow him with wisdom.' "

**878-** 'Akrama narrated that Ibn 'Abbãs, God be pleased with him, said: "God's messenger ﷺ, upon whom be peace, once embraced me and he prayed, 'O Allah, teach him wisdom.'"

**879-** 'Abdullãh bnu Omar, God be pleased with him, narrated that God's messenger ﷺ, upon whom be peace, prayed for 'Abdullãh bin al-'Abbãs, and said: "O Allah, bless him and further increase Your blessings upon him through his progeny."

**880-** Abu Huraira, God be pleased with him, narrated that God's messenger ﷺ, upon whom be peace, once came out of his house, and he met (his uncle) al-'Abbãs and said to him: "O Abul Fadhl, let me tell me the good news!" Al-'Abbãs replied: "Indeed, O messenger of Allah, please do!" God's messenger ﷺ then cheered him up when he added: "Allah, the Lord of majesty and glory, has opened this path with me, and He will bring it to its apogee through your descendants."

**881-** Jābir bin 'Abdullāh, God be pleased with him, narrated that God's messenger ﷺ, upon whom be peace, said: "In times yet to come, my *umma* (followers), will be ruled by kings who will descend from al-'Abbās, and through them Allah will further exalt and strengthen this religion."

**882-** Al-A'amash narrated that Mujāhid said: "Ibn 'Abbās, God be pleased with him, also used to be called 'the Ocean of Knowledge,' because of the undiminishing wealth of knowledge he possessed."

**883-** Maimoun bin Mihrān narrated that 'Abdullāh bin 'Abbās, God be pleased with him, told him, that God's messenger ﷺ, upon whom be peace, once placed his hand over his head, and prayed: "My Lord, endow him with wisdom, and teach him *ta'wīl*."[1] God's messenger ﷺ, upon whom be peace, then placed his hand over Ibn 'Abbās's chest, who felt its chill in his spine, as God's messenger ﷺ prayed: "O Allah, fill him with wisdom and knowledge."

Maimoun further added: "Ibn 'Abbās remained the primary expounder of knowledge of this *umma*, until Allah, the Lord of majesty and glory, took back his soul."

**884-** Abu Bakr al-Talhi narrated that Ibn 'Abbās, God be pleased with him, said: "God's messenger ﷺ, upon whom be peace, prayed many times for my benefit, and he said to me, 'Indeed, you are a blessed man, and an excellent interpreter of the Qur'an."

**885-** Abu Hāmed bin Jabla narrated that Ibn al-Hanifa, daughter of Abu Hanifa, said: "Ibn 'Abbās is indeed the foremost gnostic and savant of this *umma* (nation of believers)."

**886-** Sa'īd bin Jubair narrated that Ibn 'Abbās said: "I was a young boy, when Omar bin al-Khattāb, God be pleased with him, used to bring me along with him during the frequent gatherings of the elders of Badr. One day, some of the elders objected to my presence, and they said to Omar, 'Why do you have to bring this boy with you? We too have young children!' Omar replied, 'He is one of those whom you have learned about his notable fortune.'"

Ibn 'Abbās further said: "According to my understanding, I think that he only brought me there to confirm to them the gift which

---

[1] i.e., How to interpret and explain the meaning of the Qur'anic revelation.

Allah, Blessed be His Name, has bestowed upon me. When we sat down, Omar bin al-Khattāb, God be pleased with him, asked the people, 'How would you interpret the meaning of the Qur'anic verse, ❮ When the help of Allah comes, and victory is proclaimed. And when you see people entering the religion of Allah in masses, then celebrate the praises of your Lord, and ask for His forgiveness, for surely He is oft-forgiving. ❯ (*Qur'an 110:1-3*)?' Some of the people replied, 'In this *sura* (chapter), we are commanded to praise Allah, the most exalted, and to ask for His forgiveness when He grants us victory and triumph.' Others remained silent, while some replied, 'We do not know!' Omar turned to me and said, 'O Ibn 'Abbās, would you say the same thing?' I replied, 'No!' He further asked me, 'Then how would you interpret it?' I replied, 'This was the announcement of the end of the term of God's messenger ﷺ, upon whom be peace, in this world. In this verse, Allah, most blessed is His name, announced, ❮ When the help of Allah comes, and victory is proclaimed.[1] ❯ that will be the sign of the end of your term in this world. ❮ Then celebrate the praises of your Lord, and ask for His forgiveness, for surely He is oft-forgiving. ❯ Omar, God be pleased with him, commented, 'I only know the explanation which you have just offered.' "

**887-** Ibn 'Abbās, God be pleased with him, narrated that Omar bin al-Khattāb, God be pleased with him, was sitting with some of the elder Meccan émigrés, among other companions of God's messenger ﷺ, upon whom be peace, and a discussion about the 'Night of Power' took place. Omar listened as some of the elders debated and gave their opinions and interpretations of this miraculous night, and as to which of the nights of the of fasting month of Ramadan it denotes. Omar turned to Ibn 'Abbās and said: "What happened to you O Ibn 'Abbās? Why are you silent? Say something. Do not let your youth and respect for the elders prevent you from sharing your understanding."

Ibn 'Abbās then said: "O Prince of the Believers, surely Allah is One and unique, and He likes odd numbers. In this respect, He, Blessed be His Name, also chose a series of septets, and He made

[1] i.e., Recapturing Mecca from the unbelievers.

the week revolve around seven days; He created the human being in seven stages; He made our livelihood depend on seven types of elements; He created seven firmaments above us; and beneath us, He created two earths, each one consisting of seven layers; He revealed the Opening Chapter of the Qur'an, *al-Fātiha*, comprising seven couplets; He forbade seven types of sanguineous marriages involving family members; He allotted a universal division of inheritance to seven categories of relatives; and furthermore, in paying obeisance during our prayers, we prostrate on seven parts of our bodies; God's messenger ﷺ, upon whom be peace, circumambulated the holy *Ka'ba* seven times; he further encompassed the distance between the Hills of *Safa* and *Marwa* seven times, and he pelted Satan at *Jamarāt* seven times while proclaiming the glory of Allah as per His admonition in the Qur'an. Therefore, I think that the 'Night of Power' must be one of the last seven nights of the month of Ramadan. God knows best."

Omar, God be pleased with him, was astonished by the elaborate exegesis Ibn 'Abbās presented, and he commented: "No one had agreed with me with regard to the 'Night of Power,' and as I heard it from God's messenger , upon whom be peace, except this young boy whose hairline is not yet fully etched. Indeed, God's messenger ﷺ, upon whom be peace, did say, 'Seek it during the last ten days of the month of Ramadan.' "

Omar, God be pleased with him, then turned to the crowd of elders and said: "O ye people! Is there amongst you anyone who can rehearse this exegesis as told by Ibn 'Abbās?"

**888-** Sulaimān bin Ahmad narrated that Abi Bakr al-Huthali said: "I once visited al-Hassan, son of 'Ali, God be pleased with both of them, and he said to me, 'Surely Ibn 'Abbās has had such an unequaled and deep knowledge of Qur'anic interpretation. In fact, Omar, God be pleased with him, used to speak of Ibn 'Abbās, saying, 'He is the versed young spokesman of the elders. His tongue is most inquisitive, and his heart fathoms best. He once stood up at our pulpit, — (or maybe Omar said 'the eve of 'Arafa' during the pilgrimage season), — and he read *Surat'ul Baqara and Surat Āl Imrān* (Qur'an, Chapter II and Chapter III), and he explained them verse by verse to the senior pilgrims. — Indeed he was an engaging speaker, and his copious and energetic words poured profusely with eloquence, and with utmost clarity.' "

**889-** 'Ãmer al-Sha'bi narrated that Ibn 'Abbãs, God be pleased with him, said: "My father, al-'Abbãs, once said to me, 'My dear son, I noticed that the Prince and Commander of the Believers, Omar bin al-Khattãb, God be pleased with him, often invites you to visit with him, he also solicits your friendship, and requests your opinion, as well as do other people among the wise companions of God's messenger ﷺ, upon whom be peace. Therefore, I would like you to hearken to my words, and to honor these three qualities, 1) Beware of Almighty Allah and do not let Omar put your truthfulness to test; 2) never expose any of his secrets; and 3) do not backbite anyone in his presence.' "

'Ãmer then said to Ibn 'Abbãs: "By God, each one of these advisements equals one thousand good deeds." Ibn 'Abbãs replied: "I swear by Allah, the most exalted, that these advisements are worth more than ten thousand good deeds each!"

**890-** 'Akrama Ibn 'Ammãr narrated that following the Battle of the Camel, 'Abdullãh Ibn 'Abbãs said: "When one of the tribes of dissenters boycotted and opposed the legitimacy of 'Ali's reign over the Muslim caliphate, I said to 'Ali, 'O Prince and Commander of the believers, allow me to forgo leading the next congregational prayer, and give me permission to go and speak with these people, perhaps I can find out what is troubling them!' 'Ali replied, 'I fear for your life!' Ibn 'Abbãs said, 'Do not worry. God willing, nothing will happen to me.' "

Ibn 'Abbãs continued: "I had never met this tribe of people before, so I wore my best Yemenite raiment, and I went to see the leaders of this group. I reached their precinct during the peak of the mid-afternoon, and they were resting. I therefore made my presence known, and I sought permission to see them. When I entered, I saw a most descent gathering of people, and the marks of honor and piety on their faces were salient from long nights of devotion; there hands were callus, — like those of camels' hoofs, — from hard labor, and their faces were radiant and had the imprints of long prostrations. As I was entering the room, their elder said, 'Welcome, O Ibn 'Abbãs, what brings you here today?' I replied,

'I have come to talk to you about the companions of God's messenger ﷺ, upon whom be peace, who had received the divine revelation, and about which they had the best of understanding.' "

"Some of the people were upset, and they shouted, 'Do not talk to him!' Others said, 'Rather let's talk to him and find out what he has to say!' Hence, I sat down, and I inquired, 'Tell me, what do you hold against the cousin of God's messenger ﷺ, upon whom be peace, his son-in-law, and who was the first to believe in him among the early companions?' They replied, 'We disagree with him on three main issues!' I asked, 'What are they?' They replied, 'First of all: 1) 'He judges people by the law of God's religion, when Allah, the Lord of majesty and glory, says, ❬ The judgment belongs to no one but Allah. He reveals the truth, and He is the best of judges ❭ (*Qur'an 6:57*).' I asked, 'What else?' They replied, 2) 'He wars, but then he refused to take neither prisoners nor war spoils! If such people he fights had in fact rejected the truth (i.e., *kuffār*), then their property would have been lawful to plunder, and if these people are believers, then it would have been unlawful to fight against them to begin!'"

Ibn 'Abbās interjected: "And what else? " The people replied: 3) "He also has ceded the title *'Amïr ul-Mu'mineen'* (the Prince and Commander of the believers), therefore, if he is not the Commander of the believers, then would he be the commander of the unbelievers?"

Ibn 'Abbās continued: "I said, 'Do you see! If I rehearse unto you excerpts from God's Book, the meaning of which are clearly articulated and well defined, and if I narrate to you some of the traditions of your prophet ﷺ, upon whom be peace, as well, — *sunna* (traditions) which you do not refute, and all of which support the sound basis of his actions, would you then agree to reverse your position?' They replied, 'Indeed, we would!' I then said: "As to your saying that he judges people by the law of God's religion when judgment belongs solely to Allah, and to no one else! May I remind you that Allah the most exalted says, ❬ O ye who believe! Do not kill a hunt once you have entered the sacrament of the pilgrims, whoever does so intentionally, he has to make an offering of a domesticated animal in charity equal to the one he has killed, in atonement, and which offering he must bring to the Ka'ba (for distribution to the poor and the needy), and let two just men from among you judge him by the book (*hadyan*) ... › (*Qur'an 5:95*). In another verse dealing with a domestic dispute between a wife and a husband, Allah, the most exalted says, ‹ ... and if you fear estrangement that could lead to their separation, then appoint (two) judges, one from her family, and one from his family; and if they intend reform (for the better), then Allah will guide them to reconciliation. Surely Allah is all-knowing, and well-acquainted › (*Qur'an 4:35*)."

Ibn 'Abbãs continued: "Now, I ask you in the name of Allah, and I plead with your sound reasoning, tell me, iş the need to judge between two people by the law of God's religion with respect to sparing bloodshed, to save human lives, and to foster peace and unity between men, less important to call for the arbitration of a judge than to do so vis-a-vis the life of a rabbit worth one quarter of a Dinar?" The people replied: "Indeed not! Surely it is more important to seek arbitration to spare bloodshed, to save human lives, and to foster peace and unity between people" Ibn 'Abbãs then asked: "Then did I fare correctly on this subject?" They replied: "Indeed you did."

Ibn 'Abbãs further continued: "As to your question referring to his warring against the dissenters and refusing to take neither prisoners nor war spoils, now hear me well, if you fight your own mother and plunder her property as you would when you fight others, then in fact, you would have turned blasphemous *kuffãr*; and if you claim that she is not your mother, then there too, you would have surely apostatized and become atheistic *kuffãr* . In fact, Allah, the Lord of majesty and glory, says, ‹ The prophet is more entitled to direct the interests of the believers then they do, and his wives are their mothers › (*Qur'an 33:6*). Now, it seems that you are vacillating between two misguided stances, therefore, either choose one or the other! What do you think, did I fare correctly on this subject as well?" They replied: "Indeed you did."

Ibn 'Abbãs resumed his exposé: "As to your allegation that he has waived the title *'Amïr ul-Mu'mineen'* (Prince and Commander of the believers), may I remind you here of a similar episode, when on the day of the Truce of Hudaibiyya, God's messenger ﷺ, upon whom be peace, called 'Ali to write down an agreement between him and the contending Tribe of Quraish, and he said to 'Ali, God bless his countenance, 'Write down, 'This is what Muhammad, the messenger of Allah, has litigated as a covenant between him and the Tribe of Quraish ...' Immediately, the leader of the Quraishi delegation interjected, 'Nay! By Allah, if we knew that you were God's messenger, we would not have warded you and your followers off the Sacred House, nor would we have fought you! Just write 'Muhammad, the son of 'Abdullāh.' God's messenger ﷺ, upon whom be peace, replied, 'By God Who is my Witness, I am the messenger of Allah, and regardless of whether you belie me or not.' Then he turned to 'Ali, God bless his countenance, and said, 'O 'Ali, write down, Muhammad, the son of 'Abdullāh.' Now tell me, surely God's messenger ﷺ, upon whom be peace, is better than 'Ali, God bless his countenance, and yet, to break a fleeting impasse, and in order to score a peace treaty, he agreed to satisfy the demand of the contenders. Hence, what do you think, did I fare correctly on this subject as well? They replied: 'Yes indeed, you did.' "

Narrating this incident, Ibn 'Abbās, God be pleased with him, added: "On that day, twenty thousand men of that group desisted from their dissension, while four thousand persisted in upholding their opposition, and they carried out their war against 'Ali, God bless his countenance, and the believers."

**891-** Sa'īd bin Jubair narrated that the caliph Mu'āwiya once received a letter from the Byzantine emperor, Hiraclius (c. 575-641 C.E.), inquiring about three things, and in turn, Mu'āwiya wrote a letter to Ibn 'Abbās, God be pleased with him, asking him to clarify the meaning of, 1) The 'Lintel' (*mijarra*); 2) the 'Bow' (*qaws*); and, 3) a unique place on earth, where the sun had risen only once, never before that day, nor after which did the sun ever again rise thereupon?

In his reply to Mu'āwiya, Ibn 'Abbās, God be pleased with him, wrote: "1) As to the Lintel, this is the main gate where the heavens will split open on the Day of Resurrection; 2) as to the Bow, this is the safety frame of the earth, which prevents its inhabitants from drowning; and 3) finally, as to the only place on earth, whereupon the sun had risen only once, never before that day, nor after which did the sun ever rise there again, that is the seabed, where the sea split open before the Children of Israel, for them to cross during their flight from Pharaoh and his army, and where Pharaoh's army drowned."

**892-** Abu Bakr bin Khallãd narrated that a man went to 'Abdullãh bnu Omar, God be pleased with him, and asked him about the meaning of the verse indicating that ‹ The heavens and the earth were a seamless one piece each, and We caused them to cleave › (*Qur'an 21:30*). 'Abdullãh bnu Omar looked around, and he pointed to an old man sitting in the mosque, and said: "Go to that Shaykh and ask him, and then come back and tell me what he says!" The man went and found that Shaykh to be Ibn 'Abbãs, God be pleased with him, and when he asked him the question. Ibn 'Abbãs replied: "The heaven was a seamless one piece, and it did not rain, and the earth was a seamless one piece, and it did not allow anything to grow upon it. Hence, Almighty Allah, the Lord of majesty and glory, caused them to cleave, thus allowing the sky to rain, and the earth to sprout."

The man went back to 'Abdullãh bnu Omar and told him what he heard, 'Abdullãh then commented: "Indeed, Ibn 'Abbãs is endowed with knowledge. He spoke the truth, and they were thus." 'Abdullãh also added: "I used to wonder how bold is Ibn 'Abbãs to offer Qur'anic interpretations, but now I know for fact that surely he is endowed with knowledge."

**893-** Abu Hãmed bin Jabla narrated that Abi Sãlih said: "I once witnessed a gathering at the house of Ibn 'Abbãs, God be pleased with him, and if the Tribe of Quraish ever had to take true pride in something, then this event should have been the one. On that day, the crowds packed the entire narrow street leading to his door causing an impasse, where no one was able to go forward nor was any one able to return to his own house. I walked in, and I informed him about the flocks of people standing outside his door, and I told him that they were seeking permission to come in, and to present him with some pressing questions. Ibn 'Abbãs, God be pleased with him, asked me to get him some water to take his ablution, and after I did, he sat down and said, 'Go to that door and say to the people, 'Whoever has questions about the Qur'an, or about any of its seven vernacular phonetic roots (*hurüf*), then come in and ask as much as you want.' Hence, I went out to the people, and I gave them permission to enter, and the first group of people kept on flocking into the house, until they filled the main room as well as the entire house to capacity. Whatever they asked Ibn 'Abbãs, he satisfied their thirst for knowledge, and he even expounded upon their quest. When he finished answering their questions, he said to them, 'Have compassion on your brethren who are still standing up outside on their feet.' "

"The people left, and Ibn 'Abbãs turned to me again and said, 'Go to that door, and call out, 'Whoever has questions about the Qur'an or about its interpretations, then come in.' So I did, and I gave them permission to enter, and again, the second group of people entered, and they filled the room and the entire house. Whatever they asked him, he had the answer, and he further expounded on their subject as well. When he finished answering them, he again said, 'Have compassion on your brethren who are still standing up outside on their feet.' "

"As soon as the people left, Ibn 'Abbãs turned to me and said, 'Go out and ask the people, 'Whoever wishes to ask questions about *halãl* (the lawful), *harãm* (the unlawful), or any other questions regarding understanding *fiqh* (Islamic jurisprudence), then he may come in.' So I did announce to them what he asked me to announce, and again, the people flocked into the house, until they filled it and the room to capacity, and they began to pour out their questions. Ibn 'Abbãs, God be pleased with him, replied to each one of their individual, personal, as well as general questions, and he further expounded on the subject. When they had no further questions, he said to them, 'Your brethren, your brethren! Have compassion on those who are still standing up outside on their feet.' "

"The people left, and Ibn 'Abbãs turned to me and said, 'Give access to those who have questions about the divine *farã'idh* (ordinances), the like precepts, or other related religious obligations,' and so I did, and the next group entered, and they filled the house and the room to capacity, and no mater what they asked him, Ibn 'Abbãs had the right answer, as well as he further expounded on the subject. Ibn 'Abbãs then said to them, 'Your brethren, your brethren! Have compassion on those who are still standing up outside on their feet.' "

"Again, after the people left, he turned to me and said, 'Give access to those who have questions about the Arabic language, poetry, and any exceptional or uncommon expressions.' So I did, and the next group entered, and they filled the house and the room to capacity, and no mater what they asked him, he had the right answer, as well as he further expounded on the subject."

The narrator, Abi Sãli<u>h</u>, further said: "Therefore, if the entire Tribe of Quraish ever wants to take true pride in something, then surely this extraordinary event should be the one, for I have never witnessed such an audience gathering to hearken to a man of this caliber since that day."

**894-** 'Atã' narrated: "I have never seen a house that has as much kitchen utensils and drinking cups than the residence of 'Abdullãh Ibn 'Abbãs."

**895-** In another narration also referring to the house of Ibn 'Abbãs, 'Adiyy said: "I have never seen a house that has more knowledge and bread than the house of 'Abdullãh Ibn 'Abbãs."

**896-** Also in a similar narration, 'Abdullãh bin 'Abdu-Ra<u>h</u>mãn, son of Abi <u>H</u>ussain, said: "I have never seen a more hospitable house with as much food, drink, fruits, and knowledge, than that of the house of 'Abdullãh Ibn 'Abbãs, God be pleased with him and with his father."

**897-** Bishr bin Müsa narrated that Ibn 'Abbãs once wore a most expensive robe he bought for one hundred Dinars.

**898-** Bishr bin Müsa narrated that a man once insulted Ibn 'Abbãs who replied with utmost serenity and a remarkable poise: "You have made me the subject of your insults, and yet, I have three good qualities, 1) When I read a verse from the revealed Book of Allah, I wish that everyone would get out of its meaning as much as I do; 2) when I hear of a Muslim ruler or a judge, who has rendered a just verdict, I become extremely happy for his justice, although, it is most probable that I may never seek him for justice; 3) and thirdly, when I hear that it rained in a distant Muslim land, I become extremely happy for its people, although I do not have a single sheep grazing freely thereat."

**899-** Sa'ïd bin Jubair narrated that Ibn 'Abbãs, God be pleased with him, once said: "Even should Pharaoh say to me, 'May God bless you,' my reply will be, 'May God bless you as well.' "

**900-** Bishr bin Müsa narrated that Ibn 'Abbãs, God be pleased with him, said: "Even should a mountain infringes upon another mountain, the transgressing mountain will be leveled by God's decree."

**901-** Habïb bin al-Hassan narrated that Ibn 'Abbãs, God be pleased with him, said: "Whenever lust, lewdness, and contumacious sexual freedom dominate a society, then, the two punishments, *moutãn* (destruction and death) will ravage the land and swipe the people by the multitudes."

**902-** Sa'ïd bin Jubair narrated that Ibn 'Abbãs, God be pleased with him, said: "Should you have to stand before a man of awesome authority, or come before a tyrant you fear his oppression, then pray, 'Allah is the greatest. Surely Allah is mightier than His entire creation. Surely Allah is more powerful than what I fear, and what causes me terror and fear. I seek refuge in Allah Whom there is no god but He, Who holds the seven firmaments and prevents them from falling upon the earth and crushing it, except by His leave. I seek refuge in Him from any evil that may spur from His creation — so and so, — and from his subjects, followers, or entourage of jinn or humans. My Lord, be my Neighbor, and protect me against their evil. Most sublime and majestic is Your approbation, and to place a servant who beseeches Your protection under the banner of Your safety. Surely Your neighbor is strong by You. Blessed is Your Name, for there is no God except You.' " Ibn 'Abbãs then added: "Recite this prayer thrice."

**903-** Al-Dhahhãk narrated that Ibn 'Abbãs, God be pleased with him, said: "Whenever a servant says *Bismillãh* (In the Name of Allah), he has thus remembered Allah. Whenever he says *Al-Hamdu Lillãh* (All praises are due to Allah) he has thus thanked Him. Whenever he says *Allahu Akbar* (Surely Allah is the greatest) he has thus glorified Him. Whenever he says *Lã iLãha Il-Allah* (Indeed there is no god except Allah) he has thus testified to His Oneness. Whenever he says *Lã Hawla wa lã Quwwata illa billãh* (Surely there is no will or power to effect anything except by Allah's leave), he has thus accepted Islam, and he would have bought his own salvation (Arb. *Istislãm*) with this testimony, a resplendent light that will shine upon his face, and a magnificent treasure will be the reward that awaits him in the heavenly garden of paradise."

**904-** 'Abdul-Hamïd bin Ja'far narrated that someone saw Ibn 'Abbãs, God be pleased with him, eating the fleshy seeds of the pomegranate fruit one at a time, and he asked him: "O Ibn 'Abbãs, why do you do that?" He replied: "It has come to my knowledge, that there is not a single pomegranate tree on earth which flowers are not pollinated by a pomegranate fruit from the heavenly garden of paradise, and by doing so, I am constantly hoping that perchance, I will find and eat that perfect seed!"

**905-** 'Amru bnu Ahmad narrated that Hishãm bin 'Abdullãh al-Rãzi (who had lost his sight) was once invited to dinner at the house of Ibn al-Hanifa, and during their meal, a locust fell dead in his lap. Ibn al-Hanifa reached out and lifted it, and he handed it to Ibn 'Abbãs, saying: "O nephew of God's messenger ﷺ, upon whom be peace, this locust has fallen dead in our brother's lap." Ibn 'Abbãs, God be pleased with him, looked at it and he firmly addressed 'Akrama: "O 'Akrama!" He exclaimed: "At your command, sir!" Ibn 'Abbãs said: "It is written on the wing of this locust, in the ancient Assyriac language, 'I am Allah. There is no God except Me, and surely there is no associate with Me. Locusts are a division of My army, and they are subservient solely to My command. I inflict them as a just punishment upon whosoever I intend among My creation.' "

**906-** Abi al-Jawzã' al-Rab'i narrated that Ibn 'Abbãs, God be pleased with him, once interpreted Allah's saying: ﴾ The Day when neither wealth nor sons will avail one from Allah's just requital, except for the one who comes before his Lord with a sound heart.﴿ (*Qur'an 26:88-89*), the second verse of which refers to the Day of Judgment, to mean: "One who attests to the truth of *Lã Ilãha il Allah* (surely there is no God except Allah)."

**907-** Al-A'amash narrated that Ibn 'Abbās, God be pleased with him, once interpreted the verse, ﴾ Allah knows the deceptive tricks of the eye, ﴿ (*Qur'an 40:19*), saying: "It means that whether you look at a women, coveting a hidden desire for her or not, Allah, the Lord of majesty and glory, knows that, ﴾ And He knows what all the hearts conceal; ﴿ meaning, regardless of whether one can arrive at committing adultery, or fails to fulfill his intention."

Al-A'amash reflected for a moment about the meaning of what Ibn 'Abbās said, and perceiving a sense of wonderment on the part of his listeners, Ibn 'Abbās quickly interrupted his string of thoughts, and he added: "Wouldn't you like me to tell you about the meaning of the next verse?" Al-A'amash replied: "Indeed!" Ibn 'Abbās, God be pleased with him, then read: "﴾ And Allah judges with justice and truth ﴿ (*Qur'an 40:20*), meaning, that He has the absolute and immutable power to justly reward good for good, and evil for evil; and ﴾ As to those besides Him, some (people) call upon them to fulfill their prayers, they indeed have no power to affect any judgment whatsoever. Surely Allah is the One Who hears and sees everything¤" (Qur'an *40:20*).

**908-** Nāfi' Ibn Omar narrated that someone asked Ibn 'Abbās, God be pleased with him: "What was the sign that affected the heart of Joseph?" (i.e., when Zulaikha, the wife of the Egyptian minister, intended to seduce him, and) with passion, ﴾ She took hold of him, and he took hold of her, ﴿ — and nothing could have stopped them from committing such an evil and shameful act — ﴾ had he not seen the sign of his Lord ﴿ (*Qur'an 12:24*)." Ibn 'Abbās replied: "When Joseph realized that the woman was pulling him down with her and inducing him to commit an evil act, he pulled out and sat down for a moment to cool his urge. At that moment, a voice spoke captiously to him, saying, 'O Joseph, do not become like the bird that once had feathers, and when it committed adultery, it sat in hiding, having no feathers to cover itself!' " Hearing that, Joseph, immediately, harried to the door to escape, but to no avail, Zulaikha's husband was standing at the door ..." *the story; Qur'an 12:25-27.*

**909-** Imam Ahmad bin Hanbal, God bless his soul, that Ibn 'Abbās, God be pleased with him, once interpreted the verse ﴾ O ye who believe (in God), govern with justice as the witnesses of

Allah ❯ (*Qur'an 4:135*), he said: "This is similar to the case of two men who come before a judge anticipating a just verdict, while in his heart, the judge leans towards one party against the other."

**910-** Imam Ahmad bin H̲anbal, God bless his soul, narrated that Ibn 'Abbãs, God be pleased with him, said: "As the Day of Judgment nears, a voice will announce continuously, 'The Hour of Reckoning is coming! The Hour of Reckoning is at hand!' Every living and dead creature will hear that harbinger of the Hour calling. The caller will also say, 'To whom does the kingdom belong today? It belongs to the One, the All-powerful and Irresistible sovereign Lord.' "

**911-** 'Abdullãh bin Omar al-Ja'fi narrated that Ibn 'Abbãs, God be pleased with him, once gave a sermon during the pilgrimage season, and he began by reciting *Surat'ul Baqara* (Qur'an; the Cow, Chapter II), and which chapter he read verse-by-verse, interpreting their meaning, and explaining their connotations. Hearing him, one of the pilgrims called Shaqïq said to himself: "I have never seen or heard a man speaking with such clarity of understanding and insight as he does. Even should the entire nations of Persia and the Byzantine kingdoms hear him today, they would surely accept Islam as their religion."

**912-** Ish̲ãq bin Bishr bin Juwaybir narrated that Ibn 'Abbãs, God be pleased with him, said: "O sinners! Do not feel immune to punishment for your sins, for such attitude is a greater sin than the original one. When you do not feel ashamed of yourselves before the two guardian angels who are situated at your right and left sides, that too is a more awesome sin than the original one. To laugh after committing a sin, not knowing what punishment is awaiting you is a more ominous sin as well. To feel excited about what you have gained by committing your sin is yet a greater sin. To feel sorrow for missing an opportunity to gain the forbidden fruit of a sin, is again a greater sin. To feel apprehensive, or afraid, when the wind blows against your window curtains, in fear of being exposed, is yet a greater sin, and when your heart does not shiver, and dismisses the knowledge that you are never away, not even for a fraction of a second, from the sight of Allah, the Lord of majesty and glory,

— that is yet a more awesome sin! O unfortunate ones! Do you understand what was the sin of God's prophet Job, peace be upon him? Do you know why did Allah subject him to unbearable physical afflictions and destroyed everything he owned? It is because Job had mainly refused to help a poor man who sought his assistance to help him against an injustice he suffered. Job failed to respond as one of God's prophets should have done, and regarding that case, Job did not enjoin what is right and just, nor did he reprove the offender concerning the rights of this poor man! Therefore, Allah afflicted Job with awesome and unparalleled calamities."

**913-** Wahab bin Munbih narrated that Ibn 'Abbãs, God be pleased with him, was sitting in his house with some visitors, when he was informed of an argument taking place between two groups of people near the gate of the Tribe of Bani Sahm. Wahab added: "I believe that they were arguing about fate," (Arb. *qadar*). Hearing that, Ibn 'Abbãs, God be pleased with him, immediately handed his shepherd staff[1] to 'Akrama, and he placed one arm over his shoulder, and the other arm he placed over the shoulder of T̲ãwous, and along with the other visitors, altogether, they hurried to where the gathering was taking place.

When they arrived, both groups were happy to see him. They immediately opened the way to him, welcomed him, and they invited him to sit down, but Ibn 'Abbãs, God be pleased with him, preferred to remain standing up on his feet.

According to the narration of Abu Shahãb, Ibn 'Abbãs, God be pleased with him, then said: "Pay attention to your best learned ones in this gathering!" Right away, some of the people looked up to Ibn 'Abbãs and moved closer to him, while few others remained aloof. Ibn 'Abbãs then added: "Don't you know that Allah, the Most High, has servants who are silenced by neither dumbness nor sickness, but rather, they remain silent in reverence to His majesty, and their knowledge of His omnipresence, being the all-Hearing, and the all-Seeing Lord. In fact, such are the true gnostics, the true knowledgeable ones, the most eloquent speakers, the most concise explainers, the most noble ones among all people, and they are most

[1] Shepherd staff: acrosier; Arb. *mihjana*

cognizant and vigilant of the days of Allah, the Lord of majesty and glory. Every time they remember the majesty and glory of Almighty Allah, their Lord, they lose their minds, their hearts become shattered, and they become speechless. As soon as they regain their composure, they hasten to Allah, the Lord of majesty and glory, Blessed be His Name, and they offer every noble deed and sincere devotion for the sake of His pleasure."

**914-** 'Abdu-Rahmãn bin Mahdi, in his narration of the above incident, he quoted Ibn 'Abbãs, God be pleased with him, to have also said: "They regard themselves as worthless scapegrace who are wasting their unique opportunities in this world to satisfy their own ephemeral indulgences, and yet, they are most exalted and strong in their devotion. They see themselves as the companions of the unjust ones and the damned sinners in hell-fire, and yet, they are the most true and sincere worshipers of their Lord, and they are devoid of pretension. To their perception, their unbounded offerings for the sake of God Almighty are never enough, they accept no limitations for His sake, they do not put limits on what is acceptable to please Him, and they do not parade their faith and understanding so that no one would recognize their goals by their endeavors. They sit where you regularly find them and wonder who are these people, or what are they doing there! When you look at them, you find them industrious, concerned, solicitous, tenderhearted, fearful of their Lord, reverent of His majesty, and they are indeed most pious."

Having said that, Ibn 'Abbãs, God be pleased with him, then went back to his house in the company of his guests.

**915-** Sa'ïd bin Jubair narrated that during a gathering at his house, Ibn 'Abbãs, God be pleased with him, said: "I wish there is someone here who has knowledge of the guarded and most sacred unseen fate (*qadar*), whom I would certainly seek to open his brain and to find out what he knows!" Someone said: "Why is that?" Ibn 'Abbãs replied: "Because Allah, the most high, has created a most sacred preserved tablet, and He made it of a white pearl. Its cover is made of a red ruby, its pen is made of effulgent light, and its width stretches in-between the heavens and the earth. Allah, most exalted is His Name, gazes upon it three hundred and sixty times each and every single day. With one look, He initiates a new creation, with another look, He gives a new life, and with a third look, He causes death, and similarly, with each look, He raises the status of someone, devalues that of another, He strengthens someone and humiliates another, and throughout the entire day, He does whatever He wants."

**916-** Abi Ghālib al-Khalji narrated that Ibn 'Abbās, God be pleased with him, said: "Persevere and be coherent with the obligatory religious commands Allah has enjoined upon you, and then, complement such *farā'idh* (mandatory duties) with whatever supererogatory performances He makes accessible to you, for such are His rights upon you. Solicit His help in order to meet such obligations and pray to Him to help you to offer them correctly, for nothing can prove the truthfulness and sincerity of the servant's intention and his eagerness to receive Allah's final comforting reward, versus one's struggle against what he may dislikes, except the conclusion of his life in this world, and that will surely affect the exposure of one's real intentions when he meets his judgment day. Furthermore, always remember that Allah, the Lord of majesty and glory, is the supreme King, and He does whatever He wants."

**917-** Sa'īd bin Jubair narrated that Ibn 'Abbās, God be pleased with him, said: "Allah, blessed be His Name, has decreed, for each and everyone of His creation, a lawful share of basic sustenance he needs in this world, and regardless whether such a person is a true believer or an obdurate sinner and an atheist. If the servant awaits to receive his share of lawful earnings with patience, Allah will deliver them to him with His blessings, and if the servant becomes anxious, looses patience, and lay hands on what is unlawful instead, Allah will subtract from his decreed lawful share an equal amount to what he takes unlawfully, and about which he will be reckoned on the Day of Judgment."

**918-** 'Akrama narrated that Ibn 'Abbās, God be pleased with him, once commented on the verse, ❬ Do people think that they will be left to merely say, 'We believe,' and that (simply) thus they could eschew the trials that bring their claims to questioning? ❭ (*Qur'an 29:2*), saying: "In earlier times, Allah, blessed be His Name, would send a prophet to a nation, and the prophet will dwell with them until the end of his life in this world. Once Allah, the most exalted, takes back His prophet's soul, some people would oppose any further revelations, and they would argue, 'We only follow the teachings of such prophet and the exalted character and spiritual gifts God Almighty endowed him with.' Consequent to their claim, Allah, Blessed be His Name, would subject them to adverse trials, and whosoever among them holds firm to his beliefs, subscribes correctly to what God's prophet brought them, and indeed follows his traditions, will prove to be truthful, and whosoever wavers and acts otherwise will prove to be a liar."

**919-** 'Ali bin al-Hussain narrated that Ibn 'Abbãs, God be pleased with him, said: "Once upon a time, there lived a man who did not believe in fate (*qadar*), and he called it fallacy. Regarding other matters, the man appeared to be descent, and he was kind to his wife and family. One day, the man visited the local cemetery, and there he found a human skull on which it was written, 'Must be burned and its ashes scattered in the wind.' The man placed the skull in a basket, he took it to his wife, and he asked her to keep the basket in a safe place for later. The man then treated his wife kindly before he took off on a short business trip. During his absence, some neighboring women visited his wife, and during their conversation, they said to her, 'O mother of so and so, how can you say that your husband is kind to you? Tell us, did he leave you anything before he went on his journey?' The wife replied, 'Indeed, he left me a basket for safekeeping.' The women said, 'Of course, it probably contains the skull of a woman he once loved!' The wife became angry, and in a jealous fit, she brought out the basket and opened it to find out what it contained, and to her surprise, she discovered the skull her women neighbors told her about. The neighboring women further inquired, 'O mother of so and so, do you know what you must do with it in order to nullify its effects on him? — You must burn it, and then scatter its ashes in the air.' Immediately the wife took the entire basket and put it to fire, and then she scattered its ashes in the air. Upon returning from his journey, the husband found his wife upset, and somehow, in the course of their conversation, he asked his wife about the basked, and she told him what happened. Immediately the man shook in fear, and he exclaimed, 'I believe in Allah, and I believe that fate is true.' "

**920-** Al-Hassan narrated that Ibn 'Abbās, God be pleased with him, said: "There was a man, before your time, who lived a most pious life, and for eighty years, he devoted his entire life to the worship of Almighty Allah, most exalted and blessed is His name. One day, the man committed a single sin which act extremely distressed him, and he feared the punishment of his Lord. Hence, he left his domicile and wandered throughout the wilderness, the deserts, and the mountains, crying out, 'O mighty wilderness, whose grains of sand are countless, whose thorny bushes are dense and plenteous, whose wildlife is endless, and whose hillsides are enormous, would you have a place for me to hide from my Lord, the Lord of Majesty and glory?' The wilderness replied — by God's leave —, 'O man! I swear to Allah that there is not a single weed of grass or tree within me which is not guarded by an angel for its safekeeping up till the Day of Judgment, therefore, how can I hide you from Allah, the omnipresent sovereign Lord, most exalted is He, Who hears and sees everything?' The man left in despair, and he sought the ocean, he stood in aghast at its shores, and cried out, 'O mighty ocean, whose water is abundant, whose aquatic animals and plants are innumerous, would you have a place for me to hide from my Lord, the Lord of Majesty and glory?' The ocean replied — by God's leave —, 'O man! I swear to Allah, that there is not a single pebble on my floor or beneath it, or a fish in my waters, that is not guarded by an angel in charge of its safekeeping up till the Day of Judgment. Where do you want me to hide you from Allah, the sovereign Lord, most exalted is He Who hears and sees everything?' The man immediately ran away in fear and in despair until he reached a mighty mountain. There again he stood up terrified and he cried out, 'O mighty mountains! O skyscrapers whose caverns and grottos are countless, do you have a place for me to hide from my Lord, most exalted is He?' The mountains replied - by God's leave, - 'O man! We swear to Almighty Allah, the Lord of majesty and glory, that there is not a single pebble or cavern within us, which is not guarded by an angel in charge of its safekeeping up till the Day of Judgment! Where do you want us to hide you from the Lord of the universe Who hears and sees everything?' The man stood dumbfounded, and staggering in bewilderment, he remained thereat in worship, offering penitence, asking for forgiveness for his sin, and soliciting God Almighty's acceptance of his repentance until the end of his life when the angel of death came to harvest his soul. At that juncture, the man cried out in utter fear, 'My Lord! Take back my soul to evanesce, and take back my body to annihilation, and do not ever bring me back to life on the Day of Resurrection for judgment.' "

**921-** Imam Ahmad bin Hanbal, God bless his soul, narrated that 'Abdullãh bin Abi Malîka said: "I once traveled with Ibn 'Abbãs, God be pleased with him, from Mecca to Madina. On the road, halfway through the night, Ibn 'Abbãs would descend his ride, and he would stand up in prayers until dawn." Ayoub asked Abi Malîka: "How was his reading of the Qur'an?" He replied: "That night, he read from *sura*(*Qãf*), and when he reached the verse, ❮ And when the death stroke came in truth and justice, (as promised, he was told), 'This is what you were trying to evade! ❯ (*Qur'an 50:19*). Ibn 'Abbãs, God be pleased with him, sobbed while repeating this verse over and over."

**922-** Imam Ahmad bin Hanbal, God bless his soul, narrated that a man saw Ibn 'Abbãs, God be pleased with him, hold the tip of his tongue, before he let go of it and said: "Woe to you, what an evil visitation will befall you if you do not take heed! Either tell what is good and beneficial and you will win, or shut up and you will be safe." The man said: "O Ibn 'Abbãs. Why do I see you holding the tip of your tongue, and saying to it such and such ...?" Ibn 'Abbãs replied: "It came to my knowledge that on the Day of Reckoning, nothing will cause a man bitterness, rancor, and regret more than what his tongue had uttered in this world!"

**923-** 'Akrama narrated that Ibn 'Abbãs, God be pleased with him, said: "To financially support an entire Muslim family in need for a whole month, or even for a week, or as long as Allah wills, is more dear to my heart than to attend the pilgrimage in Mecca, year after year; and to offer a plate of food to a brother in Allah, blessed is His Name, is more worthy to my heart than to spend a single Dinar in support of a *Jihãd* campaign for Allah's sake."

**924-** Al-Dhahhāk narrated that Ibn 'Abbās, God be pleased with him said: "When the Dinar and the Dirham were first minted in the form of metal coins, Iblis, the first accursed Satan, held them happily, he then placed them over his eyes and said to them, 'You are the fruit of my heart, and the delight of my eyes. Through you, I will drive people to become tyrants, I will cause them to become agnostics (*kuffār*), and lead them to hell-fire. I accept from the son of Adam if he would only become attached to you, and worship you, and that's even if he would become indifferent to the balance of the pleasures of this world.' "

**925-** Sufyān al-Thawri narrated that Ibn 'Abbās, God be pleased with him, once said: "The human folks (Arb. *nās*) have gone, and what seems to remain are nothing but creatures of the jungle."[1] Someone asked: "What do you mean by *nasnās*?" Ibn 'Abbās replied: "Those who imitate humans, but are not humans."

**926-** Mujāhid narrated that Ibn 'Abbās, God be pleased with him, said: "There will come a dark time when people's sense of judgment will be suspended, and their brains will no longer be able to function, to the point that one will not find a single person to reason with."

**927-** Abu Bakr bin Khallād narrated that Mu'āwiya once said to Ibn 'Abbās, God be pleased with them both: "You seem to be following the traditions of 'Ali!" Ibn 'Abbās replied: "I follow neither the traditions of 'Ali nor those of 'Uthmān, I only follow the *sunna* tradition of God's messenger ﷺ, upon whom be peace."

**928-** Imam Ahmad bin Hanbal, God bless his soul, narrated that Abi Rajā' once pointed to his cheek and said: "Ibn 'Abbās's cheeks were marked with two deep lachrymal lines, the flow of his tears had engraved."

**929-** Imam Ahmad bin Hanbal, God bless his soul, narrated that Tāwous once said: "I have never met someone who is more revering of the sacred limits Allah has made inviolable as Ibn 'Abbās, God be pleased with him. I swear to Allah, blessed is His name, that at any single time, if I had to ponder upon Ibn 'Abbās's overwhelming reverence with respect to what Allah has made sacred, I would not be able to control my crying."

[1] Arb. *nasnās*; i.e., copycat, monkeys

**930-** Hafs bnu Omar, Abu Omar al-Barmaki narrated that Maimoun bin Mihrãn said: "I witnessed the funeral of 'Abdullãh Ibn 'Abbãs, God be pleased with him, at the city of Tã'if. When his coffin was laid down for the funeral prayer, a white bird flew in, and lighted on his body, and then, the bird entered in-between the layers of his shroud. We immediately looked for the bird to let it out, but we couldn't find it, and we gave up searching for it. Once we had finished the funeral prayer and had laid the body in the grave, the entire congregation heard a distinct voice, although no one was to be seen, reciting the verse, ❬ O Peaceful soul, return to thy Lord gratified to receive His blessings. Enter the ranks of My blessed servants, and come into My paradise ❭" (*Qur'an 89:30*).

## 42- 'Abdullãh Bin al-Zubair

It is related that spirituality also connotes courage when meeting with tribal arrogance involving pride in number and possessions. In This section, God willing, we will narrate few of the rare accounts of a heroic companion named 'Abdullãh Bin al-Zubair, God be pleased with him, a paragon of righteousness and a champion of truthfulness, whose palate tasted a touch of the prophet's blessed saliva,[1] and whose spiritual fabric and example are surely a rare inspiration that perhaps can enhance our clarity and heighten our understanding of this glorious divine path of Islam.

'Abdullãh Bin al-Zubair, God be pleased with him revered the high honor and exalted station of parenthood, he was regularly seen at the mosque standing up in prayers most of his nights, and he was most observing of extra voluntary fasting year around. 'Abdullãh Bin al-Zubair also memorized the entire holy Qur'an by heart, and he ritually trod on the heals of God's prophet ﷺ, upon whom be peace, as well as he regularly sought the friendship of the most loyal, the blessed witness and attestor to the truth of God Almighty, the blessed companion Abu Bakr al-Siddïq, God be pleased with him.

---

[1] Arb. *tahnik*: A tradition consisting of giving the newborn a tiny bit of date, among other fruits when available, chewed by a pious person or the patriarch of the family. At the time of God's messenger ﷺ, upon whom be peace, he himself applied such practice for some of the newborn children in his family among others.

'Abdullãh Bin al-Zubair, God be pleased with him, is the son of Asmã', daughter of Abu Bakr, God be pleased with him, the sister of 'Aisha, God be pleased with her, the loyal spouse of God's messenger ﷺ, upon whom be peace, as well as he was the grandson of the prophet's aunt, Safiyya, God be pleased with her.

**931-** Hishãm bin 'Urwa narrated, re Fãtima bint al-Munthir, that Asmã' bint Abi Bakr was pregnant with 'Abdullãh bin al-Zubair when she emigrated from Mecca to join God's messenger ﷺ, upon whom be peace, in Madina. Sometime after she arrived there, Asmã', God be pleased with her, gave birth to a boy, and even prior to nursing him, she carried him to God's messenger ﷺ, upon whom be peace, to give him a name, and for the newborn to receive his blessings. Upon her arrival to his house, Asmã' placed the newborn infant in his lap, and God's messenger ﷺ, upon whom be peace, rejoiced as he held the infant, and asked members of his household to bring him a dried date. It took the people nearly an hour to find one, and when they did, God's messenger ﷺ took a tiny piece of it, he chewed on it finely and inserted it in the infant's mouth. God's messenger ﷺ then named the boy 'Abdullãh bin al-Zubair, and he prayed for him. This was the first thing the infant tasted in this world.

**932-** Al-Hussain bin Muhammad al-Harrãni narrated that Um Ja'far bin al-Nu'mãn, once visited Asmã' bint Abu Bakr after the martyrdom of her son, 'Abdullãh bin al-Zubair, God be pleased with him, and when his name was mentioned, Asmã' said: "The son of al-Zubair used to observe long nights in prayers, he fasted most of his days, and he used to be called, 'The Pigeon of the Mosque."

**933-** Habib bin al-Shahid narrated that Ibn Abi Malika said: " 'Abdullãh bin al-Zubair used to fast a stretch of seven days at a time, besides observing perpetual night vigil in prayers, and even on the seventh day of his demanding religious performance, he would be physically the most fit among us, and he was our model to emulate."

**934-** Abu Bakr al-Talhi narrated that Mujãhid said: "Whenever 'Abdullãh bin al-Zubair, God be pleased with him, rose to prayers, he stood up motionless, just like a wooden stick, and as though he was detached from the outer world, out of his impeccable piety and intense reverence for God Almighty."

**935-** Ibn Juraij narrated that 'Atã said: "When Ibn al-Zubair stood up in prayers, he became deeply absorbed, to the degree that one could compare him to a node of reed stick."

**936-** 'Abdullãh, son of Imam Ahmad Ibn Hanbal, God be pleased with him, narrated that Ibn al-Munkadir once described 'Abdullãh bin al-Zubair, God be pleased with him, in prayers in-between battles, he said: "When you saw Ibn al-Zubair praying, you would think of a branch of a tree, moving only by the force of wind, while the shelled stones of the mangonels from the enemy's side fell around him from every direction, and yet, he never moved!"

**937-** Abu Sa'ïd al-'Absi narrated that Muhammad bin 'Abdullãh al-Thaqfi said: "I heard a sermon given by 'Abdullãh bin al-Zubair during the pilgrimage season. He was still wearing his pilgrim's garb (*ihrãm*) when he stood up on the eve of the eighth day of the pilgrimage (*tarwiya*), and then, he began by resounding the adequate revering hymns of the pilgrims (*talbiya*),[1] Ibn al-Zubair then praised Allah, blessed is His name, and he acknowledged His attributes of benevolence, then said, 'O ye people, you are the delegations who have come from distant corners of the world, responding to Almighty Allah's call, and surely He is the most worthy of honoring His delegations. Therefore, whosoever came here to ask Allah for His bounty, indeed he has come to the right place, his prayers will be fulfilled, and his efforts will not be in vain. The proof of your words lies in your actions, your intentions must be made clear, and your hearts must be pure. During these days, realize that the proof of Allah is Himself. On these days, the sins of the penitents are forgiven, and indeed, you have come from distant horizons, soliciting no business, asking for no money, and intending no comfort in this world. In fact, you have come this far, soliciting to receive what He has reserved for you by responding to His call, and you will surely receive them.' "

---

[1] Talbiya, Arb.: responding to Almighty Allah's call to humanity to perform the pilgrimage to His sacred House in Mecca, and as it was proclaimed by God's prophet Abraham, upon whom be peace. Also see Account 845, pp. 334.

Al-Thaqfi continued: "Al-Zubair then closed his sermon by recalling the *talbiya* prayer of the pilgrims, and the people repeated that after him form some time. I must say here that throughout my entire life, never have I seen as many people in tears of piety and joy as on that day."

**938-** Sufyãn bin 'Uyaina narrated that 'Abdullãh bin al-Zubair, God be pleased with him once said: "When Allah revealed the verse ‹ And on the day of your resurrection for judgment, you will settle your disputes in the presence of your Lord › (*Qur'an 39:31*), I asked God's messenger ﷺ, upon whom be peace, 'O messenger of Allah, will we on the Day of Judgment have to encounter a replay of what took place between us in this world, including descriptions of the nature of our sins?' He replied, 'Indeed, and you will hear that playback until everyone is acquitted by paying back what he owes, and until everyone receives justice.' "

**939-** Imam Ahmad Ibn Hanbal, God be pleased with him, narrated that 'Abdullãh bin al-Zubair, God be pleased with him, said: "When Allah revealed the verse ‹ And (on that Day), you will be asked to account for (all) the blessings (you received in the world)› (*Qur'an 102:8*), I asked God's messenger ﷺ, upon whom be peace, 'O messenger of Allah, what blessings will we be asked about? Surely we have nothing here but water and palm dates!' He replied, 'Indeed, you will be asked about that as well.' "

**940-** Al-'Abbãs bin Sahl, son of Sa'ad al-Sã'idi al-Ansãri, narrated that his father heard 'Abdullãh bin al-Zubair delivering a sermon at the sacred mosque in Mecca, during which he said: "O people, God's messenger ﷺ, upon whom be peace, used to say, 'If the son of Adam had a valleys filled with gold at his disposal, he would desire to own a second one, and if he is to be given what he wants, he would surely like to have a third one, although, nothing will eventually fill the hollowness of the son of Adam but dirt (when he lies in his grave), and Allah will show mercy to whoever repents (from greed).' "

# V
# Under the Canopy of The Prophet's Mosque

## The People of Suffa
## (*Ahlu Suffa*)[1]

Earlier in this book, we spoke about the spiritual and ascetic nature (*nusk*), and the applied devotion (*'ibāda*) of some of the blessed close companions of God's messenger ﷺ, upon whom be peace, who were deeply engrossed in their worship and love for the one and sole Lord of the universe, and who were most solicitous of His kindness and favors. We also read confirming testimonies of some of the leading shaykhs,2 teachers, and eminent Imams who were renowned for their truthfulness, devotion and constant remembrance (*zikr*) of their Lord.

From the aforementioned testimonies, the reader must have recognized that such unique and most pious people are indeed the paragons of virtues, knowledge and deeds, as well as they are the proof of guilt against those who are fascinated by this ephemeral world and its deceptive attractions, and who bask in its pleasures and crave its comforts.

In this section, God willing, we will narrate few of the authentic accounts of another group of extraordinary believers who also lived during the time of God's messenger ﷺ, upon whom be peace, and whose character and devotion are testimonies that had to be protected by several Qur'anic decrees, and which divine attestations were also given to cast out any personal opinions regarding their ranks, faith, spirituality, and trueness of their devotion.

---

[1] E. awnings; ledge; *Suffa*: a simple semi-rooflike structure made of the branches and fibers of palm trees, raised at the mosque of God's messenger ﷺ, upon whom be peace, and it served as shelter for new visitors to Medina, whom no one knew, or those who wished to retreat at the mosque to worship.

[2] Arb. sing. shaykh; pl. mashāyekh.

The few testimonies we are about to narrated were delivered or witnessed by a special group of people who have resigned to their Lord, and they were free from attachment to anything but His acceptance and to the everlasting favor of remaining in His nearness. On the other hand, they recognized well that they cannot receive such blessings without His shield to protect them against the mundane deceptive attractions and calamitous fascinations which are the fabric of this ephemeral world.

Allah, blessed is His Name, made them models of true asceticism and the apotheosis of trueness to one's Lord for those who want nothing but Him (*fuqara' ila-Allah*), and who are in constant need of His favors, and indeed, it is He that made the chosen companions the paragons of knowledge and wisdom. In fact, the truism of *ahlu suffa* was proven when they renounced the comfort of this world and lived in utter abnegation of its pleasures. They had no family, children, or money. No commerce or circumstances ever distracted them from their perseverance and constant remembrance of their Lord, and hence, they dedicated their entire lives to contemplation, worship, and penitence. They never regretted the pleasures they renounced in this life, and they never rejoiced anything but the strength they were endowed with to continue their striving for the ultimate reward. Their utmost happiness was to be engaged in worshipping their beloved Lord and Master, and their uttermost sorrow was to ever fail their test, or to fall short of correctly performing what they committed their lives to do.

Such are the ‹ Men whom neither business nor trading can divert them from remembering Allah › (*Qur'an 24:37*). The material comforts they declined in this life did not drive them to despondence, nor did they ever become confused by the lean portion they took from it. Their Master and King protected them against the evil consequences of indulging in the ephemeral pleasures of this world, and He assisted them to live a pure and a simple life. Thus, He helped them to shun off any attraction to the lures of committing injustices or becoming tyrants. On their part, they refused to feel sorrow for themselves because of what they missed in this world, and instead, they regarded it as insignificant and passing, and they did not take pride of a company that is fated to return to dirt.

**941-** 'Abdullāh Ibn Wahab narrated that 'Amru Bnul Harïth commented on the Qur'anic verse ❮ Should Allah have expanded the portion allotted to His servants (in this world), they would definitely fill the land (they can have control over) with injustice,❯ (*Qur'an* 42:27), and referring to the people of *suffa*, He said that, ❮ This is because they said, 'If we only had such and such...'❯ (*Qur'an 26:102 / 39: 58*), and perhaps on their part, they may have once desired the comfort of this world."

**942-** 'Abdullāh bin al-Mubãrak narrated that Abi Hãni said: "I heard 'Amru bnu Harïth say that this verse was revealed concerning the people of *Suffa*, and perhaps at one time they had some inclinations and desire for the world. He then recited the verse, ❮ Should Allah have expanded the portion allotted to His servants (in this world), they would definitely fill the land (they can control) with injustice. Hence, He allots their portions in balanced measures as He wills, for surely He is well acquainted with His servants, and He sees everything. ❯ (*Qur'an 42:27*).

Al-Hãfiz Abu Na'ïm al-Asfahãni, God bless his soul, in his commentaries about *ahlu suffa*, said: "Allah, the Lord of majesty and glory, moved their focus away from the world. He made the world look insignificant and small in their eyes. Furthermore, He restricted their access to it in order to protect them against its lures, and to help them eschew transgression and injustices against their own souls or others. Hence, He kept them guarded under the shield of His protection, He lightened their burdens, and guarded their focus against aberrations, so that no wealth in this world could inhibit their concentration and dedication to worship Him, and nothing could lure their hearts or drive them to abandon their stations."

**943-** 'Abdu-Rahmãn bnu Abi Bakr narrated: "The people of *suffa* were mostly poor, and God's messenger ﷺ, upon whom be peace, used to say, 'Whosoever can afford to prepare a meal for two people, should apportion a share to feed a third person,[1] and whosoever can afford to prepare a meal for four people, should apportion a share for a fifth or a sixth person and take it to them.'"

'Abdu-Rahmãn bnu Abi Bakr then said: "On that evening, Abu

---

[1] i.e.,from the people of *Suffa*.

Bakr al-Siddïq, God be pleased with him, prepared a meal for three people and he took it to the mosque, while God's messenger ﷺ, upon whom be peace, prepared enough food for ten people."

**944-** Mujãhid narrated that Abu Huraira, God be pleased with him, said: "God's messenger ﷺ, upon whom be peace, once came by me and said, 'O Aba Harr!' I replied, 'At your command O messenger of Allah.' He continued, 'Run to the people of *suffa* and invite them to share this meal with us.' " (*Cf. 69:1025*)

Abu Huraira, God be pleased with him, continued: "The people of *suffa* are the guests of Islam, they had no home or family to go to, nor did they have any money or possessions. Whenever God's messenger ﷺ received a collection of charities, he never took anything for himself, instead, he immediately sent them in their entirety to the people of *suffa*. However, whenever he received a gift, he took a small share of it for his family, and he sent the balance to them."

**945-** Abu 'Amru bnu Hamdãn narrated that Talha bin Omar said: "Whenever someone new came to Madina to see God's messenger ﷺ, upon whom be peace, and if he had an acquaintance, he would stay with him, or if someone recommended him to a family, he would stay with them, otherwise, he stayed at the mosque in the company of the people of *suffa*. It happened that when I arrived to Madina, I stayed at the mosque of God's messenger ﷺ, in the company of the people of *suffa,* and everyday, a man came to the mosque, accompanied with two porters carrying a load of palm dates for our basic needs."

**946-** Sulaimãn bin Ahmad narrated that when Fãtima, God be pleased with her, gave birth to al-Hussain, she went to her father, God's messenger ﷺ, upon whom be peace, inquiring: "O messenger of Allah, do I have to I offer two sheep as *'Aqïqa* for my newborn son?" He (knowing her financial strait at that time) replied: "Just shave his head and donate a charity equal to the weight of the babe's hair in silver to the overflowing number of visitors and to the indigents to share among themselves."

**947-** Muhammad bin Ahmad bin al-Hassan narrated that Fadhãla bin 'Ubaid said: "God's messenger ﷺ, upon whom be peace, would be leading the congregational prayers, when suddenly one or more people from among the visiting Arabs (i.e., *ahlu suffa*) would blackout and fall on his face out of hunger and exhaustion, and some local Arabs would comment, 'May be he is possessed!'"

**948-** 'Abdullāh bin Wahab narrated that Abu Huraira, God be pleased with him, said: "Among *ahlu suffa* there were at least seventy men who were extremely poor and did not have even a single large enough robe to cover themselves!"

**949-** 'Abdullāh bin Muhammad bin Ja'far narrated that Abu Huraira, God be pleased with him, said: "I stayed with *ahlu suffa* for sometime, and one day, when God's messenger ﷺ, upon whom be peace, sent us some dried dates, we were so hungry, and I took two dates at a time. When my companions noticed that, I turned to them and said, 'It is all right if you eat two dates at a time, for I am eating them like that.'"

**950-** Abu Muhammad bin Hayyān narrated that one day after the *fajr* dawn prayers, God's messenger ﷺ, upon whom be peace, came and he inquired from the people of *suffa*, saying: "How are you doing this morning" They replied: "Well." God's messenger ﷺ, upon whom be peace, said: "Indeed you are well today, but a day may come, when you maybe served one plate of grapes after another fruit is served, and when you will decorate your homes extensively and drape their walls and windows (to exhibit a grandiose look) with material fit for the Ka'ba!"

Amazed by his statement, the people of *suffa* asked: "O messenger of Allah, will we ever come upon such status in this world, and yet remain observant of our religious practices?" He replied,: "Yes, somehow you will!" The people of *suffa* then rejoiced and said: "Then this should be good for us, and should we live to see such a day, we will surely be generous in our charities, and we will free slaves from bondage!" God's messenger ﷺ, upon whom be peace, pondered for a moment and he then said: "Nay! Surely you are better today. When such a day comes, you will have developed jealousy and perfidy towards one another, you will be divided with indifference towards one another, and you will even grow enmity and hatred towards one another."[1]

[1] This is an excerpt from the long account of a morning conversation between God's messenger ﷺ, upon whom be peace, and the people of *suffa*, narrated by Mu'āwiya.

**951-** In another narration of the above account reported by Abu Yahya al-Rãzi that al-Hassan said: "One day I built an extension to the canopy for the poor visiting Muslims, and as soon as I completed my work, and without any hesitation, all the Muslims of Madina proceeded to supply its dwellers with generous contributions and to the best of their means. Every morning, God's messenger ﷺ, upon whom be peace, used to pass by the dwellers of *suffa* and say, 'Peace be upon you, O people of *suffa*.' They would reply, 'And peace be upon you, O messenger of Allah.' He would then inquire, 'How are you doing this morning?' Their reply was, 'We are well, O messenger of Allah,' and he would comment, 'Surely you are better today than the day when you will be served with one tray of fruit after another, and when you will wear one garment in the morning and another one later on in the day, and when you will drape your homes like the Ka'ba!' The people of *suffa* commented, 'Then it is fine when Allah, the most exalted showers us with His gifts, and we should then be extremely grateful!' God's messenger ﷺ, upon whom be peace, replied, 'Nay! Surely you are better today!'"

The number of people who resided under the *suffa* of the mosque of God's messenger ﷺ, upon who be peace, varied depending on times of the year and conditions. At times, the visitors to Madina were fewer in number, and sometimes, the number of tribal delegations compounded, and mostly, they too had to stay at the mosque. However, in general, the regular inhabitants of the *suffa* at the prophet's mosque were poor people and ascetics who chose to remain near unto him, and to leave the world behind them. They were known to be poor and to have nothing, and often, none of them had more than a single robe, and rarely did any of them sampled more than a single meal per day.

**953-** Imam Ahmad bin Hanbal, God bless his soul, narrated that Abu Huraira, God be pleased with him, said: "I saw seventy people from *ahlu-suffa* in prayers, each of them having a single robe only and no cloak to cover it. Some wore a worn out *jubba*, others had it a little too big, while some had it so short that it barely covered beneath their knees, and when one of such people would bow in *ruku'* (obeisance), he would gather up his garment and hold to it tight in fear that parts of his body maybe exposed."

**954-** 'Abdullāh bin Muhammad bin Ja'far narrated that Muhammad Ibn Seerīn, God be pleased with him, said: "Whenever God's messenger ﷺ, upon whom be peace, retired for the evening, it was customary that each one of the companions would invite one of the dwellers of *suffa* to his home to share a meal. Some invited two, some invited three, and perhaps up to ten people at a time, and so forth, each according to his means, except for Sa'adu bnu 'Ubāda, who used to bring his family up to eighty guests at a time to feed them."

**955-** Abu Bakr al-Talhi narrated that 'Uqba bnu 'Ãmer said: "Some of us periodically stayed at the mosque along with the people of *suffa*, and one day, God's messenger ﷺ, upon whom be peace, came out of his house and said to us, 'Who amongst you would like to go out daily to the plains and to come back home with two wholesome camels, all lawful, without a sin in doing so, and without a quarrel in his household?' We replied, 'O messenger of Allah, surely we would all like to do that!' God's messenger ﷺ, upon whom be peace, further said, 'Then why wouldn't one of you make an extra effort to come regularly to the mosque before dawn, and to learn even a couple of verses from the Book of Allah, or merely read a couple of verses from it, and that would be more advantageous than his daily bringing home two, three, or four camels, or even any number of camels for that matter?'"

The above narration of 'Uqba states clearly that God's messenger ﷺ, upon whom be peace, used to instruct the people to avoid and to desist from occupying themselves with worldly concerns, or to wish for worldly material success. It also indicates that he ﷺ also directed them to seek what is more befitting to their status as believers and as God's people, and that which is more soothing to their hearts and minds. God's messenger ﷺ also instructed the companions to constantly remain in a state of remembrance (*zikr*) of Allah, the return of which endeavors is a must to develop clarity, understanding, and to behold His light, and only thus can they be protected against danger and eventual ruination in this world. Furthermore, engaging in *zikr*, the remembrance of Allah, will occupy their minds and hearts from unwarranted insinuations and mental suggestions which otherwise would cloud their innermost secret soul (*sirr*) and their most needed focus on their more serious path involving their duty towards their Creator, and shortly after that, the required mandatory standing before Him for reckoning on the Day of Judgment.

**956-** Rabī'a bin Abi 'Abdu-Rahmān narrated that Anas bin Mālik said: "One day, Abu Talha came to the mosque, and he found God's messenger ﷺ, upon whom be peace, standing up and rehearsing the Qur'an to the people of *suffa,* and Talha also that God's messenger ﷺ had tied a stone under his belt to control his hunger. The people had a single concern and reason for congregating at the mosque, and that was to understand in depth the meaning of the message revealed in the Book of Allah and to learn it, and their appetite could only be satisfied by regularly hearing the resonance of the divine speech."

**957-** Ja'far bin Muhammad bin 'Amr narrated that Abi Sa'īd al-Khidri, God be pleased with him, said: "We were a group of poor Muslims who lived under the *suffa* canopy of the prophet's mosque, and we spent our time studying the Qur'an at the hand of a man from among us who also regularly prayed to Almighty Allah on our behalf. One day, God's messenger ﷺ, upon whom be peace, came by us, and he saw our condition. I assumed that God's messenger ﷺ did not know any of the present people by name, and when the people saw him coming, they felt reverence, and some of them even tried to hide behind the others to cover up some shame they felt about their torn out rags. God's messenger ﷺ, upon whom be peace, then pointed out and invited the people to form a circle around him, and when they did, he asked them, 'What were you studying?' They replied, 'This man was reading the Qur'an for us, and he also prays for us!' God's messenger ﷺ sat there for a moment, and he then said, 'Go back to what you were doing,' and before we left, he prayed, 'All praises are due to Allah Who made among my followers a group with whom I am commanded to constrain myself and to keep my soul content in their company.' *(cf. Qur'an 18:28)* He then added, 'Let the poor ones among the believers hearken to the glad tidings that they will enter the heavenly paradise five hundred years before the rich ones. The poor ones will be enjoying its blessings, while the rich ones will be facing their reckoning.'" [1]

[1] This is an excerpt of a long account narrated by Ja'far, re Thābit al-Banāni, re Salmān al-Fārisi.

**958-** In another narration of the above account, Imam Ahmad bin Hanbal, God bless his soul, narrated that Thābit al-Banāni said: "Salmān al-Fārisi, God be pleased with him, was once sitting in a group of people at the mosque remembering Allah when God's messenger ﷺ, upon whom be peace, came by. When the people saw him, they immediately stopped. He asked them, 'What are you doing?' They replied, 'O messenger of Allah, we regularly gather here to remember Allah, and to celebrate His praises.' God's messenger ﷺ then said, 'Continue to do what you were doing, for I saw the divine mercy descending upon you and I wanted to come here and to share with you what I saw.' He then added, 'All praises are due to Allah Who made among my followers a group with whom I am commanded to constrain myself and to keep my soul content in their company.' "[1]

❁❁❁❁❁

The achievers of such status and honor of poverty have signs, and those who follow in their footsteps, up to and beyond the hour of resurrection, are surely the princes of faith among the believers. The truthful banners of their commitment cannot be denied, their innermost hearts are a monumental witness and are filled with the omnipresent divine truth, for indeed, the Omnipresent, the all-Hearing, and the all-Seeing Lord is their divine Guardian and Guide, and His most blessed messenger ﷺ, upon whom be peace, is their ambassador and monitor. In fact, such blessings are the luck of the few privileged ones who eagerly renounce the comfort of this world, and unrelentingly challenge its arrogance and deceptive nature.

To their credit, the true ones anxiously seek the ulterior permanent comfort and perfection of the hereafter. Their desires spew up the harmful effects one acquires from drinking in the cup of this unreal and grossly false ephemeral world, they uncompromisingly reject its entertainment and pretentiously ornate deceptive games. Furthermore, the true believers are mere spectators who attentively observe the magnificent and all-encompassing perfect work of the permanent omnipotent Lord of the universe. They sense

---

[1] Also reported by Salmān al-Fārisi, ibid 957

the inevitable coming of what is next; — that is the permanence of the hereafter, wherein, they eagerly desire the never ending and most lasting satisfaction in the nearness of the Lord of the universe. They continuously contemplate the divine promise of the most glorious visit of their Lord in the heavenly paradise, and the everlasting sublime satisfaction therein of gazing upon His most effulgent and magnificent divine countenance.

To have such clear goals and, God willing, in order to attain them, how can one achieve such blessed station unless he accepts the divine choice for him, to experience such yearning and to renounce anything but Him? Surely one must be most content with Allah, blessed is His Name, that the magnificent and most exalted One has chosen poverty for him in this transient short-lived world, and He has lightened his burden through this short journey to allow him to attain inexhaustible wealth and ever lasting comfort in the hereafter. In fact, Allah, blessed is His Name, chose to strip his servant's real needs of anything but Him, and to drive his focus and yearnings exclusively towards Him, while firmly guarding his heart against failure or distraction. What a blessings! This is the effective channel which protects the hearts and keeps them pure, and this is the channel that elevates the servant to gather among the blessed ones, the meek and the poor ones in the heavenly paradise, and this is indeed a most kind and subtle divine treatment which is destined exclusively for the true ones who are free of ostentatiousness, and who, even in this world, are nigh unto their Lord, blessed is His Name. Such people take true advantage of their time, they avoid mixing with addled and confused people, they guard their precious moments against pacifying the prejudiced minds of those who refute the functionality of the Divine Attributes, and they ardently strive towards dealing exclusively with the Lord and Sustainer of the entire creation, — thus emulating the wise and faithful pious traditions of the sire of all the ambassadors and messengers of the Almighty Lord, Allah's most blessed messenger, and the seal of His prophets, Muhammad ﷺ, upon whom be peace.

**959-** Muhammad bin 'Uthmān al-Wāsiti narrated that Ibn 'Abbās, God be pleased with him, said: "Whenever God's messenger ﷺ, upon whom be peace, liked someone's character and intentions, he would order him to spend more time in supererogatory prayers."[1]

Indeed, the true ones have sought shelter under the *suffa* (canopy) of the prophet's mosque, and they made it their designated resting stop. Thereat, they received the blessings and protection it receives from the Lord of the divine Throne. The archangel Gabriel descended regularly upon the prophet's mosque to bring the divine revelations, and thereat, within its blessed sanctuary, myriads of angels and heavenly beings descend from the highest heaven to pay their respect, to pray, and to invoke special blessings upon God's messenger ﷺ, upon whom be peace, and upon his followers, and thus it will be until the Day of Resurrection. Hence, the *suffa* of God's prophet's mosque will always be the believers' sanctuary, and its pietistic environment cleanses them of their turbidity, it washes away the opacity of their minds, and it helps the exaltation of their souls in rank.

Within the compounds of their blessed sanctuary, and during their extended retreat, not even a speck of imperspicuity ever clung to their minds or cluttered their understanding to falter their devotion, or to impede their spiritual progress. In fact, such highly blessed and exalted surroundings became a shield that protected them against temptations that otherwise attract the inexperienced and the feebleminded, or temptations that seduce the thirsty and solicitous of ephemeral worldly pleasures and its erroneous deception. Therefore, the true ones were endowed with strong faith and determination to accept the gift of the divine guardianship, and to abide without wavering in the company of God's messenger ﷺ, upon whom be peace, and to mingle with his blessed and wise companions. Such was what the awesome God prepared them to cherish. Hence, their abode was the transitional garden (*rawdha*) of bliss in this world, and in a spiritual sense, their drink was drawn from the paradisiacal river of tasneem, ﴾ A source from which the near ones (to their Lord) drink ﴿ (cf. *Qur'an 83:27*).

---

[1] i.e., to draw more spiritual benefits out of his faith.

**960-** 'Abdullãh, son of Imam Ahmad bin Hanbal, God bless his soul, narrated that Abi Sãlih commented on the meaning of the verse, ❮ Their drink is drawn from (the river of) *Tasneem*...❯ (*Qur'an 83:27*), saying: "This is the most blessed and exhilarating drink in paradise. To the near ones, it nurses their souls with the divine inspiration, and to the common people of paradise, it stimulates and enchants their spirit."

In truth, if we were to inquire in more details into the real lineage and origin of the people of *suffa*, we must not fail to realize that in fact these special blessed people have come from the most noble ancestry and the most renowned tribes. They have come from the furthest corners of the world, and they traveled away from their homes, they relinquished their social status, they bid farewell to their families, they forsook their worldly pleasures and comforts, and they sought the company of God's blessed messenger ﷺ and the seal of His prophets Muhammad, upon whom be peace.

Guided by divine inspiration, the inhabitants of *suffa*, the noble guests of the prophet's mosque made that decision, — which ultimately proved to be the Magnificent and Awesome God's own choice, — and although they may have lived under the canopy of the prophet's mosque, and appeared as the poor ones and the unknown, and while they were sometimes treated as foreigners, homeless, and needy, towards whom some people were most critical, and sometimes, others provided them with the leftover of their food, they in fact, the people of su*ffa*, had surely gathered under the most awe-inspiring conditions that provided their true spiritual nourishment and enhanced the status of their spiritual nearness to their Lord, and they were the elite and the choice of God Almighty Himself, as they embodied the devout souls of the perfect believers.

Their real cloak was made of effulgent light, and their utmost pleasure and spiritual nourishment consisted of invoking, celebrating, and cherishing the divine attributes. In reality, they cherished nothing in this world other than being under the canopy of the prophet's mosque ﷺ, upon whom be peace, and their temperaments could not adjust to a better quiescence than that of being physically in the proximity of God's messenger ﷺ, upon whom be peace, stationing at the threshold of his door. Their essence, their innermost souls, and their faces were resplendent with the light of the divine gift, and they were purified by their invocation, gratitude, and constant yearning to attain the promised ultimate award. They tore themselves apart from the illusioned ones about the attractions and deceptive comfort of this world, and they remained absorbed in their worship and in their unrelenting focus upon their Lord. They were the exclusive subject of the divine guardianship, and they were sustained at an irrecoverable range from the company of those who bask in convivial functions for mere entertainment and distraction, and others who gather in oblivion of reality but to their own detriment.

The true ones forsook what is built to be destroyed, — a downgraded version of the original creation, — and they renounced the ephemeral comfort and pleasures which are the real cause of one's ultimate downfall. They discarded the company of an avowed enemy whose perfidy he does not hide, and they were never complaisant in their determination to defend their faith. To do so, they sought refuge and protection in the divine guardian Lord Himself, Who alone can repel such adversities.

As to their material comfort in this world, the people of *suffa* had nothing to cover themselves with but mere rags. They were satisfied to be the witnesses of the dawn (*falaq*) as it breaks, and they were content to solicit none but their Creator and Lord. They worshipped no one besides Him, they associated no one with Him, and they subsisted purely upon His love and blessings. The heavenly angels desired and sought their company, myriads of angels descended from the highest heavens to worship the awesome Allah in the blessed ambiance of the prophet's mosque, and in the company of his blessed companions. God's messenger ﷺ, upon whom be peace, was commanded to constrain himself with them, to keep his soul content in their company, to sit with them, and to share the divine blessings with them, for thus only were they able to satisfy their yearning for their Lord, and to serve their spiritual journey.

**961-** Abu Bakr al-Talhi narrated that Khabāb bnul-Art once spoke in reference to the Qur'anic verse, ❮ Do not segregate or evict (from Allah's House) those who call on their Lord morning and evening, seeking His countenance ... ❯ (*Qur'an 6:52*), and he spoke of two people, Al-Aqra' bin Hābis and 'Uyaina bin Hisn al-Fazāri, who once harbored hypocrisy and often fought and betrayed the believers, and who primarily embraced Islam for ambitious selfish reasons, but later on, and by the grace of Almighty Allah, they were guided to true Islam after they repented to the Allah, the magnificent Lord, and Who, in His divine compassion, called them in another Qur'anic verse, *al-mu'allafati qulūbuhom.*[1] (i.e., those whose hearts have recently been reconciled to the truth.)

Khabāb bnul-Art said: "Al-Aqra' bin Hābis and 'Uyaina bin Hisn al-Fazāri once came to the mosque, and they found God's messenger ﷺ, upon whom be peace, sitting in the company of Bilāl, 'Ammār, Suhayb, and Khabāb (himself), along with other believers from among the poor and the meek who were known as the dwellers of *suffa*. When al-Aqra' and 'Uyaina saw that, they despised the group, and they requested a private audience with God's messenger ﷺ, upon whom be peace, and they initially spoke to him with utter disrespect regarding the class of his company, indicating, 'We want you to grant us a special set of rules concerning who sits with you when we come here. Make that a rank which will become recognized by the dignitaries among the various delegations of Arab tribes, besides others, who come to see you, so that they would recognize our status in this city. In fact, delegations of various noble tribes come regularly to see you, and we feel ashamed that they should see these paupers and slaves sitting in our company! Hence, when we come to see you, ask these people to leave, and when we take off and get back to our businesses, then you may sit with them as much as you want!' " God's messenger ﷺ replied, 'Let it be so!'[2] The two men delighted that their condition was accepted, and they hastily demanded, 'Then write down your promise and make it an official decree!' "

The narrator, Khabāb bnul-Art, continued: "We were all sitting there observing the ramifications when God's messenger ﷺ, upon whom be peace, asked 'Ali to bring a paper to write on, but suddenly, the arch angel Gabriel, peace be upon him, descended bringing the

---

[1] [*Qur'an 9:60*]

[2] God's messenger ﷺ, upon whom be peace, as the perfect and most noble teacher, perceived a chain of events that will become a lucid lesson for every believer, therefore, he replied thus to their condition in order to draw them in to sit down with him, and for them to learn the correct religious stance.

divine revelation, ❮ Do not segregate or evict (from Allah's House) those who call on their Lord morning and evening, seeking His countenance. You are not accountable for them, nor are they accountable for you, and should you turn them away, you would have committed an extreme injustice ❯ (*Qur'an 6:52*). '"

"In His revelation, Almighty Allah then mentioned al-Aqra' bin Hābis and 'Uyaina bin Hisn al-Fazāri, saying, ❮ And thus We put to trial (the faith and character of) some people verses others (to frustrate their vainness), so that they will come to (hear themselves) say, 'Are these the people whom Allah chose to favor over us?' Alas, Does not Allah know best those who are truly grateful (from those who are not)? Therefore, when those who believe in Our signs come to see you, say, 'Peace be upon you. Your Lord has decreed upon Himself to favor you with His mercy, and that should any of you commit a wrongdoing out of ignorance, and then repents and amends his act, he will surely find Allah oft-forgiving and most compassionate ❯ (*Qur'an 6:53-54*)."

"God's messenger ﷺ, upon whom be peace, immediately discarded the paper 'Ali had just brought, as he called us to himself, and he kept on looking at us, as he cheerfully greeted us, 'Peace be upon you, peace be upon you.' Hence, we happily drew closer and nestled by him, and we blithesomely sat so tightly close to him to the point that our knees touched his knees."

"From that day on, God's messenger ﷺ, upon whom be peace, kept us in his proximity and under his direct watch; he regularly sat with us, and whenever he needed to attend to his other duties, he simply left us. This joyous privilege went on until the day when Allah, the Lord of majesty and glory, revealed His command, ❮ Apply yourself with patience to remain in the company of those who call upon their Lord morning and evening, seeking His countenance. Keep them constantly under your watch, and do not let your focus dither beyond their circle. Do not solicit (the company of those who seek) the pump and glitter of this lower life (form); Nor obey anyone whose heart We have made unaware of Us, and We caused them to forget to remember Us, those who follow their own whims and desires, and whose condition have degenerated to the point that it can only effect their ultimate loss. ❯(Qur'an *18:28*)"

Khabãb commented: "The above verse refers to al-Aqra' bin Hãbis and 'Uyaina bin Hisn al-Fazãri. Almighty Allah then spoke of the parable of two men and their quest for the world, and He directed His blessed messenger ﷺ, upon whom be peace, to reply, ❮ Say: 'The truth comes from your Lord.' Let whosoever wants to believe in it, believe in it, and let whosoever wants to reject it, reject it. Surely, we have prepared for the unjust ones a fire whose (smoke and blazes) will hem them in like a corridor whose walls and roof stand high (beyond reach). Therein, if they scream for relief, they will be given water like melted brass that will scald their faces. Alas, what a dreadful drink it is, and how uncomfortable is such couch to recline on! As to those who believe (in Our message) and who do righteous deeds, We surely do not leave unrewarded the work of someone who does good. Such ones will be rewarded with gardens beneath which rivers flow. Therein, they will be adorned with bracelets of gold, and they will wear green garments of fine silk and brocade, and therein, they are consoled in safe havens, — Aah, what a gratifying reward, and how comfortable is such a couch for reclining! ❯ (*Qur'an 18:29-31*)."

Khabãb added: "Since that revelation, we enjoyed sitting all day long in the company of God's messenger ﷺ, upon whom be peace, and when we recognized the hour in which he usually attended to his other duties, we asked to be excused, and thus allowed him to attend to his other duties, otherwise, he would sit with us forever, and until we had all retired, and only then would he turn to his other duties."[1]

**962-** In another narration of the above tradition, Abu 'Amru bnu Hamdãn narrated that Salmãn al-Fãrisi, God be pleased with him, said: "*Al-mu'allafati qulübuhom* (those whose hearts were recently reconciled with the truth),[2] once came to the mosque along with others of their class, and they sought a private audience with God's messenger ﷺ, upon whom be peace. Their leader said, 'O messenger of Allah, why wouldn't you sit regularly on an exclusive raised chair in the forefront of the mosque, and meanwhile, ask these people

---

[1] *Also reported by Omar bin Muhammad al-'Anqazi.*

[2] *ibid.* i.e., al-Aqra' bin Hãbis and 'Uyaina bin Hisn al-Fazãri.

and their foul-smelling *jubba* (mantels)[1] to pull away from us into a furthermost corner (of the mosque), so that we can hearken attentively to your teachings and learn from you!' "

It is then that Allah, the Lord of majesty and glory, sent down the revelation, ❮ (Just) rehearse (to them) what is revealed to you from the Book of your Lord. Nothing can ever change His Words, and you will not find refuge except in Him! Apply yourself with patience to remain in the company of those who call upon their Lord morning and evening, seeking His countenance. Keep them constantly under your watch, and do not let your focus dither beyond their circle. Do not solicit (the company of) those who seek the pump and glitter of this lower life-(form); nor obey anyone whose heart We have veiled and caused to forget to remember Us. Those who follow their own whims and desires, and whose condition has degenerated to the point that it can bring about their ultimate loss. Say: 'The truth comes from your Lord,' hence, whosoever wants to believe in it, let him believe in it, and whosoever want to reject it, let him reject it. Surely We have prepared for the unjust ones a fire whose (smoke and blazes) will hem them in like a corridor whose walls and roof stand high (beyond reach). Therein, if they cry out for relief, they will be given water like melted brass that will scald their faces. Alas, what a dreadful drink it is, and how uncomfortable is such couch to recline on! As to those who believe and do righteous deeds, surely We do not leave unrewarded the work of someone who does good. Such ones will be rewarded with gardens of eternity beneath which rivers flow. Therein, they will be adorned with bracelets of gold, and they will wear green garments of fine silk and brocade, and therein, they are consoled in safe havens, — Aah, what a gratifying reward, and how comfortable is such a couch for reclining! ❯ (*Qur'an 18:27-31*)."

Salmān al-Fārisi, God be pleased with him, continued: "Immediately, upon receiving this revelation, God's messenger ﷺ, upon whom be peace, stood up and left the circle, and he went searching for them. Moments later, he found most of the people of

[1] meaning Abu Tharr al-Ghafāri and Salmān al-Fārisi, among other poor and weak Muslims, and at that time, this group of pious Muslims had nothing to wear but mere woolen rags they took for cloaks.

*suffa* sitting at the far back of the mosque, remembering Allah and invoking His praises. When he saw that, God's messenger ﷺ, upon whom be peace, exclaimed blithely, 'All praises be to Allah Who did not let me die before He had enjoined upon me to abide with constancy in the company of the chosen ones among my *umma* (of followers). Henceforth, and by Allah, living is living in your company and until death comes.' "

In fact, there were several similar incidents that took place regarding the people of *suffa,* and they vary in details depending on the narrators. However, all the narrators agree to witnessing the above episodes, the firm and decisive divine response to people's faulty attitude, and the lessons the believers must learn from them. Moreover, all of the narrations agree to the reason behind the Qur'anic revelation and Almighty Allah's directives to His blessed messenger ﷺ, upon whom be peace, on this subject.

**963-** In another narration reported by Sa'ad bin Abi Waqqãss, God be pleased with him, he said: "We were six people sitting in the company of God's messenger ﷺ, upon whom be peace, including myself, Ibn Mas'oud, a man from the tribe of Huthail, and two more people, I forgot their names, when a delegation of hypocrites (from Madina) came and said to him, 'You must distance these people from you, for they are such and such....' At that moment, it appeared that God's messenger ﷺ, upon whom be peace, felt for us as he pondered when the divine revelation came down, ❮ Apply yourself with patience and remain in the company of those who call upon their Lord morning and evening, seeking His countenance ... ❯ (*Qur'an 18:28*).

**964-** Jurair narrated that 'Abdullãh bin Mas'oud said: "God's messenger ﷺ, upon whom be peace, was sitting in the mosque with Suhayb, Bilãl, Khabãb, and 'Ammãr, along with some poor common Muslims when a group of people from the Tribe of Quraish passed by, and they said to him, 'O messenger of Allah, have you chosen this class of people from among your entire followers for your closest ones! Do you want us to follow such people? ❮ Are these the ones whom Allah has chosen from among all of us for His utmost favors?❯ (*Qur'an 6:53*). Get rid of them, and perhaps if you do that we may follow you!' (*Cf. Qur'an 6:54*)

'Abdullãh bin Mas'oud, God be pleased with him, added: "It is then that Allah, the Lord of majesty and glory revealed, ‹ Forewarn with this revelation those who are fearful of the Day when they are (raised from the dead and are) gathered before their Lord (for their final Judgment). Surely they do not have a protector besides Him, nor can any intercessor (intervene on their behalf except by His leave). Therefore, perhaps such warning will help them be at their guard. Do not evict (or set apart) those who call on their Lord morning and evening, seeking His countenance. You are not accountable for them, nor are they accountable for you. Therefore, should you turn them away, you would be bearing the actions of the unjust ones › (*Qur'an 6:51-52*)."

**965-** Mu'ãwiya bin Qurra narrated that 'Ã'ith bin 'Amr said: "Salmãn, Suhayb, and Bilãl were once sitting together when Abu Sufyãn passed by them. One of them looked at him and commented with anger, 'Surely the swords have not done justice to the enemy of Allah!' Abu Bakr also was there when he heard that remark, and he said to them, 'Are you saying this to the most respected shaykhs, the patriarch of the Tribe of Quraish and its sire?' Abu Bakr immediately went to God's messenger ﷺ, upon whom be peace, and he told him what he heard. God's messenger ﷺ replied, 'O Abu Bakr, perhaps you hurt their feelings, or maybe you offended them with your comments. I swear by Him Who controls the destiny of my soul that if you have offended them, you would have brought the wrath of your Lord upon yourself!' Abu Bakr immediately hastened back to the mosque, and he said to the company of *suffa*, 'Dear brothers! Perhaps I offended you with my comments!' The people replied, 'Surely not! O Abu Bakr, you definitely did not offend us, may Allah forgive you.' "

**966-** Hamïd bin Anas narrated that God's messenger ﷺ, upon whom be peace, said: "With this knowledge, Allah will raise some people in stations, and He will make them eminent leaders and illustrious models. Their work will become widely known, and it will be admired and studied by others for ages. The angels will seek their company and huddle around them, and the angels's wings will constantly rub against their shoulders."

**967-** 'Abdullãh, son of 'Amru bnul 'Ãss narrated that God's messenger ﷺ, upon whom be peace, said: "Do you know who will be the first to enter the heavenly paradise?" The people replied: "Surely Allah and His messenger know best!" He continued: "These will be the poor ones among the émigré, and following their example (in this world), ruses and deceptions can be overcome. They die having a yearning they may not be able to satisfy. The angels will say, 'Our Lord, we are Your angels, the guardians of Your infinite treasures, and the inhabitants of Your glorious heavens, and we hope to be the first to enter the heavenly paradise. Please do not let them enter paradise before we do!' Allah, the Lord of majesty and glory, will reply, 'These are My true devout servants and they have never associated anyone with Me. When they died, they still had some yearnings in their hearts they were not able to satisfy, and yet they persevered in their devotion, and they denied themselves the need for it.' Immediately, ❮ The angels will then flock in to congratulate them, entering through every gate, proclaiming, 'Upon you is Peace, for you have surely persevered with patience, so blessed is your final abode. ❯ (*Qur'an 13:23-24*).

**968-** Abu Muhammad bin Hayyãn narrated that Muhammad bin 'Ali, son of al-Hussain, the son of 'Ali bin Abi Tãlib, peace be upon all of them, commented on the above Qur'anic verse with another verse, saying: ❮ Those are the ones who will be awarded to dwell in the highest haven because of their patience and perseverance, and therein, they will be met with congratulations and peace ❯ (*Qur'an 25:75*).

## 43- Aows bin Aows al-Thaqafi

He came to the city of God's messenger ﷺ, upon whom be peace, during his later days. Aows bin Aows al-Thaqafi arrived to Madina along with the delegation of the Tribe of Thaqïf when they embraced the religion of Islam and made their covenant with God's messenger ﷺ, upon whom be peace. Along with other alliances (*Mãliki and al-Ahlãf*), Aows bin Aows al-Thaqafi stayed at al-Quba mosque, North of the city of Madina, and not along with *ahlu suffa* as occasionally held by some narrators.

**969-** 'Abdu-Rahmān bin Ja'far narrated that Aows bin Huthaifa al-Thaqafi, said: "We arrived to Madina and met with God's messenger ﷺ, upon whom be peace, who placed *al-ahlāf* as guests to al-Mughīra bin Shu'ba, and he placed us as guests at the Quba Mosque (near the outskirts of Madina). At night, after the *'Isha* prayers, God's messenger ﷺ, upon whom be peace, used to visit us and talk to us."

## 44- Asma' bin Hāritha al-Aslami

**970-** Abu Huraira, God be pleased with him, said: "I always thought that Asmā' and his sister Hind were attendants of God's messenger ﷺ, upon whom be peace, because they mostly remained near his door, and they continuously hastened to his service."

**971-** 'Abdullāh bin Muhammad al-Baghwi said: "I read in the book of Muhammad bin Sa'ad al-Wāqidi the name of a young man called Asma' bin Hāritha who lived among the people of *ahlu suffa* in Madina, and who died the year sixty after *Hijra* in the city of Basra, Iraq, at the age of eighty."

**972-** Abu Fārouq al-Khattābi narrated, re Asma' bin Hāritha, that God's messenger ﷺ, upon whom be peace, once said to him: "Go to your people and order them to fast for this day."[1] Asma' replied: "What if I find that they already had their breakfast?" God's messenger ﷺ, upon whom be peace, said: "Then ask them to withhold from eating, and to fast for the remainder of the day."

## 45- Al-Agharr Al-Mazini

**973-** Abu 'Amru bnu Hamdān narrated, re al-Agharr al-Mazini, (also known as al-Agharr son of Mazeenah, his mother), that God's messenger ﷺ, upon whom be peace, was teaching the people to regularly ask for God's forgiveness, and he said: "I feel my heart heavy unless I ask for Allah's forgiveness at least one hundred times a day."

**974-** Abu Bakr bin Khallād narrated that Abi Burda said: "I heard a man from the Tribe of Juhaina, called al-Agharr al-Mazini

---

[1] This happened to be the day of 'Āshura, the tenth day of the first lunar month, called in Arabic Muharram.

telling 'Abdullãh bnu Omar, God be pleased with him, that God's messenger ﷺ, upon whom be peace, said, 'O ye people, repent to your Creator and Originator, for I repent to Him one hundred times a day.' "

**975-** Jãbir narrated that Bilãl, God be pleased with him, said: "In one extremely cold night, I called up for prayers at dawn but no one responded. I called again, and no one came out. God's messenger ﷺ, upon whom be peace, then said to me, 'What happened to the people?' I replied, 'Perhaps the cold weather prevented them from answering the call to prayers!' God's messenger ﷺ, upon whom be peace, then raised his hands and he prayed, 'O Mighty Allah, I beseech You to abate the cold weather for their sake.' Bilãl added, 'I bear witness that since that day, I saw the people fanning themselves to keep cool at the *fajr* dawn congregational prayers."

## 46- Al-Barã bin Mãlik

Al-Barã' bin Mãlik is the brother of Anas bin Mãlik, God be pleased with both of them, and he also was one of the blessed people of *suffa*. Al-Barã' had a soft heart, and he liked poetry and music, though he was a most courageous and a skilled fighter, and he earned his martyrdom during the Battle of Tastar.

**976-** Muhammad bin Hayyãn narrated that God's messenger ﷺ, upon whom be peace, said: "Perhaps there is amongst you a disheveled man who wears worn out rags, and towards whom no one cares to pay attention, and yet, should he ask Allah for anything, Allah will surely satisfy his prayer. Among such people there is al-Barã' bin Mãlik."

**977-** Thumama narrated, re Anas bnu Mãlik, that his brother al-Barã' had a beautiful voice, and sometimes, he used to sing short poems in the *rajaz* meter before God's messenger ﷺ, upon whom be peace. One day, he was traveling in the company of God's messenger ﷺ when they came by a group of women on the road, and God's messenger ﷺ said to him, 'Be gentle, be courteous, and beware not to captivate the attention of these women (with your songs)."

**978-** Anas bin Mãlik narrated that some years after the passing of God's messenger ﷺ, upon whom be peace, on the day of the Battle of Tastar, people came to al-Barã' and aroused his feelings, saying: "O Barã', you should make a vow with your Lord today!" Al-Barã' then prayed: "My Lord, I implore You by Your holiest oath to grant us victory over them, and to grant me to rejoin the company of Your prophet ﷺ, upon whom be peace"

**979-** Imam Muhammad Ibn Seerïn narrated that Anas bin Mãlik found his brother al-Barã' dying after the battle, and when Anas saw him laid on his back, sighing in his wounds and intoning with a short breath, Anas exclaimed: "O my beloved brother!" Al-Barã' looked towards his brother and smiled as he said: "Can you imagine me dying on my bed now that I have eliminated one hundred ruthless dissenters in hand-to-hand combat, besides those I helped other warring believers to terminate!"

## 47- Thawbãn Mawla Rasul Allah ﷺ

Thawbãn also lived at the *suffa*, and he was an excellent companion, a modest, chaste, content and a most loyal Muslim, and people used to enjoy his good-natured humor. Among the narrations also referenced to him, we note the following:

**980-** Zaid bin Aslam narrated, re Thawbãn, that a Jewish rabbi once came to God's messenger ﷺ, upon whom be peace, and said: "I wish to ask you a question!" God's messenger ﷺ replied: "Ask." The rabbi said: "Where will the people be on ﴾ The Day when the earth will be transformed into another earth (matter), as well as will the heavens... ﴿ ? " (*Qur'an 14: 48*). God's messenger ﷺ, upon whom be peace, replied: "People will be standing under an opaque veil beneath the Bridge of Judgment." The rabbi further asked: "Then who among the people will receive first access to the crossing?" God's messenger ﷺ, upon whom be peace, replied: "The poor ones among the *muhãjireen* (émigrés)."

**981-** In another prophetic saying quoted by Thawbãn, Abi Qalãba narrated that God's messenger ﷺ, upon whom be peace, said: "The best spent Dinar (in charity) is one which one spends to take care of his family, to feed his horse for Allah's pleasure, or a Dinar which is spent to feed one's companions for Allah's pleasure."

## 48- Thãbit bin al-Dhahhãk

The name of Thãbit bin al-Dhahhãk was mentioned by Abu Zaid al-Ash'hali, and he was of the early Medinite (*Ansãr*) people of *Shajara*, i.e., those who made their covenant with God's messenger ﷺ, upon whom be peace, under the Tree, near Mecca, prior to his *Hijra* (migration) to Madina. (*Cf. Qur'an 48:18*)

**982-** 'Uthmãn bin Abi Shaiba narrated, re Thãbit bin al-Dhahhãk, that God's messenger ﷺ, upon whom be peace, said during that meeting: "Whosoever accuses a Muslim of being a disbeliever (*kufur*) is equal in sin to his murderer."

**983-** Abi Qalãba narrated, re Thãbit bin al-Dhahhãk, that God's messenger ﷺ, upon whom be peace, said: "Whosoever lies using the oath of Islam is not a Muslim but rather a liar."

## 49- Huthaifa bnu Asyad al-Ghafãri

Abi Sarĩha al-Ghafãri mentioned that Huthaifa bnu Asyad was among the early Medinite (Ansãr) people of the Tree of the Covenant (*Shajara*), and who also lived at the *Suffa* of the prophet's mosque.

## The Ten Major Signs of The Last Hour

**984-** 'Abdullãh bnu Ja'far narrated that Huthaifa bnu Asyad al-Ghafãri said: "We were discussing the Last Hour when God's messenger ﷺ, upon whom be peace, came and sat with us, and he said, 'The Last Hour will not take place until ten major signs have occurred: 1) The Cataclysmic Cloud; 2) The emergence of the pseudo Messiah[1] (Arb. *Dajjal*, the Deceiver); 3) The emergence of the Behemoth (uncommon beast, Arb. *dãbba*); 4) The sun rising from the West; plus three major unprecedented earthquakes; 5) I- One in the East, 6) II- One in the West; and, 7) III- One in the Arabian Peninsula; 8) The resurgence and last conquest of Gog and Magog; and finally, 10) A major extraordinary volcanic fire that will erupt from the South of Eden, and which will drive all people to the Gathering Grounds, a portentous sign of the Day of Judgment."

---

[1] The pseudo Messiah; also a portent sign of the Advent of Jesus; the second coming of God's prophet and messenger Jesus, the son of Mary, upon both of whom be peace. Cf. Sahih Bukhãri, Vol. IV, see Hadith 567-568, pp. 436.

**985-** Huthaifa bnu Asyad al-Ghafāri narrated that God's messenger ﷺ, upon whom be peace, said: "O ye people, I am to precede you to the *Ākhira* (i.e., the thither eternal life), and (on the Day of Judgment) ye will flock in crowds to my *Hawdh*,[1] and I will ask you about your management of two major responsibilities,[2] and therefore, consider that as you interact with them. As to your first major responsibility, this is the glorious Qur'an, the Book of Allah, — the causal and effective end of its rope is in Allah's Hand, and the other end is in your hands; therefore, hold fast to its admonition and you will never go astray, and do not innovate. Your next major responsibility is to follow the example of, and to show kindness to my household,[3] for the Kind, Subtle, and the all-Acquainted Lord has informed me that these two (i.e., the Qur'an and the prophet's family) will never separate, and they will always remain in unity until they reach my *Hawdh*."

## 50- Habīb bnu Zaid

Zaid bin 'Āsim al-Ansāri reported that Habīb bnu Zaid was one of *Ahlu Suffa*, but yet, other records show that he was of *Ahlul Quba* mosque in Madina.

**986-** Zaid bin 'Āsim al-Ansāri narrated that Musailama al-Kazzāb (i.e., the liar) captured Habīb bnu Zaid, and that he personally interrogated him, saying: "Do you bear witness that Muhammad is the messenger of Allah?" Habīb replied: "Yes I do." Musailama then asked him: "Do you bear witness that I am the messenger of Allah as well?" Habīb replied: "I can't hear you!" Consequently, and after an awful and terrifying torture, Musailama finally mutilated and killed Habīb bnu Zaid."

## 51- Nasiba, Um Habīb of 'Aqaba

**987-** Habīb bnul Hassan narrated that during the caliphate of Abu Bakr, God be pleased with him, a woman called Nasiba, Um Habīb of 'Aqaba, joined the Muslim army campaign against

---

[1] *Hawdh*: The Pond of God's messenger h; a single sip of its water will quench one's thirst eternally; also known as the heavenly Pond of Eternal Youth.

[2] Arb. *Thaqalayn*: They also refer to the Qur'an and the prophetic *Sunna* traditions.

[3] i.e., *Ahlu Suffa*, Cf. Qur'an 42:23

Musailama al-Kazzãb, and she fought most courageously until Musailama was killed, and finally, she returned to Madina wearing a badge of ten wounds she earned during the battle.

## 52- Hãritha bin al-Nu'mãn

**988-** Abu Huraira narrated, re 'Aisha, the mother of the believers, God be pleased with her, that God's messenger ﷺ, upon whom be peace, said: "In my sleep, I saw myself in Paradise, and I heard the voice of a Qur'an reader from among my followers. I inquired, 'Who is that?' And I was told, 'This is Hãritha bin al-Nu'mãn' God's messenger ﷺ then added, 'Such is trueness to one's Lord, and such is the true one to his Lord.' "

**989-** Sa'ïd bin al-Musayyib narrated that Abu Huraira, God be pleased with him, said: "Hãritha bin al-Nu'mãn was most faithful to his mother, and such loyalty and trueness (*birr*) have earned him his exalted station in Allah's sight."

**990-** Abu 'Amru bnu Hamdãn narrated that Hãritha bin al-Nu'mãn, God be pleased with him, lost his sight to cataract at an old age, and he stayed with *Ahlu Suffa*, at the prophet's mosque. Hãritha sat by a corner close to the Prophet's chamber, and he tied a rope to it, to guide him to walk to the congregational prayers. Next to the end of his rope, Hãritha always had a bowl of dried dates, and whenever a beggar came to the mosque, Hãritha would use the rope to guide him to the bowl, and he would personally give the mendicant some dates. Whenever his family said to him, 'Let us help you to give the mendicant want you want to give him!' Hãritha would reply, 'I heard God's messenger ﷺ, upon whom be peace, say, 'To personally hand out your charity to a mendicant will ward off a possible evil death (should it be written as one's fate).'"

## 53- Hãzim bin Harmala al-Aslami

**991-** Khãlid bin Sa'ad narrated that Hãzim bin Harmala al-Aslami was walking when someone called him to God's messenger ﷺ, upon whom be peace, and who said to him: "O Hãzim, I oft invoke the prayer of *Lã Hawla wa lã Quwwata illã Billãhi'l 'Aliyyil 'Azeem* (Surely there is no will or power except what Allah, the glorious Lord, affects), for it is one of the greatest treasures of Paradise."

## 54- Al-Hakam bnu 'Umair

**992-** Abu 'Amru bnu Hamdãn narrated, re al-Hakam bnu 'Umair, that God's messenger ﷺ, upon whom be peace, said: "Be like guests in this world, consider the mosques as your homes, train your hearts to be gentle, train yourselves to be overly contemplative and to readily cry (when remembering what is coming). Let not your difference in opinions and ideas be the cause of you divisiveness. Surely you ambitions are driving your enterprising minds to build abodes you do not live in; to amass wealth beyond your immediate needs, and still, your minds anticipate and hope in what is beyond their reach."

**993-** Al-Hassan bin Sufyãn narrated, re al-Hakam bnu 'Umair, that God's messenger ﷺ, upon whom be peace, said: "It is enough of a depravity in one's religious claims: 1) To often indulge in sins; 2) to be short tempered; 3) to lack forbearance; 4) to have meager knowledge; 5) to sleep like a decaying cadaver at night; 6) to idle during the day; 7) to be lazy; 8) anxious; 9) impatient; 10) stingy; 11) hesitant; and 12) to exasperate easily."

**994-** Sulaimãn bin Ahmad narrated, re al-Hakam bnu 'Umair, that God's messenger ﷺ, upon whom be peace, said: "You must shy from Almighty Allah in everything you do. Cover your heads and shield them against their ruinous inclinations, as well as to protect their advantageous knowledge. Be careful about what you feed your stomach, be discreet about what the wombs conceives, and always remember death and its trials, whosoever does that, paradise will be his eternal abode."

## 55- Harmala bin Ayãs

**995-** 'Abdullãh bin Ja'far narrated that Harmala bin Ayãs said: "I once visited God's messenger ﷺ, upon whom be peace, along with a group of my neighbors, and as we were taking leave, I asked him, 'O messenger of Allah, advise me.' He replied, 'Always beware of Allah, and when you sit in the company of people, should you hear something you like, then act upon it, and should you hear something you dislike, then avoid it.' "

**996-** Hayyãn bin 'Ãsim narrated that Harmala bin Ayãs visited God's messenger ﷺ, upon whom be peace, and when he was leaving, he asked him: "O messenger of Allah, command me." God's messenger ﷺ, upon whom be peace, replied: "O Harmala, do what is morally correct, and avoid what is morally despised."

## 56- Khabãb Bnul Art

**997-** Abu Bakr al-Talhi narrated that a group of the companions of God's messenger ﷺ, upon whom be peace, visited Khabãb bnul Art,[1] during his last illness, and they said to him: "Rejoice, O Khabãb, soon you will reunite with God's messenger ﷺ, upon whom be peace." Khabãb replied: "How is that? Here is the bottom of the house, and there is its ceiling. Hasn't God's messenger ﷺ, upon whom be peace, told us, 'Suffice yourselves in this world with as little provisions as a traveler carries with him on a short journey,'"[2]

## 57- Khumays bnu Huthãfa al-Sahmi

**998-** Abu Bakr bin Mãlik narrated that Omar bin al-Khattãb, God be pleased with him, said: "Khumays bnu Huthãfa al-Sahmi[3] (Hafsa' husband) was a close companion of God's messenger ﷺ, upon whom be peace, and after Khumays died, I met Abu Bakr, and I said to him, 'If you wish, I will give you Hafsa the daughter of Omar in marriage.' Abu Bakr remained silent, and he gave a polite answer to think about it, and for a while, he did not speak to me on the subject. I became worried for her, but few nights later, God's messenger ﷺ, upon whom be peace, asked for the hand of Hafsa in marriage, and it was thus arranged. I later met Abu Bakr, and when he saw me, he immediately said, 'Perhaps you were upset with me regarding Hafsa your daughter, and because I did not return to you with a prompt answer!' I replied, 'Yes I did!' Abu Bakr then said, 'Surely nothing prevented me from coming back to you with a positive answer except that I had heard God's messenger speak of her after the death of her husband, and it is not my nature to divulge the secrets of God's messenger ﷺ, and should he ever let go of her, I will certainly marry her.'"

---

[1] Cf. Chapter III; Section 19, pp. 125

[2] Also see Chapter III, Section 30-Salmãn al-Fãrisi, Account 438, pp. 193

[3] Cf. His wife was Hafsa, the daughter of Omar bin al-Khattãb. He died in Medina, and later on, God's messenger h, upon whom be peace, married her.

## 58- Khãlid bin Yazïd al-Ansãri

This is Khãlid bin Yazïd al-Ansãri, the son of Abu Ayoub al-Ansãri, God be pleased with him, the noble host of God's messenger ﷺ, upon whom be peace, when he stayed at his house upon his arrival to Madina, and where he stayed until he built the mosque, and his blessed chamber thereat.

Khãlid bin Yazïd fought at the Battles of Badr and 'Aqaba, and he maybe considered of the dwellers of 'Aqaba, and not of *Ahlu Suffa*. Khãlid died in the city of Constantinople,[1] and he was buried near its walls. Here are a couple of the prophetic traditions referenced to his narration:

**999-** Abu Bakr bin Khalãd narrated, re Khãlid bin Yazïd al-Ansãri, God be pleased with him, that God's messenger ﷺ, upon whom be peace, said: "Tow men would go to the mosque to pray, and when they leave, one will have his prayers weigh in his favor, giving him advantage over his brother, and the second man's prayers will not be worth the weight of an atom."

Abu Hamïd al-Sã'idi asked: "O messenger of Allah, how can that be?" God's messenger ﷺ replied: "That's if his discernment functions better than the other!" Abu Hamïd asked again: "And How is that?" God's messenger ﷺ replied: "Perhaps one is more demanding of himself and he is more keen with respect to abstaining from what Allah forbids, and he eagerly hastens to do good. Hence, his prayers will be more advantageous, and even if he does not volunteer as much supererogatory prayers in comparison with what the other man offers."

**1000-** Habïb bin al-Hassan narrated, re Abu Ayoub al-Ansãri, God be pleased with him, that a bedouin Arab once came to God's messenger ﷺ, upon whom be peace, and said: "Teach me, but be brief!" God's messenger ﷺ replied: "1) When you stand up in prayer, do so like someone who bade farewell to this world; 2) do not utter a word if you know that you will have to apologize for it; and 3) finally, give up all hopes and desire for what others have."

**1001-** Sulaimãn bin Ahmad narrated that Abu Ayoub al-Ansãri, God be pleased with him, was sitting at the mosque in the company

[1] Constantinople: Modern Istanbul, Turkey

of a group of believers, when God's messenger ﷺ, upon whom be peace, came out of his house, and he sat with them, expressing a distinct joy as he said: "Today, my Lord granted me to choose between two gifts, either to have seventy thousands of my followers enter paradise without reckoning, or a special gift He will league for me!" Someone asked: "O messenger of Allah, what would such a special gift Almighty Allah would league for you?" God's messenger ﷺ did not reply, and he went back to his chamber. He then returned to us and said: "My Lord has compounded His endowment upon me, and now it includes an extra seventy thousand believers along with each one thousand from the first group, and furthermore, He also included the special gift He will league for me."

Abu Rahm then asked Abu Ayoub al-Anṣāri, God be pleased with him: "And what would such a special gift Almighty Allah would league for His messenger ﷺ?"

The people then scattered around, and some became skeptical about the authority and meaning of the prophetic narration, while others spoke wrong of Abu Ayoub's factualness. Seeing that the people were uncomfortable with what they have just learned, Abu Ayoub then called them back to him and said: "Let me clarify what this special gift Almighty Allah would league for His messenger ﷺ and not as I think, but in fact, as surely I know from the explanation I learned from God's messenger ﷺ, upon whom be peace, himself. This gift represents a favorable answer of a special prayer, Allah's messenger prayed, and which Allah granted him. He prayed: 'My Lord, grant me that whosoever bears witness that there is no god except You, attesting that You have no associate or partner, and that Muhammad is Your servant and messenger, believing thus with all his heart, and attesting to it with his tongue, paradise will be his ultimate destination."[1]

## 59- Khuraym bnu Fātik al-Asadi

**1002-** His forefather is Ahmad bin Sulaimān al-Marouzi. Khuraym lived in Ibriq, Iraq, and one day, he was awakened in the middle of the night by an anonymous voice, admonishing him: "Seek

[1] Also narrated by Sa'īd bnu Maryam, Muhammad bin Sahl, and Ibn 'Asākir.

refuge in the One and only Lord of majesty, the Eternal, Whose favors are abounding, and Whose glory is everlasting. Regularly read the divinely revealed verses, glorify the divine Oneness, and fear nothing after that."

Khuraym immediately traveled to Madina, and when he arrived to the mosque, it happen that God's messenger ﷺ, upon whom be peace, was standing on the pulpit delivering a sermon. On that day, Khuraym embraced Islam at the hand of God's messenger ﷺ, and he stayed along with *Ahlu Suffa,* and later on he fought in the Battle of Badr.

**1003-** Abi Ishāq narrated, re Khuraym bnu Fātik al-Asadi, that God's messenger ﷺ, upon whom be peace, once looked at him and said: "What kind of a man are you, had it not been for two good habits you care about!" Khuraym replied: "O messenger of Allah, if I knew that I had even a single good habit I'll be most satisfied with that. Tell me, what are they?" God's messenger ﷺ replied: "Your caring to correct the way to wear your *izār* (wrapper), and the way you trim your hair!" From that day on, Khuraym cut his hair short, and he made sure that he wore his *izār* correctly.[1]

**1004-** Khuraym's forefather was Abi al-Hassan 'Ali bin Omar al-Darqutni. One day, Khuraym bnu Aows al-Tā'ī was sitting with a group of believers at the mosque when God's messenger ﷺ, upon whom be peace, prophesied: "It has come to my knowledge, and the veils were lifted before my eyes to reveal that Islam will soon reach the City of al-Hīra in Iraq, and I saw a young woman called al-Shaimā' by herself, wearing a black veil, riding on a blond mule, and trying to escape." Khuraym immediately asked: "O messenger of Allah, should we conquer al-Hīra, and should I be the first to lay eyes on her as you have just described, can I marry her?" God's messenger ﷺ replied: "Yes, she is yours."

Some time later, Khuraym bnu Aows joined the Muslim army, and he fought under the leadership of Khālid bin al-Walīd, God be pleased with him, when they sought Musailama al-Kazzāb,[2] and defeated him and his followers.

---

[1]Apparently, prior to that event, Khuraym wore his *izār* (wrapper) loosely, and he had long hair. Hence, psychology worked.

[2] Cf. 50- Habīb bnu Zaid, account #968

Following that campaign, Khãlid proceeded to al-Hïra, Iraq, and as they neared the gates of the city, Khuraym bnu Aows laid eyes on a young woman wearing a black veil, and riding on blond mule, just as described by God's messenger , upon whom be peace, and he fell in love with her at first sight. Her brother 'Abdul Masih then came out, and when he learned of Khuraym's intention to marry his sister, he said, 'Let Allah be my witness that I will not give her away for less than Ten hundred dirhams!" Immediately Khuraym paid him one thousand dirhams, and said, 'I swear to Allah, that even should you have asked for one hundred thousand dirhams, I would have paid them for her sake."

The companions Muhammad bin Maslama and 'Abdullãh bin Omar, God be pleased with them, became the witnesses of this marriage which took place near the gates of the city of Hira, and later on, the woman's brother 'Abdul Masih said, 'I did not know then that one can count money to exceed ten hundred dirhams!' "

**1005-** Abu Muhammad bin Hayyãn narrated that Khuraym bnu Aows al-Tã'ï said: "I migrated from Tabük to God's messenger ﷺ, upon whom be peace, and I embraced Islam at his hand. One day, al-'Abbãs, the uncle of God's messenger ﷺ said to me, 'I wish to say something good about you.' I replied, 'You may only pray to Allah to help me keep my mouth shut!' "

## 61- Khubaib bnu Yasãf

Also among the dwellers of *Suffa*, there lived Khubaib bnu Yasãf, the son of 'Utba, Abu 'Abdu-Rahmãn. This is also confirmed by 'Abdullãh al-Hãfiz al-Naisaburi and by Abu Bakr bin Abi Dãwoud.

**1006-** Abu Ja'far al-Rãzi narrated, re Imam Muslim, that Khubaib bnu Yasãf said: "I first met God's messenger ﷺ, upon whom be peace, when I came along with a man from my tribe to see him. At that time, God's messenger ﷺ was preparing for a campaign, and when I realized that, I said to him, 'We shy to see our people preparing for battle, when we are deprived of such honor!' God's messenger ﷺ replied, 'Have you accepted Islam?' We replied, 'No we have not.' He then said, 'We do not accept the assistance of polytheists!' On that day, we embraced Islam at his hand, and we joined the army. During the battle against the polytheists, I fought a man who wounded me, and finally, I managed to kill him. Later on, I happened to marry the man's daughter who had embraced Islam. At times, when she is upset with me, she would say, 'I wish you were never bereft of the company of a man who begot this ornament[1] which you yoke over your shoulders!' Hearing that, I would reply, 'May you never be bereaved of the man who hastened the delivery of your polytheist father into hell-fire!' "

## 62- Dakïn bin Sa'ïd al-Mazeeni

Also among the dwellers of *Suffa*, there lived Dakïn bin Sa'ïd al-Mazeeni, or al-Khath'ami, who came to God's messenger ﷺ, upon whom be peace, in the company of four hundred men, and God's messenger ﷺ fed all of them. Later on in his life, Dakïn migrated to the City of Küfa, in Iraq.

## The Miracle of Feeding the Hungry

**1007-** Qays bin Abi Hãzim narrated that Dakïn bin Sa'ïd said: "I first cam to God's messenger ﷺ, upon whom be peace, in the company of four hundred men, and we asked him to feed us. God's messenger ﷺ then turned to Omar bin al-Khattãb, God be pleased with him, and said, 'O Omar, take these men to your home and feed them, and let them take away whatever is left.' Surprised by this unusual request, Omar replied, 'O messenger of Allah, I have no more than a mere small measure of dry date that would barely feed me and my children for a meal in this hot day of summer!'

Abu Bakr al-Siddïq, God be pleased with him, also was sitting there, and at once, he spoke firmly: "O Omar, hear the orders and obey them." Omar replied: "I hear and Obey."

Omar, God be pleased with him, then led us to his house, and he asked the men to enter in small groups. Omar then took out his keys to open the door, and as soon as he entered, there was a huge pile of dates in the middle of the room, and he had to climb on it to serve the people.

---

[1] meaning herself.

Dakïn bin Sa'ïd further said: "I was the last man to enter his house, and there was still a huge pile of dates to take away with us."[1]

## 63- Rufã'a Abu Lubãba al-Ansãri

The narrators also have mentioned the name of Rufã'a Abu Lubãba al-Ansãri, and some say that his name is Bashir bin 'Abd al-Munthir, of the Tribe of 'Amru bnu 'Awf. Rufã'a also was among the dwellers of *Suffa,* and it is said that he is related to the family of the great Muslim scholar Abu 'Abdullãh al-Hãfiz al-Naysaboori.

**1008**- 'Abdullãh bin Muhammad bin al-Akili narrated, re 'Abdu-Rahmãn bin Yazïd, re Lubãba (i.e., Bashir bin 'Abd al-Munthir), that God's messenger ﷺ, upon whom be peace, said: "Surely Friday is the best day of the week, and it is greater than the two (major Muslim) festivals of *Eid'ul Ad-ha* and *Eid'il Fitr*. Friday has five characteristic traits: 1) Adam was created on a Friday; 2) Adam descended to the earth on a Friday; 3) and Allah took back his soul on a Friday. 4) On Friday, there is an auspicious hour, during which a Muslim's prayers are accepted, unless one asks for something which Allah forbade; and finally, 5) every Friday, there isn't a heavenly angel, heavens, earth, mountains, or winds, nor oceans but are afraid that the Last Hour would take place on that Friday."

## 64- Abu Razïn

**1009**- Salma bin 'Abdu-Rahmãn, re his father, narrated that God's messenger ﷺ, upon whom be peace, once said to a man called Abu Razïn: "O Abu Razïn, when you are alone, keep your tongue moving with *Zikrullãh,*[2] for you will be in prayers (*salãt*) as long as you keep the remembrance of Allah. Do so during the daylight hours, and you will receive their reward, and do it during the time of supererogatory hours, and you will receive the reward of such hours. O Abu Razïn, When people strive to stand up to pray during

[1] This hadïth is authenticated as *sahih,* and is also narrated and referenced by several narrators. Cf. Signs of the Prophet; by Imam Abu Na'ïm al-Asfahãni, re Ismã'ïl bin Abi Khãlid.

[2] *Zikrullãh,* Engaging in the remembrance of Allah: Invoking His divine Attributes, and reading the Qur'an.

the night and fast during the day, endeavor to counsel and advise the Muslims. O Abu Razïn, when the people carry on *Jihãd* (struggle) to defend the faith, and if you wish to receive equal reward to theirs, then take shelter in the Allah's mosque, make it your duty to call to the prayers, and receive no wage for your work."

**1010-** Ibrãhïm bin 'Abdullãh narrated, re 'Abdul Malik bin Muhammad bin 'Adiy, re 'Abbãs bin al-Walïd, re his father, re 'Uthmãn bin 'Atã, re al-Hassan bin Abi Razïn that God's messenger ﷺ, upon whom be peace, said to his father Razïn: "Let me tell you about the foundation of success on this path, and how to receive the full benefit of this world and those of the hereafter! Constantly attend to the circles of Zikr, and as long as you can, when you are alone keep your tongue moving with *Zikrullãh;* love in Allah, and abhor for Allah's sake. O Abu Razïn, did you know that when a man leaves his house intending to visit his Muslim brother, seventy thousand angels will accompany him, and all the way, they will invoke *salawãt* (divine blessings) upon him, praying, 'Our Lord, he only went out to implement Thy command of fostering the bond of unity. Our Lord, deliver him into the infiniteness of Thy mercy and compassion.' "

God's messenger ﷺ then added: "If you can employ your body to do such work, then endeavor to do so."

## 65- Zaid bin al-Khattãb

**1011-** Sulaimãn bin Ahmad narrated, re Nãfi', re 'Abdullãh bin Omar, that on the day of the battle against Musailama al-Kazzãb and his followers, Omar bin al-Khattãb said to his brother Zaid: "Use my shield." Zaid replied: "But my dear brother, I desire the reward of martyrdom as much as you do!" Hence, both of them walked into the battlefield without a shield.

**1012-** Ishãq bin Ibrãhïm narrated that 'Abdullãh bin Omar said: "Abu Lubãba - Zaid bin al-Khattãb - once saw me pursuing a snake to kill it, and he said to me, 'Don't do that, for the messenger of Allah forbade us of killing limbless reptiles."

## 66- Safīna Abu 'Abdu-Rahmān

**1013-** Ja'far bin Muhammad bin 'Amr narrated that Safīna Abu 'Abdu-Rahmān said: "Um Salma bought my freedom from bondage, and she released me on the condition that I serve God's messenger ﷺ, upon whom be peace, as long as I live, and I replied to her, 'I surely do not wish to ever be away from God's messenger ﷺ as long as I live."

## The Miracle of the Shipload

**1014-** Sulaimān bin Ahmad narrated that Safīna Abu 'Abdu-Rahmān said to Sa'īd bin Jamhān: "My name is Safīna (*Arb. Ship*)." Sa'īd asked: "Why are you called Safīna?" He replied: "God's messenger ﷺ, upon whom be peace, one day called me Safīna when we were traveling with a group of believers. Deep through our journey, the companions were no longer able to carry their cumbersome luggage, and which began to slow down their journey. God's messenger ﷺ then turned to me and said, 'You carry their luggage for them, for surely you are a ship (*safīna*) today. God's messenger ﷺ then ordered me, 'O Safīna, spread down your shawl,' and I did as he told me. The companions then placed their entire cargo over my shawl, and miraculously, I was able to lift the entire load at once, and yet, they did not weigh a thing. On that day, even should I had to carry the loads of one, two, five, or as much as six pack animals would carry, that would not have been heavy for me."

**1015-** 'Abdullāh bin Ja'far narrated, re Safīna, that a man invited God's messenger ﷺ, upon whom be peace, and 'Ali, God bless his countenance, to a meal. When God's messenger ﷺ arrived, he saw a special tent raised in the house, but he did not enter the house. Later on, Fātima, God be pleased with her, said to 'Ali: "Ask God's prophet about what prevented him from entering the house?" When 'Ali asked him, God's messenger ﷺ replied: "It is not my custom nor that of any prophet before me to enter an embellished house!"

## 67- Sa'ad bin Mālik

**1016-** Abi Sa'īd al-Khidri narrated that the family of Sa'ad bin Mālik once complained about scarcity of their means, and Sa'ad bin Mālik sought to talk to God's messenger ﷺ about it. When Sa'ad reached the mosque, God's messenger ﷺ, upon whom be peace, was standing on the pulpit delivering a sermon, wherein he said: "O ye people, isn't it time for you to refrain from asking others for your needs. Surely whosoever abstains from asking, Allah will suffice him, and whosoever exhibits contentment, Allah will satiate his needs with little. I swear by Him Who holds in His Hand the destiny of Muhammad, that there is no wealth greater than exercising patience, and yet, if you insist on asking me, I will offer you whatever I find available to me."

Hearing that, Sa'ad prayed with the congregation, and then returned to his home.

## 68- 'Abdullāh bin Ja'far

**1017-** Abu Dāwoud narrated that 'Abdullāh bin Ja'far, God be pleased with him, said: "Allah looked into the hearts of humanity, and He sent Muhammad ﷺ, upon whom be peace, to His creation. He sent him with His divine message, and He chose him by His divine omniscience. Allah then looked into the hearts of people next to His messenger ﷺ, and He chose his companions, and He made them his supporters. Therefore, what the believers judge as good, then it is good, and whatever the believers find as ugly, Allah judges it accordingly."

❁❁❁❁❁

Also among the many prophetic sayings referenced to the narrations of *Ahlu Suffa*, we cite the following:

**1018-** 'Abdullāh bin Muhammad bin Ja'far narrated, re Salmān al-Fārisi, God be pleased with him, that God's messenger ﷺ, upon whom be peace, said: "Whenever the heart of a believer quivers on Allah's path, his sins will fall off like the clusters of dates fall off their tree."

**1019-** Abu Wā'il narrated, re 'Abdullāh bin Mas'oud , God be pleased with, that God's messenger ﷺ, upon whom be peace, said: "People are two types: 1) A learned person, and, 2) a student, and there are no benefits in anyone except them."

**1020-** 'Abdullãh bin Mas'oud narrated that God's messenger ﷺ, upon whom be peace, said: "Whenever a servant takes a step forward, Allah will question him about the reason why he took it!"

**1021-** Abi 'Amr al-Kindi narrated, re Salmãn al-Fãrisi, God be pleased with him, that God's messenger ﷺ, upon whom be peace, said: "I will intercede on behalf of any two men who fraternize in Allah from the day I was sent (as Allah's messenger), and until the day of Resurrection."

**1022-** 'Abdullãh bin Mus'ab narrated, re Mus'ab bin Sa'ad, that his father Sa'ad bin Abi Waqqãs asked God's messenger ﷺ, upon whom be peace: "O messenger of Allah, who among the believers will be most tried?" God's messenger ﷺ replied: "The prophets, then those next to their station, then the next, and then the next, etc. The trial of each man will depend on the strength of his faith and adherence to his religion. If the person is strong, then his trials will be more difficult, and if his faith is faint and his adherence to his religion is flimsy, then his trials in this world will measure up to his state. Like that, the believer will keep on suffering adversities until he walks on the surface of this earth chaste and without a sin."

**1023-** Abu Bakr bin Khallãd narrated, re Sa'ad bin Abi Waqqãs, that God's messenger ﷺ, upon whom be peace, said: "Allah loves a servant who is pious, satisfied with little, rich in virtues, and affectionate."

**1024-** 'Abdullãh bnu Mas'oud said: "We were sitting with God's messenger ﷺ, upon whom be peace, when a rider arrived, and he drove his horse close to God's messenger ﷺ, upon whom be peace, and said, 'O messenger of Allah, I have come to ask you a question, and I drove for nine consecutive days and nights, and until my horse became exhausted. God's messenger ﷺ asked the man, 'What is your name?' The man replied, 'I am Zaid ul-Khayl.' (i.e., a bounty hunter) God's messenger ﷺ commented, 'Nay, surely you are Zaid ul-Khair,' (i.e., the stretch of bounty). Now, ask your question, maybe a difficult question was once probed, and perhaps we had an answer for it!' "

Zaid then said: "Tell me about the sign of Allah in a person He wants, and the sign of Allah in someone He does not want?"

God's messenger ﷺ, upon whom be peace, replied: "How did you wake up this morning?" Zaid replied: "I woke up this morning having love in my heart for what is good, for the people who do good, and for the people who act upon it, and if I practice what I know to be good, I realized the benefit of its reward, and if I miss, I yearn for it!"

God's messenger ﷺ, upon whom be peace, then said: "This is the sign of Allah in someone He wants as well as it is His sign in someone He does not want. Should Allah intend for you to be among those He does not want, He will allow to walk that step, and then He does not care in which valley you vanish."

## 69- Abu Huraira

Finally in this book comes the name of the great companion Abu Huraira, the most renowned companion of *Ahlu S̲uffa,* the blessed dwellers under the canopy of the prophet's mosque. Abu Huraira, God be pleased with him, lived at the mosque and he never resided anywhere else during the lifetime of God's messenger ﷺ, upon whom be peace. Abu Huraira was unofficially the monitor who assisted God's messenger ﷺ in attending to the needs of the residents, the new comers, and the guests, and he was one of the poorest of the entire group. He exercised extreme patience towards his inordinate poverty, and he retired to the shades, were he mostly sat and prayed. Abu Huraira was an ascetic by nature, he did not care about planting trees, nor did he concern himself with the flowing of the rivers, and he did not care to socialize with rich people or to befriend merchants. Abu Huraira was a wise man, he forsook the ephemeral comforts of this world, and he aspired for the true and everlasting benefits of the One Who is worthy of worship.

**1025-** Sulaimān bin Ahmad narrated that Abu Huraira, God be pleased with him, said: "Let Allah, Whom there is no god but He, be my Supreme Witness, that I used to tie a pebble under my belt to quieten the noise of my grumbling stomach. One day, I sat on the sidewalk waiting for Abu Bakr to come out, and when I saw him, I intentionally asked him a question about a Qur'anic verse, hoping that he would stop and perhaps tread for few steps with me, and eventually ask me to share some food with him, but he did not. Soon after that, Omar came by, and again, I asked him about a verse from the Qur'an, but he did not respond. Finally, Abu'l Qãsim,[1] God's messenger ﷺ, upon whom be peace, walked by, and he came out smiling, and said, 'O Aba Hirr!' I exclaimed, 'At thy command O messenger of Allah, order me.' He said, 'Follow me.' I replied, 'At thy command O messenger of Allah,' and I hurried after him. He then entered his house, and when we reached the door, I asked permission to enter, and he gave me permission. God's messenger ﷺ then saw a small pitcher of milk on the floor, and he asked his family, 'Where did this milk come from?' His family replied, 'So and so offered it to us as a gift.' God's messenger ﷺ then turned to me and said, 'O Aba Harr! I replied, 'At thy command O messenger of Allah, order me.' He said, 'Quickly, call all *Ahlu Suffa* (the dwellers of the mosque) and invite them to this.' "

Later on, Abu Huraira explained: "*Ahlu Suffa* were the guests of Islam. They never asked any one for anything, and they cared for nothing in this world. Whenever God's messenger received a charity, he did not touch it, and he immediately sent it to them, and whenever he received a gift, he would call for them, and he would share it with them."

**1026-** Imam Muhammad Ibn Seerïn narrated that Abu Huraira said: "Sometimes I fell unconscious in-between the minbar (pulpit) of God's messenger ﷺ, upon whom be peace, and the chamber of 'Aisha. People would say, 'May be he is mad!' However, Allah knows best, that I am not mad, but rather my hunger made me thus fall."

**1027-** Abi Salma narrated that Abu Huraira once said to a gathering of people: "You say about me that 'Abu Huraira narrates many prophetic saying spoken by God's messenger ﷺ, upon whom be peace,' and you say, 'Why wouldn't *al-Muhãjireen* (the émigrés) and the *Ansãr* (the dwellers of Madina) relate these prophetic saying, and why weren't they aware of them?' My explanation is that my brethren from among the émigrés were mostly busy trading in the markets, and my brethren from among the *Ansãr* were mostly busy managing their businesses, and meanwhile, I was a poor man, living

[1] Abu'l Qãsim: God's messenger's patronym, upon whom be peace ﷺ, referring to his firstborn son al-Qãsim who was born in Mecca from his first wife Khadija, God be pleased with her, and which child died in his enfancy.

amidst the meek dwellers of *Suffa* for the price of my food. Therefore, most of the time, I was present near God's messenger ﷺ, upon whom be peace, and I heard his words when the other companions were absent, and I remembered everything he said, when they forgot."

**1028-** Abu Bakr bin Khuzaima narrated that Abu Huraira, God be pleased with him, said: "On the road to God's messenger ﷺ, upon whom be peace, to embrace Islam, I said to myself, 'What a long and a toiling night is awaiting you, and yet, it is your only way to escape from the circle of the atheists.' On my way there, one of my slave-servants ran away, and I couldn't catch him, but after I arrived and embraced Islam at the hands of God's messenger ﷺ, upon whom be peace, and while sitting with him, the young slave suddenly appeared, and God's messenger ﷺ said to me, 'Here is your slave!' I replied, 'He is now a free man, and I hereby release him from his bondage for the pleasure of Allah.' "

**1029-** Abu Bakr bin Khallãd narrated that Abu Huraira, God be pleased with him, said: "I grew up as an orphan, and I migrated as a poor man, and then, I served the daughter of Ibn Ghazwãn and my wage was my daily food."

**1030-** Qutaiba bin Sa'ïd narrated that Abu Huraira, God be pleased with him, once delivered a sermon, wherein he also said: "All praises be to Allah Who made this religion the archetype of moral code for humanity, and at the end, Who made Abu Huraira an Imam, after Abu Huraira was working as a servant for the daughter of Ibn Ghazwãn for merely his stomach fill, and she gave him a free ride when he needed it."

**1031-** Abu Hãmed bin Jabla narrated that Mudharib bin Hazan said: "I once heard a voice perpetually glorifying Allah, and I pursued the source of it, and I found it coming from Abu Huraira, God be pleased with him. I asked him, 'What are these hymns of glorification you are calling?' Abu Huraira replied, 'In gratitude!' I asked, 'For what?' He replied, 'For previously working as a servant for the daughter of Ibn Ghazwãn for merely my stomach fill, and she gave me a free ride when I needed it. When the people mounted their horses, I used to follow them, and when they stopped, I served them. Almighty Allah then gave her to me to be my lawful wife, and today, when the people mount their rides, I ride with them, and when they stop, I still serve them."

**1032-** Imam Ahmad bin Hanbal narrated that 'Uthmān bin Muslim said: "We used to have a servant who stayed a lot in the company of Abu Huraira, and when Abu Huraira greeted him, he used to say, 'May the peace of Allah always be with you. Surely your endurance will soon be rewarded with relief, and may Allah increase the wealth of the one who hates you.' "

**1033-** Imam Muhammad Ibn Seerïn narrated that Abu Huraira, God be pleased with him, used to say to his daughter: "Do not wear gold, for I fear for you from the blazes of hell-fire!"

**1034-** Bishr bin Müsa narrated that Abu Huraira said to his daughter: "Tell those who ask you, 'My father refused to adorn me with gold, and he thus shielded me from the flames of the blazing fire.'"

**1035-** Imam Muhammad Ibn Seerïn narrated that the Commander and Prince of the Believers, Omar bin al-Khattāb once called Abu Huraira to serve in his government, but Abu Huraira declined the offer. Omar became upset, and he said: "You do not like to serve, while someone better than you have asked for it." Abu Huraira replied: "Who do you mean?" Omar replied: "I am talking about Yusuf, the son of Ya'qoub, peace be upon both of them." Abu Huraira then said: "You are talking here about Yusuf, the prophet of Allah, and the son of Ya'qoub, the prophet of Allah, and here I am, Abu Huraira, the son of Umayya, and I am afraid of three and two things!" Omar interrupted: "Why wouldn't you say five things?" Abu Huraira replied: "I am afraid to say more than what I know, and surely I am afraid to make the wrong judgment, and then the whip of divine justice will lash at my back by the Book, my money will be confiscated, and the honor of my family will be insulted and defamed!"

**1036-** Sulaimān bin Ahmad narrated, re Abu Huraira, God be pleased with him, that God's messenger ﷺ, upon whom be peace, said: "Should one of you now spread his shawl on this floor and hearken to what I will say, and then, when my speech is concluded, he will surely understand the meaning and remember this speech word by word."

Abu Huraira immediately spread his shawl on the floor, and he listened carefully. Some years later, Abu Huraira used to say: "As soon as God's messenger ﷺ, upon whom be peace, finished talking, I embraced the shawl before I placed it again over my head, and from that day on, not a single word of what he said then has ever escaped me."

**1037-** Sa'ïd bin Abi Hind narrated, re Abu Huraira, God be pleased with him, that God's messenger ﷺ, upon whom be peace, once asked him: "Why wouldn't you ask me for a share of the possessions your friends always ask of me?" Abu Huraira replied: "I only wish to ask you to teach me some of the knowledge which Allah has taught you."

Abu Huraira added: "I then took off my head shawl, and I spread it on the floor in-between him and myself. God's messenger ﷺ, upon whom be peace, then spoke to me, and I understood what he said word for word. When he stopped talking, he said to me, 'Now you may hold unto your shawl.' I immediately embraced my shawl, and I placed it over my head, and since that day, not a single word of what he said ever escaped me ."

**1038-** Abu Bakr bin Khallād narrated that Abu Huraira, God be pleased with him, said: "The people are saying that 'Abu Huraira seems to be practically the sole narrator of prophetic sayings.' Let me tell you, I swear by Him Who holds the destiny of my soul, that should I tell you everything I heard from God's messenger ﷺ, upon whom be peace, you would most likely throw your trash over my head, and you would never talk to me again."

**1039-** Qutaiba bin Sa'ïd narrated that Abu Huraira, God be pleased with him, said: "I have learned directly from God's messenger ﷺ, upon whom be peace, and I have memorized prophetic sayings and knowledge that can fill five large bags. By now, I have share with you, and I have only opened two of them, and should I open the third bag, and should you hear what he said, you would surely stone me to death."

**1040-** Imam Ahmad bin Hanbal, God bless his soul, narrated that Abu Huraira, God be pleased with him, said: "Let me point out to you an easy and a cool booty." The people replied: "O Abu

Huraira, what is it?" He replied: "Offer voluntary fasting during the wintertime."

**1041-** Abu 'Amru bnu Hamdãn narrated, re Abu Huraira, God be pleased with him, that God's messenger ﷺ, upon whom be peace, said: "To fast the month of Ramadan plus three days in each month equals a lifetime of fasting."

**1042-** Imam Ahmad bin Hanbal, God bless his soul, narrated that Abu Huraira, God be please with him, used to often pace the floor of his house and say: "Woe unto my stomach, if I cloy its cravings, it sickens me, and if I ignore them, it insults me." (i.e., exposes his hunger in public by roaring.)

**1043-** Imam Ahmad bin Hanbal, God bless his soul, narrated that Abu Huraira, God be please with him, said: "I ask for Allah's forgiveness and I repent to Him twelve thousand times per day. — Surely each believer does so following the scale of his religious adherence."

**1044-** Imam Ahmad bin Hanbal, God bless his soul, narrated that Na'ïm bin al-Muharrar, the grand son of Abu Huraira, God be please with him, said: "My grandfather used to have a long string on which he tied two thousand nuts, and he would not go to sleep unless he had recited his prayers."

**1045-** Ahmad bin Bindar narrated that Abu Huraira cried during his last illness, and when asked about it, he said: "Surely I am not crying being attached to your world, but rather for the long journey awaiting me, and the little provisions I have prepared for it. This mourning, I am descending upon either a paradise, or hell, and I have no idea towards which of the two I will be taken!"

**1046-** Muhammad bin Ishãq narrated that Abu Huraira, God be pleased with him, said: "You may expect destruction to befall you when you begin to adorn your mosques, and embellish your Qur'ans."

**1047-** 'Abdullah, son of Imam Ahmad bin Hanbal, God bless his soul, narrated that Abu Huraira, God be pleased with him, said: "Woe unto the Arabs from a forthcoming inescapable evil! Woe unto them, when a day comes, and callow youths govern them according to their own whims, and who will kill in anger."

Abu Huraira, God be pleased with him, then said: "Cheer up O Europeans (*furunj*), even should the religion of Islam be hung on a high suspended chandelier, you will surely have nations from among you who will embrace it correctly."

**1048-** Abi Salma visited Abu Huraira, God be pleased with him, during his last illness, and he prayed: "O Allah cure Abu Huraira!" Abu Huraira immediately prayed: "O my Lord, never send it back again to this world." He then added: "O Salma, soon will come a day when people would prefer to be dead than to have red gold."

**1049-** Al-Hassan bin Müsa narrated that Abu Huraira, God be pleased with him, also said during his last illness: "When you see six signs in this world, should one of you have control over the release of his soul, then do so, for this is why I prefer to die today rather than to live, for I am afraid that of such trials to reach me; 1) When the brazen insolent governs you; 2) when the government can be sold out; 3) when atrocities, cruelty, and bloodshed become of no importance; 4) when families are broken apart; 5) when the hafts of swords are broken; and 6) when a new generation of Muslims compete in flutelike singing of the Qur'an."

Many more people dwelled at *Suffa,* God be pleased with them, and many a times, they were quoted as part of the chain of transmitters of prophetic Hadith. Among the most known, we also note herein the names of these blessed companions, may Allah be pleased with all of them:

**70-** AL-SĀ'IB BIN KHALLĀD
**71-** AL-TAFĀWI AL-DŪSI (also known as Abu Nadhra)
**72-** HAJJĀJ BNU 'AMRU
**73-** HANZALA BIN ABI ĀMER
**74-** JARHAD BIN KHUWAYLID
**75-** JĀRIYA BIN JAMIL
**76-** JU'AYL BNU SURĀQA AL-DHIMRI
**77-** KHUMAYS BNU HUTHĀFA AL-SAHMI[1]

[1] Cf. His wife was Hafsa, the daughter of Omar bin al-Khattāb. He died in Medina, and later on, God's messenger ﷺ, upon whom be peace, married her.

**78-** Sa'ad bnu Abi Waqqās, (*Cf. Section 3*)
**79-** Sa'īd bin 'Āmer al-Jamhi
**80-** Safwān bin Baidhā'
**81-** Sālem bin 'Ubaid al-Ashja'i
**82-** Sālem bin 'Umair
**83-** Salmān al-Fārisi (*Also see Chjapter III. Section 30*)
**84-** Shaddād bin Asyad
**85-** Shaqrān Mawla Rasūl Allah ﷺ
**86-** Thakhfa bin Qays
**87-** Talha bnu 'Amru
**88-** Thābit bin Wadī'a
**89-** Thuqayf bnu 'Amru

All praises are due to Allah, the Lord and Sustainer
of the universes,
and peace and blessings upon
our master Muhammad ﷺ, upon whom be peace,
and upon his family and followers.
By the grace of Almighty Allah,
and with His help, this volume of
The Beauty of The Righteous
& Ranks of The Elite
was completed this
Friday, July 28, 1995 C.E.
Rabī'ul Awwal 1, 1416 A.H.

والله ولي التوفيق

# Index of Selected Quotes & Points of Reference

# Partial Index of Narrators, Witnessing Companions, & Later Commentators

# General Index


**A**

'Abd Shams 89
'Ãbid 23
Aaron 10, 11, 60
Ablution 85, 135, 183, 184, 202, 255, 260, 344, 352
Abraham 8, 20, 21, 119, 145, 156, 158, 191, 204, 234, 239, 419
Abrãr 65
Abyssinia 88, 93, 97, 136
Adam 8, 22, 111, 155, 166, 228, 418
Ahlu Suffa 371
'Aina 341
Ãkhira 3
Ãl al-Bait 172
Al-'Atïq 32. See also Abu Bakr Al-Siddïq
Al-Baqara 111
Al-Najãshi 98
Al-karrubiyyoun 118
Allahu Akbar 44, 62, 75, 188, 223, 355
Allegories 20, 59, 72, 68
Ambivalent 24
Ansãr 27, 91, 161, 394, 410
'Aqïq 83
'Aqïqa 374, 417
'Aql 23, 59, 119, 131, 141
Al-Khulafã al-Rãshideen 120
Arabian Peninsula 49, 51, 89, 93, 125, 168, 170, 176, 190, 286, 394
'Ãrif 25, 65
'Ãrif -billãh 65
Ascetic
Asceticism. See Ascetic
Ascetic 24, 47, 86, 88, 103, 142, 252, 259, 371, 409
Ascetic detachment 19, 25, 43, 60, 64, 106, 169
Asceticism 74
Asceticism 11, 24, 26, 372
Asfiyã 19, 68
'Asr 329
'Atã bin al-Sã'ib 200, 310
Atheist 4, 256, 270, 295, 300, 350, 361, 411
Athkhar 127
Awliyã 10, 19, 230
Awrãd 62

**B**

Badr 58, 93, 97, 105, 121, 163, 168, 345, 399, 401
Bani 'Abbãs 183
Bani Huthayl 96
Bani Jamh 132, 257
Basïra 65
Basra 76, 161, 273, 278, 314, 391
Bãtin 23
Battle of Siffeen 123
Beginningless beginning 66
Bequeath 177, 218, 219
Birr 338
Bismillãh 355
Bread 48, 49, 58, 64, 85, 187, 196, 211, 226, 253, 262, 281, 297, 354
Burdah 126

**C**

Calamity 3, 421
Changes of Colors 161
Charity 30, 37, 42, 70, 76, 78, 85, 87, 99, 116, 123, 147, 153, 155, 177, 178, 187, 188, 191, 192, 194, 207, 222, 223, 245, 253, 257, 263, 264, 282, 311, 314, 317, 318, 319, 320, 325, 349, 374, 393, 396, 410, 417
Constipation 324
Contentment 17, 22, 25, 159, 172, 232, 287, 343, 407
Cornerstone (hajar) 310

**D**

Dajjãl, or the pseudo Massiah 292
Dajla, Tigris river 183
Dãrën 7
Day of Judgment 17, 28, 41, 49, 51, 52, 63, 65, 75, 109, 117, 119, 148, 149, 152, 170, 196, 198, 199, 205, 213, 214, 215, 233, 243, 244, 268, 274, 279, 304, 311, 338, 356, 358, 361, 363, 369, 378, 394, 395, 417
Day of Reckoning 6, 14, 41, 53, 71, 140, 142, 153, 157, 168, 205, 208, 213, 249, 274, 297, 313, 364
Day of Resurrection 6, 10, 30, 33, 38, 80, 92, 153, 173, 177, 199, 225, 227, 237, 238, 241, 270, 277, 280, 304, 340, 351, 364, 381, 408
Deceptive attractions 291, 292, 297, 420
Deen 252, 421
Dharrã 242
Dhuha 260
Digestive system 324
Disheveled 7, 392, 420
Divine benevolence 5
Dunya 35, 38, 65

**PEARL PUBLISHING HOUSE**
**P.O. Box 28870**
**Philadelphia, PA 19151 U.S.A.**

**Tel. (215) 877-4458 / Fax (215) 877-7439**